Race and Education
1954 – 2007

Race and Education
1954 – 2007

Raymond Wolters

University of Missouri Press   Columbia and London

BP53

Library of Congress Cataloging-in-Publication Data

Wolters, Raymond, 1938–
    Race and education, 1954–2007 / Raymond Wolters.
        p. cm.
    Includes bibliographical references and index.
    Summary: "Retracing Supreme Court decisions on race and education
beginning with the *Brown v. Board of Education* decision, Wolters distinguishes
between desegregation and integration and shows how devastating educational
and cultural consequences resulted from subsequent Supreme Court decisions
that conflated the two and led to racial balancing policies that have backfired"
—Provided by publisher.
    ISBN 978-0-8262-1828-5 (alk. paper)
    1. School integration—Law and legislation—United States.   2. Discrimination
in education—Law and legislation—United States.   I. Title.
    KF4155.W66 2008
    344.73'0798—dc22   2008034656

♾™ This paper meets the requirements of the American National Standard for
Permanence of Paper for Printed Library Materials, Z39.48, 1984.

Designer: Jennifer Cropp
Typesetter: The Composing Room of Michigan, Inc.
Printer and binder: The Maple-Vail Book Manufacturing Group
Typefaces: Palatino and Caslon

7/22/10

Contents

Preface

When I was a younger professor, my goal was to discover new information and to tell stories that had not been told previously. From 1969 until the mid-1990s, my published works were based largely on information that had been culled from manuscripts, microfilm, court reports, and interviews. I thought of my approach as different from that of scholars who spent much of their time interpreting or commenting on information they had come across while reading materials from a library.

This book, however, is a work of synthesis as well as research. Chapters 3 and 4 are based on fieldwork that I have done in five school districts, and Chapter 5 draws on my own research with legal documents. In other chapters, I have drawn on general accounts and the monographic studies of other scholars.

My interpretation differs from the conventional wisdom. Many people consider *Brown v. Board of Education* (1954) the high point in the jurisprudence of the U.S. Supreme Court. They also regard school desegregation and integration as policies whose value is beyond question. This work, on the other hand, shows that *Brown* was based on a dubious understanding of Constitutional history and social science. It also concludes that, in terms of educational benefits, desegregation has been problematic, and integration a failure.

Scholars associated with what is sometimes called "the civil rights community" claim that research has shown that the academic achievement of black students improves, and that of whites does not decline, if students are assigned to schools where the enrollments are racially balanced and predominantly white. They also say the social advantages of attending racially balanced schools are well documented. They say there has been only minimal "white flight" from court-ordered integration.

The civil rights scholars have circulated statements to this effect, statements that have been signed by hundreds of professors and submitted to various courts. Many of the signatories have not done research on the relevant subjects, but the number of signatures is testimony to the views that prevail in academe.

Despite the prevalence of these views, other scholars have taken exception to one aspect or another of the civil rights consensus. I believe the quality of the work of what might be called "the dissenting scholars" is superior to that of the "civil rights scholars." I have an especially favorable opinion of the scholarly work of David J. Armor, James S. Coleman, Christine H. Rossell, Abigail M. Thernstrom, Stephan Thernstrom, and Herbert J. Walberg.

Opinions differ as to the quality of the research, but there is no doubt that the evidence is subject to conflicting interpretations. Chief Justice John G. Roberts noted this in the opinion he wrote in 2007 for a Supreme Court case, *Parents Involved v. Seattle*. James E. Ryan, a law professor at the University of Virginia, has summarized the situation. In one lawsuit after another, those who favor the policy of racial balance call upon "experts who paint a . . . positive and optimistic picture of the benefits of integration." In response, "those challenging the plans hire experts who testify and present studies showing that the social and academic gains from integration are limited at best."[1]

I have not been associated with either side in these legal battles. Rather than join one of the teams, I have persisted in the role of a conventional history professor. Every year I teach hundreds of undergraduate students who enroll in introductory courses on American history and the history of the civil rights movement, and smaller numbers of students who sign up for other courses in American history. Then, when I am not working with students, I write books and articles. I do so as an independent scholar who is not bucking for entrée or status in any group or professional association.

My work and much of my social life revolve around my university, the University of Delaware. My three sons attended the U of D. I have season tickets for the Blue Hens' home football games. I try to become acquainted with as many students as possible. I have been the faculty advisor for a number of student organizations. When I walk to the Blue and Gold

---

1. *Parents Involved v. Seattle*, 127 S.Ct. 2738 (2007), 2755; James E. Ryan, "The Limited Influence of Social Science Evidence in Modern Desegregation Cases," *North Carolina Law Review* 81 (May 2003): 1690–91.

Club at lunchtime, as the carillon plays the alma mater, I know the words to the song. My summer retreat is located only twenty-one miles away from campus at the head of the Chesapeake Bay.

In addition to identifying with my university and locale, I have persisted in regarding myself as essentially a writer who is trying to tell interesting stories. Whether the story is based primarily on my own research, as was the case in years past, or also incorporates the work of many other scholars, as is the case with the present volume, my goal has been to combine narration, evocation, and explanation within a descriptive chronology.

To make the story of desegregation and integration comprehensible, I have explained the arguments on both sides of these controversial questions. Not everyone will be pleased with this approach, for it has led me to elucidate the rationale of people who were and are committed to policies that are out of fashion—policies such as segregation and the conservation of the white race.

In the modern world, in some circles, it is considered rude to suggest that nature has something to do with inequalities in educational achievement. Rather than emphasize the importance of race or heredity, many writers on both the left and right accentuate the importance of environmental factors. Those on the left often attribute inequality to various sorts of oppression: capitalism, sexism, racism, and so on. Those on the right point to social pathologies: illegitimacy, welfare dependency, dysfunctional cultural values, and the like. Both groups are prone to finding fault with teachers and schools.

To understand the opposition to desegregation and integration, however, one must understand that many of those who opposed these policies did so for racial reasons. In the 1950s segregationists predicted that desegregation and integration would fail because of racial differences in average IQ—differences that some of them attributed to dissimilarities in the size and structure of the brain. More recently, some critics have pointed to variations in the distribution of DNA. White racialists have also feared that desegregation and integration would lead to the demise of their race.

When the manuscript version of this book was being reviewed, the University of Missouri Press asked for assessments by scholars with expertise on the topics at hand. One of these scholars began his report by saying, "This is an impressive work, by many standards, and it should be published." But this scholar then added, "If the author is going to present arguments for racial inferiority, even though they are factual, historical occurrences, then . . . I fear the book will be branded as neo-racist work and may not achieve the attention that it otherwise deserves." This scholar noted: "If the author believes this proposition"—that the Negro race, on average, suffers from an "'inherent' (or genetic) mental inferiority"—then "I would not recommend publication."

The careful reader will note that I have mentioned problems with the evidence that segregationists cited.[2] With respect to craniology, some of the studies were done in Africa, without the modern equipment needed for reliable measurements. Other studies did not control for prenatal and postnatal nutrition. Still others did not use identical methods for fixing and processing the brains that were studied. As for IQ, it may be that the African Americans' experience with slavery, segregation, and discrimination accounts for the fact that their IQ, on average, trails that of white Americans by about 15 points.

The evidence on this subject is not conclusive, and since I am not an expert on either psychometrics or craniology, I am an agnostic when it comes to the significance of IQ tests and the extent and import of differences in brain size. My personal opinion is similar to that of Dwight Ingle, the chairman of the Department of Physiology at the University of Chicago. In 1963 Ingle wrote, "The concept that White and Negro races are approximately equally endowed with intelligence remains a plausible hypothesis for which there is faulty evidence. The concept that the average Negro is significantly less intelligent than the average White is also a plausible hypothesis." Ingle went on to say that he considered the evidence of the second hypothesis "somewhat stronger."[3]

Some people consider it bad taste to mention that the races differ, on average, in academic achievement and in the distribution of IQ and DNA. I believe, however, that these variances must be discussed if one is to understand the debate and the controversy over school desegregation and integration.

My discussion of racial differences is not extensive, and I mention the subject here primarily to answer the Press's anonymous expert. Speculation about racial differences is only one of many sets of ideas and experiences that must be discussed and pondered in order to understand the history of American education.

2. See pp. 95–99.
3. Dwight Ingle, "Comments on the Teachings of Carleton Putnam," *Mankind Quarterly* 4 (1963): 28–29.

Acknowledgments

The University of Delaware has supported my scholarly work ever since I joined the faculty as an instructor in 1965. In the course of researching and writing this book, I received valuable suggestions from David J. Armor, Robert L. Hampel, Paul D. Moreno, and the anonymous readers for the University of Missouri Press. Beverly Jarrett, the director and editor-in-chief at the Press, handled the review process and contractual arrangements with her customary good judgment, and Julianna Schroeder showed once again why she has become my favorite editor. I am especially indebted to my wife, Mary Wolters, for her love and support through the years.

Race and Education
1954 – 2007

Introduction

In its landmark *Brown* decisions of 1954 and 1955, the U.S. Supreme Court required public schools to deal with students on a racially nondiscriminatory basis. Later, the Court changed this policy. In its *Green, Swann, and Keyes* decisions of 1968, 1971, and 1973, the Court obliged school districts to assign students by race to achieve more racial mixing than could be achieved by racially neutral policies. Then, in its *Milliken* decision of 1974, the Court qualified and limited the amount of mixing that would be required, and in a series of decisions handed down since 1991 the Court returned to the policy that *Brown* had established. The first policy, the policy of *Brown*, should properly be called *desegregation* while the second approach, that of *Green, Swann,* and *Keyes*, should be designated *integration*.[1]

I believe the Court was on the right track and was acting in harmony with the opinions of most Americans when it insisted that agencies of the government should not discriminate on the basis of race. I further believe the Court veered in the wrong direction when it equated desegregation with integration. Yet this view is out-of-step with the opinion that prevails among most scholars at leading universities. The great majority of academics who write about school desegregation and integration present an inverted interpretation. They laud the "progressive" opinions that the Supreme Court handed down between 1968 and 1973, and they censure

1. *Brown v. Board of Education*, 347 U.S. 485 (1954); *Brown v. Board of Education*, 349 U.S. 294 (1955); *Green v. New Kent County*, 391 U.S. 430 (1968); *Swann v. Charlotte-Mecklenburg*, 402 U.S. 1 (1971); *Keyes v. School District No. 1*, 413 U.S 189 (1973); *Milliken v. Bradley*, 418 U.S. 717 (1974); *Oklahoma City v. Dowell*, 111 S.Ct. 630 (1991); *Freeman v. Pitts*, 60 USLW 4286 (1992); *Missouri v. Jenkins*, 63 USLW 4486 (1995); *Parents Involved v. Seattle*, 127 S.Ct. 2738 (2007).

1

the policy of nondiscrimination. Political correctness has reached a point where a scholar is likely to be marginalized if he or she supports either the policy that the Supreme Court required in *Brown* or the return to that policy which the Court has implemented since 1991.

Older readers will recall the orthodoxy that prevailed in the Deep South in the 1950s and early 1960s, when southern whites were ostracized if they did not oppose school desegregation. Younger people have read or heard about this era of "massive resistance." The historian James W. Silver summed up the prevailing ethos in the title of his 1964 book, *Mississippi: The Closed Society.*[2]

A quite different orthodoxy prevails today, at least on many campuses. At university conferences on civil rights, the speakers usually share the same basic assumptions. They equate desegregation with racially balanced integration. They rarely discuss the problems that have accompanied integrated education, unless the problems can be attributed to white racism. They say that research has shown that students benefit from attending schools with racially balanced enrollments. Conversely, they say that the educational disadvantages of attending racially imbalanced schools are well documented.

The academic orthodoxy was on display in 2006–2007, when the Supreme Court considered two cases that dealt with the practice of assigning students to public schools on the basis of race. In these instances, students in Louisville, Kentucky, and Seattle, Washington, were so assigned in order to achieve enrollments that approximated the racial balance of their respective communities. The racial discrimination was open and acknowledged. Nevertheless, 553 social scientists submitted a legal brief in support of the practice. Sixty historians did likewise, as did nineteen former chancellors of the University of California.[3]

Mainstream scholars implicitly criticize the *Brown* Court for distinguishing between desegregation and integration and for requiring only the former. Instead of censuring this policy, however, I consider it a sensible adaptation to American pluralism. Whatever one's judgments may be, the facts are clear. There was nothing in the decision of the Supreme Court or in the extensive notes of the justices and their clerks to indicate that *Brown* sought to achieve racially balanced enrollments in the nation's public schools. To be sure, officials and lawyers for the National Associa-

2. James W. Silver, *Mississippi: The Closed Society* (New York: Harcourt, Brace and World, 1964).
3. *Brief of 553 Social Scientists, Parents Involved v. Seattle*, U.S. Supreme Court, 2006; Jack Greenberg, counsel of record on behalf of 60 scholars, ibid.; Goodwin Liu, counsel of record, on behalf of nineteen former chancellors, ibid.

tion for the Advancement of Colored People (NAACP), the organization that backed the *Brown* lawsuit, "hoped to engineer a society that learned and worked together, not one that co-existed in parallel worlds." One of the lawyers, Robert L. Carter, has written that the NAACP "fashioned *Brown* on the theory that equal education and integrated education were one and the same."[4]

Nevertheless, although the NAACP won *Brown*, the NAACP did not write the *Brown* opinion. That opinion required *desegregation*, not *integration*. Any doubt about this was removed in 1955 when Chief Justice Earl Warren worded the implementation order, known as *Brown II*, to condemn "discrimination" not "racial imbalance." The defendant school districts were told that *Brown* stood for "the fundamental principle" that there should be no "racial discrimination in public education," and they were ordered to proceed "with all deliberate speed" toward establishing schools that would be "freed of racial discrimination." In *Cooper v. Aaron*, a 1958 case that concerned Little Rock, Arkansas, the Court reiterated that *Brown* had established that children had "constitutional rights . . . not to be discriminated against in school admission on grounds of race or color."[5]

For more than a decade, *desegregation* was understood to mean the disestablishment of segregation. Until 1968 the Supreme Court recognized that the proper remedy for compulsory separation was to end such separation. It did not insist that compulsory inclusion must begin. There was no demand that enrollments at individual schools must be balanced to achieve approximately the same racial proportions that existed in a city, county, or state.

4. Robert A. Garda Jr., "Coming Full Circle: The Journey from Separate but Equal to Separate and Unequal Schools," *Duke Journal of Constitutional Law and Public Policy* 2 (2007): 7; Robert L. Carter, "A Reassessment of *Brown v. Board*," in Derrick Bell, ed., *Shades of Brown* (New York: Teachers College, 1980), 27. Elsewhere I have maintained that prior to 1934 the NAACP itself favored a policy of nondiscrimination rather than integration. As long as W. E. B. Du Bois and like-minded leaders were in charge, the NAACP condemned unfair discrimination while also fostering racial identity, pride, and community. Du Bois envisioned a pluralist system of parallel worlds, with blacks and whites living "side by side in peace and mutual happiness," with each developing its own "peculiar contribution to the culture of their common country." Diane Ravitch has also noted that the dispute over *desegregation* and *integration* involves more than the meaning of words. It touches on "the nature of the relationship of Black people to the rest of American society." See Raymond Wolters, *Du Bois and His Rivals* (Columbia: University of Missouri Press, 2002), 2, 4, 253, and passim; Du Bois, "The Conservation of Races" (1897), reprinted in Herbert Aptheker, ed., *Pamphlets and Leaflets of W. E. B. Du Bois* (White Plains, N.Y.: Karus-Thomson Organization, 1986), 7; Ravitch, "Desegregation: Varieties of Meaning," in Bell, *Shades of Brown*, 46.

5. *Brown v. Board of Education*, 349 U.S 294 (1955); *Cooper v. Aaron*, 358 U.S. 1 (1958).

Brown pertained to Topeka, Kansas, which, in response to the Supreme Court's ruling, assigned all students, regardless of race, to the nearest neighborhood school. This did not lead to proportional mixing in each school because the residential areas in Topeka were racially imbalanced. Nevertheless, the Supreme Court expressed no objection or reservation when a unanimous federal district court accepted the Topeka desegregation plan, saying, "Desegregation does not mean that there must be an intermingling of the races in all school districts. It means only that they may not be prevented from intermingling or going to school together because of race." Topeka's neighborhood schools were considered constitutional because they were race-neutral. Under the new plan, students were being assigned to schools on the basis of their residence, not their race. Although one of the schools in Topeka was "inhabited entirely by colored students," the District Court noted, "no violation of any constitutional right results because [children] are compelled to attend the school in the district in which they live."[6]

When *Brown* had been before the Supreme Court, the litigation from Topeka was consolidated with similar lawsuits from Wilmington, Delaware, Summerton, South Carolina, and Prince Edward County, Virginia. And here, too, the federal courts distinguished between desegregation and integration. "Discrimination is forbidden but integration is not compelled," the Delaware court declared, as Wilmington assigned its children to racially imbalanced neighborhood schools. Again, the Supreme Court looked on with tacit approval. And in the South Carolina case, the Supreme Court entered no objection when the district court ruled that desegregation was required but integration would not be imposed. "It is important that we point out exactly what the Supreme Court has decided and what it has not decided. . . . The Constitution . . . does not require integration. It merely forbids discrimination."[7]

Desegregation, but not integration, was also what the Supreme Court had in mind when, in a series of brief opinions, it invalidated laws that required segregation of municipal swimming pools, tennis courts, and the like. The Court did not explain its rationale in these cases, but it prohibited the segregation "in light of *Brown*." In these cases the Supreme Court insisted that the municipal facilities must be desegregated, in the sense that no person could be denied admittance solely on the basis of race. It

6. *Brown v. Board of Education*, 139 F.Supp. 468 (1955), 468–69; Christine H. Rossell, "The Convergence of Black and White Attitudes on School Desegregation," *William and Mary Law Review* 36 (1995): 614–15.

7. *Evans v. Buchanan*, 207 F.Supp. 820 (1962), 823–24; *Briggs v. Elliott*, 132 F.Supp. (1955), 777.

did not require that, in order to qualify as "desegregated," the proportions of black and white swimmers or tennis players must be approximately the same as the proportions of blacks and whites in the larger community.[8]

The U.S. Congress concurred when it passed the Civil Rights Act of 1964. Section 407 authorized the attorney general to initiate school desegregation actions, and Section 401 defined *desegregation:* "'Desegregation' means the assignment of students to public schools and within such schools without regard to their race, color, religion, or national origin, but 'desegregation' shall not mean the assignment of students to public schools in order to overcome racial imbalance."[9]

Yet the Civil Rights Act was hardly in place when the Supreme Court changed its policy. In *Green v. New Kent County* (1968), the Court held that *Brown,* when understood properly, required school districts to take affirmative steps to achieve balanced racial enrollments. Rejecting the idea that racially neutral methods of dealing with pupils constituted full compliance with *Brown,* the Court held that school districts must achieve as much mingling as was possible.[10]

New Kent was a small rural county in Virginia—one with only thirteen hundred students enrolled in its public schools. But in *Swann v. Charlotte-Mecklenburg* (1971) the Supreme Court applied the rationale of its *Green* opinion to a North Carolina district that enrolled more than eighty thousand students. The *Swann* Court also sanctioned busing as one of the methods that should be used to achieve racially balanced enrollments.[11]

Because of legalistic qualifications, *Green* and *Swann* initially were understood to require racially balanced integration only in southern districts that had formally operated segregated schools in the 1950s. But in *Keyes v. School District No. 1* [Denver] (1973), the Supreme Court modified its rationale so as to pave the road to busing for racial balance outside the South.[12]

These cases and qualifications will be discussed in the chapters that follow, but for this introduction the key point is that the judicial reinterpretation of desegregation touched off a wave of public dissatisfaction that swept the nation and reminded many observers of the mood that had prevailed in the South in the 1950s. In 1970 President Richard M. Nixon issued an extraordinary eight-thousand-word statement that said, essentially, that *Brown* was right but *Green* was wrong—that the decision to end

8. *Florida ex rel Hawkins et al.,* 347 U.S. 1971 (1954).
9. Public Law 88-352 (1964).
10. *Green v. New Kent County,* 391 U.S. 430 (1968).
11. *Swann v. Charlotte-Mecklenburg,* 402 U.S. 1 (1971).
12. *Keyes v. School District No. 1,* 413 U.S. 189 (1973).

segregation was correct but the decision to require integration was a mistake. Polls indicated that the great majority of Americans agreed with President Nixon on this point. The compulsory transportation of schoolchildren out of their neighborhoods to increase racial mixing touched off widespread, bitter resentment. Busing gave rise to dissent, demonstrations, and white flight. Eventually, it also contributed to a decline in the quality of public education and to a realignment in politics.[13]

When the Supreme Court encountered opposition after its *Brown* decision of 1954, the justices allowed the nation time to adjust to new principles, saying that desegregation should be implemented "with all deliberate speed" and at "the earliest practicable date." When the busing cases of the early 1970s also gave rise to complaints about judicial "usurpation" and "tyranny," the Court again drew back. It did so in *Milliken v. Bradley* (1974), a case that concerned busing for racial balance in the metropolitan region near Detroit.[14]

Milliken will also be discussed in the chapters that follow. For now, suffice to say that *Milliken* limited the extent of busing for racial balance. The *Milliken* Court reiterated that busing could be required within individual school districts. But *Milliken* also placed legal roadblocks in the way of busing students across the district lines that divided most cities from their suburbs. The decision was by the narrowest of margins, 5–4, but it was crucially important. Because of *Milliken,* most busing plans would not encompass the suburbs. Busing would continue in many cities, and also throughout metropolitan areas that had county-wide school districts rather than separate districts for the city and its suburbs. Outside the South, however, most areas had separate districts. And because of disparities in the pattern of residential settlement, with whites disproportionately concentrated in the suburbs and blacks in the cities, most black and white children would not attend racially balanced schools.

After *Milliken,* the Supreme Court waited to see how things would work out. In 1977 and 1979 the Court considered two cases from Ohio, and then it stepped back and for more than a decade refused to consider any more school desegregation cases. Then, when the Court revisited the issue in

13. In 1974 Ben J. Wattenberg summed up the findings of the Gallup organization: "In 1970 Gallup began polling on school busing: the question dealt with 'busing of Negro and white school children from one school district to another.' The response was 86–11% against. In 1971, the same question yielded a 76–18% 'against,' with blacks also in opposition 47–45%. In the years since, those ratios have remained roughly constant; massive white opposition, a split black view." *The Real America* (Garden City: Doubleday, 1974), 252.

14. *Brown v. Board of Education,* 349 U.S. 294 (1955); *Milliken v. Bradley,* 418 U.S. 717 (1974).

the 1990s, the justices required school districts to achieve the sort of de-segregation that the *Brown* Court had in mind, not the sort of balanced integration that *Green, Swann,* and *Keyes* had envisioned. In additional litigation that culminated in 2007, the high court again affirmed that the Constitution prohibited racial discrimination, even if the discrimination was being used "affirmatively" to achieve racially balanced enrollments.

This book also describes the educational policies that were in vogue at the time of *Brown* and during the ensuing decades. Three years after *Brown,* the Soviet Union launched the first space satellite, and the emphasis in American education shifted. In response to *Sputnik,* and spurred by educational reformers such as Hyman G. Rickover and James B. Conant, schools began to pay more attention to developing the academic abilities of the brightest students. Educators implemented more systematic approaches to grouping students by ability, and advanced placement and honors courses were added to the curriculum of many high schools. These policies had a disparate impact, with African American and Hispanic students less likely to be enrolled in advanced courses than Caucasians or Asians. But in the 1950s most people did not regard ability grouping as a sophisticated method of "intellectual segregation." They considered it, rather, a practical way to accommodate students with widely varying levels of ability. Some observers even said that ability grouping facilitated desegregation, because it allowed for democratic interaction in social activities and introductory courses while also providing advanced instruction in some academic areas.

By the late 1960s, the social context for American education had changed again. By then the United States had sent a man to the moon, and most Americans felt confident about their nation's primacy in science and technology. In the meantime, however, people had become increasingly concerned about the race riots that had plagued many cities. Educators accordingly shifted their emphasis. Instead of stressing the importance of developing the full potential of the brightest students, schools increasingly focused on uplifting (and pacifying) the downtrodden. As historian Diane Ravitch has noted, civil rights activists brought their demands to the schools and, before long, "the pursuit of excellence was overshadowed by the needs of the disadvantaged."[15]

New educational theories then came to the fore. Prior to the late 1960s, the conventional wisdom held that responsibility for doing well in school devolved primarily on pupils and their families. Teachers were expected

15. Diane Ravitch, *The Troubled Crusade: American Education, 1945–1980* (New York: Basic Books, 1983), 233–34.

to maintain order and present information clearly, but most people assumed that students learned more if they were smart, hardworking, and from families that appreciated the importance of education. If children fell behind in school, it was thought that they did not have much aptitude for academic work, did not try hard, or received little support from their families.

As the nation became increasingly concerned with uplifting disadvantaged youths, several educational reformers shifted the burden of responsibility. Instead of attributing low achievement to the students' lack of ability or effort, or to the environment that prevailed in the students' homes or neighborhoods, they placed the blame on the schools—especially the schools of the nation's inner cities. This message was conveyed in the writings of several scholars whose work will be discussed in the text of this book—Kenneth B. Clark, Helen Gouldner, Frank Reissman, Ray C. Rist, and Robert Rosenthal. Weak students would do better, these scholars said, if teachers had more confidence in the students and more sympathy for the cultural values that prevailed in the students' neighborhoods.

Among the educational reformers of the 1960s and 1970s, none was more influential than the sociologist James S. Coleman, whose theories will also be discussed. It was Coleman, above all others, who built the bridge that led from desegregation to integration. Unlike some other educational reformers of his era, Coleman did not rail against teachers and schools. Rather, he stressed the importance of the students' peers. After analyzing the results of tests that were given to some 570,000 students at 4,000 schools, Coleman reported that black students who attended majority-white schools scored higher than other blacks. According to Coleman, this was because the students' attitudes toward school were influenced by the attitudes that prevailed among their fellow students. Coleman said that youngsters were more likely to consider schoolwork important if their peers were serious about their studies, and middle-class youths were more likely to appreciate the importance of academic work. Since most white students were from the middle class, and most blacks were not, Coleman recommended that students should be assigned to create schools with enough middle-class youngsters to create a peer culture that favored education, and a substantial number of lower-class students who could benefit from being exposed to such peers. The policy implications were obvious, and Coleman came to be known as "the scholar who inspired busing."[16]

16. *National Observer*, 7 June 1975, 1.

Coleman eventually changed his mind. After additional research he acknowledged that it had been "wishful thinking" to believe that the schoolwork of lower-class students would improve if they were exposed to more middle-class peers. Nevertheless, many of Coleman's fellow sociologists continued to regard racially balanced integration as a nostrum. In their aforementioned legal brief of 2006, 553 social scientists assured the Supreme Court that racially balanced integration improved the "critical thinking skills" and boosted the "achievement levels of African American students." Not only that, the 553 said, racially balanced integration also "promote[d] cross-racial understanding, "reduce[d] racial prejudice," and increased the likelihood "that individuals . . . will work more productively with individuals of other races."[17]

Here is another point where this author differs from many of his fellow professors. My own fieldwork in five school districts, and other studies that will be discussed in the body of this book, point to conclusions that differ from those of "the 553." If a summary statement about the effects of integration on academic achievement and race relations were phrased cautiously, the summary would say that the evidence is mixed and variable. If the statement was bold and candid, the bottom line would be that the negative effects of integration usually outweighed the positive.

Although much of this book deals with legal matters and educational sociology, it also describes how school desegregation and integration actually worked out in several towns, cities, and counties. In this respect, the present work differs from many articles that have appeared in law reviews and from social science studies that are more statistical or theoretical in their orientation. The methodology of this work is "inductive" rather than "deductive." Instead of basing conclusions on reasoning from generally accepted principles, or on deducing from statistics, the conclusions in this work are based on observation of what happened in several individual cases.

Many legal writers have gone beyond the adage that the provisions of the Constitution mean "whatever the Supreme Court says they mean." They say the Constitution should be understood to mean whatever the Supreme Court's opinions can be interpreted to mean. When it comes to school desegregation, they pass over the *Brown* Court's repeated assertion that the question before it concerned whether the Constitution prohibited separation that resulted from official state policies. They ignore the Court's statement that *Brown* established the "fundamental principle" that "racial discrimination" was unconstitutional. They disregard *Brown*'s

---

17. Ibid.; *Brief of 553 Social Scientists*, 2006.

holding that students should be treated "on a racially nondiscriminatory basis." Instead, they point to a general statement—*Brown*'s assertion that "separate educational facilities are inherently unequal." That, they say, summarizes "the ideals for which *Brown* stands." They say that "the logic of *Brown*" requires racially balanced integration. Anything less, they say, amounts to a "failure to live up to the promise and vision that animated the [*Brown*] decision." Nothing save racially balanced integration will satisfy "the deepest promises of the American system."[18]

Meanwhile, articles in the social science journals reiterate that the benefits of racially balanced integration far outweigh any costs. Thus a 1981 article in the *Harvard Educational Review* repeated a view that James S. Coleman had long since recanted: "one of the most effective ways to improve children's cognitive skills is to put them in an environment with other children who want to acquire cognitive skills and whose families support such learning." In 2006, after crunching a mountain of statistics, other pro-integration researchers told the Supreme Court that "quantitative research has demonstrated that attending integrated schools improves the racial attitudes and life opportunities of students." By then, however, the justices recognized that the social science evidence for integration was, at best, conflicting and inconclusive. Writing for the majority of the Court, Chief Justice John G. Roberts noted that there was no consensus among scholars when it came to "whether racial diversity in schools in fact has a marked impact on test scores . . . or achieves intangible socialization benefits."[19]

This book describes the course of desegregation and integration in several communities. Much went awry when desegregation and integration were implemented. In the course of describing and discussing these problems, this book also touches on two topics that many writers consider

18. I have paraphrased a famous statement that a former Chief Justice, Charles Evans Hughes, made in a speech on May 3, 1907: "We are under a Constitution, but the Constitution is what the judges say it is." William Lockhart, Yale Kamisar, and Jesse Choper, *Constitutional Law*, 3d ed. (St. Paul: West Publishing, 1970), 7; *Brown v. Board of Education*, 349 U.S. 294 (1955); *Brown v. Board of Education*, 347 U.S. 485 (1954); Amicus Brief of William Chafe et al., *Parents Involved v. Seattle School District* (U.S. Supreme Court, 2006); Charles T. Clotfelter, *After Brown: The Rise and Retreat of School Desegregation* (Princeton: Princeton University Press, 2004), 7; Cheryll D. Cashin, "American Public Schools Fifty Years after *Brown*," *Howard Law Journal* 47 (2004): 343; John Charles Boger, "Willful Colorblindness: The New Racial Piety and the Resegregation of Public Schools," *North Carolina Law Review* 78 (2000): 1794–95.

19. Richard J. Mumane, "Evidence, Analysis, and Unanswered Questions," *Harvard Educational Review* 51 (1981): 486; Amicus Brief of Amy Stuart Wells et al., *Parents Involved v. Seattle*, U.S. Supreme Court, 2006; *Parents Involved v. Seattle*, 127 S.Ct. 2738 (2007), 2755.

taboo—the shortcomings and misbehavior of some disadvantaged minority students. That is yet one more way in which this work departs from the prevailing academic orthodoxy.

This history of school desegregation and integration arrives at a paradoxical conclusion. *Brown v. Board of Education* was one of the most important events in the history of twentieth-century America. It was a landmark that separated the era of Jim Crow segregation from that of the modern United States. *Brown* put the nation on the road toward dismantling segregation and removing racial barriers. But, ironically, desegregation has been far less successful in education than in other areas of American life.

Nondiscriminatory policies have been a boon to athletics, the arts, and interstate commerce. Such policies have caused but few problems in public accommodations. In education, however, desegregation was problematical from the start, and integration has been a failure. This book describes some of the problems and failures, but for this introduction it should suffice to say that, more than five decades after *Brown*, the "achievement gap" between the average black student and the average white has proved to be intractable. At the time of *Brown*, many assumed that, with desegregation, black students would make better scores on standard achievement tests. At the time of *Green*, *Swann*, and *Keyes*, others hoped that integration would lead to academic progress. As it happened, however, the gap in academic proficiency has persisted and has become, indeed, one of the most comprehensively documented facts in American educational history. Because racial differences in academic achievement proved to be impervious to amelioration through either desegregation or integration, many educators eventually embraced other approaches to improving the situation. By the end of the twentieth century, most informed observers had lost faith in the efficacy of desegregation and integration and had turned to different ways to achieve equality of educational opportunity. The present volume could be subtitled, "The Age of Desegregation and Integration." A companion work-in-progress will deal with the contemporary "Age of School Reform."

1

Constitutional History and Social Science

Brown v. Board of Education (1954) and Stell v. Savannah Chatham (1963)

Brown v. Board

The full significance of *Brown v. Board of Education* (1954) will be apparent only with the passage of more time. In at least three respects the Supreme Court's ruling was a blessing. By ending *de jure* segregation, *Brown* was a boon to American foreign policy; it reconciled the nation's official policies with its basic principles; and it gave many individual African Americans opportunities that would not have been available if *Brown* had not dealt a fatal blow to the Jim Crow system. Most writers have emphasized these benefits. America would not have remained a viable society if blacks had continued to be consigned to separate water fountains and to seats at the back of the bus.

But *Brown* was also a bane. It was problematical in terms of constitutional history and social science, and the quality of American education eventually suffered because of the tensions and disorder that followed in the wake of desegregation and because of the unintended consequences of educational innovations that were implemented to "make integration work." *Brown* also established a precedent for judicial policy making in areas that had nothing to do with race or education. As a result, the Supreme Court was politicized while America's schools still faced daunting challenges in the twenty-first century.

When state or local governments insisted that black children must attend separate schools, those governments placed their stamp of approval on the doctrine of racial inferiority. Government officials were understood to be saying that the intellectual and cultural standards of African Americans were so different from those of Caucasians, and so inferior, that the races should not go to school together. This amounted to officially disparaging the Negro race, a humiliation that reinforced the message that mean-spirited white people conveyed when they refused to shake hands; when they did not address black men as "Mister" but rather as "boy," "Howard," or "nigger Jones"; and when they called black women "aunt" or perhaps by their first name but never "Mrs." Nevertheless, in the early 1950s neither Congress nor many state legislatures were prepared to end segregation.

Segregation also tarnished the reputation of the United States at a time when the nation was vying with the Soviet Union for influence in the Third World. American diplomats assured foreign leaders that segregation was a regional rather than a national practice, a relic of times past, a policy that was on the way out. The Justice Department's amicus brief in *Brown* argued that desegregation was in the national interest because of foreign policy. *Brown* gave the U.S. government the decision it had been hoping for, and the State Department quickly made use of the ruling. Within an hour after the Supreme Court released its opinion, a Voice of America radio broadcast trumpeted the news abroad.[1]

Brown also legitimized and helped to shape views that were emerging as a moral consensus among white Americans. In the Deep South many whites opposed desegregation, but elsewhere most whites accepted the principle that the government should not discriminate. *Brown* condemned an entrenched injustice and helped to prepare the way for the civil rights movement.[2]

Although *Brown* struck down an injustice, the rationale of the Supreme Court was spurious. In 1953, when the *Brown* litigation was pending, the Court asked opposing counsel whether the framers of the relevant section of the U.S. Constitution, the equal protection clause of the Fourteenth Amendment, had contemplated and understood that their handiwork would render segregated schools unconstitutional. Or had the framers, as a possible alternative, intended that either Congress or the Supreme Court

1. Mary L. Dudziak, "Desegregation as a Cold War Imperative," *Stanford Law Review* 41 (November 1988): 61–120; Dudziak, *Cold War and Civil Rights: Race and the Image of American Democracy* (Princeton: Princeton University Press, 2000).

2. For discussion of polls conducted in 1942, 1956, and 1963 by the National Opinion Research Center, see Herbert H. Hyan and Paul B. Sheatsley, "Attitudes toward Desegregation," *Scientific American* 211 (July 1964): 16–23; and Andrew M. Greeley and Paul B. Sheatsley, "Attitudes toward Racial Integration," *Scientific American* 225 (December 1971): 13–19.

could abolish segregation in light of future conditions? The questions suggested that the Court wanted to rule against segregation but feared that
doing so could be justified only by the sort of judicial activism that several of the justices had denounced during the years of the New Deal. The justices therefore asked the NAACP to provide historical evidence to protect
the Court against the charge that it would be legislating if, without regard
to historical intent, the Court discovered a new meaning in the amendment. The Court asked for additional information about the Thirty-ninth
Congress, which submitted the amendment to the states in 1866, and about
the subsequent state ratifying conventions.

The NAACP then employed several historians, three of whom later expressed ambivalence if not regret over their role in the venture. At the
outset, the black historian John Hope Franklin noted "the difference
between scholarship and advocacy" and expressed concern about "the
temptation to pollute . . . scholarship with polemics." So did the white
historian C. Vann Woodward. But Franklin and Woodward nevertheless
prepared papers that maintained that segregation frustrated the egalitarian intent of the Fourteenth Amendment. In 1963, Franklin confessed that
he had "deliberately transformed the objective data provided by historical research into an urgent plea for justice." And Woodward later retracted his earlier statements that the Fourteenth Amendment was prompted
by egalitarian intentions. In time Woodward conceded that, given the sen-
timents that prevailed when southern public schools were established in
the 1860s and 1870s, the alternative to segregated schools was not integration but no schools for blacks.[3]

The most important historical work in the *Brown* litigation was done
by the constitutional scholar Alfred H. Kelly. Yet when Kelly delved into
the historical records, he discovered that "unhappily, from the NAACP's
point of view, most of what appeared there at first blush looked rather
decidedly bad." To begin, there was the fact that the Congress that submitted the Fourteenth Amendment to the states also established segregated schools in the District of Columbia. It hardly seemed likely that
Congress intended to destroy the states' right to maintain segregated
schools when that very same Congress provided a system of segregated

3. John Hope Franklin, "The Dilemma of the American Negro Scholar," in Herbert
Hill, ed., *Soon One Morning* (New York: Alfred A. Knopf, 1975), 74, 73; Richard Kluger,
Simple Justice (New York: Alfred A. Knopf, 1976), 788; C. Vann Woodward, *Thinking
Back* (Baton Rouge: Louisiana State University Press, 1986), 96–97. On this point, see
also Howard N. Rabinowitz, "More Than the Woodward Thesis: Assessing *The Strange
Career of Jim Crow,*" *Journal of American History* 75 (December 1988): 842–56; and Rabin-
owitz, *Race Relations in the Urban South* (New York: Oxford University Press, 1978).

schools in the federal district. In addition, although a few states discontinued segregation after endorsing the amendment, most continued with segregation and some introduced segregation contemporaneously with passage of the amendment. They did not think there was any conflict between the two actions. All things considered, it seemed clear that neither the Congress nor the ratifying states understood that the Fourteenth Amendment would destroy the states' right to maintain segregated schools. Alexander M. Bickel, a leading authority on the original understanding of the Fourteenth Amendment, concluded that "The evidence of congressional purpose is as clear as such evidence is likely to be." Congress neither intended nor expected the Fourteenth Amendment to prohibit segregation.[4]

At first Kelly's role was to alert the NAACP to the difficulties posed by the historical record. Only then could the NAACP formulate "an adequate gloss on the fateful events of 1866 sufficient to convince the Court that we had something of a historical case." "It was not that we were engaged in formulating lies," Kelly later wrote. "There was nothing as crude and naïve as that. But we were using facts, emphasizing facts, bearing down on facts, sliding off facts, quietly ignoring facts, and above all interpreting facts in a way to do what [NAACP lawyer Thurgood] Marshall said we had to do." Initially Kelly, like John Hope Franklin and C. Vann Woodward, hoped it would suffice to emphasize the general spirit of humanitarianism and social idealism that allegedly "dominated the rise of the abolitionist movement and which by implication thereby had determined the objectives of the radical Republicans who had written the Fourteenth Amendment." Eventually, Kelly also added something of a conspiracy thesis: that John A. Bingham, a principal author of the Fourteenth Amendment, had purposely used the broad language of the equal protection clause with the secret intention of making it constitutional for a later federal government to prohibit segregation.[5]

It was a dubious argument. There was no evidence that Bingham camouflaged an undisclosed purpose. Even if such evidence had been discovered, it would not have been conclusive, for the doctrine of ratification presumes that the states understand what they are ratifying. Kelly later admitted that he had "manipulated history in the best tradition of Amer-

4. Alfred H. Kelly, "An Inside View of *Brown v. Board*," paper delivered to the American Historical Association, 28 December 1961, reprinted at the request of J. Strom Thurmond, *Congressional Record*, 87th Congress, 2d Session, 11 September 1962, 19023; Alexander M. Bickel, "The Original Understanding and the Segregation Decision," *Harvard Law Review* 69 (November 1955): 59.
5. Kluger, *Simple Justice*, 895; Kelly, "Inside View," 19025, 19024.

ican advocacy, carefully marshaling every possible scrap of evidence in favor of the desired interpretation and just as carefully doctoring all the evidence to the contrary, either by suppressing it when that seemed plausible, or by distorting it when suppression was not possible." Kelly recalled that he was "facing for the first time in my own career the deadly opposition between my professional integrity as a historian and my wishes and hopes with respect to a contemporary question. . . . I suppose if a man is without scruple this matter will not bother him, but I am frank to say that it bothered me terribly."[6]

While Kelly and other historians were working for the NAACP, Justice Felix Frankfurter asked Alexander Bickel, then a law clerk at the Supreme Court, to undertake yet another examination of the historical record. Unlike Kelly and the others, Bickel concluded that the Congress that submitted the Fourteenth Amendment neither intended that segregation be abolished nor foresaw that, under the language they were adopting, it might be. The most that could be said for the NAACP was that the framers of the Fourteenth Amendment realized that they were writing a constitution, and understood that constitutional language always contains a certain elasticity that allows for reinterpretation to satisfy the requirements of future times. Like some modern "deconstructionists," Bickel argued that, through wordplay, constitutions can (and should) be interpreted without regard to original intent to mean whatever the interpreters want them to mean.[7]

Bickel's argument was clever but not new. It essentially reiterated an opinion that Chief Justice Charles Evans Hughes had expressed in 1934, when Hughes rejected the contention that the Supreme Court should interpret the great clauses of the constitution according to their original intent. According to Hughes, "it was to guard against such a narrow conception that Chief Justice Marshall uttered the memorable warning—'we must never forget that it is a *constitution* we are expounding—a constitu-

---

6. Alfred H. Kelly, "Clio and the Court: An Illicit Love Affair," *Supreme Court Review* (1965): 144, 119–58; Kelly, "Inside View," 19024. In *The Southern Case for School Segregation* (New York: Crowell-Collier Press, 1962), 133–34, James J. Kilpatrick offered this assessment of the work of the NAACP's historians: "They produced a 235-page brief. It must stand as a pathetic monument to what happens when historians cease to be historians and take up the unlicensed practice of the law. The conclusions there drawn, that the 'proponents of absolute equalitarianism emerged victorious in the Civil War and controlled the Congress that wrote the Fourteenth Amendment,' are a bitter travesty upon the actual course of events. For it is plain to any objective student . . . that no such thing occurred. The visible, palpable, unrelenting, unavoidable truth is that [Charles] Sumner and [Thad] Stevens and their fellow radicals did not control the Congress in 1866; they did *not* get what they wanted in the Fourteenth Amendment."
7. Kluger, *Simple Justice*, 827.

tion intended to endure for ages to come, and consequently to be adapted to the various crises of human affairs.'"[8]

The *Brown* Court may have had something like Bickel's exegesis in mind when it termed the historical evidence "inconclusive." Or perhaps the justices simply meant to say that, in their opinion, the evidence was so diverse that it was hard to determine the historical truth.[9]

Ironically, other historians might have fashioned a better historical argument for *Brown*. According to Robert H. Bork, the Supreme Court should have noted that the purpose of the equal protection clause was to ensure that African Americans were not significantly disadvantaged by state laws; that at the time and for some years thereafter it was assumed that separate schools could be equal; but by 1954 it had become apparent that the separate facilities provided for blacks were not as good as those provided for whites. The Court could then have ruled that to achieve the equality that the Fourteenth Amendment had promised, it was necessary to desegregate the public schools. In this way *Brown* could have been defended as consistent with the original understanding of the equal protection clause.[10]

Michael W. McConnell has presented another originalist argument for *Brown*. Since Section 5 of the Fourteenth Amendment gave Congress the authority to enforce the amendment with appropriate legislation, McConnell maintained that contemporary congressional debates were germane to the original understanding with respect to segregated schools. He then noted that on eighteen recorded votes in the early 1870s a majority of either the House or Senate voted to prohibit school segregation, although "because of procedural problems and Democratic filibustering, a two-

8. Hughes's statement was made in *Home Building and Loan Association v. Blaisdell*, 290 U.S. 398 (1934), 443; and Marshall's in *McCulloch v. Maryland*, 4 Wheat 316 (1819), 407. Expressing a contrary point of view, the constitutional scholar Charles Cooley observed: "A cardinal rule in dealing with written instruments is that they are to receive an unvarying interpretation and that their practical construction is to be uniform. A Constitution is not to be made to mean one thing at one time, and another at some subsequent time when circumstances may have changed as perhaps to make a different rule in the case seem desirable. A principal share of the benefit expected from a written Constitution would be lost if the rules they established were so flexible as to bend to circumstances or be modified by public opinion." Agreeing with Cooley, Chief Justice Roger B. Taney once stated: "Any other rule of construction would abrogate the judicial character of this court, and make it the mere reflex of the popular opinion or passion of the day." Cooley and Taney's statements are quoted in Kilpatrick, *Southern Case*, 129–30 and 130–31.

9. *Brown v. Board of Education*, 347 U.S. 483 (1954), 489.

10. See Robert H. Bork, *The Tempting of America* (New York: Free Press, 1990), 74–84. Charles L. Black Jr. made a similar argument: "The Lawfulness of the Segregation Decisions," *Yale Law Journal* 69 (1959–1960): 421–30.

thirds vote was required at key junctures and the support for [school desegregation] fell just short of two-thirds."[11]

Yet these arguments were not developed until years after *Brown*. Bork and McConnell were distinguished conservative scholars and federal judges, and each recognized that by the time they achieved prominence no one could be confirmed for a federal appointment without supporting *Brown*. They therefore had practical reasons for defending *Brown* on originalist grounds. Whether or not Bork and McConnell are correct, the point is that in 1954 the justices of the Supreme Court would have welcomed an originalist defense of desegregation, but they were unable to conceive of one. Instead, the justices apparently thought that there was no warrant for their ruling in the historic Constitution. Instead, they mentioned the impossibility of "turn[ing] back the clock to 1868 when the Amendment was adopted." They said they had to "consider public education in the light of its full development and its present place in American life."[12]

Years later, after the ruling in *Brown* had become sacrosanct, some liberal activists endorsed the argument that *Brown* could not be reconciled with the original understanding. They sensed that if it was understood that *Brown* could not be reconciled with the original meaning of the Fourteenth Amendment, then many people would conclude that something was wrong with the idea that the Constitution should be interpreted in accord with the intentions of the framers. Thus in 1982 Michael J. Perry admitted that *Brown* (and some other Supreme Court decisions) could not plausibly be defended as interpretations of the Constitution. But Perry praised the modern Court for taking a "noninterpretivist" approach to constitutional law. According to Perry, the justices of the Court were modern "prophets" selected by an "American Israel" and authorized to strike down laws they deemed mistaken. In 1997 David Garrow similarly praised *Brown* for its "repudiation of historical intent." By ignoring "the burdens and limitations of history," by freeing the Court from "the Constitution's historical limitations," *Brown* established a precedent that later Courts could cite to justify overruling the decisions of elected legislators with respect to abortion, criminal justice, equality, religion, and other matters.[13]

11. Michael W. McConnell, "Concurring in the Judgment," in Jack M. Balkin, ed., *What Brown v. Board of Education Should Have Said* (New York: New York University Press, 2001), 164.

12. *Brown v. Board of Education*, 347 U.S 483 (1954), 492.

13. Michael J. Perry, *The Constitution, the Courts, and Human Rights* (New Haven: Yale University Press, 1982); Grover Rees III, "Prophets without Portfolio," *National Review*, 2 September 1983, 1078–82; David Garrow, "From *Brown* to *Casey*," in Austin Sarat, ed., *Race, Law, and Culture* (New York: Oxford University Press, 1997), 74–84.

Meanwhile, conservatives lambasted *Brown* for subverting democracy by departing (as, indeed, the Court thought it was) from the original understanding in order to achieve a socially desirable end. On the fiftieth anniversary of the Supreme Court's ruling, Thomas Sowell found little to celebrate. By then, he said, it had become "painfully clear that the educational results of *Brown* have been meager for black children" and, in addition, "the kind of reasoning used in *Brown* has had serious negative repercussions on our whole legal system, extending far beyond issues of race and education." George F. Will joined in lamenting the "myriad reverberations" from *Brown*. Will complained especially about *Brown*'s tendency to aggrandize the judiciary—to invest judges with "a prestige that begot arrogance," with a belief that judges should find that policies they considered mistaken were also "unconstitutional." Paul Craig Roberts lamented that *Brown* "ushered in kritarchy—government by judges."[14]

After asserting that the history of the Fourteenth Amendment was inconclusive, the *Brown* Court held that "in the field of public education the doctrine of 'separate but equal' has no place." One year later, the Court ordered school districts to "make a prompt and reasonable start" toward admitting students to public schools "on a racially nondiscriminatory basis."[15]

Brown was ambiguous, however, when it came to the question of whether the Constitution prohibited separation that was not the result of official state policy. At two points in his opinion for the Court, Chief Justice Earl Warren wrote that the case concerned the official, legal segregation of children in public schools "solely on the basis of race" and "solely because of race"—thereby implying that there was no Constitutional problem if the races failed to mingle because of unofficial and nonracial factors such as choice or residence in racially imbalanced neighborhoods.[16]

This offered reassurance to many Americans, a reassurance that was related to a paradox that lies at the core of the nation's racial thought. As the Swedish scholar Gunnar Myrdal noted in his classic study *An American Dilemma* (1944), even before *Brown* most whites opposed bigotry and supported equal rights. They were troubled by the contradiction between

14. Thomas Sowell, "Where Rhetoric Beats Reasoning," *Wall Street Journal,* 13 May 2004; George F. Will, "Good and Bad Things Came with *Brown v. Board of Education*," *Sacramento Bee,* 16 May 2004; Paul Craig Roberts, "Fifty Years of *Brown*: The Age of Kritarchy," Vdare.com, 16 May 2004.

15. *Brown v. Board of Education,* 347 U.S. 483 (1954), 493, 494; *Brown v. Board of Education,* 349 U.S. 294 (1955), 300.

16. *Brown v. Board of Education,* 347 U.S. (1954), 493, 494.

egalitarian principles and the reality of racial discrimination. They wanted their practices to be consistent with their ideals. But they also feared that desegregation would lead to an increase in miscegenation, which they feared partly because they felt a sense of racial identity and pride, and partly because of what they considered the low cultural and social standards of African Americans. Many whites who opposed official segregation also insisted on their right to freedom of association when it came to choosing friends, associates, and neighborhoods. They recognized that the moral, intellectual, and cultural standards of whites left something to be desired, but they would not accept African Americans socially until American Negroes approached these standards in large numbers.[17]

These views were not always expressed openly, but many white homeowners left their neighborhoods if more than a token number of blacks moved in, and most white parents with sufficient means removed their children from schools that became predominantly nonwhite. Most white Americans apparently favored a system of segmented development in which people voluntarily chose to live in communities that were predominantly of their own race. Nor were whites alone in this respect. Marcus Garvey and Malcolm X also spoke in favor of racial communities, and W. E. B. Du Bois once recommended that Negroes and Caucasians should live "side by side in peace and mutual happiness," with each group making its own "peculiar contribution . . . to the culture of their common country." In 1995 Supreme Court justice Clarence Thomas affirmed that "the Constitution does not prevent individuals from choosing to live together, to work together, or to send their children to school together, so long as the state does not interfere on the basis of race."[18]

At first *Brown* seemed to be consistent with this sort of pluralism. Because it held that government officials could not separate blacks from whites "solely" on the basis of race, *Brown* was initially understood to require only that states must desist from official racial discrimination. In the 1950s and early 1960s, hardly anyone favored the formal assignment of students (or the employment of workers) on the basis of race so as to achieve more racial mixing than could be achieved by racially neutral policies. *Desegregation* would be required, but *integration* would not be imposed. Until the late 1960s, *Brown* was understood to forbid the public

17. Gunnar Myrdal, *An American Dilemma* (New York: Harper and Brothers, 1944); *Congressional Quarterly Almanac*, 20 (1964), 372 (remarks of Louisiana Senator Allen Ellender).

18. W. E. B. Du Bois, "The Conservation of Races" (1897), reprinted in Herbert Aptheker, ed., *Pamphlets and Leaflets by W. E. B. Du Bois* (White Plains, N.Y.: Kraus-Thomson Organization, 1986), 7; *Missouri v. Jenkins* 515 U.S. 70 (1995), 121.

schools from practicing any sort of racial discrimination. In the 1950s and early 1960s, most civil rights activists said that race and color were irrelevant to the proper consideration of a person's worth. They sought the advancement of blacks but assumed this could be accomplished if the schools treated students as individuals, without regard to race, color, or creed.

The idea that official racial discrimination was prohibited also seemed to be implied in *Bolling v. Sharpe* (decided the same day as *Brown*), in which the Supreme Court ruled against segregation in the public schools of the District of Columbia—on the grounds that racial classifications were too arbitrary to satisfy the requirements of the due process clause. That *Brown* prohibited official racial discrimination also seemed to be the message in several *per curium* decisions in which the Court later invalidated laws requiring segregation of municipal parks and recreational facilities. In 1955 Chief Justice Warren declared that *Brown* had affirmed "the fundamental principle that racial discrimination in education is unconstitutional"; and the Supreme Court's implementation order was worded so as to condemn "discrimination" rather than "segregation" in education. Three years later, in *Cooper v. Aaron* (1958), a case that arose in Little Rock, Arkansas, the Court held that *Brown* had established that children have "constitutional rights . . . not to be discriminated against in school admission on grounds of race or color." Civil rights activists and sympathizers understood this to mean that the Court had declared that official classification by race was unconstitutional.[19]

In response to the decisions of the Supreme Court, lower federal courts affirmed that racial discrimination was prohibited and that the Constitution required the government to treat each person as an individual without regard to race. Stated most fluently, perhaps, by Circuit Judge John J. Parker in *Briggs v. Elliott* (1955), this point of view was frequently called the *Briggs* dictum. For more than a decade it was the authoritative construction of *Brown*: "It is important that we point out exactly what the Supreme Court has decided and what it has not decided. . . . The Constitution . . . does not require integration. It merely forbids discrimination."[20]

19. *Bolling v. Sharpe*, 347 U.S. 497 (1954); *Florida ex rel Hawkins et al.*, 347 U.S. 971 (1954); Andrew Kull, *The Color-Blind Constitution* (Cambridge: Harvard University Press, 1992), 162; *Cooper v. Aaron*, 358 U.S. 1 (1958), 17.

20. *Briggs v. Elliott*, 132 F.Supp. 776 (1955), 777. In an especially blunt statement, the Fifth Circuit Court of Appeals affirmed: "The Fourteenth Amendment does not speak in positive terms to command integration, but negatively, to prohibit governmentally enforced segregation." *Holland v. Board of Public Instruction*, 258 F.2d 731 (1958). As will be noted below, federal courts followed the *Briggs* dictum in implementing *Brown* in Topeka and Wilmington (whose litigation had been consolidated with *Brown*) and in Washington (whose litigation was decided the same day as *Brown*).

Echoing this view, Congress passed the Civil Rights Act of 1964, which endorsed the common understanding that official discrimination should not be tolerated but racial mixing need not be compelled. Section 407 of the Civil Rights Act authorized the attorney general to initiate school desegregation actions, and section 401 defined desegregation: "'Desegregation' means the assignment of students to public schools and within such schools without regard to their race, color, religion, or national origin, but 'desegregation' shall not mean the assignment of students to public schools to overcome racial imbalance." *Brown, Briggs,* and the Civil Rights Act were understood to be about *de jure* segregation and not about *de facto* racial imbalances and concentrations.[21]

Some critics raised objections to the reasoning displayed in the opinion (as distinguished from the holding) of *Brown;* and some others cautioned that, in a democracy, important changes should not be instigated by unelected judges, appointed for life. But the great majority of influential Americans considered the outcome of the case so morally right, and so clearly in the interests of whites as well as blacks, that *Brown* became a venerated symbol. By the mid-1960s *Brown* was revered for having brought an end to official segregation. Because it relieved blacks from stigma and whites from guilt, the Supreme Court received the thanks of a grateful nation. *Brown* became the example par excellence of what the black activist and legal scholar Derrick Bell has called "interest convergence" as a motivation for racial policy making. In this instance, Bell explained, "the interest of blacks" was "accommodated" because it "converge[d] with the interests of whites in policy-making positions."[22]

The celebration of *Brown* would not have been so widespread if Americans had had a better understanding of all that the opinion of the Supreme Court could be interpreted to imply. After holding that the relevant historical evidence was inconclusive, and after repeatedly stating that the litigation arose from segregation compelled by law, the *Brown* Court engaged in psychological and sociological theorizing that later was held to mean that actual racial mixing was called for, not just an end to state-enforced segregation. Both *Brown* and the later rulings were influenced by social science arguments that, given the evidence available at the

21. Public Law 88-352 (1964), 246.

22. Derrick Bell, "*Brown v. Board of Education* and the Interest-Convergence Dilemma," *Harvard Law Review* 93 (1980): 518; Bell, *Silent Covenants: Brown v. Board of Education and the Unfulfilled Hopes for Racial Reform* (New York: Oxford University Press, 2004), 58, 70.

time, could best be characterized as not clearly erroneous; social science arguments which, after subsequent research, came to be regarded as either dubious or mistaken.

Specifically, *Brown* held that racial isolation damaged the confidence of black youths and depressed their ambitions and self-esteem. It said that the segregation of black students generated "a feeling of inferiority as to their status in the community that may affect their hearts and minds in a way unlikely ever to be undone." It approvingly repeated the conclusion of a Kansas court: that segregation tended "to [retard] the educational and mental development of Negro children and to deprive them of some of the benefits they could receive in a racial[ly] integrated school system." *Brown* embraced what is sometimes called "the harm and benefit thesis." It held that school segregation harmed black students and implied that desegregation would help African Americans develop more self-esteem and do better academically.[23]

In so holding, the *Brown* Court placed its imprimatur on the social science of the Swedish scholar Gunnar Myrdal, whose work the Court cited approvingly in a footnote. In his classic book *An American Dilemma*, Myrdal ignored the strengths of African American life and culture—strengths that black leaders such as W. E. B. Du Bois and Marcus Garvey, among others, had emphasized. Instead, Myrdal maintained that white discrimination had so damaged blacks as to render their culture, values, and communities almost deranged. According to Myrdal, "in practically all its divergences [from the dominant white society] American Negro culture is . . . a distorted development, or a pathological condition." Segregation damaged blacks, and the extent of the damage was reflected in the way blacks lived. "The instability of the Negro family, the inadequacy of educational facilities for Negroes, the emotionalism of the Negro church . . . provincialism . . . high Negro crime rate . . . and other characteristic traits are mainly forms of social pathology which, for the most part, are created by the caste pressures."[24]

In time, Myrdal's views became something of a liberal orthodoxy. To overcome the warping effects of discrimination and segregation, Myrdal and others called for both desegregation and integration. "We assume," Myrdal wrote, "that it is to the advantage of American Negroes as individuals and as a group to become assimilated into American cul-

23. Bell, *"Brown v. Board,"* 495, 494. For a discussion of the harm and benefit thesis, see David J. Armor, *Forced Justice: School Segregation and the Law* (New York: Oxford University Press, 1995), 59–116.

24. Myrdal, *American Dilemma,* 928–29.

ture, to acquire the traits held in esteem by the dominant white Americans."[25]

As Myrdal saw it, white prejudice and discrimination had depressed the Negro's standards of living and morality, and whites then pointed to the low standards as justification for discrimination. One way to break this cycle was to fashion desegregation so as to encourage equal status contact between blacks and whites. If whites interacted with blacks of similar status, they would discover a common humanity that transcended race. If desegregation were structured properly, whites would discover that racial prejudice was irrational.[26]

At first, the Supreme Court obfuscated on the requirements it was establishing. As noted, for more than a decade *Brown* was understood to require only desegregation—the disestablishment of official segregation, the assignment of children to public schools without regard to their race. However, beginning in the late 1960s (and continuing for about twenty-five years), the Supreme Court reinterpreted *Brown* to require school boards to develop affirmative policies to achieve racial mixing in schools where such mixing was not achieved in sufficient degree by racially neutral policies. In imposing integration, the Supreme Court seemed to embrace the views of Gunnar Myrdal.[27]

In endorsing Myrdal's social science, the *Brown* Court and subsequent Supreme Courts turned away from the main line of argument that attorney Thurgood Marshall had presented in his legal briefs for the NAACP. Marshall had acknowledged that the Constitution allowed for some discrimination against groups (as with the all-male military draft and restrictions on the freedom of minors), but Marshall said the due process and equal protection clauses required not only that discrimination must be justified but also that especially weighty evidence was necessary to justify racial discrimination. Marshall said no such evidence had been presented in *Brown*. Therefore, according to Marshall, racial segregation fell within a group of unreasonable classifications that the due process and equal protection clauses prohibited. Marshall even suggested that it was

25. Ibid., 929.
26. This thesis was developed most influentially by the Harvard psychologist Gordon W. Allport in *The Nature of Prejudice* (Cambridge: Addison-Wesley, 1954).
27. For a different view, see Reva B. Siegel, "*Brown* at Fifty: Equality Talk: Antisubordination and Anticlasification Values in Constitutional Struggles over *Brown*," *Harvard Law Review* 117 (March 2004): 1470–547. If I understand this article, it maintains that *Brown* did not prohibit all official racial classifications because the Supreme Court of 1954 did not wish to suggest that it was forbidding laws against miscegenation. Even if this is so, I believe *Brown* was generally understood to have said it was unconstitutional for the public schools to classify students by race.

just as arbitrary and capricious to discriminate against people with dark skins as it would have been to discriminate against people who had blue eyes or blond hair.[28]

Marshall and other NAACP lawyers made these points repeatedly and unequivocally. They said that classifications based "solely on race or color" were "arbitrary and unreasonable" and "the very kind the equal protection clause was designed to prohibit." They said it was their "dedicated belief" that the Constitution was "color-blind." They said that the Fourteenth Amendment had "stripped the state of power to make race and color the basis for governmental action." And they also renounced discrimination as a remedy for previous discrimination. They said they were

> not asking for affirmative relief. . . . The only thing that we ask for is that the state-imposed racial segregation be taken off, and to leave the county school board . . . to assign children on any reasonable basis they want to assign them on. . . .
>
> What we want from this Court is the striking down of race. . . .
>
> Do not deny any child the right to go to the school of his choice on the grounds of race or color. . . . [D]o not assign them on the basis of race. . . . If you have some other basis . . . any other basis, we have no objection. But just do not put in race or color as a factor.[29]

The Supreme Court embraced this rationale in *Bolling v. Sharpe,* a companion case that was decided with *Brown* on May 17, 1954. The *Bolling* case rose from the District of Columbia and was decided separately for legal reasons. The Fourteenth Amendment (which asserted that no *state* could deprive a person of the equal protection of the laws) did not apply to the federal government. But the Fifth Amendment prohibited the federal government from depriving citizens of liberty without due process. In *Bolling* the Court recognized that "discrimination may be so unjustifiable as to be violative of due process." It said that "classifications based solely upon race must be scrutinized with particular care, since they are contrary to our traditions, and hence constitutionally suspect."[30]

28. Leon Friedman, ed., *Argument: The Oral Argument before the Supreme Court in Brown v. Board of Education of Topeka, 1952–1955* (New York: Chelsea House, 1969), 38, 45.
29. Kull, *Color-Blind Constitution,* 157; G. W. Foster Jr., "The North and West Have Problems, Too," *Saturday Review,* 20 April 1963, 72; Friedman, *Argument,* 47, 375, 402.
30. *Bolling v. Sharpe,* 347 U.S. 497 (1954), 499. Because *Brown* held that the Fourteenth

In *Brown*, however, the Court said nothing about the arbitrariness of racial classifications. Instead, the Court pointed to the damage that segregation supposedly did to blacks. It said that segregation so victimized black students as to make an equal education impossible.

Perhaps it would have been better if *Brown* had repeated the rationale of *Bolling* and the implications of the *per curiam* rulings; if *Brown* had simply said it was inherently arbitrary for government officials to classify and discriminate on the basis of race; if it had endorsed the major argument that Thurgood Marshall had presented in *Brown,* or the dictum that Judge Parker would announce in *Briggs,* or the definition that Congress later provided in the Civil Rights Act of 1964. Instead, after citing evidence from the social sciences, *Brown* held that segregation was unconstitutional because it damaged blacks psychologically. Later this rationale and holding would lead the Court to affirm that *Brown* mandated not only what most people at the time thought it required (no racial discrimination) but also something quite different (affirmative racial assignments to achieve more racial integration that could be achieved through racially neutral policies).[31]

Some of the NAACP's lawyers had reservations about using evidence from social science, but they knew that different minds might be persuaded by different arguments, and that therefore successful lawyers often presented all the arguments they could muster, neglecting none. Thus, at the behest of attorney Robert L. Carter, the NAACP got in touch with psychologist Kenneth B. Clark, who then prepared a statement that eventually was signed by thirty-two prominent anthropologists, psychologists, and sociologists—a statement that declared that black children were psychologically injured if they attended segregated schools. Regardless of the condition of the separate facilities, the social scientists said, segregation had a belittling effect upon the self-esteem of African American students. According to the social science statement, segregated black students reacted with "feelings of inferiority," which led to "a generally defeatist attitude and a lowering of personal ambitions." "In producing such effects," the statement said, "segregated schools impair[ed] the ability of the child to profit from the educational opportunities provided

---

Amendment prohibited states from maintaining racially segregated public schools, the justices also considered it "unthinkable that the same Constitution would impose a lesser duty on the Federal Government."

31. See Raymond Wolters, *The Burden of Brown: Thirty Years of School Desegregation* (Knoxville: University of Tennessee Press, 1984); and Wolters, *Right Turn: William Bradford Reynolds, the Reagan Administration, and Black Civil Rights* (New Brunswick: Transaction Publishers, 1996).

him." The statement further maintained, "under certain circumstances" (among them an absence of competition and special efforts to ensure that the academic status of the black and white students would be equal) "desegregation not only proceeds without major difficulties, but has been observed to lead to the emergence of more favorable attitudes and friendlier relations between races."[32]

The statement reflected a paradigm shift in social science. An earlier generation of scientists, influenced by a Social Darwinian belief that the races were at different stages of evolutionary development, tended to regard Negroes as innately inferior to Caucasians in terms of analytical intelligence. By the 1930s and 1940s, however, new scientific theories were coming into vogue, and many social scientists believed that racial differences in intelligence test scores and societal achievements resulted from the accidents of history and the influence of culture rather than from any innate differences in mental abilities. The NAACP's social science statement emphasized that "the available scientific evidence indicates that much, perhaps all, of the observable differences among various racial and national groups may be adequately explained in terms of environmental differences."[33]

In addition to suggesting that desegregation would boost the self-esteem and academic achievement of blacks, the NAACP's social scientists and lawyers also said that segregation gave whites a false sense of superiority and denied blacks the opportunity to learn the social skills needed for effective interaction with the dominant group. They said that segregation reinforced racial prejudice, increased mutual hostility and suspicion, and made outbreaks of racial violence more likely. With desegregation, they said, these problems would be ameliorated.

The NAACP's social science statement was consistent with much of the research of the 1930s and 1940s. The social scientists were not merely activists who were motivated by moral and political concerns rather than scientific data. Nevertheless, many of their assertions have since been discredited. Eventually, as historian John P. Jackson noted in 2001, "the psy-

32. See James T. Patterson, *Brown v. Board of Education: A Civil Rights Milestone and Its Troubled Legacy* (New York: Oxford University Press, 2001), 44: "Some of the people around [Thurgood] Marshall wondered about such research. Both [Jack] Greenberg and Spotswood Robinson were skeptical. Another top lawyer, William Coleman, pounded the table in opposition to using the research." "The Effects of Segregation and the Consequences of Desegregation: A Social Science Statement," in Philip B. Kurland and Gerhard Casper, eds., *Landmark Briefs and Arguments of the Supreme Court of the United States* (Arlington, Va.: University Publications of America, 1975), 49:4–5, 15–17.
33. "Effects of Segregation," 52.

chologists involved in *Brown* [came to be] viewed as liberal reformers who cloaked their political wishes in the guise of social science." That their testimony was unfounded became "the dominant understanding of the case."[34]

Numerous post-*Brown* studies later established that black students do not suffer in terms of self-esteem. In fact, according to one review of the literature, "research is nearly unanimous in reporting either no racial differences in self-esteem or differences favoring blacks over whites." Perhaps this is because most American youths consider academic achievement less important than street smarts, athletic prowess, and success with the opposite sex. Yet, because blacks lag behind whites in average academic performance, the self-esteem of blacks attending predominantly white schools is substantially lower than the self-esteem of those who attend predominantly black schools. Contrary to the prediction of the NAACP's social science statement, "segregation *protects* self-esteem [of blacks], while the impact of desegregation is to lower self-esteem."[35]

David J. Armor has provided a concise summary of the extensive research on self-esteem. At the time of *Brown*, "low self-esteem was seen as the major psychological mechanism to lower academic performance of black children." Subsequent research, however, indicated, first, that the self-esteem of black students was as high as that of whites; and second, that "segregated" black students were more likely to have a positive self-image than "desegregated" black students. According to Armor, "The research on black self-esteem . . . not only fails to support the harm and benefit thesis . . . but indeed seems to turn the thesis on its head." Attending predominantly black schools did not harm the self-esteem of black students. Instead, attending predominantly white schools led to lower self-esteem—either because blacks were experiencing racial prejudice, or because they found themselves at a disadvantage in comparison with white students.[36]

Given the relatively low average socioeconomic status of blacks, it may seem surprising that blacks did not suffer from low self-esteem. But the

34. John P. Jackson Jr., *Social Scientists for Social Justice* (New York: New York University Press, 2001), 2. Jackson himself dissented from this "dominant understanding."

35. Marylee C. Taylor and Edward J. Walsh, "Explantions of Black Self-Esteem," *Social Psychology Quarterly* 42 (1979): 242; Roy L. Brooks, *Integration or Separation? A Strategy for Racial Equality* (Cambridge: Harvard University Press, 1996), 2–3, 12–13, 16–18, 18–21, 23–24, 218–20, 231–33; Edgar G. Epps, "The Impact of School Desegregation on Aspirations, Self-Concepts, and Other Aspects of Personality," *Law and Contemporary Problems* 39 (spring 1975): 307.

36. Armor, *Forced Justice*, 99–101.

subculture of blacks allowed most African Americans to buffer the negative evaluations of mainstream whites. In *An American Dilemma*, Gunnar
Myrdal had noted that blacks tended to attribute their problems and low
status not to any personal failings but to racism and the American system.
In another classic work, *Equality of Educational Opportunity* (1966), James
S. Coleman also reported that blacks had self-esteem levels at least equal
to whites. The self-esteem of blacks was probably enhanced further as the
civil rights movement of the 1960s and 1970s placed increased emphasis
on black pride and black power.[37]

The NAACP's social scientists were mistaken when they informed the
Supreme Court that blacks were suffering in terms of self-esteem, and
they were naively optimistic when they told the Court that the conditions
for successful desegregation could "generally be satisfied in . . . public
schools." Given the racial gap in average academic achievement, there
was no likelihood that black and white students, on average, would be of
equivalent academic status. Moreover, because competitiveness is deeply
embedded in the American culture and because teachers are expected to
give higher grades to better students, competition could not be eliminated from the classroom. There was no way to create the circumstances that
the NAACP's social scientists themselves identified as essential for the
success of desegregation.[38]

Thus further research cast doubt on some (although not all) of the assertions of liberal social science. Critics took particular exception to the
work of psychologist Kenneth B. Clark, whose testimony in the *Brown*
case had been especially striking and influential. When the Supreme
Court cited "modern authority" in social science, as it did in footnote 11
of the *Brown* opinion, the Court first mentioned the work of "K. B. Clark."
During the previous decade Clark had published articles that dealt with
the effect of segregation on the self-esteem of black youths, and the
NAACP's lawyers thought that the "general scientific findings would
have more weight in a courtroom if it could be demonstrated that they
also applied in the specific cases . . . before the court." To that end, Clark
showed black and white dolls to sixteen black children selected at random
from segregated schools in Summerton, South Carolina, whose litigation
had been consolidated with the *Brown* litigation from Topeka, Kansas.
Clark then reported that nine of the sixteen children, when asked which
doll was the "nice one," selected the white doll, and that only eleven said

37. Myrdal, *American Dilemma,* 144; James S. Coleman et al., *Equality of Educational
Opportunity* (Washington: Government Printing Office, 1966).
  38. "Effects of Segregation," 59.

the black doll was the one that looked more like themselves. From this Clark inferred that segregation had a detrimental effect on the personalities of black children.[39]

Certainly Clark's presentation was vulnerable, as several commentators soon noted. Richard Kluger, a celebrant of the *Brown* decision, conceded that "sixteen children were not very many to start with, and if even one or two of them had undergone atypical experiences or traumas in their young lives, the overall test results would have been thrown out of kilter." Sociologist Ernest van den Haag scoffed that Clark's sample of students was not only too small for gauging any damage to the ego structure of blacks, but also "this number would be too small to test the reaction to a new soap."[40]

Others weighed in with additional criticisms. The legal scholar Edmond Cahn, a champion of the *Brown* decision (but not of the *Brown* opinion), noted that Clark's doll test did not purport to demonstrate "the effects of *school* segregation, which is what the court was being asked to enjoin. If it disclosed anything about the effects of segregation on the children, their experiences at school were not differentiated from other causes." Cahn thought it dangerous to base constitutional rights on social science as flimsy as that presented by Kenneth Clark. Psychologist Bruno Bettelheim also wondered "how far a good cause can be served by unsubstantiated or even spurious arguments made in its favor." Bettelheim supported the civil rights movement, but as a Jew who had attended nonsegregated public schools in Germany and Austria, he took exception to Clark's "familiar presumption that meeting children of different races and religions in school leads to better racial and religious relations." According to Bettelheim, "the seeds of racism and ultra-nationalism" had taken "firm root" in Germany's integrated schools, "while most children who went to Catholic parochial schools turned out (even under the Nazis) to be much less prejudiced." The educational success of Asian, Catholic, and Jewish students in the United States also cast doubt on the contention that racial or ethnic separation inevitably impaired educational development.[41]

Thus the NAACP's social science statement, and especially Kenneth

39. *Brown v. Board of Education*, 347 U.S. 483 (1954), 499n11; Kenneth B. Clark, "The Desegregation Cases," *Villanova Law Review* 5 (1960): 229; Trial Transcript, *Briggs v. Elliott*, Civil Action 2657, U.S. District Court, Columbia, South Carolina.

40. Kluger, *Simple Justice*, 446; Ernest van den Haag, quoted in Clark, "Desegregation Cases," 238.

41. Edmond Cahn, "Jurisprudence," *New York University Law Review* 30 (1955): 163–64; Bruno Bettelheim, "Discrimination and Science," *Commentary* 21 (April 1956): 384–86.

Clark's doll tests, were subjected to withering criticism. Nevertheless, perhaps because most scholars in the field sympathized with the purpose that animated this research and testimony, Clark's professional reputation was not damaged. Clark later enjoyed a lengthy career as a professor at the City University of New York, with stints teaching at Harvard, Columbia, and Berkeley. He became a member of the Board of Regents of New York State and a member of the Board of Directors of the Rand Corporation and of several foundations. He became a trustee of the University of Chicago and a consultant to the State Department. Eventually, Clark became the president of the American Psychological Association.

More immediately, Clark had the satisfaction of knowing that his doll test and social science statement made a crucial contribution to the NAACP's victory in *Brown*. The Supreme Court had found the NAACP's historical argument inconclusive, but it picked up its ears when the NAACP's social scientists said that segregation fostered feelings of inferiority that hampered the education of blacks. Historian Alfred Kelly conceded, "[Clark's] black and white dolls won the case, not the historians." In tribute to the NAACP's premier psychologist and most influential witness, some social scientists referred to *Brown* as the "Ken Clark law."[42]

The lawyers for South Carolina probably would have confronted Clark had they known that the Supreme Court would later rely on his doll studies. But since the doll test involved so few children, attorney Robert McCormick Figg recalled, "I didn't press the matter. [Clark's] numbers were small and unimposing." John W. Davis, the lead attorney for South Carolina, was especially skeptical of the social science evidence, confiding in one letter: "I think I have never read a drearier lot of testimony than that furnished by the so-called educational and psychological experts." "I can only say that if that sort of 'fluff" can move any court, 'God save the state!'" Instead of stressing social science, Davis made a legal argument. With citations to eighty years of precedents, Davis said that the right of a state to maintain segregated schools had been affirmed so frequently by

42. Kelly, "Inside View," 19026; C. P. Armstrong, S. S. Crutchfield, W. E. Hoy, and R. K. Kuttner, "Legal Testimony and Scientific Evidence," *Mankind Quarterly* 4 (October–December 1963): 105. *Brown* has been interpreted in many ways, and some able commentators have denied the social science provenience of the opinion. Edmond Cahn's already cited law review article, "Jurisprudence," is one example. For more recent, differing assessments of the influence of social science, see Sanjay Mody, "Brown Footnote 11 in Historical Context," *Stanford Law Review* 54 (2002): 793–829; and Michael Heise, "*Brown v. Board of Education,* Footnote 11, and Multidisciplinarity," *Cornell Law Review* 90 (2005): 279–320.

the highest authorities, including the Supreme Court, that the matter should be considered settled.[43]

Despite his confidence in the legal precedents, Davis briefly took exception to the social science evidence in general and to Professor Clark's doll studies in particular. He noted that Clark's testimony was especially suspect because Clark had not told the courts that he had previously shown black and white dolls to 134 black children who attended segregated schools in Arkansas and to 119 black children who attended desegregated schools in Massachusetts. Nor had Clark informed the courts that the proportion of black students who preferred the white dolls was actually higher in the desegregated northern schools than in the segregated southern schools. Thus if the doll test was a valid means of indicating what sort of schooling enhanced black self-respect, the data tended to favor segregated schools.[44]

The result of Clark's South Carolina doll test also was at odds with results that Clark reported in *Belton v. Gebhart,* a desegregation case in Delaware. In Delaware, only 12 of 41 black children identified the black doll as "bad," while 25 refused to make any identification of a bad doll. But in contrast to the situation in South Carolina, where Clark inferred psychological damage if children said the black doll was bad, in Delaware Clark said that children who refused to pronounce a negative judgment were "seeking to avoid coming to grips with the personally disturbing problem of racial status." Whatever choice a child made, Clark interpreted it as evidence of psychological damage. As Edmond Cahn noted, "If Negro children say a *brown* doll is like themselves, he infers that segregation has made them conscious of race; yet if they say a *white* doll is like themselves, he infers that segregation has forced them to evade reality."[45]

The results of other tests were even more damaging to the NAACP's case. When Clark asked children to color the drawing of a boy or girl, "nearly 80 per cent of the southern Negro children [who had been educated in all-black, segregated schools] colored their preferences brown, whereas only 36 per cent of the northern Negro children did. Furthermore, over 20 per cent of the northern [black] children colored their pref-

43. Kluger, *Simple Justice,* 446, 687; William H. Harbaugh, *Lawyer's Lawyer: The Life of John W. Davis* (New York: Oxford University Press, 1973), 498, 499.

44. Argument of John W. Davis, in Kurland and Casper, *Landmark Briefs,* 49:336; Ernest van den Haag, "Social Science Testimony in the Desegregation Cases—A Reply to Professor Kenneth Clark," *Villanova Law Review* 6 (fall 1960): 69, 71; Herbert Garfinkel, "Social Science Evidence and the School Segregation Cases," *Journal of Politics* 21 (1959): 37–59; Harbaugh, *Lawyer's Lawyer,* 500.

45. Trial testimony of Kenneth Clark, quoted in Jackson, *Social Scientists,* 141; Jackson, ibid., 142; Cahn, "Jurisprudence," 163.

erences in a bizarre color, while only five per cent of the southern [black] children did." Such results suggested that desegregation created more psychological problems than it solved. This led psychologist Bruno Bettelheim to conclude that the NAACP would have been wiser if it had steered clear of bogus science and had based its case on legal and ethical principles.[46]

The *Brown* Court nevertheless placed its *imprimatur* on the social science of the NAACP. The Court even listed Kenneth Clark as *primus inter pares*—the first among a group of scholars whom the Court cited as "modern authority" in social psychology. The headline in the *New York Times* called *Brown* "a sociological decision," and the *Times*'s best-known columnist, James Reston, wrote that the "Court's opinion read more like an expert paper on sociology than a Supreme Court opinion. It sustained the argument of experts in education, sociology, psychology, and anthropology." At a victory celebration, Thurgood Marshall called out William Coleman and Robert Ming, two NAACP lawyers who had initially questioned the wisdom of using social science evidence in *Brown*. Then, in jest but also to acknowledge the important role that social science played in the case, Marshall asked Coleman and Ming to bow down to Kenneth Clark and admit that they had been wrong.[47]

Stell v. Savannah

The Supreme Court's opinion in *Brown* took segregationists by surprise, for they had not only considered the NAACP's social science to be of slight consequence, they had also expected *Brown* to be decided on the basis of historical evidence and legal precedents. Yet when these expectations proved to be mistaken, segregationists enlisted social science in their own behalf and pointed to what John W. Davis called "a large body of respectable expert opinion to the effect that separate schools, particularly in the South, are in the best interests of children of both races as well as of the community at large." "If the Court wanted scientific data," historian William H. Tucker has written, "the segregationists would supply the data with a vengeance. Since the plaintiffs' experts had testified that segregation was damaging to the personality and self-esteem of black children, the opposing scientists would marshal their own evidence to show that

46. Bettelheim, "Discrimination and Science," 386, 384.
47. *New York Times,* 18 May 1954, 1; Jack Greenberg, *Crusaders in the Courts* (New York: Basic Books, 1994), 199.

integration was even more harmful to the young black psyche." In response to the NAACP's argument that racial differences in scholastic performance were environmentally based and in reply to the implication that desegregation would lead to improvement in black educational achievement, segregationists would cite IQ studies that showed that the differences were intractable and other studies that suggested that the differences probably resulted from heredity. When the academic performance of black students either did not improve after desegregation, or improved very little, segregationists insisted that the *Brown* Court had been "hoodwinked by biased evidence."[48]

Much of the evidence for segregation was presented in *Stell v. Savannah-Chatham Board of Education* (1963). Segregationist lawyers carefully chose Savannah because they knew that the presiding judge, Frank M. Scarlett, supported segregation. They therefore expected Judge Scarlett to allow them to introduce social science evidence over the objections of the NAACP, which now maintained that cases should be decided on the basis of legal precedents (that is, *Brown*), and that social science evidence was irrelevant and should be excluded.[49]

In *Stell* the segregationists began with Robert Osborne, a professor of psychology at the University of Georgia. Osborne gave testimony to the effect that whites in Savannah, on average, scored significantly higher than blacks on tests of reading and mathematics, with the differential increasing from less than two grade levels at age eleven to more than three grade levels at age seventeen. Osborne said that "in regions . . . where the Negro population is relatively small there may be no problem of balancing the schools in terms of race." But he predicted trouble ahead "if public schools are ordered to integrate *en masse.*" If white schools in Savannah did not "lower the educational standards and level of instruction," there would be "a 40 to 60 percent Negro failure rate." The only alternatives would be to institute a system of grouping students by academic achievement, which would lead to "*de facto* segregation," or "to apply differential marking and evaluation systems to the two groups."[50]

The segregationists next presented their star psychologist, Henry E. Garrett, a former president of the American Psychological Association.

48. Kluger, *Simple Justice,* 690; William H. Tucker, *The Science and Politics of Racial Research* (Urbana: University of Illinois Press, 1994), 150.

49. *Stell v. Savannah-Chatham Board of Education,* 220 F.Supp. 676 (1963). Carleton Putnam included lengthy excerpts from the *Transcript of Proceedings* in his book *Race and Reality: A Search for Solutions* (Washington: Public Affairs Press, 1967), 76–85.

50. R. Travis Osborne, "Racial Differences in Mental Growth and School Achievement," in Robert E. Kuttner, ed., *Race and Modern Science* (New York: Social Science Press, 1967), 405–6.

Garrett was a man of patrician bearing who had taught at Columbia University for thirty years before moving to the University of Virginia. Summarizing the findings of several scholarly studies, Garrett told the court that on IQ tests American Negroes regularly scored from fifteen to twenty points below the average for American whites, that only 25 percent of African Americans overlapped the average white on most mental tests, and that the difference was even greater on "tests of an abstract nature . . . involving reasoning, deduction, comprehension." Garrett recognized that "inequality in social status" made it difficult to obtain a fair comparison of black and white Americans, but he reported that the gap in test scores did not disappear when black and white subjects were paired in terms of fourteen social and economic factors. The persistence of the gap, and the regularity of results from many studies, made it "extremely unlikely [in Garrett's opinion] that environmental opportunities can possibly explain *all* the differences." According to Garrett, "the differences between the two racial groups in a variety of mental tests are so large, so regular and so persistent under all sorts of conditions that it is almost unthinkable to conclude that they are entirely a matter of environment."[51]

Garrett also mentioned additional points that would receive more emphasis in the years ahead. He said that massive integration would "pull achievement down" and "ruin the white schools." He opined that "neither group would be happy," since "one group would be challenged above its ability level and the other group would not be challenged enough." And he said that as a result of "bringing the groups together . . . under classroom conditions," many African American students would become frustrated, "and frustration leads to aggression and aggression leads to broken windows and muggings and crime." In their legal briefs for *Stell v. Savannah*, segregationist lawyers Carter Pittman and George Leonard also warned that black students would bring with them "a severe increase in disciplinary problems resulting from the more prevalent use of violence, vile profanity, lascivious sexual behavior, thefts, vandalism . . . and other anti-social conduct."[52]

In *Stell* the segregationists also maintained that differences in academic achievement resulted largely from differences in brain structure. Robert

51. Ibid., 672–73; Putnam, *Race and Reality*, 58–59; Henry E. Garrett, "Negro-White Differences in Mental Ability in the United States," *Scientific Monthly* 65 (9 October 1947): 333; Frank McGurk, "A Scientist's Report on Race Differences," *U.S. News and World Report*, 21 September 1956, 95; Henry E. Garrett, "Racial Mixing Could Be Catastrophic," *U.S. News and World Report*, 18 November 1963, 93.

52. Testimony of Henry E. Garrett, quoted in I. A. Newby, *Challenge to the Court: Social Scientists and the Defense of Segregation, 1954–1966* (Baton Rouge: Louisiana State University Press, 1967), 205, 199.

E. Kuttner, a professor of biology at the Creigthton University Medical School, gave testimony on this point. But the segregationists' star witness was Wesley Critz George, emeritus professor of anatomy at the University of North Carolina Medical School and the president of the North Carolina Academy of Science. After summarizing several scholarly studies on the relation of brain weight, body size, and intelligence throughout the animal kingdom, George informed the court that the average weight of the brains of Caucasians was about 1,380 grams, that of Negroes about 1,240 grams, with the difference especially pronounced in the prefrontal area where abstract thought occurred. George further stated that these differences were "no doubt . . . inherited," the result of evolutionary development in geographically distinct regions over periods of time best described in geological terms. According to George, schools could modify these differences only "to a minimal degree."[53]

Some segregationists considered the racial differences in anatomy to be especially important. Most people already knew that blacks lagged whites on academic tests, but the segregationists sensed that many observers attributed this to differences in environment and opportunity. Yet if blacks and whites differed in brain structure, the segregationists reasoned, more people would recognize that racial differences in IQ and academic achievement were inherent and hereditary.

Professor George's summary of the anatomical evidence was striking—so striking that it caused NAACP attorney Constance Motley to weep audibly in the courtroom. But George's testimony was not conclusive with respect to school segregation, for even segregationists conceded that there was a considerable overlap in brain weight (as there was in IQ scores), with about 20 percent of African Americans exceeding the white average. Thus the NAACP could argue, as it had in *Brown,* that children in desegregated schools could be grouped by ability, regardless of race. "Put the dumb colored children in with the dumb white children," Thurgood Marshall had said to the Supreme Court in 1955, "and put the smart colored children with the smart white children."[54]

Segregationists therefore called on their own social scientists, who ar-

53. *Stell v. Savannah-Chatham,* 229 F.Supp. 667 (1963), 673; Putnam, *Race and Reality,* 84, 82–83; Wesley Critz George, *The Biology of the Race Problem* (New York: National Putnam Letters Committee, 1962).

54. Putnam, *Race and Reality,* 83; Friedman, *Argument,* 402. In their Social Science Statement, however, the NAACP stated a different view: "Actually, many educators have come to doubt the wisdom of class groupings made homogeneous solely on the basis of intelligence. Those who are opposed to such homogeneous grouping believe that this type of segregation, too, appears to create generalized feelings of inferiority in the child who attends a below average class, leads to undesirable emotional conse-

gued that racial segregation was psychologically beneficial to African American schoolchildren, including those of superior intelligence. In *Stell v. Savannah* their star witness on this point was Ernest van den Haag, a psychiatrist and professor of social philosophy at New York University. Van den Haag was also the author of one of the earliest articles that had criticized Kenneth Clark. Writing in the *Villanova Law Review* in 1960, van den Haag had noted that Clark himself, in articles written before *Brown*, had reported that black children in segregated schools were "less pronounced in their preference for the white doll" and more often thought of the colored dolls as "nice." Van den Haag suspected that Clark had intentionally misled the courts and deliberately deceived the NAACP's lawyers. "Else how could they present as an expert witness to demonstrate the damages of school segregation a man who has actually demonstrated only the damages of desegregation?"[55]

In *Stell v. Savannah*, van den Haag essentially maintained that African American children would be happier if they were educated in all-black schools. He granted that there was something to "the common sense view that Negroes are humiliated . . . by segregation," but he thought it would be even worse to send black students to school with hostile whites who would "resent . . . the imposition." Van den Haag said that "being resented and shunned personally and concretely by their white schoolmates throughout every day would [not] be less humiliating to Negro children than a general abstract knowledge that they are separately educated because of white prejudice." "If the gifted Negro child is transferred into a hostile white school environment, I doubt that there would be an educational advantage."[56]

In making this argument, van den Haag harkened back to points that the black scholar and civil rights leader W. E. B. Du Bois had made in 1935. "The proper education of any people includes sympathetic touch between teacher and pupil," Du Bois had written. But racial prejudice was so deeply entrenched that it was difficult to find white teachers who regarded blacks as their equal. Consequently, Du Bois wrote, black students in the desegregated North were often "admitted and tolerated," but they were "not educated" because they did not receive "decent and sympathetic education in the white schools." Indeed, "the treatment of Negro

quences in the education of the gifted child, and reduces learning opportunities which result from the interaction of individuals with varied gifts." Kurland and Casper, *Landmark Briefs*, 49:55.

55. Van den Haag, "Social Science Testimony in the Desegregation Cases," 77, 79.

56. Ibid., 69, 71; Ernest van den Haag, "Intelligence or Prejudice?" *National Review*, 1 December 1964, 1061.

children in [desegregated] schools . . . is such that they ought to demand a thorough-going revolution in the official attitude toward Negro students, or absolute separation in educational facilities." Du Bois complained that he had "repeatedly seen wise and loving colored parents take infinite pains to force their little children into schools where the white children, white teachers, and white parents despised and resented the dark child, made mock of it, neglected or bullied it, and literally rendered its life a living hell. Such parents want their child to 'fight' this thing out,— but, dear God, at what cost!" Du Bois thought it would be better for the NAACP to seek equalization of funding and facilities instead of pressing for integration. He doubted the wisdom of trying to compel "a rich and powerful majority of the citizens to do what they will not do." He conceded that mixed schools with good and sympathetic teachers and fellow students would be ideal. But "a mixed school with poor and unsympathetic teachers with hostile public opinion and no teaching of truth concerning black folk, is bad."[57]

Du Bois was not defending segregation. He was, rather, stressing that there was "no magic" in mixed schools and that black children would not benefit if they were placed in schools that did not treat them fairly. Du Bois insisted that integration was not a panacea. He cast doubt on the value of educating black children in predominantly white schools.[58]

Van den Haag argued in addition that because of deficiencies at home most poor black students needed a special curriculum that would provide elementary instruction on matters that most middle-class white children picked up automatically. He thought that "instruction in schools for Negroes should attempt to remedy the disadvantages suffered by students coming from a culturally deprived home environment." "At least for the time being, the needs of Negro children would be met best—i.e., to their advantage and without disadvantage to others—by separate education geared to meet the obstacles presented by lack of opportunity and unfavorable environment." Such schools could also facilitate the cultivation and celebration of the African Americans' unique heritage.[59]

Van den Haag also emphasized the importance of what he called "acceptable group identifications." He said that "the sense of achievement essential to a healthy personality in a superior pupil is caused by excelling in a group with which he has a strong identification"; that such sense would be "limited or destroyed" if students were placed "in a group with

57. W. E. B. Du Bois, "Does the Negro Need Separate Schools?" *Journal of Negro Education* 4 (July 1935): 328, 329, 330, 330–31, 329, 335.
58. Kluger, *Simple Justice*, 691.
59. Van den Haag, "Intelligence or Prejudice?" 1061.

which such identification is lacking"; that a goal of education "should be to strengthen the degree to which Negroes identify with their own sub-group rather than with other groups." Van den Haag said that the integration of able black students would have especially unfortunate effects on the black rank-and-file. He predicted that, with integration, the best black students would move into predominantly white classes, and black children of ordinary aptitude "would be deprived of the natural leadership of their group, would lose a sense of group achievement, be subjected to a demoralizing sense of rejection and . . . would suffer feelings of inadequacy or inferiority."[60]

Once again, van den Haag was asserting views that in some ways were similar to opinions that W. E. B. Du Bois had expressed in the 1930s. Du Bois had then urged African Americans to "stop being stampeded by the word *segregation*." What they should be concerned about was *discrimination*; discrimination as practiced, for example, when public schools "refus[ed] . . . to spend the same amount of money on the black child as on the white child for its education." But Du Bois said that segregation and discrimination did "not necessarily go together," and he insisted that there should "never be an opposition to segregation pure and simple unless that segregation does involve discrimination."[61]

Du Bois urged blacks to protest against official segregation. But he also urged them to "go to work" to make sure that black schools were as good as possible. If the Negro could not "educate his children in decent schools with other children, he must, nevertheless, educate his children in decent Negro schools and arrange and conduct and oversee such schools." Du Bois complained (with some exaggeration) that "the NAACP and other Negro organizations have spent thousands of dollars to prevent the establishment of segregated Negro schools, but scarcely a single cent to see that the division of funds between white and Negro schools, North and South, is carried out with some approximation of justice." For too many African American leaders, Du Bois wrote, "the fight against segregation consists merely of one damned protest after another; . . . the technique is to protest and wail and protest again, and to keep this up until the . . . walls of segregation fall down."[62]

Du Bois also thought it was a mistake to emphasize *integration* as the

60. *Stell v. Savannah-Chatham*, 220 F.Supp. 667 (1963), 674–75.
61. *Crisis* 41 (January 1934): 20, italics added.
62. *Crisis* 41 (June 1934): 183; Du Bois, "Does the Negro Need Separate Schools?" 332. In *From Brown to Bakke: The Supreme Court and School Integration, 1954–1978* (New York: Oxford University Press, 1978), 25, J. Harvie Wilkinson noted that Du Bois was not alone in making this point. "There had long been disagreement—even within the

best solution to America's racial problems. He was convinced that "not for a century and more probably not for ten centuries, will any such consummation be reached." "No person born will ever live to see . . . racial distinctions altogether abolished." Indeed, Du Bois dismissed integration as "the absurd Negro philosophy of Scatter . . . Escape." He insisted, "the problem of 12,000,000 Negro people, mostly poor, ignorant workers, is not going to be settled by having their more educated and wealthy classes gradually and continually escape from their race into the mass of the American people." To the extent that occurred, Du Bois predicted, the black masses would be left without leaders and would "sink, suffer and die." Du Bois called on the black "talented tenth" to stay in their black communities and serve as role models and missionaries of culture. He urged "the better class of Negroes [to] recognize their duty toward the masses." "[T]heir chief excuse for being [is] the work they may do toward lifting the rabble."[63]

Some of van den Haag's views were similar to those of Du Bois, although not identical, and both men had opinions that resembled those of sociologist A. James Gregor. Like van den Haag, Gregor rejected Kenneth Clark's assertion that "segregation has detrimental psychological effects." On the contrary, Gregor wrote, Clark's own evidence "tends to support racial separation in the schools." It showed that there were "*more* serious [psychological] impairments . . . in '*integrated*' situations." "If the evidence available to the Court in *Brown v. Board of Educ.* demonstrates anything at all, it demonstrates that the personality impairment suffered by Negro children is less in a racially insulated environment than with congregation." Gregor warned that "a Negro child who systematically observes his group performing at a lower level . . . in integrated situations . . . can hardly avoid assessing [his group] as inferior in some significant sense. This leads to the characteristic negative evaluation of his own group on the part of the Negro child."[64]

Gregor (and Du Bois) also thought that blacks and whites both identi-

---

NAACP high command—about whether to argue an 'equalization' strategy within the confines of *Plessy* or to take the bolder and riskier course of asking the Court to overrule separate but equal altogether." See also Kluger, *Simple Justice,* 658–64, 677–80.

63. *Crisis* 41 (April 1934): 117; W. E. B. Du Bois, "A Negro Nation within the Nation," *Current History* 42 (June 1935): 269; Du Bois, *The Philadelphia Negro* (1899; reprint, Millwood, N.Y.: Kraus-Thomson Organization, 1973), 392, 393. For more on Du Bois and integration, see Raymond Wolters, *Du Bois and His Rivals* (Columbia: University of Missouri Press, 2002).

64. Kenneth B. Clark, quoted by A. James Gregor, "The Law, Social Science, and School Segregation," *Western Reserve Law Review* 14 (1963): 626, 632, 633.

fied with their race. Like Du Bois, who said most African Americans possessed an instinctive preference for one another, a consciousness of kind
"which they cannot escape because it is in the marrow of their bones,"
Gregor maintained that most whites also possessed a sense of racial identity. More than that, Gregor thought that mankind possessed an inherent
drive to form in-groups and out-groups. He said that people had "a gener-
ic tendency . . . to identify with those like themselves" and an instinctive
"disposition to limit contact with outgroup members." Admittedly, this
tendency could be influenced by "social and political circumstances."
Sometimes group consciousness was focused on religious beliefs or class
standing, but often it revolved around race. Indeed, Gregor said, throughout history there had been little mixing on terms of equality when people
came into protracted contact with groups of markedly different "racial liv-
ery." In making this argument, Gregor was squarely in the mainstream of
social science. In *The Nature of Prejudice* (1954), the influential Harvard
psychologist Gordon W. Allport had argued along similar lines. Allport
had entitled one chapter "The Normality of Pre-judgment." In it he maintained that the formation of in-groups was a natural phenomenon and
was often accompanied by the rejection of out-groups.[65]

Thus Gregor was not surprised to learn that when schools were integrated, as many were outside the South, "each racial group tended to go
its own way with little social interaction." Neither blacks nor whites could
expect to find sympathetic, congenial support in schools that were dominated by members of the other race. Gregor maintained, in addition, that
mixing was likely to produce separation if one of the groups, as seemed
to be true of African Americans, possessed a "subculture" that was characterized by "minimal academic aspirations." Gregor, indeed, was one of
the first sociologists to use a new term: "white flight." He observed that
white homeowners fled residential integration at the first inkling of "sociological problems." And white students behaved similarly. "The deteri-
oration of the standards of local schools, the increased incidence of delin-

65. W. E. B. Du Bois, "The Future and Function of the Private Negro College," *Crisis* 53 (August 1946): 235; Gregor, "Law, Social Science, and School Segregation," 629,
630; A. James Gregor, "On the Nature of Prejudice," *Eugenics Review* 52 (1961): 217–24;
Allport, *Nature of Prejudice*, 17–28; John P. Jackson Jr., "The Scientific Attack on *Brown
v. Board of Education*, 1954–1964," *American Psychologist* 59 (September 2004): 533. "In
contrast to some of the more pessimistic writers on the subject," Walter A. Jackson has
written, "Allport proclaimed himself an unabashed meliorist and insisted that it was
possible to reduce discrimination by changing public policy and to lessen prejudice
through a variety of educational strategies." *Gunnar Myrdal and America's Conscience:
Social Engineering and Racial Liberalism, 1938–1987* (Chapel Hill: University of North
Carolina Press, 1990), 288–89.

quency and crime . . . provide . . . sufficient rational motive for white flight."[66]

In *Stell v. Savannah,* the lawyers for the NAACP did not try to refute the segregationists' arguments. Constance Baker Motley briefly mentioned that many experts in anatomy, psychology, and sociology did not agree with the opinions expressed by the segregationists' scientists, but Motley did not call any witnesses. Instead, she objected to the use of scientific testimony. Her position resembled that taken by John W. Davis when *Brown* was being litigated: "that social science testimony was specious and irrelevant since the Supreme Court had already decided the constitutional issues involved in the case." Motley said the law was settled because *Brown* had held "that segregation itself injures Negro children in the school system. That is what the Supreme Court's decision is all about, so we do not have to prove that."[67]

Judge Scarlett held otherwise. Ruling for the segregationists, Scarlett noted that the preponderance of testimony in his courtroom was to the effect that racial differences in academic achievement were of such magnitude as to make it difficult for most black children to be educated in predominantly white classrooms. Scarlett wrote that he had heard "no evidence whatsoever . . . to show that racial integration of the schools could reduce these differences." And he concluded that "superior" black students (those who admittedly could keep up with whites academically) would suffer psychologically if separated from their fellow African Americans. Scarlett acknowledged that his findings differed from those of the Supreme Court in *Brown,* but he nevertheless concluded that the segregationists had made a reasonable case for separating the races in school.

The Fifth Circuit Court of Appeals then reversed Judge Scarlett's decision. Circuit Judge Griffin Bell explained that "no inferior federal court may refrain from acting as required . . . even if such a court should con-

66. Gregor, "Law, Social Science and School Segregation," 629–30; A. James Gregor et al., "Interracial Housing and the Law: A Social Science Assessment," in Alfred Avins, ed., *Open Occupancy vs. Forced Housing under the Fourteenth Amendment* (New York: Bookmailer, 1963), 147; George A. Lundberg, *Selective Association of Ethnic Groups in a High School* (New York: International Association for the Advancement of Ethnology and Eugenics, 1965).

67. Newby, *Challenge to the Court,* 207; *Stell v. Savannah,* 220 F.Supp. 667 (1963), 676. Mark Tushnet has emphasized the importance of this point. One of Thurgood Marshall's goals was to establish precedents that were favorable to the NAACP. Once this was accomplished, as in *Brown,* the NAACP could demand "the rule of law"—and forgo the presentation of evidence from the social sciences. See Tushnet, *Making Civil Rights Law: Thurgood Marshall and the Supreme Court, 1936–1961* (New York: Oxford University Press, 1994).

clude that the Supreme Court erred." Bell went on to say there was "no constitutional prohibition against an assignment of individual students to particular schools on a basis of intelligence, achievement or other aptitudes," but "race must not be a factor in making these assignments." According to Bell, the problem with racial segregation was that "many of the Negro pupils overlap many of the white pupils in achievement and aptitude but are nevertheless to be segregated on the basis of race. They are to be separated, regardless of how great their ability as individuals, into schools with members of their own race because of the differences in test averages as between the races. Therein is the discrimination. The individual Negro student is not to be treated as an individual and allowed to proceed along with other individuals on the basis of ability alone without regard to race."[68]

68. *Stell v. Savannah-Chatham*, 333 F.2d 55 (1964), 61, 62.

2

School Reform in the 1950s

The Road Not Taken

During the decade after *Brown v. Topeka Board of Education,* there was only limited compliance with the order of the Supreme Court. Writing in the *New York Times* in 1964, Claude Sitton noted that "98.9 per cent of the 2,901,671 Negro students in eleven Southern states still attend all-Negro schools." Yet an emphasis on "how far [the South] yet has to go" obscured the fact that, after *Brown,* desegregation was widely implemented in several border states and the District of Columbia. Desegregation was facilitated in these areas because the 1950s was a decade when certain trends were ascendant in the public schools.[1]

To understand the course of school desegregation, one must understand that *Brown* came down at a time when most elementary students were assigned to neighborhood schools. Since most residential areas were predominantly but not exclusively inhabited by members of one race or the other, assigning children to neighborhood schools led to some racial mingling—but not to anything like the mixture that would have been required to reflect the racial proportions of the larger region or state.

At the same time, most teenagers attended comprehensive high schools that tended to have large enrollments comprising all the youngsters from an extended area. When an extended area was inhabited primarily by people of one race, even comprehensive schools had only a rather small amount of racial mingling. There would be more mixing if the extended area was racially diverse, but teenage blacks and whites tended to have

1. *New York Times,* 16 January 1964, 73.

different interests and different levels of preparation. Because the grades, test scores, and interests of black teenagers differed, on average, from those of their white counterparts, students at large comprehensive high schools tended toward separate classes in some academic subjects even as they mixed proportionately in some general classes and in some extracurricular activities.

Beginning in the mid-1960s, liberal integrationists would take exception to both neighborhood elementary schools and to comprehensive high schools. They would demand that schools take affirmative steps to achieve a "better" racial balance in each school *and* in each classroom. One should understand, however, that there were few such demands at the time of *Brown* or during the decade thereafter. Especially after 1957, when the Soviet Union launched the first space satellite, *Sputnik,* there were quite different demands that the United States increase and systematize the grouping of high school students. It was understood that grouping by academic ability would work against achieving racial balance in the classrooms. But winning the competition with the Soviet Union seemed more important at that time than achieving racially balanced integration.

Far from pushing for integrated education, educational reformers of the 1950s and early 1960s criticized American education for being insufficiently rigorous and for neglecting to challenge the best students. They found fault with teachers who allegedly thought their job was "not so much to teach history or algebra, as to prepare students to live happily ever after." One best-selling critique was entitled *Quackery in the Public Schools.* Another influential book bore the title *Educational Wastelands.* At the grass roots there were demands for even more grouping of students by ability in states as dissimilar as Louisiana, Massachusetts, and New Jersey, and in cities as different as Denver, Minneapolis, Pasadena, and Eugene, Oregon.[2]

Some educational reformers even raised questions about the value of one of the signature achievements of American education, the comprehensive high school. They noted that, unlike the situation in Europe, where most students were sent to vocational schools and only a minority continued with academic education after the age of fourteen, in the United States teenagers with vastly different vocational and professional ambitions were taught on the same campus. Critics said that the majority al-

2. *Time* magazine, as quoted by Diane Ravitch, *The Troubled Crusade: American Education, 1845–1980* (New York: Basic Books, 1983), 72; Albert Lynd, *Quackery in the Public Schools* (Boston: Little, Brown, 1953); Arthur Bestor, *Educational Wastelands* (Urbana: University of Illinois Press, 1953); David Hulburd, *This Happened in Pasadena* (New York: Macmillan, 1951).

most inevitably set the tone in comprehensive schools, and that this privileged students who were adept socially, especially boys who were athletes and girls who were stylish, while youths who excelled only in academic work were relegated to the margins. Some critics said that to be fair to high-achieving students, American high schools should be reformed in accord with the European pattern. They said it was not possible for comprehensive schools to do a good job for both students who would go to work immediately after high school and for students who were college bound. They said the European system of different, specialized high schools was a better approach.

Hyman G. Rickover

Admiral Hyman G. Rickover was the most influential proponent of this view. Rickover's specialty was nuclear propulsion, and he was widely known as "the father of the atomic submarine." Yet when the journalist Edward R. Murrow once asked the usual questions about the way nuclear power and weapons affected naval strategy and thinking, Rickover interrupted the questioning to say: "Why don't you ask questions about the really important things?" Rickover proceeded to say that education was "even more important than atomic power in the Navy, for if our people are not properly educated in accordance with the terrific requirements of this rapidly spiraling scientific and industrial civilization, we are bound to go down." In an essay for the *New York Times*, Rickover added: "Rarely have the ideas dominating education anywhere been so wholly at odds with the needs of society."[3]

Rickover recognized that, in theory, several different educational programs might be combined simultaneously in a single comprehensive high school. In practice, however, this was not easily done. If schools established special courses for talented students, the parents of those who were not included in the hard courses often lobbied against the establishment of a program they considered "elitist." Consequently, differentiation could be achieved only through an elective system, which Rickover faulted for two reasons. Without proper guidance from school authorities, many able students would settle for easy courses. At the other extreme, many parents who were ambitious for their children would

3. *New York Times*, 9 August 1959, 1; Edward R. Murrow, preface to Hyman G. Rickover, *Education and Freedom* (New York: E. P. Dutton, 1959), 5–6; *New York Times*, 2 February 1971, 37.

push forward youngsters who were not ready for demanding academic work.[4]

Rickover also complained that instead of emphasizing the mastery of factual information, comprehensive schools spent too much time on "a vast amount of marginal stuff." He considered it a waste of time for schools to try to teach children the meaning of democracy by participating, deciding, and planning together. Rickover wanted schools to concentrate on services that only schools could provide—reading, writing, and arithmetic in the elementary schools; history, science, and mathematics in the secondary schools. He thought it mistaken to assume responsibility for family values, dating etiquette, or drivers' education. He feared that if schools accepted responsibility for tasks that were beyond their purview, the additional efforts not only would fail but also would compromise the primary purpose of academic education.[5]

According to Rickover, comprehensive schools suffered from two maladies: an excess of egalitarianism and "a lot of amateur sociology and a lot of amateur psychology." He said that Americans had failed to reconcile "our commitment to equal educational opportunity" with "the sad but indisputable fact that of all the species on earth, human beings are the most unequally endowed." Americans would "not face up to the fact that, beyond the most elementary level, children simply vary so greatly in their capacity to absorb a given body of knowledge that keeping them in the same class [or school] shortchanges every ability group." Instead of following the European practice of streaming teenage students in different directions, Americans had developed the comprehensive high school, where students spent "a lot of time [learning] how to date, how to answer a telephone, how to set a table, and all the rest of that nonsense." The nation had done so, Rickover alleged, "so that children might not separate when their educational paths take them naturally into different directions." He considered it preposterous to assert, as some educators did, that "comprehensive education will in adult life bind rich man, poor man, beggar man, thief, doctor, lawyer, and Indian chief into a warm togetherness of shared educational experience."[6]

Rickover's skepticism about comprehensive schools was part of a larger opposition to what he called "progressive education." He conceded that progressives were on the right track insofar as they brought a relaxed and friendly atmosphere into the nation's classrooms, but Rickover re-

4. Rickover, *Education and Freedom*, 134–35.
5. *New York Times*, 2 June 1960, 1.
6. Ibid., 12 September 1959, 7; 1 February 1971, 31; 3 September 1962, 17.

jected the suggestion that teaching should begin with subjects already known to the pupils. According to Rickover, "[John] Dewey's insistence on making the child's interest the determining factor in planning curricula" inevitably led to a transformation of American education—away from domination by teachers who were experts in specific subjects like mathematics or history and toward generalists who taught students how to deal with "the minutiae of daily life"—how to behave as responsible citizens, how to balance a budget, how to use modern technology. Rickover took particular exception to the progressives' assertion that there was "no aristocracy of 'subjects' . . . mathematics and mechanics, art and agriculture, history and homemaking are all peers." He disputed John Dewey's claim that "the primary business of the school is to train children in cooperative and mutually helpful living." He scoffed at "[William Heard] Kilpatrick of Teachers College, principal disciple of Dewey, [who] remarked that he 'was not troubled . . . so long as the child is working fruitfully at some self-propelling social interest and . . . is interacting wholesomely in his social milieu.'" Because of progressive educators like Dewey and Kilpatrick, Rickover wrote, American students were "deprived of the tremendous intellectual heritage of Western civilization which no child can possibly discover by himself."[7]

As an expert on nuclear power, Rickover had long been aware of what he called "the potential military advantages of outer-space control." Especially after 1957, when the Soviet Union launched the first space satellite, he tried to "awaken America to the danger facing the nation." He hoped that *Sputnik* would be "the catalyst which brings about drastic and long-overdue reforms in utilizing the nation's intellectual resources." Rickover said that progressive education had set its aims too low, at adjusting children to life rather than at developing intellectual potential that might change life for the better. He called for "a thoroughly reorganized educational system with totally different aims and considerably higher scholastic standards." He said that America's educational system should be revamped "to equip us for winning the educational race with the Russians."[8]

"What can we do?" Rickover asked. "To make our education the best in the world," Rickover advised the United States to stop pushing academic education "on children who either cannot or will not keep up with their studies." Instead, the nation should learn "from Europe's educational experience." Instead of wasting "the best years of our children in the name

7. Rickover, *Education and Freedom*, 139, 143, 153.
8. Ibid., 158, 165, 166, 180; *New York Times*, 7 December 1957, 30.

of democracy and of the sacred comprehensive school," Americans should accept "the incontrovertible fact that children are unequally endowed with intelligence and determination and that it is impossible to educate the slow, average, and fast learners together." Instead of trying to educate the gifted student "with the dolts," the able student should be pushed ahead "as fast as he can go." When slow and fast learners were grouped together, Rickover wrote, "the slower group sets the pace." And when "above-average children are kept from advancing at the speed appropriate to their ability," some "lose interest" and others developed "a false sense of superiority which convinces them that they are so smart they will never need to apply themselves to anything." According to Rickover, "The most effective step we can take immediately is to unshackle our talented youth from the lock step of the average and below-average pupil."[9]

In speeches throughout the country and especially in an influential book of 1959, *Education and Freedom,* Rickover placed special emphasis on two points: that America's "cult of mediocrity" led to neglect of talented students, and that high schools should hire the most knowledgeable teachers available, "regardless of the 'union card requirements' of educational training and teaching techniques." Rickover lamented that internationally renowned scientists could not teach in most American high schools because they had not taken enough courses on how to teach. According to Rickover, "the certification racket"—requirements that teachers must take several courses in educational methods and then return to colleges of education "again and again during the summers for more . . . 'oceans of piffle'"—drove away many able prospective teachers. Rickover acknowledged that in all professions there were certain "tricks of the trade." Trial lawyers, for example, had to pay attention to their appearance and voice, but this professional "know-how" was acquired on the job and was not taught in law schools. So it should be with education. Unfortunately, Rickover said, the emphasis in most education schools was not on knowledge of subject matter but on teaching methods.[10]

As a step toward reforming American education, Rickover called for the establishment of twenty-five demonstration high schools in various sections of the country. Students would be chosen on the basis of their scores on a comprehensive examination. And since "an average teacher cannot successfully teach an above-average student," the schools would

9. Rickover, *Education and Freedom,* 188, 176, 166, 134, 117, 115; *New York Times,* 20 April 1958, 32; 24 March 1958, 1.
    10. *New York Times,* 23 November 1955, 25; 24 March 1958, 1; Rickover, *Education and Freedom,* 200, 201, 202.

be staffed by teachers with high IQs and "thorough mastery of one or two subjects." These schools would then serve as examples that might be widely emulated. In addition, Rickover called for national academic standards. He understood that, because of America's tradition of states' rights and local control, the federal government probably could not establish national standards for the high school diploma; but he recommended that this be done by a private agency that included scholars in the most important academic fields.[11]

Rickover's criticism of the comprehensive high school and of progressive education took most educators by surprise, since for many years progressive education had been identified with all that was good in American education. Many progressives found it hard to understand how their movement had fallen into disrepute. William G. Carr, the executive secretary of the National Education Association (NEA), took exception to Rickover's emphasis on the importance of mastering factual knowledge, saying that "storing the memory with knowledge" should not be "the controlling aim of our schools," since "a man with much knowledge and no social adjustment is at best an unhappy misfit and at worst a dangerous one." Theodore Brameld, a professor of education at Boston University, similarly maintained that the "psychological doctrine [of] the mental storehouse" was "outmoded" and "obsolete." According to Brameld, modern psychology had shown that students did better if classrooms were not dominated by the teacher, if there were "group projects" and "cooperative learning." Brameld also believed that research on childhood learning had shown that hard studying must be mixed with periods of recreation. In addition, Brameld wrote, "children should learn the meaning of democratic freedom by participating, deciding and planning together."[12]

Other educators developed additional points. At Teachers College, Columbia University, Professor John J. Norton complained that Rickover had failed to take into account that American schools had "radically different purposes from those of the class-structured institutions of Europe." Rickover's program would be "a calamity," Norton said, a "march back toward the traditional anti-democratic, class-structured system of Europe." A. Harry Passow, another professor at Teachers College, also rejected Rickover's contention that "only as our schools pattern themselves on European systems will they be able to provide for the talented stu-

11. Rickover, *Education and Freedom,* 208; *New York Times,* 23 November 1957, 8; 12 September 1959, 7; 9 April 1961, E11; 3 September 1961, 17.
12. *New York Times,* 27 April 1958, E9; 1 February 1959, BR1.

dent." For the sake of democracy, Passow said, "quality education for the talented can and must be provided within the framework of universal education." Passow insisted that this could be achieved if comprehensive schools were structured properly. It was not necessary to "throw out the baby with the bath water."[13]

Sidney Hook, a professor at New York University and one of John Dewey's most prominent disciples, offered yet another criticism of Rickover. According to Hook, the admiral's real concern was not with education but with winning the Cold War. Hook scoffed that Rickover's book *Education and Freedom* should have been entitled *Education for Victory in the Next War*. Lawrence G. Derthick, the U.S. Commissioner of Education, also rejected the implication that "to equal or surpass the Russians in some missile feat we must design an educational system like theirs."[14]

James B. Conant

In the end, the comprehensive high school endured and American education was not reshaped according to the European model. Much of the credit for this should go to James B. Conant. At one time Conant had been a world-class chemist; after that he spent twenty years as the president of Harvard University. Still later he served as U.S. high commissioner for Germany and as the American ambassador to the Federal Republic of Germany. During the 1950s, Conant was, according to the *New York Times*, "the most influential voice in American education," "the nation's one-man education reform movement." Eventually, he saved the comprehensive school by addressing some of the problems.[15]

Rejecting Rickover's contention that American schools could do justice to talented students only if the schools were patterned after the European fashion, Conant insisted that quality education for top students could and should be provided within the framework of the nation's democratic tradition. He warned that the European system of secondary education would "threaten the democratic unity provided by our public schools." He stressed that the United States had developed a system "where the future leader and manual worker have gone to school together at age fifteen to seventeen"—"something that exists nowhere in the world outside of the United States." He thought it wonderful that so many American

13. Ibid., 23 May 1958, 27; 25 March 1958, 25; 16 April 1958, 32.
14. Ibid., 20 February 1960, 21; 5 April 1959, 54.
15. Ibid., 13 January 1965, 75; 27 January 1964, 116.

teenagers attended the same schools—"the boy who will be an atomic scientist and the girl who will marry at eighteen; the prospective captain of a ship and the future captain of industry." Conant wished to preserve this uniquely American system. "One of the highly important objectives of the comprehensive high school," he wrote, "is the development of mutual respect and understanding between students with different abilities and different vocational interests."[16]

Nevertheless, Conant also recognized that many Americans questioned "the ability of a [comprehensive] high school to prepare a gifted [youth] adequately for university work." Responding to this concern, Conant went on record (as early as 1950) to say, "the foremost shortcoming of American education was the failure of the high school to provide adequate stimulus and instruction for the intellectually able student." He called for more emphasis on the education of gifted pupils but insisted that able students could be found at every level of family income. He pointedly asserted, "no one has estimated how much potential talent goes undeveloped in [Europe] because of the early selection of preuniversity students—a selection often influenced by the class system of European lands." Conant demanded tougher academic programs for *all* students who were preparing for college. If the academically talented were not directed into proper channels and provided with stiff academic courses, Conant said, the nation would lose potential scientists, mathematicians, and world leaders. He insisted, in addition, that comprehensive schools could be structured to serve the needs of even the most gifted students.[17]

In 1957–1958, the Carnegie Corporation indicated that it was ready to finance any project Conant might have in mind. Conant then assembled a four-member team that visited fifty-nine comprehensive high schools and published one of the most influential books in the history of American education, *The American High School Today* (1959). The timing was perfect, for public concern about education was especially keen after the Soviets launched *Sputnik* in 1957. Americans wanted to know what they could do to make their schools as good as possible.

Conant offered reassurance. "No radical alteration in the basic pattern of American education is necessary." "Without any radical change in our pattern of public high school education, public secondary schools can be made more adequate." All that was needed was candid recognition that students differed in aptitude—that only a minority of the nation's youth

16. James B. Conant, *My Several Lives* (New York: Harper and Row, 1970), 667, 670; Conant, *The American High School Today* (New York: McGraw-Hill, 1959), x, 74.
17. Conant, *My Several Lives*, 669; *New York Times*, 20 July 1958, E9; Conant, *American High School Today*, 2.

had the ability to handle demanding college prep courses. Conant said it was a mistake to criticize a school "because only 10 per cent of the senior class had elected 12th-grade mathematics." "In some schools, no larger fraction could handle the subject." "It will be a rare district where more than 25% of a high school class can study with profit twelfth-grade mathematics [or] physics."[18]

For Conant "the essence of a comprehensive school" lay in "the principle of electives." He recommended that students "should be grouped according to ability, subject by subject," and teachers should set standards so high that students who did not have the ability to handle advanced material would be "discouraged from electing these courses and prevented from continuing in the sequence." If that were done, bright students would no longer become "disinterested and bored" and average students would be less "confused and frustrated." Conant also recommended "instruction in several vocational fields as well as a diversified list of academic electives." Schools should face up to the facts of life: some youths were not willing "to do the amount of work that is implicit in my program for the academically talented," and other students lacked the aptitude needed to do such work.[19]

To serve the interests of *all* students, Conant recommended that smaller high schools should be consolidated. If a high school did not have a graduating class of at least one hundred students, he said, it would be prohibitively expensive to provide suitable courses for students who should be divided according to their ability in each subject. With a graduating class of at least a hundred, however, it would be possible to provide for academically superior children while also preserving "the democratic unity provided by our public schools."[20]

Conant was especially concerned that American high schools were not offering talented students a wide range of academic studies. "As a rule," the top students were "not being sufficiently challenged"; they did "not

18. Conant, *My Several Lives* 621; *New York Times*, 5 June 1958, 26; James B. Conant, *The Comprehensive High School* (New York: McGraw-Hill, 1967), 50; Conant, *American High School Today*, 37. Other educators disputed this point. "I see no justification whatever for the conclusion that only 15 percent of the American people can be seriously educated," said former University of Chicago president Robert Maynard Hutchings. Dr. Frederick M. Raubinger, the commissioner of education in New Jersey, also spoke against "a tendency to assume the attitude that only 10 or 15 percent of the students" were capable of advanced education in high school. *New York Times*, 15 February 1959, 22; 20 September 1959, 9.

19. Conant, *American High School Today*, 47, 49, 48, 93; Conant, *Comprehensive High School*, 13, 47.

20. Conant, *My Several Lives*, 667; *New York Times*, 5 October 1958, 135.

work hard enough." Conant lamented that some "academically talented pupils . . . elect[ed] an easy program," and, at the opposite extreme, some "overambitious parents" slowed the pace of schoolwork by demanding that children "with little academic ability" be admitted to top classes. Because weak students sometimes created disturbances that impeded the education of others, Conant thought there was nothing wrong if some youngsters dropped out of high school at age sixteen. "Take the case of the very slow readers," he explained. "If even with special attention their reading level is still low and their interest in the required general program is slight, and if the simple type of vocational training is leading directly to a job, I see no reason why a transfer to full-time work during the tenth or eleventh grade should not be applauded by all concerned." Conant specifically rejected "the dogma one often hears: that all the youth, irrespective of academic ability and interest, should complete grade twelve."[21]

Yet Conant was not merely an elitist. He was also concerned about the education of youths who wished to study a trade, and he reported that these youths were being shortchanged because many vocational programs were subpar. His most unexpected discovery, Conant said, was his own "enthusiasm for vocational education," if the quality of the trade training could be improved. After visiting high schools across America, the former Harvard president stressed the need for better vocational programs as well as for more demanding academic courses. "The problem of protecting . . . a minority" arose "not only in connection with the pupils who are scholastically able," he said, "but also in many schools in connection with the education of those boys who desire to make progress in learning a skilled trade." Like his Carnegie Corporation sponsor, John W. Gardner, Conant took exception to any society that scorned plumbing, because plumbing was a humble activity, and celebrated philosophy, because philosophy was an exalted pursuit. Such a society would have "neither good plumbing nor good philosophy. Neither its pipes nor its theories will hold water."[22]

For many reasons, Conant's analysis became the conventional wisdom of the late 1950s and early 1960s. There was, to begin, Conant's personal eminence. No other educator commanded as much respect as this highly regarded research chemist who had gone on to become president of Har-

21. Conant, *American High School Today*, 40; *New York Times*, 17 October 1961, 1; 29 January 1959, 25; James B. Conant, *The Revolutionary Transformation of the American High School* (Cambridge: Harvard University Press, 1959), 27.

22. *New York Times*, 29 January 1959, 15; statement of John W. Gardner, in Bruce Bohle, ed., *The Home Book of American Quotations* (New York: Gramercy, 1967), 290.

vard and ambassador to Germany. As one commentator noted, when Conant spoke, "the nation must take notice." And Conant said that American high school education was "sound enough to meet all challenges" and that "proposals that the European educational pattern be followed" were "ill-advised."[23]

Conant reassured families that questioned the ability of the public school to prepare gifted children for university work. He endorsed the distinctively American comprehensive high school. And he made a point of refraining from criticism of progressive teaching methods. As historian Robert Hampel has noted, Conant "said very little about course content or teachers' methods." For Conant, grouping students properly was all-important. "He did not apologize for the sorting and slotting done in schools." If Conant had any "private hesitations," they stemmed from a concern that "his own well-publicized recommendations were not tough enough."[24]

The educational establishment also appreciated Conant's emphasis on the need for additional funds. Conant knew that many people were tired of hearing "the repeated cries of 'more money for our schools.'" Yet he concluded that only 51.4 percent of comprehensive high schools were "adequately staffed." He maintained that "an excellent comprehensive high school can be developed in any school district," but only "provided . . . sufficient funds are available." To meet the needs of *all* students, he explained, comprehensive schools not only must offer a diversified array of courses but also "must be in a position to have a larger staff than would otherwise be the case." Conant lamented the inequality of school funding and thought it "obvious that the great sums of money required for improving and expanding public education can only be found through new methods of financing."[25]

Conant also found favor because he lashed out at critics of public education. Although 92 percent of American high school students attended public schools in the 1950s, Conant said that private schools threatened to undermine "the democratic unity" of the nation. "In any given locality," he wrote, "the introduction of one or more private schools alongside of a comprehensive high school tended to weaken the unity of the community." He even suggested that private and religious schools undermined support for public education. Catholic leaders such as Boston's Archbishop Richard Cushing angrily rejected that allegation, but Conant's in-

23. Conant, *American High School Today*, ix, x; *New York Times*, 15 November 1958, 25.

24. Robert L. Hampel, *The Last Little Citadel: American High Schools since 1940* (Boston: Houghton Miflin, 1986), 61, 65; Conant, *American High School Today*, xiii.

25. Conant, *Comprehensive High School*, 21, 16, 13, 2, 21, 80.

sinuation probably reinforced his popularity with most of those who were in charge of the nation's public schools.[26]

Most of all, Conant's assessment won favor because he insisted that advanced students need not be held back by the less gifted, if schools were organized properly. Critics had questioned whether comprehensive high schools could provide a good education for all young people. But Conant insisted that this could be done "under one administration and under one roof (or series of roofs)." Indeed, Conant concluded, it was being done. America was on the right track. In the mid-1950s, he wrote, ability grouping had been "a highly controversial subject," but a decade later the controversy seemed to have subsided, "for 96.5 per cent of the principals responded affirmatively" when asked, "Do you group students by ability in one or more academic subjects?"[27]

It is important that *Brown v. Board of Education* was first implemented during a decade when the writings and recommendations of James B. Conant (with assists from *Sputnik* and Admiral Rickover) were widely credited. It was a time when leading educators said that bright pupils were not working hard enough. It was a time when educational reformers demanded more challenging courses for gifted and talented students. While rejecting proposals to scrap comprehensive high schools in favor of the intellectually more rigid but socially undemocratic European idea of early sorting, American high schools offered more advanced courses and more grouping of students by ability. Small high schools were being consolidated to facilitate these changes. Throughout the country, the *New York Times* noted, "the general trend was toward stiffer courses and more homework." According to the *Times,* educational reform was then conceived as "a general effort to beef up curricula and give more opportunities to talented students."[28]

It should be noted, in addition, that regardless of what teachers taught and however they taught it, teachers of the 1950s rarely were held responsible for how much a child learned. Some students were thought to be "smart," others were known to be "hard workers," and still others were understood to be neither. Since variations in intelligence were influenced by nature and family background, the achievement of students was thought to be largely beyond the control of teachers. The responsibility for doing well in school—that is, for achievement—was assumed to lie with

26. Conant, *My Several Lives,* 468, 467.
27. Conant, *American High School Today,* x, ix; Conant, *Comprehensive High School,* 30.
28. *New York Times,* 27 April 1958, E9. In 1958, even the National Education Association, a bastion of progressivism, called for "a citizenry as willing to help the talented as to help the handicapped." *New York Times,* 5 October 1958, 135.

the children. Intellectual ability was regarded like other abilities, from sports to music. Teachers were expected to maintain order and present information clearly, but most observers assumed that the performance of students was largely a function of their aptitude and exertion. "If children failed, it was thought to be due either to their inability or their lack of effort; if they excelled, it was due to their talents and their industry. The one qualifier in this construction held that, regardless of ability, children could, through hard work, 'overachieve,' or, if they failed to work, 'underachieve.'"[29]

Informed observers at the time understood that black students trailed whites in average academic achievement, but most educators thought this was because most black children were still being educated in inferior schools. With equalization and desegregation it was thought that blacks would shed the feelings of inferiority the Supreme Court had mentioned in *Brown* and then do better in schoolwork. In the meantime it was thought that all students, blacks as well as whites, would benefit if students were grouped by ability and achievement. Such grouping facilitated desegregation, since grouping seemed to ensure that advanced students would not suffer if weaker students were admitted to their schools.

After the mid-1960s, however, the United States turned away from Rickover, Conant, and others who equated "school reform" with providing more advanced courses for gifted students. As the civil rights movement gained momentum and as race riots erupted in many cities, the pursuit of academic excellence yielded to concerns for uplifting and pacifying disadvantaged youths. The emphasis in school reform then shifted to funding for compensatory educational programs, to experiments with what was called "community-controlled education," and to busing to ensure that middle-class peers shaped the student culture at as many schools as possible.

29. Tommy M. Tomlinson, "The Troubled Years: An Interpretive Analysis of Public Schooling since 1950," *Phi Delta Kappan*, January 1981, 372–73.

3

Desegregation Begins

Topeka, Washington, Wilmington, and the Border States

The early experience with school desegregation was paradoxical. James B. Conant's educational reform movement offered assurance that schools could be desegregated without damaging educational standards. Nevertheless, the early experience was problematical. It is instructive to see how things worked out in the school districts whose cases were decided when the Supreme Court announced its *Brown* decision on May 17, 1954.

Topeka

Immediately upon receipt of the order to desegregate, Topeka assigned all children, regardless of race, to schools in the neighborhood of their residence. Since the residential areas were racially imbalanced, this did not lead to proportional mixing in each school. Yet in the mid-1950s *Brown* was not understood to require more than racial neutrality. "Desegregation does not mean that there must be an intermingling of the races in all school districts," a unanimous U.S. district court wrote in accepting the Topeka plan. "It means only that they may not be prevented from intermingling or going to school together because of race."[1]

In Topeka there was no formal grouping of students, but students did not need tests and teachers' grades to choose the level of instruction they considered best for themselves. Consequently, a form of tracking existed

1. *Brown v. Board of Education*, 139 F.Supp. 468 (1955), 470.

in Topeka (and many other cities), with academically inclined students enrolled in college prep classes while others signed up for general courses or vocational training. With the academic achievement of African American high school students trailing that of their white counterparts by about three years, on average, black youths disproportionately enrolled in the easier, general courses. Yet this caused little concern in Topeka, for white students were a majority in almost every high school class. The black proportion of the city's population was only 8.3 percent in 1950, increasing to 9.5 percent in 1980. The proportion of African American students was somewhat higher, about 14 percent, in 1955.

Yet desegregation was not free of trouble. Initially there was concern about protecting the jobs of black teachers, and many black students felt that they were victims of neglect if not outright prejudice. In responding to a NAACP survey of 1970, they complained that it was almost impossible for blacks to win election to the student government, the cheerleading squads, or the drill teams. In the classrooms, they said, some teachers were prejudiced and others made no effort to assist students with special problems. They accused some teachers of assuming that blacks were virtually uneducable.[2]

Black discontent came to a head in the spring of 1970, when the principal of one of Topeka's three high schools refused to authorize a school assembly on the Thursday of Black Culture Week. Other black assemblies and presentations had been held earlier in the week, and the principal decided that by Thursday the students needed time to catch up with class work that had been interrupted. In response, a group of black students set a fire in the school auditorium, with the blaze destroying the twenty-foot curtains, auditorium seats, the stage floor, a grand piano, and theatrical equipment. The total damage amounted to $27,446. Several African American youths were later convicted in juvenile court.[3]

In the meantime black high school students organized a citywide boycott of classes. Asserting that black students were "punished too severely for minor offenses," the protesters called for the reinstatement of students who had been expelled or suspended for participating in the mayhem.

2. Raymond Wolters, *The Burden of Brown: Thirty Years of School Desegregation* (Knoxville: University of Tennessee Press, 1984), 254–55, 322. The number of black teachers in Topeka increased from about twenty-five at the time of *Brown* to forty in 1969 and seventy-five in 1974. These teachers made up 7 percent of the overall faculty—about one-half of the black percentage of the total student enrollment—but blacks were so well represented on the staff that by 1974 minorities made up 12.5 percent of the school district's combined faculty and staff.
3. Wolters, *Burden of Brown*, 254–62.

They demanded that the school board hire more African Americans and fire twenty allegedly prejudiced white teachers and administrators, including the principals of two of the city's three high schools. The protesting students also demanded a review of school rules and assurance that no disciplinary action would be taken against any student who participated in the boycott.[4]

Even before the fire and the boycott, white students had complained about intimidation in the bathrooms, fighting in the halls, and the use of profanity. "Teachers and counselors are afraid to do anything when blacks scream obscenities in their faces," one white student said. Even Linda Brown, the first-named plaintiff in Topeka's original desegregation suit, was concerned about an increase in defiance and disrespect. Her younger sister, who taught sixth grade at Monroe Elementary School, reported that their discipline problem had gotten "out of hand. . . . The teacher tells the kids something to do and he [sic] just talks right back." Linda Brown observed similar problems at the schools her children attended. She thought it was because many parents had failed to instill proper attitudes. "We have so many broken homes now," she explained. "So many mothers are working."[5]

After the fire, some whites said the authorities should do more to maintain order in the schools. One white father maintained, "There is no excuse for a bunch of troublemakers to be able to destroy property." Another said, "the halls at Highland Park High aren't safe to walk in. . . . Negro boys walk arm-in-arm down the corridors, and the whites have to duck to get out of the way." A white mother said there was talk of a vigilante committee where she worked. "We're tired of juvenile delinquents running around loose," the woman said. "This town is really going to rip loose if those responsible for all this aren't punished." Another man declared, "The silent majority wants the school board to know they don't condone violence, disruption, or threats by any element. Those responsible should be expelled and prosecuted, and authority given back to principals and administrators who have felt their hands are tied."[6]

To reduce tensions, the school board suspended classes for seven days during the student boycott of 1970 and agreed to make school attendance voluntary, thereby enabling boycotting black seniors to graduate with their class. In addition, the board guaranteed that black, white, and Mexican American students would be given proportional representation on the

4. Ibid., 255–56.
5. Ibid., 256–57; *Topeka Capital*, 8 October 1968; *Topeka Journal*, 26 September 1968; *Washington Post*, 12 May 1974.
6. Wolters, *Burden of Brown*, 256; *Topeka Daily Capital*, 21 April 1970.

cheerleading squad, the drill team, and the student government. The board also promised to supplement the curriculum with material on the cultural contributions of minority groups, and gave assurance that in the future prospective teachers would be assessed in terms of their "sensitivity to modern life and the knowledge required to survive in culturally deprived areas."[7]

This "compromise" annoyed many whites. A petition bearing 1,840 signatures demanded that truancy regulations be enforced, and another protest condemned the school board for suspending regular classes. White resentment increased when the boycotting black seniors received their diplomas after marching into the assembly with fists clenched in the black power salute. The principal architect of the compromise, Connie Menninger, recalled that she was "really clobbered" when she ran for reelection to the school board. "Especially in the white residential districts there was a terrible ruckus. People complained about 'those liberals' and 'that Menninger woman.'" Meanwhile, inside the schools, black and white students competed for territory, with Topeka High's black students of the 1970s eventually occupying the center of the main hall before classes while whites moved to the outlying spaces—a reversal from the situation that had existed in the 1960s. Menninger conceded that because of an "undercurrent of racial tension" there was a "need to have security guards stationed in the halls" at Topeka High, where the proportion of minority students had increased to 33 percent by 1982. "White kids who haven't had much experience with blacks come into a different world at Topeka High," she said. "They have to learn to keep their cool. The black kids can be very provocative."[8]

Some whites responded by moving away from desegregation. Some parents sent their children to local parochial schools or moved to one of four predominantly white suburban school districts. Migration to the suburbs probably would have been greater if Topeka's neighborhood school policy had not made it possible for parents to ensure a middle-class socialization for their children on the west side of town. West Topeka was the major growth area of the city during the 1970s. It was an area of middle-class housing developments, an area so predominantly white that in 1984 only 97 black students were enrolled among the 1,468 youths who attended Topeka West High School. There was no well-defined black ghetto in central and eastern Topeka, but to the west the population was homogeneously middle class and overwhelmingly white. White flight

7. Wolters, *Burden of Brown*, 259.
8. Ibid., 260–61; Connie Menninger, interview with the author, 20 October 1982.

was limited in Topeka because well-fixed parents who were skeptical of liberal sociology did not have to flee the city; they simply moved to the west side of town.

Washington, D.C.

While the courts had been considering *Brown v. Topeka Board of Education,* African American plaintiffs also demanded the desegregation of public schools in the nation's capital, Washington, D.C., and the Supreme Court's decision in the Washington lawsuit was announced immediately after *Brown.* Noting that *Brown* had just held that states could no longer maintain segregated public schools, the justices also said it was "unthinkable that the same Constitution would impose a lesser duty on the Federal Government."[9]

As in Topeka, school authorities in Washington immediately desegregated the public schools. Geographic boundaries were traced around each school, and all children who lived within the boundary were assigned to the same school, regardless of race. Because most residential areas were not balanced racially, integrationists would later find fault with the policy of neighborhood school assignments. In 1954, however, the word *desegregation* was not understood to mean that black and white students should be balanced proportionately. No such balance existed in Washington's schools, but during the 1954–1955 school year members of the two races mixed together in various proportions at more than two-thirds of the District's schools. At the time, Washington was generally considered a model of desegregation. In an implementation order of 1955, an opinion known as *Brown II,* the Supreme Court itself said that African American children should be admitted to schools of their choice, "within the limits set by the normal geographic school districting."[10]

Yet there was concern about academic standards, especially among college-educated graduates who worked for the government. When citywide pupil achievement tests were given in 1955, the averages differed widely at schools that were either predominantly black or predominant-

9. *Bolling v. Sharpe,* 347 U.S. 497 (1954), 500.
10. "In November 1954, out of 41,358 white pupils, 33,691 were attending school with colored pupils. Only 7,667 in fifteen schools were attending all-white schools. On the same date, out of 64,051 colored pupils, 41,358 attended with white pupils. Only 19,043 colored pupils in 27 schools attended all-colored schools." By 1963, only 1,074 pupils attended school in four all-white schools. See Carl F. Hansen, *Danger in Washington* (West Nyack, N.Y.: Parker, 1968), 25; *Brown v. Board of Education,* 349 U.S. 294 (1955), 298n2, 300–301.

ly white. The average score for Washington's entire group of high school seniors was at the 45th percentile—5 percent under the national average. But at Armstrong, Cardozo, Dunbar, and Spingarn high schools, where only 8 of the 5,019 seniors were white, the average score was in the nation's lowest 5 percent. By contrast, at Coolidge, Western, and Wilson high schools, where only 99 of the 3,129 seniors were black, the average score was in the nation's top 5 percent. Dorothy Tripp, the principal of one of the city's schools, spoke for many teachers when she said she was "shocked at the low achievement of the Negro children who have been in the schools of Washington."[11]

Most observers assumed that with desegregation blacks would do better in school and in later life. Walter E. Hager, the president of the District of Columbia Teachers' College, predicted that within ten years Washington's pupils would meet the national norms on standardized tests. Irene C. Hypps, a black assistant superintendent, forecast that academic achievement would "become less of a problem every year, now that more attention is being given to educating children who are below their grade level."[12]

Some of the optimism stemmed from knowledge that Carl F. Hansen, the District's most influential school administrator, possessed a deep and abiding commitment to desegregation. When desegregation began in 1954, Hansen was a forty-eight-year-old associate superintendent with special responsibility for the senior high schools. He became the superintendent in 1957, and for the next decade Hansen was the dominant figure in public education in Washington.

Hansen was a strong proponent of the comprehensive high school. He thought it wonderful that almost 90 percent of high-school-aged Americans attended school, but he also warned that good students would suffer if academic subjects were watered down for the benefit of slow learners; and that weak students would be damaged if standards were set so high that only the brightest students would succeed. As Hansen saw it, American students needed instruction at a pace appropriate to their abilities. The curriculum should be geared to the needs of diverse students—

11. *Hearings before the Subcommittee to Investigate Public School Standards and Conditions in the District of Columbia, Committee on the District of Columbia,* House of Representatives, 84th Congress, 2d Session, 1956 (cited hereafter as *1956 Investigation*), 344, 161.

12. *U.S. News* 40 (3 February 1956): 40. Hypps added an important qualification: "But since the heart of the problem is the low economic level of many Negro families, the educational problem won't be solved until the economic problem is solved. . . . That will take a great many years."

those below as well as those above the national average. Consequently, Hansen urged Washington to employ more high school teachers—with some teachers especially prepared to deal with slow learners and others especially qualified to teach bright students.

Hansen's recommendation was brought to the attention of segregationists in Congress, who apparently assumed that Hansen's support for ability grouping indicated opposition to desegregation. Yet when Hansen was called to testify before a Congressional committee in 1956, it was apparent that he was no segregationist. Hansen acknowledged that teachers found it difficult to teach classes in which there was a great range in ability, but he insisted that this was "an educational problem," not a racial one. He said he had had the same problem years before when he had been the principal of a predominantly white high school in Omaha, Nebraska. Hansen emphasized that there was a range of aptitude within each race and that some black pupils scored higher than most whites. He said all students would benefit from grouping by ability.[13]

Hansen also insisted that desegregation was going well in Washington. He even wrote a pamphlet that described how well things were proceeding, a pamphlet whose theme was summarized in its title, *Miracle of Social Adjustment*. One group that favored desegregation, the Anti-Defamation League of B'nai B'rith, distributed 90,000 copies of Hansen's account. The *Washington Post* praised the booklet as a "welcome antidote to the poison spread by [segregationists]." For a decade Carl Hansen was regarded as one of the nation's most articulate advocates of desegregation. Ignoring threats to his life, he defied segregationists and traveled throughout the South speaking to various organizations.[14]

While some people were fearful of desegregation, Hansen saw the opportunity for progress. For years he had believed that ability grouping would be to the advantage of all students, but with desegregation Hansen sensed the opportunity to initiate the sort of program he had long had in mind. Hansen did not agree with those who said that, with desegregation, "the advanced student would be held back by the retarded student, the gifted by the less gifted, the white by the Negro." But he thought these "prophets of doom and gloom" could serve a useful purpose. Concern about desegregation provided the opportunity to make changes that were long overdue and should have been made solely for educational reasons.[15]

Beginning in the fall of 1956, each of Washington's high school students

13. Hansen, *Danger in Washington*, 43–45; *1956 Investigation*, 360.
14. *1956 Investigation*, 47.
15. Ibid., 365; *New York Times*, 13 October 1960; trial transcript, *Hobson v. Hansen*, Civil Action 82-66, U.S. District Court, Washington, D.C., 607–11.

was placed in one of four tracks, with the student's placement depending on motivation, grades, and test scores. There was an "honors" curriculum for especially strong students and a "basic" track for those who were especially weak. Those in between were given the choice of either the "general" or the "college preparatory" curriculum. Hansen personally had little use for the general track, which allowed able students to "get by" with easy elective courses and without courses in mathematics and foreign language. "If I could be fully authoritarian," he said, "I would require every capable pupil, college bound or not, to choose the college prep curriculum."[16]

There was some criticism of tracking when the system was introduced in 1956. "Why label students and put them in a narrow groove from which they might never escape?" some opponents asked. Yet the criticism was muted because the benefits of Hansen's program seemed beyond dispute. After desegregation, the enrollment in Washington's public schools increased from 104,330 in 1954 to 149,116 in 1969. This increase was due to an influx of black immigrants from the rural South—an influx that more than offset an 80 percent decline in the white enrollment in Washington's schools (from 40,927 in 1954 to 8,449 in 1969). In most cities the combination of a black influx and white departures led to lower scores on nationally standardized examinations. Yet to the surprise of many, the opposite occurred in Washington, where the average score improved despite the immigration of students who were increasingly from lower income black families. "On three national high school achievement tests," *Time* magazine reported in 1960, "Washington students have raised their position relative to the rest of the U.S. by 14 percentile points." During each of the five years after tracking began, Washington's high school students also improved their relative standing on the national SAT College Entrance Examinations—and this at a time when Washington sent a higher percentage of African Americans to college than any big-city school system in the nation. The rise in academic standards, coinciding with an increase in the number of blacks enrolled, was testimony to "the capacity of the Negro pupil to respond to educational opportunity," Hansen declared.[17]

16. *Washington Evening Star*, 16 June 1959; *1956 Investigation*, 205, 220–22; Carl F. Hansen, "Ability Grouping in the High School," *Atlantic Monthly* 206 (November 1960): 124.
17. Susanna McBee, "D.C. Schools' Basic Track in Trouble Again," *Washington Post* clipping, n.d., in scrapbooks of Washington Board of Education; *Time* 75 (1 February 1960): 64; *Investigation of Schools and Poverty in the District of Columbia, Hearings before the Task Force on Anti-poverty, House of Representatives, Committee on Education and Labor*, 89th Congress, 1st and 2d sessions, 1965–1966 (cited hereafter as *1966 Investigation*), 342; *New York Times*, 4 April 1960, 1.

The improvement in test scores was so extraordinary that some observers wondered if the Washington schools were not somehow "stacking" the statistics. There were rumors that the tests were not being given to students enrolled in the basic track. Hansen denied such insinuations and offered an alternative explanation. In the years after desegregation, "the leadership of the Negro community had set the tone for the parents: You see to it that your children measured up in the schools. Parents were aware that they had a special mission to perform and they communicated this feeling to their children." Hansen also gave credit to the track system. "The gifted must be challenged to their level of promise," he wrote; "the slow to theirs." In addition, Hansen thought it important that Washington's elementary schools focused on reading, writing, and arithmetic; and that most high school students concentrated on English, history, mathematics, and science. Hansen emphatically rejected the idea that "the way to help poor children is to supply them with curriculum experiences selected from their own limited backgrounds."[18]

In the late 1950s, Hansen was considered one of the nation's leading educators. According to *Time*, he had turned "the 'wreck' of Washington schools into a model that less beleaguered cities may envy." He had "confounded pessimists everywhere by raising academic standards higher than they had been under segregation." Writing in the *Saturday Review*, James Koerner reported that Hansen understandably enjoyed "the consistent support of all major groups concerned with the District's schools. . . . The tremendous progress in the Washington school system since the inception of his superintendency is proof that his ideas are effective."[19]

Nevertheless, some disturbing evidence was brought to the surface when a congressional subcommittee investigated the Washington schools in 1956.[20] Taking exception to the black students' use of vulgar language,

18. Hansen, *Danger in Washington*, 53.
19. *Time* 75 (1 February 1960): 64; 76 (31 October 1960): 53; James D. Koerner, "Carl F. Hansen," *Saturday Review* 44 (16 December 1961): 51.
20. A majority of the subcommittee were southerners, and the NAACP characterized the inquiry as a "preconceived" sally by men who believed from the start that desegregation was a mistake. The Americans for Democratic Action similarly predicted that the committee would "scavenge a 'record' of failures and horror stories about desegregation." The investigators' motives may have been questionable, but testimony given by more than fifty Washington teachers and school administrators nevertheless pointed to grave problems. The investigators may have run advance checks to find witnesses who would confirm the case against desegregation, but, as the *New Republic* acknowledged, "the disturbing evidence that came out during the hearings is not made less disturbing merely because of the prejudice and ulterior motive of . . . Southerners." *New York Times*, 19 September 1956, 74; 21 September 1956, 1; 3 October 1956, 15; 29 December 1956, 1; *New Republic* 135 (8 October 1956): 3–4.

John Paul Collins, who had worked in the District's schools for thirty-four years and had been principal of Anacostia and Eastern high schools, declared that he "heard colored girls at the school use language that was far worse than I have ever heard, even in the Marine Corps." Elva Wells, the principal of Theodore Roosevelt High School, asserted that vulgar language was the greatest cause of fights at her school. She said that so many remarks had been made to Roosevelt's girl cheerleaders during the basketball season of 1954–1955 that it had been necessary to switch to boy cheerleaders the next year.[21]

Nor was vulgarity confined to language. Arthur Storey, the principal at McFarland Junior High School, said that in crowded corridors "boys would bump against girls" and "put their hands upon them," but discipline was difficult to administer because "a boy could say, 'I was pushed.'" At Wilson High School the situation got to the point where the student newspaper published an editorial entitled, "Hands Off." At Eastern High School white girls complained about "being touched by colored boys in a suggestive manner when passing . . . in the halls." One white girl said a group of "colored boys put a knife at her back, marched her down an alley and backed her up against a wall. While the group debated as to whether they should make her take her clothes off, she broke away and ran home."[22]

Some observers feared a decline in standards of propriety, especially after one teacher reported that her students were "so preoccupied with sex that when she left the room even for a moment, sex symbols appeared on the blackboard." Others were alarmed when they heard that teenage boys "talked about girls as wives. They spoke of them as if they had all the privileges of marriage." Some also expressed concern about venereal disease and pregnancies. They noted that blacks accounted for 98 percent of the 854 cases of gonorrhea reported among schoolchildren in 1955 and 90 percent of the female students reported as pregnant. Marjory Nelson, a teacher at McFarland Junior High, expressed concern that desegregation would have "a tendency to bring white girls down to that level." Several principals discontinued dances and reduced other social events, despite the fact that black and white students tended to separate from one another in the cafeterias and in extracurricular activities.[23]

In addition, *Time* magazine noted, "teacher after teacher reported an increase in stealing, vandalism, and obscenity." Admitting that the decorum

21. *1956 Investigation*, 36, 39.
22. Ibid., 80, 271, 36.
23. Hansen, *Danger in Washington*, 164; *Time* 69 (7 January 1957): 49; *U.S. News* 43 (12 July 1957): 66–68; and 45 (12 December 1958): 66; *1956 Investigation*, 267, 73, 133, 139.

of students left something to be desired even before desegregation, Dorothy Denton, a teacher at Barnard Elementary School, said that behavior was "going from good, or medium-good, to bad, in my opinion." In 1956 John Paul Collins said there had been "more thefts at Eastern [High School] in the last two years than I had known in all my thirty-odd years in the school system." One teacher, Katherine Fowler of McKinley High School, blamed the NAACP for undermining the authority of teachers. She recalled that after she had scolded some black students who were singing in the hall and disturbing others, the students said she was picking on them because of their race. An official of the NAACP then discussed the matter with Fowler's principal, who warned the teacher to "be careful" in disciplining black students. A few weeks later Fowler came upon four black students riding noisily through the halls in a trash cart. "I started after them," she recalled, "and I am sure I did not take more than four steps before I remembered what had happened to me before, so I said: 'No, Katherine, you just let them go and let the principal of the school or somebody else . . . take care of it.' Of course . . . I felt that I was neglecting my duty. But I did not care to have that unpleasant situation again, so I neglected it."[24]

Meanwhile, many white students departed from Washington's public schools. By 1974 whites made up only 3 percent of the public school students in the District, as compared with 40 percent when desegregation began in 1954. After desegregation, the rate of white withdrawal from the public schools tripled. Between 1949 and 1953 white enrollments had declined by about 4,000 students; between 1954 and 1958, white enrollments declined by almost 12,000 students. Washington was on the way to having an almost all-black, "resegregated" public school system. In the nation's capital the era of desegregation turned out to be the interval between the time when the first blacks moved in and the last whites moved out.[25]

Yet as long as Carl Hansen's ability grouping system was in place, the great majority of Washington's middle-class black families continued to

24. *Time* 69 (7 January 1957): 49; *1956 Investigation*, 95, 36, 230–31. Carl Hansen was more skeptical. "White teachers and principals, most of them people whom I knew and respected, testified about scholastic retardation, delinquent behavior with strong emphasis on sexual aggressions such as indecent exposure, and the curtailment of normal school activities such as school dances and dramatic presentations. The testimony over the nine days of open hearings was a gruesome recounting of instances of bad behavior and low achievement among Negro pupils, as if these elements were occurring for the first time in the classrooms of the District of Columbia. The whole affair was an open gossip session in which all the neighborhood scandal was gleefully discussed." *Danger in Washington*, 43.

25. See the statistical table in Wolters, *Burden of Brown*, 16.

patronize the public schools. As the civil rights movement gained momentum, however, ability grouping seemed out of step with an increasingly egalitarian temper of the times. Hansen's program also came in for criticism as a result of three specific controversies.

One dispute grew out of Hansen's decision to establish a "back to basics" curriculum at Amidon, an elementary school in southwest Washington. Here Hansen hoped to show that, as he put it, elementary school students did not need "'an endless panel discussion' but 'firm grounding in the Three Rs.'" Beginning with the first grade, the curriculum emphasized spelling, handwriting, arithmetic, and reading (taught by the phonic method). Grammar, normally taught in the sixth grade, was introduced in the third year, along with French and Spanish. History and geography were taught individually and not grouped with other "social studies." There were no Halloween parties, no orchestra, no student government association, and field trips were held to a minimum. In addition, Hansen extended the system of ability grouping (which previously had been limited to the high schools) so that elementary pupils at Amidon were grouped with others of similar academic achievement.[26]

By 1964 Amidon's reputation had grown almost to cult level, and 300 of the school's 800 students were transfers from other parts of the District. This was possible because construction had been delayed on some nearby apartment buildings that were supposed to provide the school with much of its enrollment. Some parents transferred their children from expensive private schools at the first vacancy. The wife of an engineer who was moving her family from Texas informed a real estate firm that she wanted a home "near the Amidon school, wherever that is." The remaining students came from two military installations, a neighborhood public housing project, and nearby townhouses and luxury apartments. With a black enrollment of about 70 percent, Amidon was one of the more integrated schools in the District at a time when the black enrollment in Washington approached 90 percent and when the enrollment in most schools tended to be predominantly of one race of the other.[27]

Nevertheless, some critics took exception to Amidon's traditional education, perhaps because (as Hansen speculated) they recognized that success would discredit "the permissive child-centered [education] once associated with the term 'progressive.'" One school administrator in nearby Maryland denounced Amidon as "a sop to all the reactionary forces

26. Norman Poirier, "The Extraordinary Amidon School," *Saturday Evening Post* 237 (19 December 1964): 22–23; *New Republic* 145 (23 October 1961): 6.
27. Poirier, "Extraordinary Amidon," 22.

afloat." Writing in the *New Republic*, Christopher Jencks discounted Amidon's success. "Students in the new school will almost certainly learn more," Jencks observed. But this was because a disproportionate number were being recruited "from middle-class families who think good education important enough to bring their students to and from school. It will be no surprise when children from such families turn out to learn more than the progeny of more indifferent homes."[28]

If Hansen had been a social scientist, he would have set up a controlled experiment, with a second school staffed by progressive instructors and attended by students who voluntarily chose not to have a subject-centered curriculum. But this was not done, and progressive educators recognized that Amidon was structured to accentuate the benefits of an orderly, systematic curriculum focused on basic subject matter. When an amazing 94 percent of the students at Amidon scored above the national norms in reading and computation, a growing number of parents concluded that Amidon's approach should be implemented throughout the District.[29]

Amidon challenged the ideology that was dominant in most schools of education. Many progressives consequently wanted to discredit Hansen if they could. One opportunity to do so presented itself unexpectedly after a race riot at a high school football game. For several years the *Washington Post* had sponsored a Thanksgiving contest between the champions of the local public and parochial leagues, which usually meant that one team and its supporters were predominantly black and the other predominantly white. The year 1962 was no exception. At the end of the game, in which a crowd of 50,000 spectators, three-fourths of them black, saw St. John's defeat Eastern, several thousand blacks "brandishing sticks and other assorted implements . . . raced across the field to have a go at the whites sitting together on the other side." During the melee 346 people were injured, all but thirty of them whites. There were thirteen broken noses, two broken jaws, and twenty stabbings. Simeon Booker, an African American journalist well known for his coverage of white assaults on civil rights activists in the South, candidly stated that "the predominant number of offenders were Negro. . . . What I saw at the stadium easily could have duplicated what I saw covering the Little Rock school desegregation case, or the bus station mob during the Freedom Rides to Birmingham or the Emmett Till case in Mississippi. The difference, ironical-

28. Hansen, *Danger in Washington*, 208, 209; Koerner, "Carl F. Hansen," 51. Jencks was the author of two unsigned pieces in the *New Republic* 142 (4 April 1960): 6; and 145 (23 October 1961): 6.

29. *1966 Investigation*, 157.

ly, was that the predominant number of offenders were Negro. The explosion of hate stemmed mostly from my own people."[30]

After six weeks of probing, a mostly white investigative commission concluded that "conduct at athletic games—including the recent stadium contest—is symptomatic of the school conditions." According to the commission's chairman, "Not a single teacher . . . was surprised that the outbreak took place." "Why should we be?" asked one teacher. "We live with this brand of conduct every day in the schools." Numerous assaults were said to have occurred, most of which were never reported to police authorities.[31]

There was no consensus as to the cause of the trouble. Chuck Stone, the editor of the *Washington Afro-American,* said Carl Hansen was "a man remarkably free from racial prejudice," but Stone thought some administrators did not share Hansen's "intellectual and emotional commitment to an integrated school system." Stone thought the disorder was partly a response to white prejudice.[32]

For his part, Carl Hansen thought the problem stemmed from "the unusually large number of children from problem homes." Because so many families were broken and so many mothers were working, Hansen said, many youths did not receive adult supervision after school hours. Hansen asked for the authority to expel incorrigible pupils and to hire more male teachers. "Many of the youngsters don't have too much contact with adult males," he said. "They are in a matriarchal kind of family situation where the female, the mother, runs the show. It's a good thing for children, as they grow up, to have some close contact, some relationship, with the male of the species. That's why I want more men teachers." Hansen also arranged to have police patrolmen put on "short beat" duty so they would be available if needed at one of the schools.[33]

While not absolving unruly black students, the investigating commission emphasized a different conclusion. It blamed the disruptions on Carl Hansen's system of ability grouping. According to the commission, the basic track had become "the dumping ground for hundreds of Negro youth." These students allegedly became "discouraged at being tossed into a scrap heap, lose interest in schooling and become dropouts, the

30. *New Republic* 147 (15 December 1962): 6–7; *U.S. News* 54 (21 January 1963): 72–74; *New York Times,* 28 November 1962, 26.

31. The report was summarized in *U.S. News* 54 (21 January 1963): 72–74.

32. *New York Times,* 14 March 1962, 29.

33. *U.S. News and World Report* 54 (18 February 1963): 37–39; 54 (11 March 1963): 62–68; *New York Times,* 21 February 1963, 6.

members of a large grouping who form the 'social dynamite' to haunt our community."[34]

The commission's conclusion was extraordinary. It blamed the school system for the misbehavior of students. The Jesuit journal *America* noted that the commission's report "spotlighted the inadequacies of the public schools." After conceding that black leaders should "tackle this problem of rowdyism and juvenile delinquency," another Catholic journal, *Commonweal*, concluded that "the task of Washington's white population is no less demanding. Somehow it must find the courage to confront the fact of its irresponsible evasion of the problem of Negro rights and Negro progress."[35]

In some respects Carl Hansen and the tracking system were at odds with an egalitarian mood that gained momentum in the 1960s. Yet given the force of inertia, Hansen's system might have stayed in place a while longer had it not been for the opposition of one of the most dramatic civil rights leaders of the decade, Julius W. Hobson. Hobson's challenge to Hansen, which eventually became a lawsuit, *Hobson v. Hansen*, became another, and the most significant, of the challenges to Hansen's program.

As a young man Julius Hobson had flown thirty-five missions as an army pilot during World War II, and after the war he became a statistician and economist at the Library of Congress and at the Social Security Administration. Hobson was also a self-styled Marxist who achieved prominence as the leader of several dramatic demonstrations in the nation's capital. On one occasion he led a caravan of automobiles carrying cages of rats to Georgetown, insisting that wealthy people should share a problem they said was insoluble. On other occasions he picketed automobile dealers who refused to hire black salesmen and participated in "lay-ins" and "live-ins" at hospitals and apartment houses that served only whites. After parting from the NAACP and quarreling with the national leaders of CORE (the Congress of Racial Equality), Hobson helped to establish a new organization called Associated Community Teams (ACT). Hobson described ACT as an "organization of militants" who "went to sleep mad."[36]

During the 1960s Hobson also compiled a mass of statistics that pertained to grouping students by ability. Although by 1967 the proportion of black students in Washington was so large (92.3 percent) that African Americans made up a majority of the students in every track, Hobson con-

34. Commission Report, in files of Washington Board of Education.

35. *America* 108 (30 March 1963): 425; *Commonweal* 77 (14 December 1962): 304–5.

36. *Washington Post*, 24 March 1972, 6 April 1977; *New York Times*, 25 March 1977, sec. 4, p. 14; *1966 Investigation*, 323, 832.

demned tracking as a "vicious injustice to thousands of innocent children." He did so because statistics showed that if children were assigned
on the basis of either performance or aptitude, students from low-income
families would be assigned disproportionately to the lower tracks while
youngsters from wealthier families were assigned disproportionately to
the upper tracks. Hobson then insisted that disadvantaged youths could
not be classified correctly on the basis of tests with norms that were based
on middle-class standards. It was, he said, "a cunning and ingenious system of discrimination based on a new kind of supremacy theory: cultural
superiority"—a theory that rendered many poor blacks uneducable because it "undermin[ed] the slum child's self-respect."[37]

Hobson's theory was not widely credited in black Washington, where
only four hundred students joined a 1967 boycott he called to protest
tracking. "The trouble with Washington is that there are a lot of middle-
class Negroes here, and they are satisfied," said one protestor. Hobson admitted that there was "great apathy in Washington," that many parents
were "satisfied with Hansen." After thoroughly discussing the tracking
system in 1966, the school board continued to support the tracking program and extended Hansen's contract for an additional three years.[38]

The tide was turning against Hansen, however. Although the *Washington Post* had commended the District's public schools in 1962 for acceler-
ating the pace of academic education, after 1965 the newspaper became a
major, persistent critic of what it called "the rut system." At the same time,
some African Americans linked ability grouping with the patronizing
snobbery they associated with the light-skinned colored "aristocracy."
One said the tracking system was "dangerous to poor children" because
it had been designed to encourage middle-class African Americans to stay
with the public schools. Another complained that Hansen was "insensitive . . . to the needs of the new Negro in town," whom he identified as
"the out-group . . . not a member of the old-line Negro families. His skin
is often dark." One black woman who worked for the U.S. Office of Education, although herself a member of the old Negro elite, nevertheless opposed Hansen on the grounds that the time had come for an African
American to be in charge of the District's largely black school system.[39]

37. *1966 Investigation,* 237, 238, 241; Julius Hobson, "Using the Legal Process for
Change," in Dwight W. Allen and Jeffrey C. Hecht, eds., *Controversies in Education*
(Philadelphia: Saunders, 1974), 535; Deposition of Julius Hobson, 18 June 1966, CA 82-
66, U.S. District Court, Washington, 1965; *Washington Post,* 24 March 1967, 2 April 1967.
    38. *Washington Star,* 1 May 1967; *1966 Investigation,* 251; Wolters, *Burden of Brown,* 31.
    39. *Washington Post,* 23 October 1962, 15 October 1965; Hansen, *Danger in Washing-
ton,* 222–23.

Yet since Hobson had not won many converts in black Washington and Hansen still had the support of a majority of the school board, Hobson decided to change tactics. "I called [Hobson]," recalled one friend, "and told him we should bring suit on the basis of economic differential treatment." With guidance from his principal attorney, William Kunstler, Hobson maneuvered so that the lawsuit would be heard by one of the most liberal of all federal judges, J. Skelly Wright.[40]

After listening to testimony that ran to almost eight thousand pages, Judge Wright concluded that school tests and teachers' grades were culturally biased and "wholly inappropriate for making predictions about the academic potential of disadvantaged Negro children." The system "simply must be abolished," Judge Wright ordered. The separation along socioeconomic lines was such that Judge Wright considered the system "wholly irrational and thus unconstitutionally discriminatory." Instead of being grouped according to capacity to learn, students were in reality being classified according to socioeconomic class, "or—more precisely—according to environmental and psychological factors which have nothing to do with innate ability." With citations to psychologist Kenneth B. Clark, Judge Wright speculated that low test scores and grades were a product of the teachers' middle-class bias, and that, because students lost confidence after receiving low scores and grades, the students then performed at substandard levels. Because he considered the system so capricious, Judge Wright ruled that tracking amounted to an unconstitutional denial of liberty without due process of law.[41]

The Supreme Court has permitted policies that have a disparate impact on different economic classes, as long as the policies are not arbitrary on their face. Judge Wright, however, held that policies that are neutral on their face but affect the poor disproportionately must satisfy a higher standard that the Supreme Court had reserved for official racial discrimination. In defending its program, the school board had satisfied the standard of "minimum rationality," but Judge Wright ruled against ability grouping because school authorities had not presented "compelling" evidence that was so weighty as to be conclusive.

Because his rationale was at odds with the jurisprudence of the Supreme Court, few other judges have followed Judge Wright's approach to due process. Ability grouping has remained a constitutional option in other parts of the United States. By a vote of four to three, however, the

40. *Washington Evening Star,* 20 June 1967; Hansen, *Danger in Washington,* 94.
41. *Hobson v. Hansen,* 269 F.Supp. 401 (1967), 474, 484, 491, 513–15.

Court of Appeals for the District of Columbia upheld Judge Wright's decision. The opinion of the Court of Appeals was written by Judge David Bazelon, a jurist so widely known for his liberal and egalitarian views that Judge Wright, speaking in a different context, once opined that he and Bazelon were the two most liberal members of the entire federal judiciary. The Supreme Court then declined to review *Hobson v. Hansen*.[42]

The initial reactions to Judge Wright's opinion were mixed. Julius Hobson hailed the decision as "a sweeping victory." The *New York Times* considered the opinion "a monumental exercise in sociological jurisprudence." And Carl Hansen fumed that it was a milestone in judicial conceit. People were wrong to say, "God is dead," Hansen wrote. "He is currently sitting on the Federal Bench in Washington, D.C. His name is J. Skelly Wright." Another critique came from columnist Joseph Alsop. Writing in the *New Republic*, Alsop declared, "It is time to stop talking nonsense about Negro education." Alsop predicted that Wright's ruling would leave the schools more "resegregated" than ever because it would stimulate flight and "increase the Negro percentage in the primary and elementary schools from 93 to 98 or 99 percent." In point of fact, the proportion of black students reached 97 percent in 1973.[43]

With ability grouping banned by order of the court, Carl Hansen resigned as superintendent, and the school board hired psychologist Kenneth B. Clark to design a new curriculum. As Clark saw it, self-esteem was a crucial prerequisite for educational progress, and the teachers' expectations were the key to instilling self-esteem. Unfortunately, Clark said, many middle-class teachers, blacks as well as whites, believed that lower-class families provided such a bad home environment that it was hard to educate their children. Therefore, Clark said, the teachers concentrated their attention on talented middle-class students, thinking that the best that could be done was to salvage the few who showed some natural academic aptitude. Middle-class teachers did not seem to recognize that their pessimistic expectations induced lower-class students to perform at substandard levels. Clark insisted that teachers who believed in lower-class students would do better than those who thought poor

42. *Smuk v. Hobson*, 408 F.2d 175 (1969); J. Skelly Wright, "A Colleague's Tribute to Judge David L. Bazelon," *University of Pennsylvania Law Review* 123 (December 1974): 250–53.

43. *New York Times*, 30 June 1967, 1; 23 June 1967, 38; Hansen, *Danger in Washington*, 91; Joseph Alsop, "No More Nonsense about Ghetto Education!" *New Republic* 157 (22 July 1967): 18–23; Alsop, "Ghetto Education," *New Republic* 157 (18 November 1967): 8–23.

blacks had so many cards stacked against them that they could not measure up.[44]

To combat the power of negative thinking, which Clark sometimes described as a "self-fulfilling prophecy," Clark proposed to make the teachers' promotions and pay contingent upon their students' performance on standardized examinations. The teachers' union, however, was strongly opposed to this sort of "merit pay." The union insisted that teachers could not be fairly judged by their students' scores, because a teacher's influence would often be outweighed by what happened at home and elsewhere in the community. The president of the teachers' union asked, "What do you do about the teacher who happens to have a group of students who do not get proper food at home or come from an environment that is not conducive to learning?" Most teachers were incredulous when Clark insisted, "It is the teacher's job to make up for the deficiencies in the home."[45]

So was Hugh Scott, who in 1969 replaced Carl Hansen as superintendent of schools. Scott was a young administrator who had endorsed Clark's concepts when he was interviewed for the position. But Scott considered it "simplistic" to expect a dramatic improvement in academic scores if teachers viewed students from a different perspective. In addition, Scott said, "It makes no difference what type of plan you put in. If you don't have the cooperation of the teachers, it's not going to work." Scott backed away from Clark's proposals after he came to understand the strength of the teachers' opposition. Clark then felt betrayed. He said his plan was being "abandoned" and "interred" not just by the teachers' union but also by Superintendent Scott. As long as Scott was superintendent, Clark declared, "the plan is dead."[46]

It is hard to see how any superintendent could proceed in the face of vehement opposition from the teachers' union. Shelving Clark's plan, however, did not improve the quality of education in Washington. Instead, during and after the years of Scott's regime, the scores of top students declined from the level achieved under Hansen.

Scott resigned after four years and was succeeded in 1973 by Barbara Sizemore, whose philosophy of education was very different from that of Kenneth Clark. Whereas Clark emphasized the importance of students'

44. Wolters, *Burden of Brown*, 49–52.

45. *Washington Post*, 19 July 1970, 30 August 1970, 27 September 1970.

46. *Washington Star*, 18 April 1971, 10 December 1970, 18 March 1971; *New York Times*, 22 February 1978, 22; *Washington Post*, 20 November 1970, 10 September 1970, 21 November 1970, 20 April 1970, 19 February 1973, 31 July 1975, 31 August 1975; *Washington Teacher*, October 1970.

scores on standard tests of reading and mathematics, and proposed to reward teachers accordingly, Sizemore discontinued the use of such tests. Instead, Sizemore favored open classrooms, organized in the manner then in fashion in some English schools. Under this arrangement, students would not be required to study a particular topic chosen by the teacher. They would instead focus on matters they found especially interesting—with the assumption that with informal guidance children who pursued a student-centered approach eventually would learn to read and to cipher. Sizemore also said the "age-graded, monolingual, mono-cultural" program found in most public schools benefited only "affluent whites of European descent." It was necessary, Sizemore said, to design a distinctive Afrocentric curriculum for poor blacks.[47]

Many middle-class parents wondered if Sizemore really had anything better to substitute for the traditional course of study, but the Washington school board thought Sizemore possessed special insight into how to teach disadvantaged black youths. Yet Sizemore was fired in 1975, not because of her educational philosophy but because she did not properly handle several administrative matters. Quarterly financial statements were not prepared, and an annual report was not filed on time. Many of the buildings fell into disrepair, school supplies were misplaced, and teachers were assigned too late to permit adequate planning for classes. In October 1975, fifteen hundred employees complained of mistakes in their paychecks.[48]

The school board then turned to Vincent Reed, a former football player who had been teaching in Washington since 1956. Reed's appointment as superintendent represented something of a departure, since in the recent past the school board had hired superintendents who were noted for their educational ideas. In naming Vincent Reed to head the school bureaucracy, the board indicated that above all it wanted a competent manager. In this respect, Reed did not disappoint. His budgets were prepared on time. The delivery of books and supplies was markedly improved. In 1976 only three employees complained about mistakes in their paychecks.[49]

Reed generally received high marks for his work in restoring administrative order to Washington's public schools. Yet when standard tests were given again in 1978, after having been suspended during the years of Barbara Sizemore's superintendency, the results were not encouraging. The scores generally followed the income and educational level of neigh-

47. *Washington Post*, 23 April 1975, 5 April 1975, 16 April 1975.
48. Ibid., 15 December 1974.
49. Ibid., 3 January 1977, 24 September 1976.

borhoods, with most schools in low-income areas doing poorly while those in affluent areas did better. On the average, Washington's sixth-grade public school students were one year behind the national mean in mathematics and 1.7 years behind in reading. By ninth grade, the average Washington public school student was three years below national norms in both reading and mathematics. These numbers did not reveal much about what a particular child might achieve, but many parents thought they suggested something about the level of instruction at the junior and senior high schools. In a statement that reflected the rationale of many of the middle-class black parents who sent their children to private schools or to public schools in the suburbs, *Washington Post* columnist William Raspberry lamented, "When the averages fall low enough, so does the teaching level. Even the most dedicated teacher finally has to gear her lessons to the bulk of the class."[50]

Nevertheless in 1978, by a vote of ten to zero with one abstention, the school board reappointed Vincent Reed to a second term as superintendent. It was the first reappointment of a superintendent since that of Carl Hansen in 1966. Because the academic performance of Washington's students was so low, the abstaining board member noted that Reed's major achievements had been in management and public relations. "When we look at the students' test scores . . . it brings us back to the question of what schools are for."[51]

Partly because of the low scores, many middle-class blacks abandoned the District's public schools—a phenomenon sometimes called "bright flight." In 1981 Acting Superintendent James T. Guines explained, "most of the black middle class, the former backbone and beneficiary of the system, [had] dissociated itself from the school system as a source of instruction, although not as a source of income." As long as students were grouped by ability, Guines said, middle-class African Americans had continued to patronize the District's public schools. After grouping was abolished, however, "many middle-class black heads of households continue[d] to work in the public schools as teachers and administrators and then use[d] a substantial portion of their salaries to exercise their freedom of choice to enroll their children in expensive local parochial and private schools."[52]

What can be said by way of assessment? By the mid-1960s blacks made up 90 percent of the students in Washington's public schools, but on na-

50. Ibid., 31 August 1978, 7 and 13 September 1978.
51. Ibid., 24 November 1978.
52. Ibid., 18 January 1979, 23 March 1979, 17 May 1979.

tional tests those students approached (and in some cases exceeded) the national average. A trend that was so clearly contrary to expectations should have been acclaimed and studied carefully. Yet Judge J. Skelly Wright was so taken by egalitarian sociology that he could not let pass the opportunity to impose his views. Instead of assisting school administrators in their efforts to provide a high quality of public education, he destroyed an educational system that had been working reasonably well, and in the name of the Constitution he delivered the school system to excesses of disorder and academic experimentation. One cannot know that things might have turned out better if wiser people had made better choices. But if that possibility is admitted, then the story of public education in Washington is one that illustrates the perils of judicial arrogance.

Wilmington, Delaware

Wilmington was yet another city whose schools were desegregated by order of the *Brown* Court. Initially the litigation grew out of disputes that pertained to the city's high school for blacks, Howard High School, to two elementary schools (one for blacks and the other for whites) in the village of Hockessin, ten miles west of Wilmington, and to an all-white high school in the town of Claymont, nine miles north of Wilmington. The cases were consolidated with the litigation from Topeka when appeals were taken to the Supreme Court.

In 1954 blacks made up 27 percent of the thirteen thousand public school students in Wilmington, and desegregation proceeded in stages, beginning with the grammar schools in 1954 and extending to the junior high schools in 1955 and the senior high schools in 1956. As in Topeka and Washington, students in Wilmington were assigned to neighborhood schools, although in Delaware this policy was modified by an open enrollment policy that allowed parents to transfer their children to other schools if they wished. As in Topeka and Washington, this system was approved by a federal court, which held that, because of *Brown*, "discrimination is forbidden but integration is not compelled. . . . [I]f races are separated because of geographic or transportation considerations or other similar criteria, it is no concern of the Federal Constitution."[53]

At the time, Wilmington's school superintendent, Ward Miller, said that

53. *Evans v. Buchanan*, 207 F.Supp. 820 (1962), 823–24. In 1956–1957, only twenty children (in a school district that enrolled more than thirteen thousand students) were transferred to nonintegrated schools.

desegregation had "succeeded beyond our fondest hopes," and *New York Times* reporter Benjamin Fine wrote that "in less than three years a new way of life has taken hold in the city's schools." Fine reported that "in the early grades [the children] accept integration without question. They do not know the meaning of the word, but they certainly practice it. They take turns swinging the jump rope. . . . During the resting period in kindergarten, the children stretched out on blankets on the floor. They lay side by side, regardless of color."[54]

There was less mixing in the high schools. "White elementary school pupils invite Negroes to their homes for a glass of milk and cookies or to work on a school project," Fine reported. "But there comes a time when this stops. Sometimes it is in the fifth or sixth grade. Or it might be in junior high school. By the time they get to senior high, the social separation appears decisive."[55]

Despite some difficulties, desegregation seemed to go well. For several years after 1954, the Wilmington public schools continued to be considered as good as any in Delaware. Bill Frank, the most prominent newspaper columnist in the state, reflected the views of most informed observers when he wrote, "This is a fact. Where desegregation in Delaware has been given a fair trial . . . it has been successful in that it has not developed into any difficulty nor has it gone beyond any limit set by educators."[56]

Yet many whites apparently thought otherwise, for with desegregation they began to leave Wilmington. At the same time, a growing number of blacks moved into the city, many from the rural South. There was no single point when enrollments tipped quickly from white to black. Instead, the migrations proceeded for two decades. Total enrollment in the Wilmington public schools varied between 13,000 and 16,000 students, but the percentage of whites steadily decreased from 72.9 in 1954 to 9.7 in 1976.

In contrast to people who routinely emphasized the importance of race, residents of Wilmington and its suburbs generally said that race was of little consequence. Many of the teachers and school administrators were from northern states, especially Pennsylvania and New Jersey, and they were said to "go around pretending that race doesn't exist." The official

54. *Wilmington Morning News,* 14 February 1956, 25 June 1958; *Wilmington Evening Journal,* 21 September 1954; *Southern School News,* March 1958; *New York Times,* 13 May 1957, 1.

55. *New York Times,* 13 May 1957, 1; *Wilmington Morning News,* 28 March 1957, 29 September 1969.

56. *Wilmington Morning News,* 29 September 1955.

position was that academic problems resulted from cultural deprivation and not from any inherent deficiency in the blacks' reasoning power or imagination. "The whole thing is simply a problem of class," one white teacher said. "Most of our Negro students are simply from poor families. They act pretty much the same as white lower-class children." A reporter for the *Wilmington Morning News* maintained that problems were not caused "solely by Negroes and where they have been caused by Negroes it is not because of any peculiarity of race but because of the social and economic situations in which most Negro families have been forced to live."[57]

In an effort to retain academically talented students, the Wilmington schools moved toward further grouping of students by scholastic achievement. With desegregation there was no change in the range of ability, but there was a marked change in the frequency of distribution. Some students continued to do well in the traditional college preparatory curriculum, but a growing number needed to move at a slower pace. School officials consequently devised new programs for those with below- and above-average ability. "There are many more of the former than the latter," the *Wilmington Morning News* stated, "but special programs have been set up for each." Especially in the late 1950s, school officials in Wilmington stressed the need for programs suited "to the needs of boys and girls with superior ability." Like Carl Hansen in Washington, Wilmington's superintendent Ward Miller said that one of the major problems in American education was "an unwillingness to group pupils for instructional purposes in order that those with superior ability may progress in accordance with their capacities." To remedy this weakness, the Wilmington schools inaugurated a system where, on the basis of tests, grades, and teachers' evaluations, schools grouped pupils by subjects, "with the brilliant ones in math together, those in social studies together, and so on."[58]

After desegregation, however, and especially in the 1960s and 1970s, officials focused increasingly on the needs of disadvantaged students. As whites departed and blacks moved in, significant modifications were made in the educational program. Thomas W. Mulrooney, the director of child guidance, reported that a growing number of students came to school "unfed and clothed in rags." Many came from "unstable families and one-parent families with drinking mothers . . . who often fear to dis-

57. Herbert R. Baringer, "Integration in Newark, Delaware," in Raymond W. Mack, ed., *Our Children's Burden* (New York: Random House, 1968), 148, 149; *Wilmington Morning News*, 3 January 1963.

58. *Wilmington Morning News*, 19 August 1958; *Staff Reporter* (magazine published by Wilmington Public Schools), April 1956, September 1958, March 1961.

cipline their children." In 1965 Assistant Superintendent Muriel Crosby described the situation this way:

> These youngsters are accustomed to seeing a succession of men in the home, whose relations with the mother are transitory. *Such children lack the stability of normal family life which helps them feel important and wanted because it is centered in the welfare of the children.* The oldest children in the family are forced to assume the burden of maturity too early in life. They handle the family food budget, shopping while mother is at work. They prepare whatever food is available for younger children. They often assume full responsibility for younger brothers and sisters. . . . For many disadvantaged children moral and spiritual perversion is the result of deprivation. Cramped and crowded living space denying any form of privacy introduces the child to adult sexual behavior before he is mature enough to comprehend the significance of it. He is often victimized by adults living in his home. This is particularly true of girls, who often become mothers when they are still little more than children. Illegitimacy is an accepted pattern of life, and marriage is of little consequence in sexual relationships.[59]

To cope with this situation, the Wilmington public school system became a pioneer in providing breakfasts and clothing and in employing social workers, psychologists, doctors, nurses, and psychiatrists. The old methods of teaching would "no longer suffice to deal effectively with the kind of problems now faced in our classrooms," Superintendent Miller reported. By the early 1960s Miller was convinced that the time had come "to cut the strings which tie us to traditions and habits established through the years." To make desegregation a success, several new programs were developed. Some sought to improve family and community life. Others tried to motivate children from low-income families. In the classrooms, teachers increasingly turned toward group work that focused on projects like calculating a family budget or planning a community activity. In this way teachers could reward students who worked cooperatively as well as those who did well on tests.[60]

During the 1950s and early 1960s, when Ward Miller and Muriel Crosby were in charge of the Wilmington schools, the emphasis on innovative programs was kept in perspective. New programs were devised for a

---

59. *Wilmington Morning News,* 16 November 1959; Muriel Crosby, *An Adventure in Human Relations* (Chicago: Follett, 1965), 8–10, emphasis in original.

60. *Staff Reporter,* February 1960, February 1963.

rapidly changing city, but traditional curricula were also maintained for academic students. The goal was to teach all the children of all the people. To do this it was necessary to develop distinctive programs for strong, average, and weak students.

In 1963 Miller retired at the age of seventy, after seventeen years as superintendent of schools. During the next seventeen years, three white superintendents were succeeded by three blacks, and African Americans also became a majority of the teaching staff and board of education. As the black presence increased, the emphasis moved even more toward designing new approaches to reach disadvantaged students. "The simple teaching methods of earlier days—long on repetition and repressive discipline—would no longer be adequate to meet the new situation," white superintendent Gene A. Geisert declared. Instead of requiring students to take academic courses in the traditional sequence, black superintendent Earl C. Jackson recommended individual attention in a less competitive atmosphere. The needs of Wilmington's predominantly black students of the 1970s differed markedly from those of its predominantly white students of the 1950s. "What we had in the past worked with the students who were taught then," said James Moore, the principal of P. S. du Pont High School. But by the 1970s a large portion of the students were too far below grade level to understand traditional academic material.[61]

In the 1960s and 1970s, Wilmington's schools experimented with many of the approaches dear to the hearts of progressive educators. Project Expansion gave high school students the freedom to design their own courses of study. Project Open-Out was designed for hard-core dropouts, as was Project E.S.O., a street academy established with funds from the Du Pont Company. Beginning in 1968 several elementary schools developed a progressive program of informal education in "open" classrooms. Financed by the National Follow Through Program and sponsored by Bank Street College in New York City, this program was for low-income children in kindergarten through fourth grade. It emphasized that a child's success in learning was "inseparable from his self-esteem," and that teachers should make the child "feel important as a person" and develop his "ability to work and play cooperatively with other children." Basic skills were important, but the teacher's role was "more that of a facilitator than a lecturer or director." Teachers were told that excessive di-

61. *Profile* (magazine published by Wilmington Public Schools), April 1970, January 1971; Annual Report of Wilmington Public Schools, 1971–1972; *Wilmington News Journal*, clipping, 10 August 1973.

rection would repress their students' natural inclinations and inborn "enthusiasm for learning."[62]

In the end, though, the new programs did not solve Wilmington's educational problems. The trend in academic achievement was steadily downward. By the mid-1970s Wilmington's public high school seniors, once the best in the state, were three and one-half years below national norms on standardized tests and four years behind students in the suburbs of Wilmington.[63]

In retrospect, it would be easy to fault Wilmington's school officials for going too far in lowering academic standards. Yet their error, if it was an error, grew out of an earnest desire to teach disadvantaged students. The officials tried most of the approaches that were recommended at the time, and yet the students' academic performance declined significantly. Wilmington was caught in the grip of demographic forces that were beyond the control of local officials. As middle-class whites departed for the suburbs, their places were taken by black migrants from the rural South and, in the 1970s, by a substantial number from Puerto Rico as well. In a relatively brief period, Wilmington changed from a city of mostly middle-class families to one with a substantial number of impoverished people.

Meanwhile, there was a marked increase in the number of disciplinary problems. "It was almost as if there was something magic—or hellish—when the black enrollment reached 40 percent," recalled Jeanette McDonnal, the dean of girls at P. S. du Pont High School. "The black attitudes changed then, and the whites had reason to be frightened." Beginning in the early 1960s, there were frequent reports of petty extortion at P.S. du Pont, as older black students demanded protection money from younger students of both races. Graffiti appeared on the school's previously immaculate buildings, refuse littered the grounds, and windows were smashed. In 1968 more than one hundred white parents signed a petition asking for stronger discipline at "P.S." Spokeswoman Dorothy Worthy said her children were "getting an education all right—but not the right kind."[64]

Faculty members at "P.S." were also subjected to ill treatment. Most of

62. Annual Reports of the Wilmington Public Schools, 1968–1977; Jeffrey A. Raffel, *The Challenge of Educational Change: An Evaluation of the Follow Through Program in the Wilmington Public Schools* (Newark: University of Delaware Division of Urban Affairs, 1974), 2, 15, 22, 51, and passim.

63. Wolters, *Burden of Brown*, 187, 188.

64. Jeanette McDonnal, interview with the author, 4 August 1981; *Wilmington News Journal*, clippings, 12 July 1968, 8 November 1968.

the abuse was verbal, but some of it was physical as well. One teacher was pushed down a flight of stairs and another warded off an assault by firing a stream of tear gas at a group of students. In 1968, sixty-seven of the eighty-five members of the faculty signed a petition protesting what they called "the continuous lack of administrative support of teachers in the resolution of disciplinary problems." In 1975 the faculty at "P.S." demanded the immediate suspension of two hundred students. "I've been teaching at this school for fifteen years and when I look at it now I could just weep," one teacher said.[65]

The prevailing chaos was also evident when a black state senator, Herman M. Holloway, visited the school at the request of a constituent, who said her daughter had been raped in one of the corridors. The principal was busy when Holloway and three companions arrived, so the four men stood in a hall and observed what Holloway considered a scene of complete disorder. "Disrespect for the faculty was evident. It was . . . a scene that belonged anywhere but in a high school." Holloway was discouraged by "the ultra sloppy dress of the students, the tremendous noise of the students gallivanting up and down the corridors, the absolute lack of discipline and even the timidity of the faculty members to attempt any control."[66]

Holloway had a similar experience in 1973 when he and three other state legislators, as well as a reporter from the *Wilmington News Journal*, made unannounced visits to several city schools. Because Holloway was an African American and his associates represented the city's major ethnic groups—Polish (Casimer Jonkiert), Irish (Amos McCluney), Italian (Marcello Rispoli), and Jewish (Bill Frank)—their observations were widely credited in Wilmington. At Burnett Middle School, where the curriculum stressed independent study and open classrooms, the visitors discovered a state of disorder that they characterized as "almost unbelievable." They described the girls' lavatory at Wilmington High School as "dirtier than a pig pen" and complained that many pupils were sleeping at their desks while classes were in session. By the mid-1970s, as noted, high school seniors in Wilmington were, on average, performing at the level of eighth-grade students in the predominantly white suburbs. Helen Bayliss, a former principal of Harlan Elementary School in Wilmington, spoke for many citizens when she said it was "a real tragedy to see

65. *Wilmington News Journal*, clippings, 4 January 1969, 15 June 1968, 6 December 1968, 4 February 1975, 4 January 1969.
66. Ibid., 23 April 1970, 1 April 1975.

what education had come to." Public education in Wilmington had reached rock bottom.[67]

During the decade after *Brown*, several cities in the border states emulated Topeka, Washington, and Wilmington. By 1964 barely 1 percent of the African American students in eleven southern states were attending public school with whites. In the leading border cities, however, desegregation (but not racially balanced integration) became a reality. In St. Louis, for example, a high-level black administrator developed a plan that provided interracial schools for about two-thirds of the elementary pupils and racially mixed enrollments at six of the city's seven previously all-white high schools. A 1962 report to the U.S. Commission on Civil Rights praised the school board for "desegregat[ing] all its schools completely in the school years 1954–1955 and 1955–1956," and for more than a decade St. Louis was considered a model of desegregation.

Subsequently, however, several factors combined to cause "resegregation." In the 1950s and 1960s, many whites (and some blacks) purchased newer and more spacious homes in the suburbs, a trend that was made possible by increased prosperity, facilitated by the construction of major highways and accelerated as substantial numbers of lower-class blacks moved into middle-class neighborhoods and schools. As a result, the proportion of black students in the public schools of St. Louis increased from 30 percent in 1950 to 73 percent in 1977. Between 1970 and 1975, St. Louis lost a larger proportion of its students—about 22 percent—than any large city in the country.[68]

The same trend developed in Missouri's other major city. In Kansas City there were twelve hundred fewer white students in 1955 than there had been the year before, with two-thirds of the loss occurring among whites that had been assigned to schools in mostly black neighborhoods. With each year, more white students left Kansas City, and more blacks moved in. When *Brown* was decided, blacks made up 18.9 percent of the 63,487 students in the city's school district. Thirty years later, 67.7 percent of the 35,520 students remaining in the district were black. In 1984 whites made up 27 percent of the public school students in Kansas City and 93 percent of the students in eleven nearby suburban districts.[69]

67. *Wilmington Evening Journal*, 1 May 1973; Helen Bayliss, interview with the author, 28 July 1981.

68. *Liddell v. Board of Education*, 469 F.Supp. 1304 (1979), 1313–18; Raymond Wolters, *Right Turn: William Bradford Reynolds, the Reagan Administration, and Black Civil Rights* (New Brunswick: Transaction Publishers, 1996), 406–14.

69. Wolters, *Right Turn*, 414–26.

So it went elsewhere. Some neighborhoods in Baltimore turned over so quickly that the desegregated schools went from having a few blacks to becoming almost entirely black within a few years. In Oklahoma City several formerly white schools also became almost entirely black, although it took longer for the trend to eventuate throughout the city (with the proportion of white students eventually declining from 90 percent to 47 percent over the course of a generation). The pace of white flight was especially fast in middle-class areas with above-average incomes. It was slower in areas where working-class whites found it difficult to relocate. In the end, though, the trend was unmistakable. Desegregation led to only a limited amount of interracial mixing.[70]

70. Michael. J. Klarman, *From Jim Crow to Civil Rights: The Supreme Court and the Struggle for Racial Equality* (New York: Oxford University Press, 2004), 348; Wolters, *Right Turn*, 444–51.

4

In the Deep South

Massive Resistance and Grudging Compliance

While the border states experimented with desegregation, whites in the Deep South initially refused to comply with the Supreme Court's ruling in *Brown v. Board of Education.* Sometimes the opposition to school desegregation was a product of racism. In other instances, opponents had constitutional concerns. Some white people also worried about educational standards and predicted that (because of the differences in racial averages with respect to academic achievement) the quality of education would decline in integrated schools. Others feared the prospect of interracial dating and marriage.

Although many considerations contributed to the southern opposition to *Brown,* two theories eventually came to the fore. One was a constitutional argument that James J. Kilpatrick popularized from his perch as the editor of the *Richmond News Leader.* The other was a racial case that was made by a business-executive-turned-author, Carleton Putnam, and by a group of scientists associated with the International Association for the Advancement of Ethnology and Eugenics.

From the moment of the *Brown* decision, Kilpatrick regarded desegregation as "jurisprudence gone mad." He thought the Supreme Court had ignored eight decades of legal precedents and willfully disregarded the original understanding of the Fourteenth Amendment. Since the justices had interpreted the Constitution "to suit their own gauzy concepts of sociology," Kilpatrick recommended that the South use every possible legal means to circumvent desegregation. "Let us pledge ourselves to litigate this thing for fifty years," he wrote. "If one remedial law is ruled invalid, then let us try another; and if the second is ruled invalid, then let us enact a third. . . . If it be said now that the South is flouting the law, let it be said to the high court, *You taught us how.*"[1]

In an extraordinary series of editorials published in the *Richmond News Leader* in 1955, Kilpatrick resurrected the Jeffersonian idea of interposition as a way to stop abuses of federal power. When a Federalist congress passed the Alien and Sedition Acts of 1798, in apparent disregard of states' rights and of the First Amendment's declaration that "Congress shall make no law . . . abridging the freedom of speech," James Madison and Thomas Jefferson prepared protests known as the Virginia and Kentucky Resolves. If the federal government acted unconstitutionally, Madison and Jefferson asserted, a state had the right to interpose its authority between the federal government and its own citizens. Yet Madison and Jefferson did not have to specify the precise meaning of interposition, for the Alien and Sedition Acts expired on March 3, 1801, the day before Jefferson succeeded John Adams as president of the United States.

It was John C. Calhoun, writing in the 1820s and 1830s, who explained how states might resist federal encroachments without withdrawing from the Union. They could "interpose" or suspend the operation of a federal law considered unconstitutional pending resolution of the dispute according to the manner prescribed in Article 5 of the Constitution. In joining the Union each state had conceded that the Constitution might be amended by three-fourths of the states. Thus interposition by one state could prevail only if it was sustained by at least one-fourth of the sister states. Individual states possessed the right to set aside federal policies they considered unconstitutional, Calhoun asserted, but this right was to be checked by the power of three-fourths of the states acting in concert.

Kilpatrick thought the right to interpose could be inferred from the nature of the Constitution and its system of checks and balances. In his view the *Brown* Court, while purporting to interpret the Constitution, had actually amended the charter and in the process had arrogated powers that were reserved to three-fourths of the states. According to the logic of Madison, Jefferson, and Calhoun, however, usurpations such as *Brown* could be checked and suspended pending appeal to the people of the states that had joined to form the federal Union.[2]

---

1. James J. Kilpatrick, *The Southern Case for School Segregation* (New York: Crowell-Collier Press, 1962), 105; *Richmond News Leader,* 1 June 1955; Raymond Wolters, *The Burden of Brown* (Knoxville: University of Tennessee Press, 1984), 88–90.
2. *Richmond News Leader,* 21, 22, and 23 November 1955; James J. Kilpatrick, *The Sovereign States: Notes of a Citizen of Virginia* (Chicago: Henry Regnery, 1957).

In February 1956, Virginia's state legislature adopted an interposition resolution that asserted that, in the absence of an amendment to the Constitution, states retained the authority to operate racially segregated schools, provided such schools were substantially equal. By mid-1957, eight states had formally approved measures of interposition, and three others had protested officially against the Supreme Court's decision in *Brown*.[3]

Meanwhile, nineteen southern Senators and eighty-one members of the House of Representatives challenged the legitimacy of *Brown* with a formal Declaration of Constitutional Principles (popularly known as "the Southern Manifesto"). It described "the unwarranted decision of the Supreme Court" as the substitution of "naked power for established law." It praised states that had "declared the intention to resist forced integration by any lawful means." And it asked people outside the South "to consider the constitutional principles involved against the time when they too, on issues vital to them, may be the victims of judicial encroachment."[4]

Endorsed by many southern luminaries (including senators Harry Byrd of Virginia, James F. Byrnes of South Carolina, J. William Fulbright of Arkansas, and Richard B. Russell of Georgia), the Southern Manifesto was "a calculated declaration of political war against [*Brown*]." It shouted defiance while declaring for law and order. It became a battle cry for massive resistance.[5]

Since Kilpatrick was a journalist steeped in American history, his arguments emphasized states' rights and constitutionalism. He mentioned racial differences in average IQ and brain size, but with touches of uncertainty that befit a writer who did not pretend to be a scientist. He acknowledged that "the question of the Negro's innate inferiority has not been proved and hence is still open." Personally, Kilpatrick "incline[d] toward the view that African Americans, on average, were innately inferior to whites in intellectual ability," but he refused to assert that he knew this to be true. He insisted that, in terms of the problem immediately at hand, the question of whether the blacks' shortcomings were innate was "irrelevant." If the condition was intrinsic, Kilpatrick saw "nothing but disaster . . . in risking an accelerated intermingling of blood lines." If it

3. Numan V. Bartley, *The Rise of Massive Resistance: Race and Politics in the South during the 1950s* (Baton Rouge: Louisiana State University Press, 1969), 131.

4. *Congressional Record*, 84th Congress, 2d Session (March 12, 1956), 3948, 4004; Bartley, *Rise of Massive Resistance*, 116.

5. Alexander M. Bickel, *The Least Dangerous Branch: The Supreme Court at the Bar of Politics* (Indianapolis: Bobbs-Merrill, 1962), 256; Harry S. Ashmore, *An Epitaph for Dixie* (New York: W. W. Norton, 1957), 32.

was acquired, blacks still lagged far behind, and most whites were determined not to let their children be "guinea pigs for any man's social experiment." Kilpatrick also pointed to practical problems that he thought would beset the schools if integration were implemented at a time when one race, on average, trailed far behind the other in academic achievement.[6]

This did not satisfy the segregationists' most popular writer, Carleton Putnam. Putnam thought that Kilpatrick was mistaken to think "that the Constitution could save [the South]—that states' rights was its best defense." Putnam believed that instead of emphasizing constitutional principles, segregationists should stress the importance of differences in brain size and IQ, and they should warn that interracial mating would increase if students were sent to desegregated schools where they would be taught that racial differences were of no great significance. Putnam said that "instinctive human kindness" had prevented many southern leaders from emphasizing the importance of IQ and the size and structure of the brain, but the NAACP and its allies had left segregationists with "no choice." However much they might regret the necessity of discussing the shortcomings of the Negro, there was "a point at which . . . kindness ceases to be a virtue."[7]

Putnam was an unlikely recruit to the segregationist cause. He was born in New York, educated at Princeton and Columbia, and descended from a Revolutionary War general, Israel Putnam. After making a fortune as a founder and executive of Delta Airlines, he had written a well-regarded biography of Theodore Roosevelt. When the Supreme Court handed down its opinion in *Brown*, Putnam was absorbed with other matters and did not pay much attention to school desegregation. But he kept abreast of the news and over the course of the next few years he found the arguments for segregation more cogent than those for desegregation. After a school desegregation crisis in Little Rock (1957–1958) Putnam wrote to President Eisenhower saying that "the law must be obeyed" but *Brown* was wrong, "that it ought to be reversed, and that meanwhile every legal means should be found, not to disobey it, but to avoid it."[8]

President Eisenhower did not respond to Putnam's letter. Nevertheless, Putnam had made the case for segregation so effectively that, after the letter was published in southern newspapers, a group called "the Putnam Letters Committee" raised thirty-seven thousand dollars in contributions

6. Kilpatrick, *Southern Case,* 43, 70–73.
7. Carleton Putnam, *Race and Reason: A Yankee View* (Washington: Public Affairs Press, 1961), 20, 35, 109.
8. Ibid., 6.

to reprint the letter as a paid advertisement in newspapers outside the South. When eight northern newspapers refused the ads, Putnam concluded that the national press had closed its mind and had established a "paper curtain" to prevent Americans from hearing the truth about racial matters. To combat this, Putnam wrote two books, *Race and Reason: A Yankee View* (1961), which sold more than a hundred thousand copies, and *Race and Reality* (1967). A northerner by birth and inheritance, Putnam won acclaim in the South. In Mississippi, Governor Ross Barnett designated October 26, 1962, "*Race and Reason* Day," and in Louisiana and Virginia, the state boards of education made *Race and Reason* required reading for high school students.[9]

Putnam argued that there were substantial biological differences between the races and that these differences in anatomy, especially brain structure, were "the crux" of America's racial problems. He also feared that school integration would lead to "an ever increasing rate of interbreeding" and that this eventually would degrade American civilization. These were hardly new ideas, and one critic dismissed Putnam's work as simply another "pernicious" addition to "the rubbish pile of racist tracts." But it was an especially dangerous contribution because, as other critics observed, Putnam was "an effective writer with a fluid style and beguiling presentation"; he was making "tiresome" arguments with such "verve and literacy" that he was "enchanting a number of southern newspaper editors and even a few scientists."[10]

Putnam put a Yankee gloss on an argument that southerners had been making for years. As James T. Patterson has noted in his history, *Brown v. Board of Education* (2001), segregationists not only "raised the specter of sexually aggressive black males" but also "worried that their own children might come to enjoy the company, even sexual relationships, with blacks." This was true of elite whites as well as members of the rank and file. In 1956 South Carolina's governor James F. Byrnes, himself a former justice of the U.S. Supreme Court, insisted that "one cannot discuss [*Brown*] without admitting that, in the South, there is a fundamental objection to integration. White Southerners fear that the purpose of many

9. I. A. Newby, *Challenge to the Court: Social Scientists and the Defense of Segregation, 1954–1966* (Baton Rouge: Louisiana State University Press, 1967), 152, 165–67; Putnam, *Race and Reason*, 13; Corey T. Lessig, "Roast Beef and Racial Integrity: Mississippi's 'Race and Reason Day,' October 26, 1962," *Journal of Mississippi History* 56 (1994): 1–16.

10. Carleton Putnam, *Race and Reality: A Search for Solutions* (Washington: Pacific Affairs Press, 1967), 81; Barton Bernstein, review of *Race and Reason, Journal of Negro History* 48 (January 1963): 58–60; Newby, *Challenge to the Court*, 158; Louis Schneider, "Race, Reason and Rubbish Again," *Phylon* 23 (1962): 149.

of those advocating integration is to break down social barriers in the period of adolescence and ultimately bring about intermarriage of the races. Because they are opposed to this, they are opposed to abolishing segregation." Segregation was not based on "petty prejudice," Byrnes insisted, but on "an instinctive desire for the preservation of our race." He opined that "pride of race has been responsible for the grouping of people along ethnic lines throughout the world." He endorsed Benjamin Disraeli's assertion that no one should "treat with indifference the principle of race. It is the key to history." Although Byrnes did not dwell on racial statistics pertaining to crime, illegitimacy, and venereal disease, he said parents should try to rear their children in an atmosphere reasonably free from moral dangers. When they gave their children to school authorities for several hours each day, parents had the duty as well as the right to "control the schools their children attend." "The lives of our children must not be fashioned by some bureaucrat in Washington," Byrnes declared.[11]

Herbert Ravenel Sass, a well-regarded author from Charleston, South Carolina, also worried that "integration of white and Negro children in the South's primary schools would open the gates to miscegenation and widespread racial amalgamation." In an article in the *Atlantic Monthly*, Sass maintained that integration rested on the premise that blacks and whites were essentially alike except for skin color. Integrated schools consequently would turn out "successive generations in whom, because they are imbued with this philosophy, the instinct of race preference would have been suppressed." Some people thought this would be a good thing, the happy solution to the race problem in America. But Sass maintained that one need look no farther than Latin America to see that the fusion of racial bloodlines led to second-class societies.[12]

Not all segregationists feared miscegenation. Sociologist A. James Gregor, for one, said that people possessed an instinctive "consciousness of kind" that generally prevented widespread interracial mating. According to Gregor, "social creatures throughout the animal kingdom" manifested a "disposition to identify with only select members of [their] species."

11. James T. Patterson, *Brown v. Board of Education: A Civil Rights Milestone and Its Troubled Legacy* (New York: Oxford University Press, 2001), 88; James F. Byrnes, "Guns and Bayonets Cannot Promote Education," *U.S. News and World Report*, 5 October 1956, 104; Byrnes, "The Supreme Court Must Be Curbed," *U.S .News and World Report*, 18 May 1956, 50, 58; Howard H. Quint, *Profile in Black and White: A Frank Portrait of South Carolina* (Washington: Public Affairs Press, 1958), 25.
12. Herbert Ravenel Sass, "Mixed Schools and Mixed Blood," *Atlantic Monthly* 198 (November 1956): 45–49.

Hence, in the past "anything more than a casual or temporary contact between widely diverse races" had led, at the least, to "prejudice and discrimination and a subsequent rationalization for felt preferences." On some occasions, mixing had led either to subordination or extermination. According to Gregor, the nature of the racial separation or subordination varied from place to place, but true amalgamation occurred only rarely—and then only over the course of centuries.[13]

Nevertheless, Carleton Putnam warned that one could not break down educational barriers "without eventually breaking them down heterosexually." As an example, he mentioned the comment of an eighteen-year-old white girl who attended an integrated high school in the North: "I remember reading somewhere that a famous sociologist said that about the last person that the average white kid would be interested in is a Negro. I have news for him. Integration is a gradual process. At first it is difficult to see anything but that they are Negroes. Later you think of them as just people and then as friends. As one girl I know put it, from there it is just a hop, skip and a jump before you think of them as more than friends. Almost every white girl I knew had a secret crush on one of the colored boys. The crushes varied from warm friendship to wild infatuation. . . . One of the girls felt guilty about it but she kept on dating the colored boy. . . . She once told me that if people were going to object they shouldn't expose us to the temptation. As she put it, we're not all saints."[14]

Some integrationists also discussed this topic. Harvard professor Thomas Pettigrew, for example, wrote in 1964 that "if panmaxis—completely random mating with no regard to racial differences—were to take place in the United States, the darker skin shades of Negroes would be virtually eliminated, but there would be little noticeable effect on the skin color of Caucasians. . . . The Negro one-tenth of the nation would be 'inundated by a white sea.'" University of Minnesota professor Alan Freeman similarly described a "utopian . . . version of the integrated society." "By 2200, everyone had become a creamy shade of beige, and race had simply ceased to exist under the guiding hand of genetic entropy."[15]

Such reassurance did not satisfy Putnam, nor did it appeal to African Americans who felt a sense of racial identity and pride. W. E. B. Du Bois,

13. A. James Gregor, "On the Nature of Prejudice," *Eugenics Review* 52 (1961): 217–24.

14. Putnam, *Race and Reason*, 65.

15. Thomas P. Pettigrew, *A Profile of the Negro American* (Princeton: Princeton University Press, 1964), 27–53, 65–63; Alan David Freeman, "School Desegregation Law," in Derrick Bell, ed., *Shades of Brown* (New York: Teachers College Press, 1980), 78.

for instance had long insisted that "self-obliteration" was not "the highest end to which Negro blood dare aspire."[16]

Meanwhile, as Putnum popularized the case for segregation, a group of like-minded scientists and social scientists joined together in 1959 to establish the International Association for the Advancement of Ethnology and Eugenics (IAAEE). It was an imposing title for an organization whose purpose was to oversee and coordinate the efforts of scientific racialists. Chartered in 1959, the IAAEE's first president was Robert Kuttner, a biologist who had given testimony in *Stell v. Savannah*. The membership included most of those who had testified in *Stell* and many others: British geneticist R. Ruggles Gates, Italian sociologist Corrado Gini, and several American professors, among them George Lundberg of the University of Washington, Frank McGurk of Villanova, Aubrey Shuey of Randolph-Macon, and Charles Callan Tansill of Georgetown. With funds provided by Wickliffe Draper of the Pioneer Fund, the IAAEE set up a scholarly journal, *Mankind Quarterly*, and distributed pamphlets and other literature to a mailing list of sixteen thousand people.[17]

The revival of scientific racism surprised many observers, who thought that the Second World War and the destruction of fascism had brought an end to such thinking. The organization of the IAAEE and publication of *Mankind Quarterly* signaled that at least some authorities no longer felt "that because the study of race once gave ammunition to racial fascists, who misused it," researchers should avoid the study of racial differences. Instead, as one critic noted, the IAAEE had decided "to reopen Pandora's box."[18]

In simplified form, the scientific racists said that races could be identified by physical appearance and measurements, that some races possessed more intelligence than others, and that races that were deficient in intelligence lacked the ability to develop or even to maintain a high civilization. In support of these views, scientific racists relied on two bodies of evidence that were summarized in *Stell v. Savannah*. One pertained to IQ scores and academic achievement—where a racial gap persisted even after controlling for socioeconomic variables. The other dealt with disparities in the structure and measured weight of brains.

16. W. E. B. Du Bois, "The Conservation of Races," reprinted in Herbert Aptheker, ed., *Pamphlets and Leaflets by W. E. B. Du Bois* (White Plains, N.Y.: Kraus-Thomson Organization, 1986), 5, 4.
17. See John P. Jackson Jr., *Science for Segregation* (New York: New York University Press, 2005).
18. Carleton Coon, *The Story of Man* (New York: Alfred A. Knopf, 1954), 187–88; Henry E. Garrett and A. Thomas, replies to Juan Comas, *Current Anthropology* 2 (October 1961): 320, 330.

At first most mainstream scholars sputtered, as if they did not wish to pay the compliment of a rational response to arguments they considered unworthy. Eventually, however, egalitarian critics of scientific racism mounted a counterargument. With respect to differences in the weight and structure of the brain, egalitarians said the extant studies were dated and problematical. Some had been conducted in Africa without the modern equipment required for reliable measurements. Others did not control for prenatal and postnatal nutrition. Still others did not use identical methods for fixing and processing the brains that were analyzed. As for IQ tests, egalitarians said that allowance should be made for the African Americans' experience with slavery, segregation, and discrimination—and that this consideration could account for the fifteen-point difference in mean IQ scores.

Most of all, egalitarians turned to cultural anthropology, a field that had been germinating for decades in the seminars of a Columbia University professor, Franz Boas. At one time Boas had reported that "the average size of the Negro brain is slightly smaller than the average size of the brain of the white race," and he therefore thought it likely "that differences in mental characteristics of the two races exist." Yet even before Hitler's rise to power, Boas had come to emphasize that a people's cultural heritage—their ideas and values—shaped the way they lived. Boas acknowledged that Caucasians had developed a high civilization "which is sweeping the whole world," that Asians had developed impressive but less technical civilizations, and that Negroes lagged behind. But he insisted that "the reason for this fact" did "not necessarily lie in a greater ability of the races of Europe and Asia." Boas thought "the variations in cultural development" could be explained "by a consideration of the general course of historical events" and without recourse to innate racial differences.[19]

Boas also discounted the danger of racial amalgamation. There was no danger, he said, because the range of differences within one race greatly overlapped that of the other. He assumed that Caucasians would mix only with superior Negroes, in which case the results of racial crossings would be positive. He insisted that nothing justified the branding of an individual as inferior or superior simply because he happened to belong to one race or another.[20]

In addition, Boas trained a number of influential anthropologists (among them Ruth Benedict, Melville Herskovits, Alfred Kroeber, Margaret Mead,

19. Franz Boas, "The Real Race Problem," *Crisis* 1 (November 1910): 2, 23; Boas, *The Mind of Primitive Man* (New York: McMillan, 1911), 5, 11, 22, 29.
20. Franz Boas, "The Problem of the American Negro," *Yale Review* 10 (1920–1921): 384–95.

and Ashley Montagu), and the "Boasians" (as they were sometimes called) proceeded to detach "civilization" from race. Previously, educated people had generally considered racial inheritance responsible for at least some differences in civilizational standards. The Boasians, on the other hand, attributed the differences to history and environment. Instead of stressing the importance of race, they insisted that "patterns of culture" were primarily responsible for differences in social behavior. And by emphasizing that the range of differences within the Negro race greatly overlapped the average among Caucasians, they called into question the very concept of race.[21]

A 1950 UNESCO statement reflected Boasian cultural anthropology at its peak. It asserted that racial characteristics were limited to physical traits like hair, eyes, head shape, and physique and did not extend to intelligence, character, or personality. "For all practical purposes," the statement declared, "'race' is not so much a biological phenomenon as a social myth. . . . Biological differences between ethnic groups should be disregarded. . . . The unity of mankind is the main thing." According to Ashley Montagu, the principal author of the statement, "Whatever classification the anthropologist makes of man, he never includes mental characteristics as part of those classifications."[22]

This UNESCO statement eventually became an article of faith for many Americans, one that was repeated regularly, with feeling if not conviction. All human groups were basically the same, racial egalitarians insisted, and any differences were culturally determined products of differences in upbringing, lifestyle, and social environment. This point of view was implicit in the title of Ashley Montagu's influential book *Man's Most Dangerous Myth: The Fallacy of Race* (1942). Jacques Barzun developed the same theme in another influential book, *Race: A Study in Superstition* (1966) as did the Public Broadcasting System (PBS) in a documentary film of 2003, *The Power of an Illusion.*

Nevertheless, many geneticists and physical anthropologists rejected the argument that "race" was merely a social construct. The prominent population geneticist Theodosius Dobzhansky was one of the first to find

21. Carl Degler, *In Search of Human Nature* (New York: Oxford University Press, 1991), 81 and passim; Dinesh D'Souza, *The End of Racism* (New York: Free Press, 1995), 153 and passim; Hasia R. Diner, *In the Almost Promised Land* (Westport: Greenwood Press, 1977), 147 and passim.

22. Jenny Reardon, *Race to the Finish: Identity and Governance in an Age of Genomics* (Princeton: Princeton University Press, 2005), 28; Michelle Brattain, "Race, Racism, and Antiracism: UNESCO and the Politics of Presenting Science to the Postwar Public," *American Historical Review* 112 (December 2007): 1386–413.

fault with the UNESCO statement of 1950. Dobzhansky was a friend of Ashley Montagu, with whom he coauthored articles. But Dobzhansky insisted, "Race *differences* are facts of nature which can, given sufficient study, be ascertained objectively." The prominent physical anthropologist Carleton Coon agreed, saying that the "soft pedaling" and "prudery" of cultural anthropologists with respect to race was "equaled only by their horror of Victorian prudery about sex." Others chimed in. Henri Vallois, the director of the Musée de l'Homme in Paris, considered it ridiculous to regard race as a myth. And W. C. Osman Hill, the prosector at the Zoological Society of London, insisted,

> That range of mental capabilities is "much the same" in all races is scarcely a scientifically accurate statement. It is at most a vague generalization. It is, however, scarcely true, for temperamental and other mental differences are well known to be correlated with physical differences. . . . Even if it were true that there is "no proof that the groups of mankind differ in intelligence, temperament or other innate characteristics," it is certainly the case that there is no proof to the contrary.[23]

In response to these criticisms, in 1951 UNESCO convened another committee of racial experts, one that was composed almost entirely of physical anthropologists and geneticists. The resulting second UNESCO statement on race differed from the first statement in some important respects. The second statement did acknowledge that within a given race "capacities vary as much as, if not more than, they do between different groups." Nevertheless, instead of embracing the social constructivist view, the second statement allowed for the possibility that there were racial differences in mental traits. "It is possible, though not proved," the second statement said, "that some types of innate capacity for intellectual and emotional response are commoner in one human group than another." As Jenny Reardon has noted, the second statement "accommodated both those who wanted to de-emphasize the importance of group-level differences in intellectual and emotional traits (by pointing to the importance of differences among individuals *within* a group) and those who wanted to hold onto a belief not uncommon among geneticists and physical anthropologists that group differences in mental and psychological traits did exist."[24]

At the time of *Brown,* most population geneticists and physical anthro-

23. Theodosius Dobzhansky, *Mankind Evolving* (New Haven: Yale University Press, 1962), 267; Coon, *Story of Man,* 188; Pat Shipman, *The Evolution of Racism* (New York: Simon and Schuster, 1974), 164–65.

24. *The Race Concept* (Paris: UNESCO, 1952), 13; Reardon, *Race to the Finish,* 30. Writ-

pologists accepted the possibility (but not the certainty) that the races differed in important respects. This view was so widespread that even Ashley Montagu acknowledged that there was no proof as to the equal distribution of innate intelligence. This was quite a concession, but one that
Montagu had to make in order to maintain the respect of his professional
peers. In 1944 Montagu had written "with some degree of assurance that
in all probability the range of inherited capacities in two different ethnic
groups is just about identical." In 1961, however, Montagu asserted that
he had been misunderstood; that he had never maintained that the races
were equal in mental abilities; that he had contended only "that studies
claiming to have proven that genetic differences were the responsible
causes [for differences in test scores and standards of civilization] have
not upon critical examination been found to prove anything of the sort."
Montagu went on to say that "during thirty-five years of reading on the
subject I have *not more than once or twice* encountered a writer who claimed
that 'the races were equal in mental abilities.'"[25]

When describing mainstream views of race and science at the time of
Brown, some egalitarians have confused skepticism about racial inequality with a belief in racial equality. Professor John P. Jackson Jr., for example, has mistakenly asserted that by the middle of the twentieth century,
"most American social scientists . . . believed there were no fundamental
differences in intelligence between the races"; that "the races were, scien-
tifically speaking, equal." But this obscures a crucial distinction. It would
be correct to say that most scholars questioned the evidence that had been
presented to show that Caucasians were superior to Negroes intellectually. It did not follow that they thought the earlier claims had been disproved. Among well-informed scholars and scientists, the prevailing
view was not that the races were equal but that the evidence of Negro inferiority was not conclusive.[26]

Although most experts remained skeptical, even agnostic, about the
significance of race, with the passage of time popular opinion in the United States moved in a different direction. Whatever geneticists, physiolo-

---

ing in the *American Historical Review* in 2007, historian Michelle Brattain rebuked the
second UNESCO statement for "recant[ing] the . . . social constructivist position" and
for "return[ing] to a biological definition of race." "Race, Racism, and Antiracism,"
1388.

25. *Science* 100 (20 October 1944): 383–84; *Perspectives in Biology and Medicine* 5 (au-
tumn 1961): 132–34. Montagu could explain that there was no contradiction, since the
"range" of intelligence differs from the "distribution." The former term refers to individuals—where each race possesses a great range, from the retarded to the genius.

26. John P. Jackson Jr., *Social Scientists for Social Justice* (New York: New York University Press, 2001), 43; Jackson, *Science for Segregation*, 9–10.

gists, and physical anthropologists might think, the public increasingly embraced what the historian Walter Jackson has called a "liberal orthodoxy"—that there were no racial differences in intelligence, aptitude, or character. Thus the Harvard historian Oscar Handlin declared, "There is no evidence of any inborn differences of temperament, personality, character, or intelligence among races." And the Berkeley historian Kenneth M. Stampp asserted, in memorable language, "Negroes *are* after all, only white men with black skins, nothing more, nothing less." In 1980 the *Academic American Encyclopedia* reported that "many scientists today reject the concept of race," and in 1993 a revised edition of this encyclopedia changed the "many" to "probably most." In 1995 a group of scholars meeting in Los Angeles announced that "the concept of race . . . has no basis in fundamental human biology." And in 2004 biologist Paul R. Gross noted an extraordinary paradox. Many American intellectuals, when asked to identify their society's most serious problem, answered, "Race." But many (most?) of these intellectuals also insisted that the concept of "race" was meaningless; "that there are no biologically significant human group differences, hence no human races."[27]

Accounting for the popularity of racial egalitarianism necessarily involves some speculation. The phenomenon was probably due in no small part to the strategic brilliance of Martin Luther King Jr. King may have begun with the hope that he could convince the South and the nation that racial discrimination and segregation were morally wrong. Eventually, however, King modified his approach. In 1963 he chose Birmingham, Alabama, as the site for massive demonstrations because he calculated that the nation would be repulsed because the police chief there, Bull Connor, was likely to deal roughly with demonstrators. The next year King focused a voting rights campaign on Selma, Alabama, because he expected Jim Clark, the local sheriff there, to behave as Bull Connor had in Birmingham. King hoped that when the brutal repression of Birmingham and Selma were televised to the rest of the nation, there would be a backlash, and whites outside the South would insist that the federal government should protect civil rights demonstrators, desegregate the schools, and enact new laws to guarantee the right to vote and to end discrimina-

27. Walter A. Jackson, *Gunnar Myrdal and America's Conscience: Social Engineering and Racial Liberalism, 1938–1987* (Chapel Hill: University of North Carolina Press, 1990); Oscar Handlin, quoted by Carleton Putnam, "These Are the Guilty," *Mankind Quarterly* 4 (July–September 1963): 13; Kenneth M. Stampp, *The Peculiar Institution* (New York: Alfred A. Knopf, 1956), vii; *Academic American Encyclopedia* (Princeton: Arete, 1980), 16:33; *Academic American Encyclopedia* (Danbury, Conn.: Grolier, 1993), 16:33 ; *Los Angeles Times*, 20 February 1995, A1; Paul R. Gross, "Race: No Such Thing," *New Criterion* 22 (April 2004): 86–90.

tion in public accommodations. And this, indeed, is what came to pass. As legal historian Michael Klarman has noted, "it was the brutality of southern whites resisting desegregation that ultimately rallied national opinion behind the enforcement of *Brown* and the enactment of civil rights legislation."[28]

Civil rights also gained popularity because prior to the late 1960s most whites thought the demands of the movement were reasonable. Blacks were demanding the right to vote, an end to racial discrimination in public accommodations, and the desegregation but not the massive integration of public schools. In pursuing these goals, civil rights leaders also insisted that their movement should be nonviolent and dignified. For tactical reasons, these leaders sought to portray a contrast between "well-dressed studious blacks peacefully protesting" and, wherever possible, a violent mob of whites, "a ragtail rabble, slackjawed, black jacketed, grinning fit to kill." The freedom riders "count[ed] upon the racists of the South to create a crisis," and black leaders in Birmingham "calculated for the stupidity of a Bull Connor."[29]

There were other factors as well. The extremism of Nazi Germany had discredited racism during World War II, and during the Cold War desegregation at home was of benefit to American foreign policy. Meanwhile, because of the great migration of blacks away from the rural South and toward urban areas, more blacks were voting—and politicians were seeking their support. At the same time, the growth of the national economy had led to a larger black middle class, whose purchasing power mattered more than ever before. With economic integration throughout the nation, and especially with the increasing influence of chain stores, corporate leaders pressed the white South to accept national norms. The "nationalizing" of television and radio also had a similar effect. In addition, the New South developed patterns of settlement that resembled the situation in the North more than that of the Old South. In Dixie relatively few whites continued to live as a minority in predominantly black areas. Instead, they followed the example of their northern cousins and moved to predominantly white suburbs.

These trends provided the context in which most whites began to say that all races were equally endowed with intelligence. Politicians did not wish to alienate a growing segment of the electorate. Business leaders did

28. Michael J. Klarman, *From Jim Crow to Civil Rights: The Supreme Court and the Struggle for Racial Equality* (New York: Oxford University Press, 2004), 385; Klarman, "How *Brown* Changed Race Relations: The Backlash Thesis," *Journal of American History* 81 (June 1994): 81–118.
29. Klarman, *From Jim Crow*, 429.

not want to lose black customers. With the growing spatial segmentation of the American population, there was less reason to give offense. Most of all, most whites did not wish to be associated with massive resistance to what they considered the sane and sensible demands of the civil rights movement.

Thus racial egalitarianism emerged as a new conventional wisdom. After the 1960s most people came to understand the civil rights movement as a campaign of moral superiority that was opposed by racial bigots. In 2006, when the Intercollegiate Studies Institute published *American Conservatism: An Encyclopedia,* "conservatism" was shorn of any concern for the conservation of races. Names like Carleton Putnam and court cases like *Stell v. Savannah* disappeared from the record. Little mention was made of the intellectual arguments that had prompted many educated people to oppose desegregation in the 1950s. "Bull" Connor and his snarling police dogs were left as the most widely recognized symbols of massive resistance.[30]

Yet to understand what happened in the Deep South—especially in areas where blacks made up a large portion of the population—one must take account of the influence of writers like Putnam and Kilpatrick and the scholars associated with the IAAEE. Without the support of these writers and scholars, many white southerners would have been less likely to challenge *Brown.* As Roy Wilkins of the NAACP has noted, rank-and-file southerners were emboldened "by groups of so-called respectable people." A civil rights lawyer in Tennessee made the same point in colorful language. "What the hell do you expect these people to do when you have some 90-odd Congressmen from the South signing a piece of paper [the Southern Manifesto] that says you're a southern hero if you defy the Supreme Court?"[31]

Prince Edward County, Virginia, and Summerton, South Carolina

Opposition to school desegregation was particularly evident in the two southern communities whose legal cases had been consolidated with *Brown* on appeal: Prince Edward County, Virginia, and Summerton, South Carolina. For a decade the white citizens of these areas challenged the fed-

30. Thomas Jackson, review of "Science for Segregation," *American Renaissance,* March 2006.
31. Klarman, *From Jim Crow,* 428.

eral judiciary and refused to countenance desegregation. Then, when the federal government eventually put an end to their massive resistance, the whites of Prince Edward and Summerton established private academies that stymied efforts to integrate their schools.

Given the nature of its population and the qualities of its leaders, massive resistance was probably inevitable in Prince Edward County. In 1950 blacks made up 57 percent of the students in this predominantly rural area, and their academic achievement, as measured by average scores on standard tests, was well behind that of whites of the same age. The county's most influential white leader was J. Barrye Wall, the editor of the local *Farmville Herald*. Wall was an unfailingly polite southern gentleman who said he had "never treated a Negro with discourtesy—or been treated that way by one of them. I respect them all. But I was and am for separate education for white and black." The county's most influential black leader, the Rev. L. Francis Griffin, conceded that he "respect[ed] the local whites for the honesty of their position. Their feelings were firm and out in the open. They were not deceitful. I think it's fair to say they respected me, too. . . . It was sort of a gentleman's fight. There was no overt violence."[32]

Wall acknowledged that in communities where there were few African Americans it was "conceivable that some schools can be integrated without harm to students or to education." But Wall insisted that the problem of educating a few black students in the suburbs was entirely different from the problem of integrating 1,500 white students and 1,800 black students in Prince Edward County. The local superintendent of public schools explained, "if we are ordered to carry out horizontal integration, that is, to combine white and Negro pupils according to their present grade, the teacher who now has an aptitude range of three years among white pupils in one classroom will find a range of five to six years in a mixed class."[33]

This view was echoed by Robert T. Redd, a local teacher who later became the headmaster of the private, all-white Prince Edward Academy. Redd noted that in some respects his educational philosophy was similar to that of Washington superintendent Carl F. Hansen. "Hansen and I could have been great buddies," Redd said. "We both know you have to have a basic structured situation for most children to learn. We both believe in ability grouping." But Redd also recognized a crucial difference

32. John Egerton, *Shades of Gray* (Baton Rouge: Louisiana State University Press, 1991), 124–25.
33. *Farmville Herald*, 25 June 1954; statement of T. J. McIlwaine, quoted in Haldore Hanson, "No Surrender in Farmville," *New Republic* 133 (10 October 1955): 14.

that separated his educational views from those of Hansen. "Hansen thinks blacks can achieve as much as whites if they are taught properly. I doubt that." "You can't solve an educational problem until you identify it," Redd said, "and most people won't admit that race is a problem. Most blacks simply do not have the ability to do quality schoolwork. Some do, I admit. But only 10 to 15 percent of them score above the white median on most academic examinations. The rest are likely to become frustrated and disruptive. That's one reason why there are so many assaults and so much vandalism in schools with a sizeable enrollment of Negro students." Looking back in 1979, and referring to a congressional report entitled *Violent Schools—Safe Schools*, Redd said, "We felt back in 1951 that what is happening today would happen if the Supreme Court insisted on desegregation. . . . We felt we understood black people as well as anybody, because of our long interaction with them. We knew desegregation couldn't work because of the inherent temperamental and intellectual differences."[34]

Wall also mentioned additional points: that "the long-term aim of the NAACP is intermarriage" and that "intimate race mixing of white and colored children in the classrooms" eventually would "sign the doom of the white race and the Negro race." Robert B. Crawford, an influential businessman in Prince Edward, similarly maintained that "mixing children in school is the beginning of the end for both races. . . . It is inevitable that children who play together from the age of five will not stop at eighteen. There will be intermarriage." After visiting Prince Edward on assignment for *Commentary* magazine, James Rorty reported that "the fear of racial intermixture" was "real to the point of pathology among poor white farmers and lower middle-class villagers."[35]

Whites in Prince Edward also developed legal arguments. They conceded that the Fourteenth Amendment guaranteed equal protection of the laws, but they insisted that the Congress that had submitted the amendment and the states that had ratified it had not contemplated or understood that equal protection would require the abolition of segregated schools. If this had been the case, Congress and the ratifying states would have abolished segregation where it existed. Instead, one after the other, they established racially separate schools at the same time they endorsed the amendment. As editor Wall saw it, much of the controversy could have been avoided if advocates of desegregation had amended the Con-

34. Robert T. Redd, interview with the author, 23 July 1979.
35. *Farmville Herald*, 9 June 1959, 4 November 1955; Hanson, "No Surrender," 14–15; James Rorty, "Virginia's Creeping Desegregation," *Commentary* 22 (July 1956): 64.

stitution "in an orderly way—as prescribed by the document itself—instead of attempting in effect to amend the Constitution by judicial decisions . . . based on questionable sociological, historical, and legal evidence."[36]

Beyond this was another legal question: could unelected judges require an elected legislative body, Prince Edward's Board of Supervisors, to assess taxes for desegregated schools? White leaders in Prince Edward insisted that there should be "no taxation without representation." They also noted that various courts had previously given meaning to this principle by requiring that all bills for raising revenue should originate with the people's elected representatives. In *Brown* the Supreme Court had decided that a county could not segregate public school students on the basis of race. But the Court had not decided that counties were constitutionally required to operate public schools. Indeed, according to white Prince Edward, the judiciary would transgress the constitutional separation of powers if judges prescribed how elected legislators should spend tax money.

Among whites in Prince Edward there was little division over the need to resist desegregation. In 1955 Robert Taylor, a local contractor, expressed the prevailing opinion when he said he would rather have his children "miss a year or two of school than face the kind of bitterness and brawling that mixed schools will bring." Later he recalled, "We felt our primary duty was to provide for our children as best we could. Most blacks were so far behind our children academically and differed in mores and cultural attainment. There was nothing good that our children could gain from interaction in school with blacks." Echoing this view, 4,184 citizens, more than had voted in any previous election, signed a statement affirming that they preferred "to abandon public schools and educate our children in some other way if that be necessary to preserve the separation of the races." "If one wished to oversimplify," Richmond editor James J. Kilpatrick wrote, "it could be said that the court ruled at Noon that Negroes must be admitted to Prince Edward's public schools, to which the county replied, at 8 o'clock, there will be no public schools."[37]

Litigation dragged on for years, but there was little doubt about the resolve of white Prince Edward. After two lower courts moved toward requiring desegregation in 1959, the county closed its public schools, cut property taxes in half, and urged taxpayers to give the difference to pri-

36. *Farmville Herald,* 14 June 1962.
37. Irv Goodman, "Public Schools Died Here," *Saturday Evening Post* 234 (29 April 1961): 87; Hanson, "No Surrender," 14; Robert T. Taylor, interview with the author, 23 July 1979; *Richmond News Leader,* 1 June 1955.

vate schools. Private schools were then established for white students, and local whites offered to do likewise for blacks. Black leaders, however, discouraged blacks from accepting the offer. Roy Wilkins urged the blacks of Prince Edward to sacrifice "a few years of education in the name of freedom." Martin Luther King Jr. similarly expressed the hope that blacks would not "sell their birthright of freedom for a mess of segregated pottage." Virginia NAACP leader Oliver Hill explained, "The whole world is watching Prince Edward." If blacks permitted segregation there, it would be more difficult to achieve integration elsewhere. For their part, local whites complained that Prince Edward was being used "as a pawn in a great game of national . . . politics." By depicting Prince Edward as "a community of tyrants which has taken education from Negro children," the NAACP was reaping "propaganda advantages" and building "an appeal to the credulous for funds."[38]

A stalemate ensued, and between 1959 and 1964 there was little formal education for black children. African Americans established "activity centers" for youths who were out of school, but the director of the centers explained that they were "not in any respect . . . a substitute for schools." They were intended primarily to keep children busy. In 1963 the Ford Foundation and other northern philanthropies established private schools that enrolled 8 white students and 1,570 blacks, but even integrationists questioned whether these schools provided good basic education.[39]

Meanwhile, the courts moved slowly toward resolving the tangled issues of equity and constitutional law. Speaking for Prince Edward County, attorney Collins Denny maintained that *Brown* did not require the operation of public schools but merely prohibited discrimination if such schools were operated. Expressing a contrary view, black leaders characterized the county's policy as a clever way to avoid court-ordered desegregation.[40]

According to white Prince Edward, the fundamental question was not whether public schools were closed or children illiterate, but whether federal judges could compel a local governing body to appropriate money for public schools. This was a states' rights lawyer's dream, and the county prevailed before a panel of three judges from the Fourth Circuit Court

38. *Southern School News,* January and February 1960; Bob Smith, *They Closed Their Schools* (Chapel Hill: University of North Carolina Press, 1965), 198; Kennell Jackson, "Reducing the Kids to Dust," *Nation* 203 (14 November 1962): 522; *New York Times,* 21 May 1961, 77; *Newsday,* 19 December 1960; *Farmville Herald,* 24 March 1961; *Farmville Herald,* as quoted in *Southern School News,* January 1960, April 1962.

39. *Southern School News,* February 1960, March 1962; C. G. Gordon Moss, interview with the author, 13 May 1980; comments of L. Francis Griffin, in Egerton, *Shades of Gray,* 124–25.

40. Wolters, *Burden of Brown,* 111.

of Appeals. "The negative application of the Fourteenth Amendment is too well settled for argument," the court held in 1963. "Schools that are operated must be made available to all citizens without regard to race, but what public schools a state provides is not the subject of constitutional command."[41]

Yet the only opinion that mattered was that of the U.S. Supreme Court, and there never was much doubt about that. On May 25, 1964, ten years after *Brown*, the Court again decided in favor of the NAACP. Writing for a unanimous Court, Justice Hugo Black held that Prince Edward's public schools had been closed and private schools established "for one reason, and for one reason only: to ensure . . . that white and colored children in Prince Edward County would not . . . go to the same school." As a result of this constitutionally impermissible purpose, the Court concluded that Prince Edward had denied its citizens the equal protection guaranteed by the Fourteenth Amendment.[42]

The northern press generally praised the Court's decision. The *Washington Post* endorsed Justice Black's contention that there had been "entirely too much deliberation and not enough speed," and the *New York Times* opined that the Court had spoken with "eminently warranted sharpness in rebuking Prince Edward County for its disgraceful record." Among liberal journals, only the *New Republic* expressed any reservations. While celebrating the Court's victory over Prince Edward's "resourceful, determined, peaceable, and . . . in its tragic way successful resistance," the *New Republic* noted that "some eyebrows were raised" by Justice Black's assertion that federal courts could require local officials to levy school taxes.[43]

As expected, white southerners criticized the Court. "Never in the history of our nation has the Supreme Court intimated or held that it had the authority to compel a legislative body to levy taxes," said Virginia congressman Watkins M. Abbitt. Making a similar point, the *Richmond Times-Dispatch* said, "the manner in which the highest court in the land has arrogated to itself the 'right' to order a unit of local government to levy taxes . . . is alarming in the highest degree." In the guise of interpreting the Constitution, the Court had usurped a power that had been deliberately denied. In the process, it had established a dangerous precedent "and one that could rise to plague us in years to come."[44]

41. *Griffin v. Board of Supervisors*, 322 F.2d (196) 336.
42. *Griffin v. School Board*, 377 U.S. 218 (1964) 231.
43. *Washington Post*, 31 May 1964; *New York Times*, 27 May 1964, 38; *New Republic* 150 (6 June 1964): 5–6.
44. *Southern School News*, June 1964; *Richmond Times Dispatch*, quoted in *New York Times*, 31 May 1964, sec. 4, p. 9.

Public schools were reopened after the decision of the Supreme Court, but this did not lead to much integration—at least not initially. In 1964, only 7 of the county's 1,000 white students enrolled in public schools along with approximately 1,400 blacks. The remaining whites attended the private, all-white Prince Edward Academy. Forty years later, however, more than half of the county's white youths attended public schools. Some did so because they or their parents favored integrated education. In other cases, the parents could not afford to pay the cost of private tuition. To help families defray expenses, the private academy hired as many parents as possible—as bus drivers, secretaries, janitors, and groundskeepers. Many mothers also went to work and saved part of their income to cover tuition. This pattern of family financing evoked some amusement among integrationists. "We're going to win this one," said Clarence Penn, a black public school administrator in Prince Edward. "[Tuition] has . . . a lot of white daddies hurting and a lot of white mommies working." By the year 2000 a new and different form of segregation had developed in Prince Edward (and many other counties)—with private schools for those who were white and affluent and public schools for others.[45]

It is hard to say who won in Prince Edward. J. Barrye Wall expressed the views of many whites when he acknowledged, "we got our asses kicked in court." Yet Wall insisted, "it doesn't matter. We had to fight for what we knew was right." "We were defending the people's right to educate the races separately." According to Wall, the Supreme Court had vandalized the Constitution, but "the principles we fought for aren't settled. We lost in court—the South lost—but it's still not settled."[46]

Like many other blacks, the Reverend L. Francis Griffin also had mixed feelings. "It depends on how you look at it," he said. "If you're talking about integration, then it could be said that the whites won, because there's still a lot of segregation." Griffin nevertheless thought that African Americans had triumphed because public education had been preserved. "The South would have closed its public schools if we had not won our case in 1964," Griffin said. "Prince Edward was a beacon. If the courts had permitted the schools to remain closed the rest of the South would have followed the example. I believe you could say the black people of Prince Edward saved the South's public schools."[47]

The quality of education in the county is difficult to measure. The white patrons of the county's private academy profess to be satisfied with their

45. *New York Times*, 13 May 1974, 24.
46. J. Barrye Wall, interview with the author, 23 July 1979.
47. L. Francis Griffin, interview with the author, 25 July 1979.

school. Students there regularly scored above the national averages on standardized tests, and a disproportionately large number have succeeded in the competition for National Merit Scholarships. According to one resident of the county, "You could say we've got pretty much what we had before, only better." By 2005, however, more than half of the white students in the county were attending public schools.[48]

There has been much dispute over the quality of the education in the county's public schools. At first the enrollment was almost entirely black, and the scores on standard tests were among the lowest in Virginia. In 1972, on tests where the national average was 50 percent, the composite achievement percentiles for Prince Edward were 9 percent for grade eleven, 14 percent for grade eight, and 17 percent for grade four. In 1979, only 50.3 percent of the students at the county high school passed a minimum competency examination that the state required to qualify for a high school diploma. According to Griffin, the quality of Prince Edward's public schools in 1979 was "comparable with that of schools elsewhere in Southside Virginia—and I don't know if that's saying a lot."[49]

Since then the public schools have improved. Nevertheless, many African Americans are ambivalent about the quality of the education. Some took exception to a traditional, back-to-basics emphasis that was implemented in the 1980s. Others said the public schools were trying to attract white students away from the private academy by "hiring an excessive number of white teachers, so that white students and their parents would feel comfortable and safe in coming to the public schools." Still others faulted the public schools for failing to do more to help blacks maintain a sense of racial identity. Some complained that the return of white students undermined the confidence and academic ambition of blacks—because whites received a disproportionately large share of the academic honors at the desegregated Prince Edward County High School and thus left the impression that academic achievement was "acting white."[50]

The youngest of Griffin's children gave voice to these concerns when he campaigned for a student office in 1979. In a rousing speech to a school assembly, young Eric Griffin fretted that half the teachers were white, and he said it was not right for the school to neglect black studies and to choose whites as valedictorian, homecoming queen, and editor of the student

48. Wolters, *Burden of Brown*, 97; Lester Andrews, quoted in John Egerton, "A Gentlemen's Fight," *American Heritage* 30 (August–September, 1979), 62.
49. Wolters, *Burden of Brown*, 119, 120; Egerton, *Shades of Gray*, 125.
50. Kara Miles Turner, "'Getting It Straight': Southern Black School Patrons and the Struggle for Equal Education in the Pre- and Post–Civil Rights Eras," *Journal of Negro Education* 72 (spring 2003): 226; *Farmville Herald*, 23 June 1972.

newspaper. Offended by Griffin's remarks, most whites walked out of the assembly, while blacks cheered and chanted, "Get out! Get out! We don't want you."[51]

Young Griffin lost the election and later apologized for his remarks. Many black adults, however, continued to express concern about what they perceived to be problems with white teachers. Black residents of the county complained about "the dearth of Black students in gifted classes or receiving honors at commencement and the large number of Black children in special education courses." In 2003, Kara Miles Turner reported in the *Journal of Negro Education* that most blacks in Prince Edward believed "the detrimental aspects [of school desegregation] have outweighed the benefits." One person whom Turner interviewed complained about "the perceived inability of White teachers to interact effectively with Black children." Another said, "some White teachers [are] afraid." Yet another lamented, "It's something about White teachers that they are not reaching the little Black boys." By way of explanation, other interviewees said that teachers could no longer get up in front of a class and say, as they could in the days before desegregation, "Listen, you've got to compete against the white man." "Today teachers don't do that. They teach and go home."[52]

Summerton, South Carolina

Throughout the South most whites initially were inclined toward massive resistance. This was especially true in the towns and farming regions of what was called "the black belt"—a region of about two hundred counties in which the black percentage of the population ranged upward from about 50 percent. Farmville, Virginia, was one such town, and so was Summerton, South Carolina, where black students outnumbered whites by seven to one (about 2,400 to 350). Summerton was another of the four communities whose litigation had been consolidated for decision in *Brown*. When the Supreme Court handed down its decision, Charles N. Plowden, a white landowner and a former member of the state's General Assembly, expressed the prevailing view among local whites: "If the Court orders us to integrate, we'll close."[53]

Yet *Brown* gave district judges some leeway, allowing them to consider

51. Wolters, *Burden of Brown*, 124.
52. Turner, "'Getting It Straight,'" 225.
53. John Bartlow Martin, *The Deep South Says "Never"* (New York: Ballantine, 1957), 62; *Columbia State*, 1 September 1955.

what was practicable in light of local circumstances and requiring only that school districts "make a prompt and reasonable start" and then proceed "with all deliberate speed" toward admitting students to public schools "on a racially nondiscriminatory basis." As a consequence, there was no pressure to desegregate in Clarendon County until 1965, by which time the Prince Edward litigation had established that individual school districts could not refuse to operate public schools. By then Congress had also passed the Civil Rights Act of 1964, which undercut much of the South's legal argument against desegregation. The white South had maintained that it was improper for judges to interpret the Fourteenth Amendment in a way that differed from the original understanding, but even segregationists recognized that the Fourteenth Amendment gave Congress the authority to enforce the equal protection clause "by appropriate legislation." With this in mind, the Civil Rights Act of 1964 authorized the Department of Justice to initiate school desegregation actions, and empowered the Department of Health, Education, and Welfare to withhold federal funds from schools that were not "desegregated."[54]

With both Congress and the courts insisting on desegregation, by 1965 whites in Summerton (and throughout the South) understood that massive resistance was no longer an option. "Goaded by fear of losing urgently needed federal funds," historian John A. Garraty has written, "all but 170 of the 5,045 school districts in the South had begun to integrate classes. Probably more southern Negroes entered white schools in 1965 than in the entire 11-year period since the desegregation decision of 1954." Desegregation came to Summerton in 1965, when five black students enrolled in the previously all-white Summerton High School. About 110 white students then transferred to Clarendon Hall, a newly established, all-white private school, but 250 whites remained in the public schools. By 1969 the number of blacks attending the desegregated schools had increased to twenty-eight—approximately 12 percent of the students then enrolled in Summerton's predominantly white public schools.[55]

In the 1950s whites in Summerton had retaliated against those who sought desegregation. Harry Briggs, a black mechanic who was the first-named plaintiff in Summerton's initial desegregation lawsuit, was fired from his job at a local garage, and others who supported the cause were subjected to various sorts of economic pressure: one was denied financ-

54. *Brown v. Board of Education*, 349 U.S. 294 (1955), 298n2, 300, 301; Public Law 88–352 (1964).
55. John A. Garraty, *The American Nation* (New York: Harper and Row, 1966), 831.

ing for farm equipment, another lost his line of credit at the local feed store, and still others could not rent any land to grow cotton.[56]

By the 1960s, however, local whites were resigned to desegregation, and there were no more reprisals. After 1965 students were allowed to attend whichever school they freely chose. No request for a transfer was denied for any reason at all, and there were no reports that anyone was abused— that any parent had lost a job, or that other pressure had been exerted. The twenty-eight desegregated black students admittedly made up only a small portion of the more than two thousand black students in the district. But school authorities were assigning students on a nonracial basis. Black students were free to mix with whites if they wished. Moreover, the school board reported that the desegregated blacks generally kept up with the white children academically, and instructors such as Marian Barksdale, a music teacher, later stated that between 1965 and 1970 desegregation "worked just fine."[57]

Yet by 1968 the Supreme Court was no longer satisfied with the amount of mixing that was achieved by freedom of choice. In *Green v. New Kent County* (1968), about which more will be said shortly, the high court held that *Brown* required that students in southern school districts must be assigned on the basis of race so that the racial enrollment at individual schools was not out of proportion with the racial ratio in the school district as a whole. Therefore, after *Green*, District Judge Charles E. Simons, a federal judge who had previously held that freedom of choice was working well in Summerton, ruled that the 250 white and the 2,000 black public school students must be assigned so as to achieve racially balanced enrollments. Simons recognized that this would probably precipitate an exodus of whites from the public schools, with the result that "the public school system will have less racial integration than under the present freedom of choice plan." Nevertheless, Simons ordered massive integration because the Supreme Court had insisted on this. "Under the controlling decisions of the United States Supreme Court," Simons wrote, approximate racial balance was required, "apparently without regard to any adverse effect such move may have on the quality of the education to be provided in the public schools."[58]

Throughout the South other federal judges reached the same conclu-

56. Julian Scheer, "The White Folks Fight Back," *New Republic* 133 (31 October 1955): 24; Martin, *Deep South*, 67.

57. Marian Barksdale, interview with the author, 20 August 1980.

58. Motion for Further Relief, 19 June 1968, Civil Action 7210, U.S. District Court, Columbia, South Carolina; "Application of the Law to the Facts," ibid.; Court Order, 18 July 1969, ibid.

sion, and in many communities, as in Summerton, this precipitated a flight of whites. In Summerton the public schools became almost entirely black when all but one of the 250 whites who had been attending public schools transferred to the white private academy. In other small towns and farming regions, the pattern varied, depending on the demography. In areas where black students outnumbered whites by a large margin, as in Summerton, almost all whites left the public schools. In regions with a larger proportion of white students, there was less flight. In Manning, South Carolina, the closest town to Summerton, almost half the white students in the district (50 percent black) continued to attend public schools after the courts imposed racially balanced integration. And in 75 percent white Turbeville, the next closest town, almost two-thirds of the white youths continued to attend public schools. A demographic law appeared to be at work. Whites were more likely to attend public schools if their numbers were large enough to ensure that they would not be isolated.[59]

Atlanta

In the urban South the general trend was for federal courts to require school desegregation in the early 1960s and then proceed to insist upon balanced integration in the 1970s. In most places each phase of the process was accompanied by a great deal of white flight. There were variations, however. Memphis experienced both aspects of the usual transition, desegregation and integration, while Atlanta never underwent the second phase—the encounter with racially balanced mixing. Despite the difference, the final result was similar in the two cities. The public schools went from segregated to resegregated with short intervals for desegregation or integration.[60]

Initially, most whites in Atlanta were as strongly opposed to desegregation as the white people of Prince Edward and Clarendon counties. "If we had had a vote on closing the schools, by a popular vote," said Atlanta

59. For a graph that compares the proportion of nonwhite students with the proportion of white students in private schools in nonmetropolitan counties of the South, see Charles T. Clotfelter, *After Brown: The Rise and Retreat of School Desegregation* (Princeton: Princeton University Press, 2004), 112.

60. In this section I have drawn on the work of Kevin M. Kruse, *White Flight: Atlanta and the Making of Modern Conservatism* (Princeton: Princeton University Press, 2005); Matthew D. Lassiter, *The Silent Majority: Suburban Politics in the Sunbelt South* (Princeton: Princeton University Press, 2006); and George W. Noblit, "Patience and Prudence in a Southern High School," in Ray C. Rist, ed., *Desegregated Schools: Appraisals of an American Experiment* (New York: Academic Press, 1979), 65–88.

lawyer Griffin Bell, who in 1960 had been an aide to Georgia's governor Ernest Vandiver, "they would have been closed." Yet by then the leaders of Atlanta's municipal government and business community believed that at least some desegregation was inevitable and that massive resistance was bad for business.[61]

Atlanta's leaders noted that in Virginia many whites had seen no need for the sacrifices that would be required to maintain segregation. In the predominantly white Piedmont and Appalachian regions, and also in the white neighborhoods in and near Arlington, Norfolk, and Richmond, most whites opposed massive resistance and insisted that their public schools should be kept open. They would have preferred segregated schools, to be sure, but accommodating the few blacks who lived in their vicinities did not seem too high a price to pay for preserving public education. Because of this sentiment, in 1959 Virginia abandoned massive resistance as a statewide policy, and a small number of black students peacefully enrolled in previously all-white schools in Norfolk and Arlington. Commenting on this development, James J. Kilpatrick said that massive resistance had collapsed because whites broke ranks. "United we might have stood for a generation. Divided we are failing as surely as a cause can fail."[62]

Atlanta's mayor William B. Hartsfield was also aware of the price that Little Rock, Arkansas, had paid for its resistance to school desegregation. Because of the bad publicity, Hartsfield noted, Little Rock had lost millions of dollars. He "commissioned a study of [the] economic losses and made sure Atlanta's top businessmen all received copies. Members of the Little Rock Chamber of Commerce were even brought to Atlanta to counsel their counterparts. They displayed a letter from an industrial leader who refused to build a factory in Arkansas, explaining, 'We have no desire to be involved in the segregation problems current in that state.'" A leaflet described the "Cost of Little Rock" and warned that "resistance meant ruin." One observer said that because of the controversy over school desegregation there was "little new industry" in Little Rock, and another reported grimly, "the '2 most profitable businesses now are Moving Van companies.'"[63]

The lesson of Little Rock weighed on the minds of many businessmen in Atlanta. Fearing that their city would suffer economically if it refused to go along with desegregation, they yielded to the authority of the fed-

61. Kruse, *White Flight*, 141.
62. James W. Ely Jr., *The Crisis of Conservative Virginia: The Byrd Organization and the Politics of Massive Resistance* (Knoxville: University of Tennessee Press, 1976), 132; *Richmond Times Dispatch*, 7 May 1959.
63. Kruse, *White Flight*, 147–48.

eral courts even though this required many of them to disregard their personal convictions. "I am just as much in disagreement with the Supreme Court decision as anyone," banker Mills Lane said. "Yet you cannot look at the experience of our other Southern neighbors in any but a practical way." Members of the Atlanta Chamber of Commerce recognized that their self-interest was at stake. "They weren't a bunch of do-gooders," said member Opie Shelton. "They were hard-headed businessmen." They thought a reputation for moderation in racial matters would lead to economic progress and profits.[64]

When the beginning of school desegregation approached in 1961, the Atlanta police did everything they could to ensure that there would be no violence. Some members of the force were sent to Arkansas and Louisiana to learn what Little Rock and New Orleans did wrong. And Police Chief Herbert Jenkins planned for the first day of school with what one observer called "a care for detail that characterized the D-Day landing." "Undercover cars carried the [desegregating] students to and from school during the first days, with a black detective driving and the route detailed, street by street, minute by minute. And the schools themselves were guarded with equal care. . . . To scare off bombers, canine units patrolled the grounds. . . . A half-dozen uniformed and plainclothes policemen stood ready outside each school, with a police-woman and more officers stationed inside. A special mobile squad, paddy wagons, a helicopter, and the evening motorcycle squad would all be on call as well."[65]

At the same time Mayor Hartsfield, Chief Jenkins, and local business leaders recognized that they had "a great public relations job to do because there will be so many members of the press present and the eyes of the world will be focused on [Atlanta] during this period." The mayor and the chief therefore kept the press well informed, and local business interests treated the press to a bus tour of the city, a cocktail party, and a dinner. Reporters were astonished. According to *Newsweek,* "Old hands who had been harassed and badgered by city officials on the integration beat from Little Rock to New Orleans were awed by Atlanta's anxious efforts to cater to the working press."[66]

To placate rank-and-file whites, Atlanta's leaders also worked to keep desegregation to a bare minimum. To this end, they developed a desegregation plan that allowed only high school juniors and seniors to transfer in 1961, with desegregation expanded by one grade a year after that, working backward through the earlier grades. In addition, Atlanta re-

64. Ibid., 149.
65. Ibid., 152.
66. Ibid., 152–54; *Newsweek* 58 (11 September 1961): 31–32.

quired transferring students to satisfy the requirements of a pupil placement plan. Under the terms of this plan, transfers would be approved only for students whose scores on academic tests indicated that they possessed "scholastic aptitude" and "relative intelligence"; and only for students whose personal interviews indicated that they were not likely to provoke "friction or disorder."[67]

Although these procedures were designed to limit desegregation to token levels, they were not avowedly racial. In 1958 the Supreme Court had approved a similar plan in Alabama and, after that, many southern cities used such policies to limit the extent of desegregation. In Atlanta the school board approved only 10 of the 133 requests it received for transfers in 1961, when blacks made up about 30 percent of the 100,000 students enrolled in the city's public schools. In 1962 and 1963, the number of requests that were approved increased to 44 and 143. As pressure mounted from the federal courts, so did the number of transfers, with the school board approving more than 700 requests for transfer in 1964. Initially, the transferring students had boasted higher test scores than the average for their white classmates, and a spokesperson for the NAACP observed, "We've got a saying around here that it's easier to go to Yale than to transfer from one public school to another in Atlanta."[68]

When they entered their predominantly white high schools, the black pioneers generally encountered a pervasive ostracism. Robert Coles, a psychiatrist who was on hand to observe the desegregation of Atlanta's schools, reported that hardly any of the white students welcomed their new black classmates. "By far the largest number [of white students] are quizzical, annoyed, or would just say that they don't want them," Coles reported. White students said "that Negroes will lower standards"; "that they are not like white people, inferior and less intelligent, born and made to serve."[69]

Sometimes the disapproval was spiked with insults and barbs. According to historian Kevin M. Kruse, the treatment that Martha Ann Holmes and Rosalyn Walton received at Murphy High School was "perhaps the worst experienced by Atlanta's transfer students." "During the first week of classes, as detectives kept watch, white students remained 'stand-offish.' In the lunchroom, for instance, the two girls ate alone at a table for twelve. 'Those few Murphy students who wanted to be friendly,' a reporter noted, 'hesitated for fear of exposing themselves to the

67. Kruse, *White Flight*, 150–51, 167; Lassiter, *Silent Majority*, 96, 106.
68. Kruse, *White Flight*, 151.
69. Robert Coles, *The Desegregation of Southern Schools: A Psychiatric Study* (New York: Anti-Defamation League of B'nai B'rith, 1963), 9–14 .

heckling meted out to a "nigger-lover."' When the police disappeared, things got even worse. Students crayoned 'Nigger' on the girls' lockers and slipped crude notes inside: 'Go back to Africa, Jungle Bunny.' As the girls walked to and from classes, students would sneak up behind them and utter vulgar curses. 'I tried not even to look back at them in the halls,' Martha told a reporter, 'so they wouldn't think we were paying attention.' But things were no better in the classrooms. In Martha's physics class, for instance, the boy who acted as a teacher's aide would mark her examination booklets with a swastika or the words 'NAACP Approved.' Once, he took the liberty of lowering her grade himself. In English class, meanwhile, the boy who distributed test papers refused to hand Martha hers. He simply threw them at her. As students saw teachers ignoring such slights, they grew bolder. One afternoon, a boy at the blackboard hurled a piece of chalk at Martha, striking her directly between the eyes. After that act went unpunished, students tormented Martha with a wide arsenal of everyday items, such as pennies and berries. 'One day,' she remembered, 'I was just picking nails out of my hair.'"[70]

Yet the pattern of white resistance soon changed. An early sign of what was in store came in May 1961 when school officials received an unusual request from Sandra Melkild, a white girl from a middle-class family. Sandra sought to transfer from Northside High, which was scheduled for desegregation that year, to Dykes High, which would remain all-white. She stated her reason simply, saying she wished "to maintain freedom of association." She did not want to have anything to do with black people.[71]

The school board and the supervising federal judge ruled against Sandra's transfer, on the ground that the application was motivated by racial considerations. In the background, however, there was another concern. Judge Frank Hooper expressed the opinion that, if Sandra's transfer had been approved, there would have been wide-scale white flight. "The practical effect would be to vacate the school as to all white students desiring to transfer."[72]

Although Sandra's request was not approved, Professor Kruse has emphasized the importance of the case. For more than a decade prior to school desegregation, Atlanta's blacks had been purchasing homes in working- and middle-class white neighborhoods. Whites had tried various methods to prevent the "encroachment," but they were unable to stem the tide. For a while a white group with fascist overtones, the Columbians, had formed street patrols and engaged in various sorts of intimidation,

70. Kruse, *White Flight,* 157, 156.
71. Ibid., 161.
72. Ibid., 162.

such as "arresting" black people who were caught in a white neighborhood. But the blacks kept coming, and the Columbians eventually disappeared from the streets of Atlanta. Other white groups then emerged to lead the opposition. The West End Cooperative Corporation tried to erect a "Great White Wall" of racially restrictive covenants written into property deeds. Another group, the Mozley Park Home Owners' Protective Association, tried to prevent a black "invasion" by raising funds to repurchase homes that were sold to blacks. But these groups were also unable to stay the force of demography. The southern economy needed fewer workers on the farms, and record numbers of blacks were moving to the cities. Try as they did, whites in Atlanta were unable to maintain the racial character of one neighborhood after another. Many of them therefore decided to distance themselves. When desegregation came to Atlanta's public schools, in 1961, it was against a background of more than a decade of white flight from various neighborhoods. As school superintendent John Letson noted in 1960, "It is very evident that many white residents are moving . . . , and many white areas in the city are becoming Negro residential communities."[73]

In his impressive account of race relations in Atlanta, Kruse said little about the decline in social standards as neighborhoods passed from white to black, and nothing about misbehavior by black students at desegregated schools. In another able scholarly study of developments in Atlanta, Professor Matthew D. Lassiter also steered clear of these politically incorrect matters. Instead, Professor Kruse emphasized the importance of what might be called "white identity." Against the background of residential transition, Kruse noted, whites feared that their schools would also be inundated by a black "flood."

Regardless of how blacks behaved, Kruse implied, by 1961 many whites had come to regard freedom of association as "a fundamental right." The president of one segregationist group expressed this view when he wrote, "It is perfectly alright if people who want integration have all the integration they want, provided those who feel otherwise (including me, of course) are granted the same 'freedom of choice'" to do otherwise. Another segregationist said, "I want the negro to enjoy his freedom but I don't want any part of them. I don't want any one to tell me I've got to sit with them [or] have my children go to school with them."[74]

This interpretation is open to question. This writer wonders if the behavior of Atlanta's black students really was beyond reproach. If so, the situation in the Georgia metropolis was quite unlike that in Topeka, Wash-

73. Ibid., 47, 55, 65, 165.
74. Ibid., 163; Lassiter, *Silent Majority*.

ington, Wilmington, and other places described in this book. In those communities, white flight was prompted as much by untoward conduct as by any conscious sense of racial pride or loyalty. Yet tendencies toward white ethnocentrism have doubtless persisted despite the hegemony of racial liberalism since about 1960. When it comes to choosing friends and neighborhoods, most whites (and many blacks, too) prefer to be with one another, although modern egalitarianism seems to have obliterated these inclinations in some people and suppressed them in many more.

According to Professor Kruse, however, whites in Atlanta were almost uniquely concerned with maintaining their racial communities. Perhaps so. Certainly there is no gainsaying the extent or the speed of white flight in Atlanta. When desegregation began in 1961, about 70 percent of Atlanta's more than 100,000 public school students were white, and only ten black students were enrolled in predominantly white schools. Ten years later, 70 percent of the 110,000 public school students in the city were black. By 1985, whites made up only 6 percent of the total enrollment. Since then "the nearly completely black character of Atlanta's public school system" has been "unmistakable." Most whites moved to white suburbs, while those who remained in the city generally enrolled their children in predominantly white private schools. "As they fled from the schools in record numbers and at record speed," Professor Kruse has written, "yet another desegregated public space passed from segregation to resegregation, with barely any time spent on true 'integration' at all."[75]

Memphis

The situation in Memphis differed from that in Atlanta. Desegregation was more successful in the Tennessee city, and racially balanced integration was achieved for a short while in a few schools. But the balance turned out to be short-lived, and racial relations at the schools were always problematical.

There are able scholarly accounts of Memphis's experience with desegregation and integration. Some of the best work emerged from a study of the day-by-day experience of students at one integrated high school, Crossover High School. Beginning in 1975, George W. Noblit and Thomas W. Collins, a sociologist and an anthropologist at Memphis State University, spent two years observing events at this school. Like anthropologists and ethnographers who live among primitive tribes, Noblit and Collins

75. Kruse, *White Flight*, 239–40, 169.

closely observed (and then reported on) the customs of the "natives"—
the students and teachers at an anonymous school designated as "Crossover High."[76]

In the 1960s the students at Crossover had been predominantly white,
and almost all came from families of at least middling means. The school
was surrounded by a large park and boasted some elaborate extras, including large stone columns at the entrance and marble in the hallways.
In the past Crossover had been known as "a college prep school with high
academic standards." But the school changed dramatically after a 1971
court order paired Crossover with a formerly black high school the researchers called Feeder, which was located across the railroad tracks some
eight blocks away. Crossover then became the high school for a larger area
and Feeder the junior high school.[77]

Thanks to integration, new groups enrolled at Crossover. One was a
small group of studious blacks who were committed to success in school.
Another was a larger contingent of "blue collar whites [who] demonstrated less commitment to success in school." Yet another group, larger
than the others, was made of "lower-class blacks . . . from the housing
projects . . . [who] had a relatively strong commitment to behaviors and
attitudes and styles that are common to the street." Noblit mentioned that
"white parents complained about a lack of discipline within the school,"
but, in keeping with the custom of political correctness in academia, neither Noblit nor Collins described instances of misbehavior.[78]

The goal of court-ordered integration was to achieve an even racial balance at Crossover and a ratio of about 60 percent black and 40 percent
white at most other schools. Yet far from achieving these ratios, the imposition of balanced mixing precipitated massive white flight. In 1972
nearly 35,000 of the district's 60,000 white students left the public school
system. However, most of the whites who had been enrolled at Crossover
chose to stay rather than attend another school. This was especially true
of juniors and seniors who were only a year or two away from graduation. The white flight was much greater among students who were assigned to attend Feeder Junior High and other schools in black neighborhoods. After 1975, even the white enrollment at Crossover declined
rapidly, "indicating that all but those who were dedicated to desegrega-

76. Noblit, "Patience and Prudence," 65–88; Thomas W. Collins, "From Courtrooms
to Classrooms: Managing School Desegregation in a Deep South High School," in Rist,
Desegregated Schools, 89–114. Noblit and Collins followed the ethnographers' practice
of not identifying people or even schools by their correct names. "Crossover" was their
choice for a fictitious name.
77. Noblit, "Patience and Prudence," 77.
78. Ibid., 77–78, 70.

tion or too poor to afford private school had left the public school system." The racial ratio at Crossover shifted from roughly 50–50 in 1972 to 28 percent white and 72 percent black in 1976.[79]

Between 1975 and 1977, Noblit and Collins were on hand, observing the goings on at the school. As they saw it, Crossover tried hard—perhaps too hard—to maintain its white enrollment. For fear that Memphis would become "another Atlanta," Crossover catered to what Noblit called "the honor students"—those who "came from elite families within the city who, while being liberal enough to 'try' desegregation," were concerned about the quality of education and "not above using their influence." To reassure these whites, the school's black principals instituted strict disciplinary policies and allegedly punished blacks more severely than whites who were guilty of the same infractions. In his only specific reference to misconduct, Collins contrasted the punishment meted out to black and white boys who wore hats as they entered a classroom. The black boy was sent to the principal's office for discipline, while the white was required merely to take off his hat.[80]

In response to pressure from white families, the authorities at Crossover also did their best to maintain advanced placement courses—despite a sharp decline in the demand for such courses. The reduced demand stemmed from the decline in white enrollment and also from the fact that black students generally preferred standard classes and shunned those that were designated as "accelerated." The authorities also established two study halls to which students could repair during free periods. One, the "non-recreational study hall," was located in the library and was patronized primarily by white students. The other, located in an annex to the school, was a "recreational study hall" which "quickly became a black area."[81]

Despite the efforts to retain white students, there were persistent complaints about lower academic standards, and concerns eventually came to a head in 1974 after a highly regarded white teacher transferred to another school and was replaced by a black teacher who had had problems at several previous schools. "Almost immediately, the honor students became dissatisfied with her teaching," and they "mobiliz[ed] their elite parents." When the principal stood firmly in support of the teacher, the white parents began to reconsider their options. "As [the white parents] had originally viewed it," Noblit wrote, "their liberal ideology supported de-

79. Collins, "From Courtrooms to Classrooms," 89.

80. Noblit, "Patience and Prudence," 66, 69, 70; Collins, "From Courtrooms to Classrooms," 81.

81. Noblit, "Patience and Prudence," 70, 72, 79.

segregation even though it might result in some possible educational costs to their children." But now, they began to wonder if the costs were not too high. The following year a new black principal was hired at Crossover, a principal whom white parents generally praised. Even so, many parents transferred their children to other schools since they attributed their problems "not . . . to the new principal but to desegregation."[82]

The white exodus was also a response to changes in social life at Crossover. "Although the lack of . . . accelerated courses was the chief reason that white parents continued to withdraw their children," Noblit wrote, "a new reason emerged a few months into the second school year. White parents reported that their children were quite unhappy at the lack of social life at the school." Noblit's associate, Collins, explained that "before Crossover was paired with Feeder School, its athletic achievements were limited, but games were well attended"—by students and also by adults from the community. The same had been true at Feeder, which "had an active parent booster club" and where the surrounding "black adult community took pride in the fact that this . . . school was able to produce state-level championship teams on a regular basis." Feeder's marching band was also well regarded, and both the musicians and athletes were "a strong unifying force in the Feeder community."[83]

Court-ordered integration changed this. "White business and community leaders stopped attending games," Collins reported, and "private contributions fell off to zero." Nor did black adults take up the slack. Although they had enthusiastically supported the teams at Feeder High, most black adults "considered the loss of their Feeder School a critical setback." They considered Crossover "the white school not theirs." In the past football games at each school had regularly attracted large crowds of spectators, but attendance dwindled after the court order, sometimes to as few as forty to fifty persons.[84]

During the first year of desegregation, "the combination of athletic talent" had produced an outstanding football team. With each passing year, however, the number of white players declined until by 1975 (the fourth year of integration) only three white students remained on the football team. "In 1976 the entire team was composed of black students," as was also the case in basketball. "The white students who could compete in these sports chose to participate on all-white church sponsored teams in the City Park League. When asked to explain why they no longer tried out for the school teams in football or basketball, "the white students said out-

82. Ibid., 70–72, 74.
83. Ibid. 85; Collins, "From Courtrooms to Classrooms," 103, 98.
84. Collins, "From Courtrooms to Classrooms," 105.

right that they could not identify with the teams and now considered major sports 'a black thing.'"[85]

When it came to golf, tennis, and cross-country track, another variety of distancing was evident. These were regarded as white sports "in which few blacks were willing to compete." According to Collins, "the Crossover student body had sorted out the various sports-related activities for ethnic control."[86]

Apart from athletics, the trend was much the same. Until 1976, the twelve positions on the girls' cheerleading squad were apportioned equally between black and white students. When the quota system was abolished, however, the cheerleading squad also became all-black. With respect to school publications, the staff of the yearbook was almost all-white, while black students controlled the newspaper. Yet there were some exceptions to the general pattern of separatism. The band and choral groups at Crossover were well integrated, and there was also a good deal of racial interaction in the Reserve Officers Training Program (ROTC).[87]

Summing up the situation at Crossover High School, professors Collins and Noblit, and their editor Ray C. Rist, reached three conclusions that would have applied to integrated education more generally: (1) "Desegregation has . . . brought blacks and whites together under one roof, but segregation remains"; (2) "After 5 years, the upper whites chose to withdraw. . . . All but those who were dedicated to desegregation or too poor to afford private school had left"; and (3) Integration had not been a complete failure. The educational benefits were "few and far between," but authorities had managed "to keep the lid on—no matter what." "The level of violence and inter-racial conflict was kept to an absolute minimum."[88]

85. Ibid., 103–5.

86. Ibid., 106.

87. Collins, "From Courtrooms to Classrooms," 103, 105, 113.

88. Ibid., 113, 102; Noblit, "Patience and Prudence," 69; Rist, *Desegregated Schools,* 9. Crossover was only one high school, but the situation elsewhere was much the same. After observing the situation at a middle school in the Northeast, Janet Schofield, a committed integrationist, reported that the lunch period was often the most segregated time of the day. Over the course of one two-year period in the 1970s, Schofield mapped the seating arrangements in the school cafeteria once each week, and then reported that, on an average day, only 15 of the 250 students in the cafeteria chose to sit next to a student of another race. According to Robert L. Crain and Amy Stuart Wells, who also were committed integrationists, segregation in the cafeterias was also commonplace in the suburbs of St. Louis. After reviewing the information in some two hundred high school yearbooks, yet another scholar who favored integration, Charles T. Clotfelter, also noted that the composition of social organizations tended to be disproportionately of one race or another. Janet Ward Schofield, *Black and White in School* (New York: Praeger, 1982), 100; Amy Stuart Wells and Robert L. Crain, *Stepping over the Color Line* (New Haven: Yale University Press, 1997), 329; Clotfelter, *After Brown,* 18.

5

Desegregation Transformed

By 1966, most southern officials had grudgingly accepted the 1964 civil rights act as the law of the land. They did so because by then they considered desegregation inevitable and also because they wanted federal money—not just for education but also for research and development, for military bases and industrial contracts. The *New York Times* reported that "all but about 100 of the 5,000 districts in seventeen southern and border states" had ceased official discrimination "in order to receive Federal aid." According to the *Times*, "the South has been brought almost to a par with the rest of the country in the removal of racial barriers. *De jure* segregation has been removed. . . . Remaining is *de facto* segregation throughout the land."[1]

Most of the southern school districts embraced "freedom of choice" as their method for establishing schools that were racially nondiscriminatory. Departing from the practice that prevailed in the North and West, where students usually were assigned to the nearest neighborhood school, beginning in 1965 many southern communities allowed each student to choose his school. Many northerners were skeptical, believing, as one federal official stated, that southern districts opted for freedom of choice "because that will bring less integration than [geographical] zoning." Yet racial clustering in residence was so pronounced in the North and West that there was no more racial interaction there than there was in the South under freedom of choice.[2]

Whatever the amount of mixing, southerners said that federal courts

1. *New York Times*, 12 January 1966, 45.
2. Statement of David Seeley, quoted in *New York Times*, 9 May 1965, 40.

had repeatedly affirmed that *Brown* required only that racial discrimination be ended. And with the Civil Rights Act of 1964, Congress had not only defined desegregation but also defined what desegregation was not. Desegregation meant "the assignment of students to public schools . . . without regard to their race" but "not . . . the assignment of students to public schools in order to overcome racial imbalance." By allowing students to attend the school of their choice, southerners seemed to have done all that *Brown* and the Civil Rights Act required. Public officials were no longer practicing racial discrimination.[3]

Although it ended official segregation, freedom of choice led to only limited integration, and in most instances the mixing occurred only if Negro pupils transferred to white schools. Nevertheless, since the language of *Brown* and the 1964 Civil Rights Act required only that students be assigned on a racially nondiscriminatory basis, federal officials seemed to have no alternative but to accept freedom of choice. All the federal Office of Education could do was investigate to make sure that the choice was truly free. In 1965 the staff was increased, and investigators were sent South to make sure that parents were given adequate notice and to see that there were no reprisals or other forms of intimidation. Federal officials said they would try to "spot the phony" and see that "children do in fact have a choice and are free to make that choice." During the summer of 1967 the federal government investigated the situation in some 250 southern districts.[4]

There were abuses. In York, Alabama, a black father was fired from his job after enrolling two of his children in what had been an all-white school. In Sylvester, Georgia, a fourteen-year-old black girl was sent to reform school as a punishment for cursing a white classmate. And an instance of abuse in Drew, Mississippi, later became the subject of both a book and a feature film. The instance involved Mae Bertha Carter and Matthew Carter, two black sharecroppers who took advantage of a freedom of choice plan and sent seven of their children to what had been all-white public schools. Between 1965 and 1970, the Carter children were the only black students in their schools. In response, a segregationist landlord evicted the Carters from their house, and the Carter children were isolated at school, except for occasional taunts and name-calling. Because of such abuses, wrote

3. Public Law 88-352 (1964), 246.
4. Statement of James Quigley, *New York Times*, 9 May 1965, 40. For a similar statement by another federal official, David Seeley, see *New York Times*, 5 September 1965, 40. *Wall Street Journal*, 11 December 1967, 1.

Ralph McGill, the editor and publisher of the *Atlanta Constitution,* "there is all too often no freedom in the freedom of choice plan." According to McGill, such plans offered "a segregationist, racist-dominated community . . . an opportunity to proclaim a free choice, while they covertly employ 'persuasions' to maintain segregation or meager tokenism. . . . Freedom of choice [is] neither freedom nor a choice. It is discrimination."[5]

In other places, however, the choice was free and untrammeled, but integration was limited because hardly any white students chose to enroll in predominantly black schools and many blacks preferred to attend schools that were mostly or entirely black. In Waycross, Georgia, Christine Sarvis not only desegregated the formerly all-white schools but also was recognized for superior scholarship. Nevertheless, Christine's sister Bernadette preferred to stay at an all-black school. "She would rather be where her friends are," the girls' mother explained. In West Point, Mississippi, two black girls returned to their former school after a year of desegregation—not because of any mistreatment but because they felt more comfortable at their former school. In rural Alabama a black teenager named Richard Mock told reporters that he personally preferred his old black school, but his mother insisted that he attend a school that was predominantly white. "He had his choice and I had my choice," the mother said, "and I chose for him to go back to the white school." Richard then ran away from home and went to Los Angeles, where he got a job washing pots and pans for $105 a week. Before departing, Richard said that few black students wished to attend desegregated schools. "Unless they pass a law to make them go, they ain't going to do it."[6]

From the outset civil rights activists understood that they would have to counteract the prevailing desire to go to school with one's friends. "Particularly in the rural hinterlands," the *Wall Street Journal* noted, "free choice will require vigorous promotion among Negro parents by such organizations as the National Association for the Advancement of Colored People." In Georgia the promotion became so vigorous that the state superintendent of education asked, "How can they call it freedom of choice when the NAACP goes in and tells the Negroes they have to transfer to white schools?"[7]

5. *Wall Street Journal,* 14 August 1968, 1; 24 February 1969, 5; Constance Curry, *Silver Rights* (Chapel Hill: Algonquin Books, 1995); Chea Prince and Constance Curry, *The Intolerable Burden* (Brooklyn: Icarus Films, 2004); *Journal of American History* 92 (December 2004): 1138–40; Ralph McGill, quoted in Leon E. Panetta, *Bring Us Together: The Nixon Team and the Civil Rights Retreat* (Philadelphia: J. B. Lippincott, 1971), 79.

6. *Wall Street Journal,* 28 August 1967, 1; 11 October 1967, 1.

7. Ibid., 20 July 1965, 1; 30 August 1965, 1.

Despite the recruiting, only a minority of black students chose to attend predominantly white schools. This resulted, at least in part, from a change of mood among blacks. Prior to 1965 the prevailing emphasis had been on desegregation. But once that was achieved—once there were no official policies to prevent African Americans from attending the schools of their choice—some influential civil rights groups began to emphasize the importance of building institutions in the black community. In the late 1960s the national leaders of the Congress of Racial Equality (CORE) and the Student Non-Violent Coordinating Committee (SNCC) rejected integration as a goal and focused instead on improving schools that were predominantly black. Moreover, the transformation of CORE and SNCC was symbolic of what was happening throughout the country where local black power groups proliferated. In 1967 an editor of the *New York Times* observed, "Now the fact must be faced that a significant fraction of American Negroes—including many of the most articulate and politically active—want integration as little as the Governors of Mississippi and Alabama."[8]

There were many reasons for the changed mood. Some people assumed that most African Americans favored integration, and that black power groups had succumbed to subtle forms of white racism. Yet those who were familiar with the black experience recognized that many blacks, while condemning unfair discrimination and demanding equal rights, also wanted to maintain and foster a sense of racial identity, racial community, and racial pride. This sentiment was deeply rooted in African American history and had been key to the popularity of Marcus Garvey in the 1920s and to that of W. E. B Du Bois throughout his long life. The emergence of black-ruled nations in Africa doubtless reinforced the belief that blacks were fully capable of managing their own institutions. In the late 1960s many blacks consequently came to assert that, while segregation should be opposed, integration was not the answer to every problem. The prevailing mood was neither integrationist nor separatist. It was *pluralist*. Many African Americans insisted on equal rights. They resented and opposed compulsory segregation. But they also wanted to preserve and develop their own institutions.[9]

8. Harry Schwartz, "Black Apartheid and the American Future," *New York Times*, 31 July 1967, 26. See also August Meier and Elliott Rudwick, *CORE: A Study in the Civil Rights Movement, 1942–1968* (New York: Oxford University Press, 1968); Clayborne Carson, *In Struggle: SNCC and the Black Awakening of the 1960s* (Cambridge: Harvard University Press, 1981).

9. For more on pluralism in African American history, see Raymond Wolters, *Du Bois and His Rivals* (Columbia: University of Missouri Press, 2002).

The new mood was evident in many places. One well-publicized instance occurred in Atlanta in 1973, where the local branch of the NAACP dropped its demand for racial balance in every school in return for assurances that black educators would be appointed to more administrative positions in the school system, including the post of superintendent. While insisting that he had "not given up on school integration," the president of the Atlanta NAACP said it was necessary to be "realistic" and to recognize that, since blacks already made up 80 percent of the public school students in the city, an attempt to impose racial balance in each school was likely to precipitate white flight, with the result that there would be even less mixing after "complete integration" than before. Fearing that acceptance of this "Atlanta compromise" would be seen as backing away from the goal of full integration, the national office of the NAACP then suspended the local president and expelled the Atlanta branch. When local NAACP chapters in Knoxville, Tennessee, and Grand Rapids, Michigan, also agreed to plans that did not require the maximum theoretical amount of racial mixing, the national NAACP adopted a resolution that required local branches to adhere to the organization's national policy.[10]

The new mood was also apparent in rural Hyde County, North Carolina, where black students refused to attend integrated public schools for an entire year, 1968–1969. In part the boycott was prompted by a belief that blacks bore an unfair share of the burdens associated with desegregation. Because of white flight, integrated districts did not need as many teachers, and black teachers suffered disproportionately from the job losses, either because they were victims of racial discrimination (as African Americans tended to believe) or because the black teachers, on average, were not as well qualified as white teachers (as many whites maintained). Whatever the reason, several hundred black teachers in North Carolina lost their jobs in integrated districts. Sometimes black students also encountered hostile attitudes and unfair ability grouping in biracial schools, and black parents in Hyde County reported that there was "a decline in student motivation, self-esteem, and academic performance."[11]

Yet resentment of unfair treatment was only one of the reasons for the boycott in Hyde County. Black schools had long been important institutions in rural communities, and the boycott in Hyde County emerged from what a historian of the locale has called a "rich and vibrant heritage of African American education that had nourished . . . blacks for genera-

10. Statement of Lonnie King, quoted in *New York Times,* 2 July 1973, 15; *New York Times,* 3 July 1973, 18 and 69; 22 July 1973, 19.
11. David S. Cecelski, *Along Freedom Road* (Chapel Hill: University of North Carolina Press, 1994), 9, 8, and passim; *New York Times,* 15 June 1965, 31.

tions." From 1930 to 1961 a black graduate of Atlanta University, Oscar A. Peay, had presided over a black school that maintained high standards of quality despite economic stringencies. In the early 1960s, the physical facilities at the school were upgraded, and local blacks praised the institution for its "spirit of commitment, community, and social mission." At the Peay school they found little of the "cultural arrogance" they encountered in predominantly white schools. They were exposed instead to a curriculum that included African American studies and stressed the need for community service. When offered the choice in the mid-1960s, only a minority of Hyde County's black students transferred to formerly white schools. The majority chose to remain in schools with sympathetic black teachers and familiar "markers of cultural and racial identity." When all pupils were reassigned in 1968 to achieve integrated racial balance, the blacks of Hyde County staged their boycott and demanded a return to freedom of choice. In so doing, they brought national attention to "strong undercurrents of black ambivalence" toward racially balanced integration. "Though the size and resolve of black dissent [in Hyde County] was clearly exceptional," historian David Cecelski has written, the boycott "was basically a microcosm of school desegregation throughout the South—especially the rural South."[12]

At one time federal officials acknowledged the significance of this pluralism. In 1964 an assistant to the U.S. Commissioner of Education explained that *Brown* "did not require . . . integration, it merely required desegregation. . . . It doesn't require you to force Negro students to go to school with white students. . . . It just requires that the actions of the school district in assigning students not be based on race. . . . If you have . . . a free choice system . . . and you end up with most of the Negro students going to one school and the white kids going to another, or all of them for that matter, this could, conceivably be found to be non-discrimination, so long as it was clear that this was not by policy of the board but by choice of the students."[13]

A New Policy

In the mid-1960s the federal government changed this policy. Instead of accepting freedom of choice as long as the choice was truly free, govern-

12. Cecelski, *Along Freedom Road*, 9, 31, 173, 171, 102, 168, 11, and passim.
13. Tape recording of David Seeley, speaking to school officials in Biloxi, Mississippi, 25 July 1964, quoted in Gary Orfield, *The Reconstruction of Southern Education* (New York: Wiley, 1969), 63.

ment officials insisted that students should be assigned on the basis of race to achieve racially balanced enrollments. For about ten years after *Brown*, these officials had said that individuals should be freed from racial restrictions—that they should be treated as individuals, without regard to race, color, creed, or national origin. They said that students should not be assigned to school on the basis of race. In the mid-1960s, however, a new generation of government bureaucrats identified freedom of choice as another form of massive resistance—a surreptitious successor to closing public schools. The change—from "Freedom Now" to "Mandatory Integration"—propelled civil rights policy in a different direction. Some observers later concluded that the officials of the mid-1960s made a momentous wrong turn.[14]

In the past, the federal Office of Education had employed older educators who had spent most of their careers in state and local school systems. Yet this changed in the 1960s as the office hired younger people who had participated in the civil rights movement, who were disillusioned by the limited amount of racial interaction that freedom of choice had produced in the schools, and who generally believed, as one of them put it, that "the use of governmental power to break up the remnant of the American caste system is the most pressing public issue of this generation." The activists-turned-bureaucrats scoffed at the idea that the federal government should simply investigate to make sure that freedom of choice was a reality and not a ruse.[15]

A decisive change occurred in 1966 when Harold Howe II became the U.S. Commissioner of Education. A grandson of Samuel Chapman Armstrong, a Union army general who had founded Hampton Institute for Negroes in 1868, Howe grew up in Hampton as the son of the school's president, the Reverend Arthur Howe. Although himself educated at the elite Taft school and at Yale University, Harold Howe by the 1960s had developed the conviction that integrated public schools were the answer to the nation's racial problems. As commissioner of education he played a leading role in redefining desegregation so as to require racial balance.[16]

Howe and his staff held powerful positions, for when Congress enacts a statute the executive branch of the government becomes responsible for enforcing the law. With the Civil Rights Act of 1964, the Office of Educa-

14. This theme is implicit in my book, *Right Turn: William Bradford Reynolds, the Reagan Administration, and Black Civil Rights* (New Brunswick: Transaction Publishers, 1996).

15. Orfield, *Reconstruction of Southern Education*, xi and passim.

16. *Current Biography*, 1967, 185–88.

tion (in the Department of Health, Education, and Welfare) and the Department of Justice were authorized to insist that public schools must be desegregated. As has been noted, however, the Supreme Court, in *Brown*, had defined the goal as the admission of students to public schools "on a racially nondiscriminatory basis," and Congress had defined desegregation both positively and negatively. Desegregation meant "the assignment of students to public schools . . . without regard to their race," but "not . . . the assignment of students to public schools in order to overcome racial imbalance."[17]

Howe and his staff understood this, but they disdained the original understanding of *Brown* and the definitions of the Civil Rights Act. Instead, they regarded integration as the best method to promote the advancement of African Americans. Consequently, in drafting guidelines for enforcing the Civil Rights Act, they maintained that freedom of choice did not satisfy the requirements of the law unless it achieved substantially proportional racial mixing. "The single most substantial indication as to whether a free-choice plan is actually working," the 1966 enforcement guidelines stated, "is the extent to which Negro or other minority group students have in fact transferred from segregated schools." A scale of normally expected progress specified that schools would not be considered desegregated unless the amount of racial mixing doubled each year until racial balance was achieved. As historian James T. Patterson has noted, "eager liberal officials . . . were interpreting the law so as to strive for 'racial balance.'" They established "guidelines [that] went far beyond anything that Congress had anticipated in the Civil Rights Act."[18]

Although the civil rights bureaucrats had a fundamental disagreement with the law they purported to enforce, they were careful to avoid a candid public discussion of their ideas. When their guidelines came in for criticism, the bureaucrats defended themselves by saying that they were merely trying to end the dual system that the Supreme Court had condemned in *Brown*. This was a subterfuge, but it sufficed at the time. There was some criticism, to be sure. One member of Congress accused Harold Howe of concocting a "contemptible plot" to invert the meaning of de-

17. *Brown v. Board of Education*, 349 U.S. 294 (1955), 298n2, 300, 301; Public Law 88–352 (1964), 246.

18. U.S. Department of Education, Revised Statement of Policies for School Desegregation Plans under Title VI of the Civil Rights Act of 1964 (1966); *New York Times*, 8 March 1966, 1; 12 April 1966, 18; James T. Patterson, *Brown v. Board of Education: A Civil Rights Milestone and Its Troubled Legacy* (New York: Oxford University Press, 2001), 137, 127.

segregation, and Georgia's senator Richard Russell characterized the 1966 guidelines as "fanaticism at its very zenith." Mike Mansfield, the liberal senate majority leader from Montana, "agreed with the southern claim that Title VI forbade segregation but did not demand 'an affirmative policy of integration.'" Yet Congress did not formally repudiate the 1966 guidelines, perhaps because, as Gary Orfield has written, "very few members of Congress understood the subtleties of the enforcement debate." Many northerners also discounted criticism of the guidelines, since so much of it came from southerners who had opposed desegregation for years. Then, in *Green v. New Kent County* (1968), the Supreme Court sided with Harold Howe, endorsed the 1966 guidelines, and held that *Brown* and the Civil Rights Act required integration, not just desegregation, at least in the South.[19]

Several factors strengthened the position of integrationists. In a celebrated sociological survey of 1966, a team of researchers headed by James S. Coleman reported that black children who attended predominantly white schools learned more in school than similar black children who attended predominantly black schools. Expounding on Coleman's theory, one federal judge explained that quality of a school depended on its "class climate," and that middle-class schools were better. Since most whites were middle class, and many blacks were not, the purpose of integration was to create schools with "enough middle class students to establish the class character of the school and . . . a substantial number of lower class children to benefit from it."[20]

One year later, in 1967, the U.S. Commission on Civil Rights also reported that when either rich or poor black students were placed in classes with white youngsters, the performance of the black students was demonstrably better than if they attended school with comparable students of their own race. In accounting for this phenomenon, the Civil Rights Commission offered two explanations. It reiterated some of the points that psychologist Kenneth B. Clark had made when the Supreme Court was considering *Brown*. The commission said that "racial isolation" shattered the self-esteem of black students and thus reduced their ambition and enthusiasm for schoolwork. The commission also harkened back to one of the themes of Gunnar Myrdal's influential book, *An American Dilemma*, suggesting that the racial oppression of the past had so damaged black in-

19. Orfield, *Reconstruction of Southern Education,* 285, 274, 289, 303; *Green v. County School Board of New Kent County,* 391 U.S. 430 (1968).

20. James S. Coleman et al., *Equality of Educational Opportunity* (Washington: Government Printing Office, 1966); Judge Simon Sobelof, in *Brunson v. School Board No. 1, Claredon County,* 429 F.2d 820 (1970), 824.

stitutions as to render them incapable of socializing African Americans properly.[21]

Other social scientists took exception to the conclusions of James S. Coleman and the Civil Rights Commission, and Coleman himself eventually recanted. In the meantime, the case for integration was buoyed by yet another commission report, the report of the Commission on Civil Disorders. Popularly known as the Kerner commission for its chairman, Governor Otto Kerner of Illinois, this eleven-member body had been established by President Lyndon B. Johnson to report on and to explain the race riots that had rent the nation in the mid-1960s. In its most famous passage, the Kerner commission warned, "Our nation is moving toward two societies, one black, one white—separate and unequal." Unless drastic measures were taken to promote integration, the commission said, there would be "continuing polarization of the American community and, ultimately, the destruction of basic democratic values." Going beyond calls for an end to racial discrimination, the Kerner commission recommended "sharply increased efforts to eliminate *de facto* segregation in our schools."[22]

Integrationists received another boost from their enemies, the die-hard segregationists. As the legal historian Michael Klarman has noted, in much of the nation there was a backlash against the South. "It was the brutality of southern whites resisting desegregation that ultimately rallied national opinion." Many people were repulsed by Bull Connor's use of attack dogs and fire hoses in Birmingham, by the deceptive tactics and rioting that were used to oppose the enrollment of James Meredith at the University of Mississippi, by Alabama governor George Wallace barring young black pupils by standing in the schoolhouse door, by the need to deploy U.S. paratroopers to protect black students from jeering segregationists at Central High School in Little Rock, Arkansas.[23]

Because of this resistance, officials in the Office of Civil Rights said they were fighting against what one of them called "a bunch of racists." Whatever the legalities with respect to freedom of choice, the federal officials thought they were locked in battle against "the worst element of the Deep South." The *New York Times* expressed a prevailing northern opinion

21. U.S. Commission on Civil Rights, *Racial Isolation in the Public Schools* (Washington: Government Printing Office, 1967).

22. *Report of the National Advisory Commission on Civil Disorders* (New York: Bantam Books, 1968); *New York Times,* 1 March 1968, 1; report of the Kerner commission, as quoted by John Finley Scott and Lois Heyman Scott, "They Are Not so Much Anti-Negro as Pro-Middle Class," *New York Times,* 24 March 1968, SM46.

23. Michael J. Klarman, *From Jim Crow to Civil Rights: The Supreme Court and the Struggle for Racial Equality* (New York: Oxford University Press, 2004), 385.

when it stated editorially that it was "not Federal arrogance but hardened local prejudice" that was responsible for the criticism of the 1966 guidelines.[24]

Nevertheless, the civil rights enforcers were skating on thin legal ice. As the historian Herman Belz has noted, the rule of law requires that laws be enforced as they are written and understood, but after 1966 the Office of Education was enforcing the Civil Rights Act in a way that was at odds with the spirit and letter of the law. What is more, the enforcers knew that their efforts were contrary to the original understanding of *Brown* and the literal wording of the Civil Rights Act. The enforcers were motivated by good intentions—a desire to help blacks—as well as by a wish to retaliate against the white South. But good intentions can be pleaded for most abuses of authority. It was one thing to demand an end to racially discriminatory policies. It was something else to require that, until racial balance was achieved, southern districts had to show an annual, geometric increase in the percentage of Negroes attending school with Caucasians. Of course freedom of choice plans could be used to prevent desegregation, if the white community intimidated blacks. But the civil rights enforcers were mistaken to assume that the purpose of freedom of choice was to perpetuate segregation. The preferable but more difficult approach would have been to move against any intimidation of African Americans. By proceeding against freedom of choice instead of against intimidation, the enforcers succumbed to the blindness of zeal.[25]

The civil rights enforcers nevertheless "bet" that the Supreme Court eventually would uphold their creative interpretations of *Brown* and the Civil Rights Act. History would prove them right.[26]

Green v. New Kent County (1968)

When the 1966 guidelines were challenged in court, the initial results were mixed. In the Fourth Circuit, which included several southern states along the Atlantic seaboard, the federal appeals court rejected the guidelines. In an opinion written by Chief Judge Clement F. Haynesworth, the

24. Panetta, *Bring Us Together*, 112, ix; *New York Times*, 7 December 1966, 46.
25. Herman Belz, *Equality Transformed* (New Brunswick: Transaction Publishers, 1991), 26; *Wall Street Journal*, 27 March 1967, 14; 4 February 1969, 18; 11 February 1969, 12; 16 March 1970, 14; 2 January 1972, 14.
26. For discussion of a similar development with respect to affirmative action, see Paul Craig Roberts and Lawrence M. Stratton Jr., "Color Code," *National Review*, 20 March 1995, 40, 45; Roberts and Stratton, *The New Color Line* (Washington: Regnery, 1991); and Wolters, *Right Turn*, chapter 8.

court held that freedom of choice satisfied the requirements of *Brown* and the Civil Rights Act. Unless there was evidence of some sort of intimidation, there was no need for school authorities to assign students to achieve "a greater intermixture of the races." "If each pupil, each year, attends the school of his choice, the Constitution does not require that he be deprived of his choice."[27]

However, the Fifth Circuit Court, which had jurisdiction over cases from the Deep South, rejected freedom of choice and declared that the 1966 guidelines were "required by the Constitution and . . . within the scope of the Civil Rights Act of 1964." In an opinion written by Judge John Minor Wisdom, the court held that *Brown* imposed an "affirmative duty . . . to furnish a fully integrated education to Negroes as a class." When properly understood, *Brown* required more than an end to racial discrimination; it also imposed "an absolute duty to integrate." Paraphrasing the 1966 guidelines, Judge Wisdom declared that desegregation plans were to be judged according to the amount of racial mixing actually attained. "No army is stronger than an idea whose time has come," Judge Wisdom wrote," and for Judge Wisdom, as previously for the Office of Education, the time had come for compulsory integration. This was "commanded by *Brown,* the Constitution, the Past, the Present, and the wavy fore-image of the future."[28]

The Fifth Circuit Court said it approached its decision "with humility" and with the recognition that "as far a possible federal courts must carry out congressional policy," but it then proceeded to transform the meaning of desegregation. The essence of *Brown* and the Civil Rights Act was the principle that racial discrimination was wrong. That was the idea whose time had come. But in affirming the 1966 guidelines, the Fifth Circuit Court held that the Constitution and the Civil Rights Act required affirmative racial policies to achieve racially balanced student enrollments. As Judge W. Harold Cox noted in a spirited dissent, "The English language simply could not be summoned to state any more clearly than does the very positive enactment of Congress, that these so-called 'guidelines' . . . are actually promulgated and being used in opposition to and in violation of this positive statute."[29]

In 1968 the Supreme Court settled the conflict between the Fourth Cir-

27. *Bowman v. County School Board,* 382 F.2d (1967), 327, 329.
28. *United States v. Jefferson County Board of Education,* 372 F.2d 836 (1966), 847, 848, 849, 878; *United States v. Jefferson County Board of Education,* 380 F.2d (1967), 39.
29. *United States v. Jefferson County Board of Education,* 372 F.2d 836 (1966), 848, 883, 910; Lino A. Graglia, *Disaster by Decree: The Supreme Court Decisions on Race and the Schools* (Ithaca: Cornell University Press, 1976), 60.

cuit (where freedom of choice was still the official policy) and the Fifth (where integration had become compulsory). In *Green v. County School Board of New Kent County,* the high court unanimously sided with the Fifth Circuit and ordered southern school districts to assign students so as to achieve integration. Purporting to do no more than to apply the holding of *Brown* to the case at hand, the Supreme Court changed the constitutional mandate from a prohibition of segregation to a requirement that authorities must achieve a substantial amount of racial mixing.[30]

Situated about halfway between Richmond and Williamsburg in Virginia, New Kent was a rural county with only two schools and 1,300 students, 740 of whom were African Americans. Each of the schools was a combined elementary and high school, and prior to *Brown* the schools were racially segregated, with blacks assigned to the George W. Watkins School in the western portion of the county and whites to the New Kent School on the east side. Until 1965, Watkins continued to have an all-black student body, faculty, and staff, and New Kent remained all white. Then, to qualify for federal money after passage of the Civil Rights Act, school authorities adopted a freedom of choice plan that gave students free transportation to whichever school they wished to attend. Thirty-five black students chose to attend New Kent in 1965, 111 in 1966, and 115 in 1967, but no white student ever chose to go to Watkins. In 1967, one white teacher was employed at Watkins and one black at New Kent. Thus the Watkins School remained almost entirely black, while New Kent School was 83 percent white.[31]

Jack Greenberg, the NAACP's chief legal counsel, personally took charge of the New Kent lawsuit, and he saw to it that the legal briefs and arguments focused on the constitutionality of freedom of choice. The black plaintiffs admitted that in New Kent County each child was given the unrestricted right to attend either of the county's two public schools. Elsewhere there might be pressures to restrict freedom of choice, but in New Kent the choice was conceded to be completely free and unencumbered. Defense attorney Frederick T. Gray told the Supreme Court, "115 children of the colored race have elected to go to the white school, . . . and there is not a shred of evidence that anyone has been, in any way, abused; that any parent has lost his job; that any pressure has been exerted."[32]

30. *Green v. County School Board,* 391 U.S. 430 (1968).
31. Ibid.; Philip Kurland and Gerhard Casper, eds., *Landmark Briefs and Arguments of the Supreme Court* (Arlington, Va.: University Publications of America, 1975), 66:1–298.
32. Kurland and Casper, *Landmark Briefs,* 66:1, 225, 231–32, 259, 262; *Green v. County School Board,* 382 F.2d 338 (1967), 32.

The NAACP nevertheless argued that freedom of choice was illusory. Lawyers for the organization said that blacks could not choose freely in New Kent because of the way they had been reared. Rather than stress the persistence of a sense of black identity, community, and pride, the NAACP's lawyers said that most African Americans had decided to remain at the previously all-black school because they sensed that this was what most whites wanted them to do.

The Supreme Court agreed. During the oral argument, Chief Justice Earl Warren said the system in New Kent was "booby trapped" by "social and cultural influences that have existed for centuries there." Justice Thurgood Marshall had to be reminded that the black plaintiffs had conceded that their choice was free and unrestricted. By putting "freedom of choice" in quotation marks in the opinion he wrote for the Court, Justice William Brennan implied that blacks could not choose freely.[33]

Chief Justice Warren later observed that the New Kent case changed "the traffic light . . . from *Brown* to *Green*." In *Green* the Court held that public schools must go beyond *Brown*'s requirement that public schools must admit students on a racially nondiscriminatory basis. It ruled that authorities must also take "whatever steps might be necessary" to establish "a racially nondiscriminatory school *system*." A racially imbalanced pattern of enrollment—with one school almost entirely black and the other mostly white—was said to indicate that different schools were intended for students of different races.[34]

The essential question in *Green* concerned the point at which a school board had fulfilled its duty to provide equal protection of the laws. New Kent said it had satisfied its obligations by ceasing racial discrimination and by offering free choice. It said that "desegregation" was different from "integration," that school districts were not required to achieve racially balanced enrollments, and that the availability of free choice was sufficient quite apart from the amount of mixing that resulted. The *Green* Court ruled to the contrary, saying that the school board must take "affirmative" steps to ensure that no school would be racially identifiable. The constitutional mandate was changed from prohibiting racial discrimination to separate the races to requiring racial discrimination to mix them.

One cannot overemphasize the importance of *Green*. It transformed the meaning of desegregation. When *Brown* was handed down, federal judges

---

33. Kurland and Casper, *Landmark Briefs*, 66:223–25; *Green v. County School Board*, 391 U.S. 430 (1968), 441.

34. Bernard Schwartz, *Super Chief: Earl Warren and His Supreme Court* (New York: New York University Press, 1983), 706; *Green v. County School Board*, 391 U.S. 430 (1968), 435, 439, italics added.

had to determine what the Supreme Court had decided and what it had not decided. One after another they held that, because of *Brown*, state officials could not deny any person for racial reasons the right to attend a public school. But if the schools were open to children of all races, as Judge John J. Parker noted in *Briggs v. Elliott*, one of the cases that had been consolidated with *Brown*, there was "no violation of the Constitution . . . even though the children of different races voluntarily attend different schools, as they attend different churches. Nothing in the Constitution or in the decision of the Supreme Court takes away from the people the freedom to choose the schools they attend. The Constitution, in other words, does not require integration. It merely forbids discrimination." Similarly in *Evans v. Buchanan*, the Delaware litigation that also had been consolidated with *Brown*, Judge Caleb M. Wright wrote that *Brown* "held only that a State may not deny any person on account of race the right to attend a public school. . . . If races are separated because of geographic or transportation considerations or other similar criteria, it is no concern of the Federal Constitution." And in Topeka a three-judge federal court approved the implementation of *Brown*, saying, "Desegregation does not mean that there must be intermingling of the races in all school districts. It means only that they may not be prevented from intermingling or going to school together because of race."[35]

The Supreme Court let these rulings stand, and until *Green* the meaning of desegregation was settled. With the Civil Rights Act of 1964 Congress reinforced the general understanding that desegregation meant the assignment of students to public schools without regard to race but not the assignment in order to overcome racial imbalance.

Yet the Civil Rights Act was hardly in place when the Supreme Court changed colors. In *Green* the Court rejected the idea that racially nondiscriminatory methods of assigning pupils constituted full compliance with *Brown*. Thereafter, desegregation no longer meant assignment without regard to race; it meant assignment according to race to produce greater racial mixing. A constitutional provision that was thought to have prohibited racial assignments became the basis for requiring racial assignments.[36]

35. *Briggs v. Elliott*, 132 F Supp 776 (1955), 777; *Evans v. Buchanan*, 207 F.Supp. 820 (1962), 823–24; *Brown v. Board of Education*, 139 F.Supp. 468 (1955), 470.

36. It would be an understatement to say that the preceding paragraphs draw on Lino A. Graglia's pathbreaking book, *Disaster by Decree*. For me, reading *Disaster by Decree* was truly a "road to Damascus" experience. It changed my life. Professor Graglia convinced me that, in the area of school desegregation and integration, the conventional wisdom of liberal academics was mistaken. As will be noted in Chapter

It is hard to account for this transformation, except to say that judicial objectivity was swept along by the vogue of integration. *Green* was decided at a time when the influential sociologist James S. Coleman recommended racially balanced mixing as the best way to improve the academic achievement of black students. It was a time when the Civil Rights Commission urged Congress to enact legislation that would require balance in all the nation's public schools, when the Kerner commission touted integration as necessary for social stability, when the government's civil rights enforcers regarded themselves as a band of "young Turks" who were "cheerfully fighting" for "racial justice." One more factor should also be mentioned. Martin Luther King was assassinated on the day after the Supreme Court heard the oral argument in *Green,* and the nation experienced one of its worst periods of racial rioting during the weeks when the justices considered the case. Once again, the justices decided, it was time for decisive judicial leadership.[37]

Swann v. Charlotte-Mecklenburg (1971)

Three years after *Green,* the Supreme Court extended its transformation of the law by holding that busing could be required if necessary to achieve substantial integration. It did so in *Swann v. Charlotte-Mecklenburg Board of Education* (1971), a case that arose from an area that differed greatly from New Kent County. The Charlotte-Mecklenburg School District ranged over an area of 550 square miles in North Carolina and served 84,000 students, 29 percent of whom were African Americans who were disproportionately concentrated in some parts of the city of Charlotte. James B. McMillan, the judge of the district court, recognized that it was one thing to require, as *Brown* had, that children must be assigned to public schools on a nondiscriminatory basis; it was something else to require, as *Green* had, that school boards must take affirmative steps to achieve substantial integration. He wrote that "the rules of the game have changed, and the methods and philosophies which in good faith the Board [of Education] has followed are no longer adequate to complete the job which the courts now say must be done." Judge McMillan therefore imposed a busing program that aimed to achieve an equal dispersion of blacks and whites. He started "with the thought . . . that efforts should be made to reach a 71–29

10, it took more time, but eventually a majority of the justices of the Supreme Court reached the same conclusion.

37. Panetta, *Bring Us Together,* 221.

ratio in the various schools so that there will be no basis for contending that one school is racially different from others."[38]

On appeal, the Supreme Court affirmed Judge McMillan's ruling, but not before considering the points at issue. Justice Hugo Black wanted to overrule Judge McMillan's order because Justice Black thought busing for racial balance was at odds with *Brown*'s command, "that there was to be no legal discrimination on account of race." Justice Black also maintained that the legislative history of the 1964 Civil Rights Act established that "the purpose of Congress was to deny the courts exactly what [Judge McMillan was] urging, namely, that pupils be transported to achieve a racial balance."[39]

Chief Justice Warren Burger also wanted to reverse Judge McMillan. But Burger discovered that he and Justice Black were alone in their opposition to affirmative racial assignments. Recognizing that there were not enough votes on the Court to obtain a decision against busing for racial balance, Burger voted with the majority so that he could assign himself the job of writing the Court's opinion. He hoped to include enough caveats to limit the damage.

The integrationists on the Court allowed Burger to say that the Court "has not ruled, and does not rule that 'racial balance' is required under the Constitution"; that "the basic constitutional requirement" was "that the State not discriminate between public school children on the basis of race"; and that desegregation plans should be "feasible," "workable," "effective," and "realistic." Burger's fellow justices also allowed him to say that the objective of desegregation was to remedy the formal segregation of yesteryear. The goal was to remove the "vestiges of state-imposed segregation," Burger wrote. To this end, affirmative assignments could be required "in a system with a history of segregation," but if there were no such history, "it might well be desirable to assign pupils to schools nearest their homes." Equally important, the Court's majority allowed Burger to write that after school authorities had complied with the Court's orders, their system would be "unitary," and it would not be necessary "to make year-by-year adjustments of the racial composition of student bodies once the affirmative duty to desegregate has been accomplished." In the 1990s, another Supreme Court would make much of these statements.[40]

38. *Swann v. Charlotte-Mecklenburg*, 402 U.S. 1 (1971); *Swann v. Charlotte-Mecklenburg*, 300 F.Supp. 1358 (1969), 1372; *Swann v. Charlotte-Mecklenburg*, 306 F.Supp. 1299 (1969), 1312, 1314.

39. Bernard Schwartz, *Swann's Way* (New York: Oxford University Press, 1986), 101, 177–78.

40. *Swann v. Charlotte-Mecklenburg*, 402 U.S. 1 (1971), 31, 15, 26, 28, 23–24, 5–6, 31–32.

But the Supreme Court of 1971 made Chief Justice Burger write six drafts of the *Swann* opinion. They made him say that district judges and local authorities were required to make "every effort to achieve the greatest possible degree of actual desegregation." They made him approve busing as one way to implement the mandate of *Green*. They made him call for pro-integration techniques that could be "administratively awkward, inconvenient and even bizarre in some situations"—techniques such as the "gerrymandering of school districts and attendance zones" and the "'pairing,' 'clustering,' or 'grouping' of schools with attendance assignments made deliberately to accomplish the transfer of Negro students out of formerly segregated Negro schools and the transfer of white students to formerly all-Negro schools." They made Burger assert that if authorities had kept the races apart in the past, they must now take affirmative steps to promote racial mixing. The *Swann* opinion that finally came down in Burger's name was far from the opinion that the Chief Justice had tried to write.[41]

Because *Green* and *Swann* were at odds with the original understanding of *Brown* and with the clear wording of the 1964 Civil Rights Act, these opinions of the Supreme Court represented a tremendous victory for the civil rights bureaucrats who had disdained the original understandings and definitions. The Supreme Court of 1954 and the Congress of 1964 had sought the advancement of African Americans but held that this could be accomplished if the government and private employers treated citizens as individuals, without regard to race, color, creed, or national origin. But the civil rights bureaucrats thought (and sometimes said) that it was not enough to cease discrimination. They demanded affirmative policies to achieve more integration than could be obtained by mere nondiscrimination. "The essential weakness" with freedom of choice, one of them candidly acknowledged, was that it did not produce enough integration because "blacks seldom choose to go to white schools and whites never choose to go to black schools."[42]

Critics accused the bureaucrats of subverting the laws they were sworn to enforce. The House of Representatives approved legislation to stop the Department of Health, Education, and Welfare from cutting federal funds to school districts that had freedom of choice plans, and even many erstwhile supporters of the civil rights movement expressed criticisms. In 1967 the liberal journalist Meg Greenfield questioned the propriety of

41. Ibid., 26, 27; Schwartz, *Swann's Way*, 114 and passim.
42. Panetta, *Bring Us Together*, 169.

equating "racial balance" and "desegregation," and in 1970 a headline in the *New York Times* asserted that the "National Push for School Integration" was "Losing Momentum" (while an editorial lamented a "nationwide retreat from school integration"). Writing in the *Wall Street Journal,* Vermont Royster noted that it would be almost unthinkable to deny adults the freedom to live in a racially imbalanced neighborhood and questioned whether it was "moral for society to apply to children a policy which, if it were applied to adults, men would know immoral."[43]

Integrationists were especially taken aback by criticism from Alexander M. Bickel. In 1952 Bickel had been a clerk for Justice Felix M. Frankfurter, and at that time he had urged the Court to support the NAACP in *Brown* even though the framers of the Fourteenth Amendment had not had school desegregation in mind. Later Bickel became the Chancellor Kent professor of law and legal history at Yale and a contributing editor at the nation's most influential liberal journal of opinion, the *New Republic.* In 1970 he noted that integration could not be forced in most cities, because most urban whites could move to predominantly white suburbs if they wished. Integration could be imposed only on people who were tied to a particular community—that is, residents of small towns and rural regions. And since few blacks lived in the towns and farming areas of the North and West, massive integration was not in prospect there. According to Bickel, integration was likely to be achieved only in the small towns and rural regions of the South. Bickel wondered, however, whether it was morally right "to require a small rural and relatively poor segment of the national population to submit to a kind of schooling that is disagreeable to them (for whatever reasons . . .), when we do not impose such schooling on people in cities and in other regions, who would also dislike it."[44]

Meanwhile, rank-and-file people weighed in with letters to the editor. After conceding that freedom of choice rarely led to racially balanced mixing, one writer concluded that the persistence of racial imbalance simply established "that few people—black or white—are willing to switch from the schools in their own neighborhood. They prefer and benefit from neighborhood association. This is the real lesson from 'Freedom of Choice.'" Another writer opined, "From the beginning, history records that men have always preferred their own family, their own tribe, their

43. *Wall Street Journal,* 1 August 1969, 3; Meg Greenfield, "What Is Racial Balance in the Schools?" *Reporter,* 23 March 1967, 20–26; *New York Times,* 22 March 1970, 45; 24 March 1970, 46; Vermont Royster, "Forced Integration: Suffer the Children," *Wall Street Journal,* 26 February 1970, 16.
44. Alexander M. Bickel, "Desegregation: Where Do We Go from Here?" *New Republic,* 7 February 1970, 20–22.

own kind. Why should we expect to be different?" Yet another writer expressed the opinion that the Supreme Court had "fallen prey to the simpleminded view that if segregation is bad then integration surely must be good. Instead of integrating, however, it should have had the good sense to desegregate, which is an entirely different concept. The Court should have realized that the proper remedy for compulsory exclusion is to decree that compulsory exclusion must end. Under no circumstances should the court have decreed that compulsory inclusion must begin."[45]

Right or wrong, in *Green* and *Swann* the Supreme Court rejected freedom of choice and insisted on affirmative policies to promote the maximum amount of actual racial mixing. This was a godsend to civil rights bureaucrats. After *Green* they could assert that, far from being the willful zealots that their critics claimed, they were simply enforcing the law as determined by the U.S. Supreme Court. This was evident in the recollections of Leon Panetta, who served in 1969–1970 as director of the Office of Civil Rights in the Department of Health, Education, and Welfare. Panetta maintained that he was merely implementing the law as it had been determined by the Supreme Court. If critics regarded civil rights enforcers as "bloodthirsty integrationist[s]," Panetta later wrote, that was only because "diligence in enforcing the law could make us [appear to be] extremists."[46]

Desegregation, Integration, and Richard M. Nixon

The extremism of the civil rights enforcers had not troubled President Lyndon B. Johnson but was a problem for his Republican successor, Richard M. Nixon. In his 1968 campaign, Nixon led the South to believe that as president he would prevent compulsory integration. "Nixon Raps HEW on Schools, Favors 'Freedom of Choice,'" proclaimed one headline in the *Manning Times*, the leading newspaper of Clarendon County, South Carolina. By contrast, Nixon's Democratic rival, Hubert H. Humphrey, was said to promise "No Let Up in School Guidelines."[47]

Nixon favored the sort of desegregation that *Brown* initially was understood to require and opposed the massive resistance that James J. Kilpatrick had counseled. It was largely for that reason that Nixon lost five states in the Deep South to George Wallace in 1968 even as he prevailed

45. W. R. Bjorklund, S. W. Winters, and Robert A. Mercer to *Wall Street Journal*, 15 October 1969, 18; 4 March 1970, 10.
46. Panetta, *Bring Us Together*, 137, 172, 291.
47. *Manning Times*, 24 October 1968; 11 December 1969.

in the other six states of the former Confederacy. Recognizing that the white people of Dixie were divided over desegregation, the canny Nixon had tailored his message to appeal to southern moderates. In 1958 a group of one hundred businessmen in Norfolk, Virginia, had summarized a cardinal tenet of southern moderation when they explained, "while we would strongly prefer to have segregated schools . . . the abandonment of our public school system is . . . unthinkable."[48]

Especially in those parts of the South where blacks made up only a small part of the population—in Appalachia, in most suburbs, and even in many urban neighborhoods—few whites were willing to make the sacrifices that would be required to maintain segregation. Believing that the courts would be satisfied if the small number of blacks who lived in their vicinity were assigned to predominantly white schools, moderate whites insisted on keeping their public schools open. It was only in areas with (or near) large numbers of blacks that most whites perceived that, once desegregation began, their public schools would be engulfed by a black flood. Nixon understood that urban "rednecks" and rural and small-town "racists" favored massive resistance, but he sensed that Governor Wallace already had a lock on their votes. Nixon therefore decided to court what turned out to be an even larger number of moderate white voters elsewhere in Dixie.[49]

Yet this was not just a case of political calculation. In this instance, Nixon's personal views corresponded with his political interest. Essentially Nixon believed that *Brown* was right but *Green* was wrong—that the decision to end segregation was correct but the decision to require balanced integration was a mistake. He also sensed that most moderates would agree with him, and some extremists would understand that Nixon's position would salvage as much as was possible in the circumstances. In a North Carolina speech that sounded a theme of his campaign, Nixon declared that he personally favored freedom of choice, an objective that could still be obtained by appointing strict constructionists to the Supreme Court. It was too late in the nation's history for a president to refuse to enforce a Supreme Court decision, but Nixon conveyed the impression that if he were elected president he would find other ways to make his influence felt. If Nixon was president, the federal government would not require the sort of balanced integration that *Green* envisioned.

This impression was reinforced in 1969 when Nixon nominated Clem-

48. Matthew D. Lassiter, *The Silent Majority: Suburban Politics in the Sunbelt South* (Princeton: Princeton University Press, 2006), 33.
49. Ibid.

ent F. Haynesworth to replace Abe Fortas as an associate justice of the Supreme Court. Haynesworth was not only a southerner but, as chief judge of the Fourth Circuit Court, he was the author of the decision for freedom of choice that the Supreme Court had reversed in *Green v. New Kent County.* Nixon did not refuse to enforce *Green.* Nor did he repudiate the 1966 guidelines that the *Green* Court had endorsed. But he did the next best thing. He chose to elevate a southern judge who only a few years before had rejected the contention that freedom of choice did not satisfy the Constitution.

By a vote of 55 to 45 the U.S. Senate refused to confirm Haynesworth's nomination, the first time a Supreme Court nomination had been rejected since 1930, when the Senate turned down John J. Parker, the author of the *Briggs* dictum. Haynesworth and Parker were distinguished judges, and neither rejection reflected credit on the Senate. In Haynesworth's case the opposition came from an alliance of special interests. The NAACP objected to the judge's opinion in the *Green* case. Advocates of ethnic balance considered him an unsuitable choice for a seat that had been occupied since 1916 by a succession of Jewish justices. The American Federation of Labor took exception to Haynesworth's decision in a 1963 labor dispute. And some "good government reformers" said that Haynesworth should have disqualified himself from hearing a case that involved a company that rented vending machines from another company in which Haynesworth owned stock.

After Haynesworth's defeat, Nixon chose another southerner, Judge G. Harrold Carswell, whose nomination was also rejected after many senators concluded, with some reason, that Carswell was not a first-rate jurist. An outraged Richard Nixon publicly charged that "when all the hypocrisy is stripped away, the real issue was [Haynesworth and Carswell's] philosophy of strict construction of the Constitution, a philosophy that I share—and the fact that they had the misfortune of being born in the South." "As long as the Senate is constituted the way it is," Nixon said, he would not nominate another southerner and let him be subjected to "regional discrimination." Many senators took exception to that allegation, but the white South concluded that the president was doing his best to protect their interests.[50]

This impression was reinforced when Nixon fired Leon Panetta from his position as the director of the Office of Civil Rights. Like many civil

50. Rowland Evans Jr. and Robert D. Novak, *Nixon in the White House* (New York: Random House, 1971), 171–72.

rights bureaucrats, Panetta was a young white man from a sheltered background. At his college and law school, Santa Clara University, there had been only one black student on campus. Panetta nevertheless insisted that compulsory integration was not only required by the Supreme Court's decision in *Green* but also favored by "the entire Negro community." He seemed not to recognize that many black intellectuals and activists had turned away from integration toward pluralism. Charged with responsibility for administering HEW's guidelines, Panetta would brook "no relaxation of enforcement." He even wanted the Internal Revenue Service (IRS) to require private and religious schools to have racially balanced enrollments in order to maintain their tax exemptions. He thought it reprehensible that Richard Nixon, in his campaign for the presidency, had supported freedom of choice and thereby "actively courted the worst element of the Deep South." Panetta lamented that "the Nixon team" was executing a "civil rights retreat." The surprise is that Panetta was not fired earlier.[51]

In 1970 Nixon further appeased his constituency with an eight-thousand-word statement explaining his views on school desegregation. An editorial in the *New York Times* criticized the president for using "code words" like "the neighborhood school." But the *Wall Street Journal* said the message was "sensible" and expressed in just the right tone—one of "profound concern for the problem coupled with a wholly realistic approach." In the message, Nixon noted that "lawyers and judges have honest disagreements about what the law requires," but he said that he personally thought there was "a fundamental distinction between so-called *de jure* and *de facto* segregation." Nixon further said, "we must recognize that in a free society there are limits to the amount of government coercion that can reasonably be used." He also insisted that "federal officials should not go beyond the requirements of the law in attempting to impose their own judgment on the local school district."[52]

Having thus reassured his supporters, Nixon said no more about freedom of choice, and his administration enforced the Supreme Court's mandate of *Green v. New Kent County.* In 1970 more than one hundred U.S. attorneys, federal marshals, and other civil rights enforcers were sent to the South to monitor integration. The Department of Health, Education, and Welfare denied federal funds to southern schools that were not racially

51. Panetta, *Bring Us Together,* 15, 60, 126, 318, ix, ii–iii.
52. *New York Times,* 30 March 1970, 41; *Wall Street Journal,* 26 March 1970, 10. The text of the president's statement was printed in the *New York Times,* 25 March 1970, 26.

balanced; and the Department of Justice instituted a spate of lawsuits to abolish free choice and to require integration.[53]

As a result of this legal offensive, more racial mixing was achieved during Nixon's first administration than ever before. HEW reported that the percentage of southern blacks enrolled in schools with a majority of whites more than doubled, from 18 percent in the fall of 1968 to 39 percent in the fall of 1970. At the same time the number of southern blacks attending all-black schools declined from 67 percent to 14 percent, and the number of southern blacks enrolled in 80–100 percent black schools dropped from 79 percent to 39 percent. Meanwhile, the proportion of blacks attending all-black or predominantly black schools continued to increase outside the South. By 1970, HEW reported, there was far more racial mixing in public schools of the South than in other parts of the country.[54]

The Nixon administration claimed no credit for the mixing. After all, spokesmen explained, it was not the president or Congress but the Supreme Court that had required integration. The president was simply carrying out his obligation to enforce the law. "The highest court of the land has spoken," Nixon said. "The unitary school system must replace the dual school system. . . . The law having been determined, it is the responsibility of those in the federal government and particularly the responsibility of the President of the United States to uphold the law."[55]

Some supporters of the civil rights movement grudgingly approved the Nixon administration's record on desegregation. "Having secured his Southern base," Rowland Evans and Robert D. Novak wrote, "Nixon . . . could act more responsibly on the school desegregation question." Writing in the *New Republic*, John Osborne said the Nixon administration had a good record enforcing integration in the South—better than it was generally given credit for, and better in some respects than that of the preceding Democratic administration of Lyndon B. Johnson. The Nixon administration did not claim credit for the achievement, of course; "virtue" had been forced upon it. Nevertheless, the administration had "brought about more desegregation in the South . . . than anybody had reason to expect." The official statements were spiked with reassuring southern com-

53. John Osborne, *The Second Year of the Nixon Watch* (New York: Liveright, 1971), 123–25.
54. John Egerton, "Report Card on Southern School Desegregation," *Saturday Review* 55 (1 April 1972): 41–48; John Osborne, *The Third Year of the Nixon Watch* (New York: Liveright, 1972), 11.
55. Osborne, *Second Year*, 129.

fort, but the Nixon administration had veered away from freedom of choice. "However cynically the process of enforcement may be viewed and explained, . . . liberal critics of the Administration may as well face the fact that their image of the President . . . is outdated."[56]

Others had a different assessment. To say the Nixon administration imposed integration on the South because the courts required it was unsatisfactory, William F. Buckley wrote in the *National Review*. Nixon had a special talent for foreign policy, about which he was far more deeply concerned than racial issues. He feared that if he antagonized integrationists, who dominated the media and were influential in Congress, and who already disliked him personally, his ability to conduct foreign policy would be jeopardized. Nixon had to protect the national interest in a dangerous world, and once his political base was secure he decided not to oppose integration. "The opinion-makers have said that we must have integrated schooling, that any slowdown in that program is nothing less than moral temporizing. So, Mr. Nixon has calculated, let's get on with it, and see what happens." Buckley also pointed to "the cynical-realistic" attitude, "confirmed by all past experience that the desegregated schools will soon be resegregated again anyway, so what difference does it make?"[57]

Desegregation Moves North

By holding that integration was not required for its own sake but only to disestablish a pattern of officially compelled racial separation, *Green* and *Swann* implied that affirmative assignments would be required only in the South. Affirmative assignments could be required "in a system with a history of segregation," Chief Justice Burger wrote in *Swann*, but if there were no such history, "it might well be desirable to assign pupils to schools nearest their homes." This served a practical purpose. It minimized national attention and made busing and other affirmative policies appear as steps taken by a patient court to counteract devious southern efforts to preserve segregation.[58]

Yet from the outset many people questioned the propriety of regional differentiation. In 1968 Georgia's senator Richard Russell attached a rider to an appropriation bill requiring HEW to give as much attention to civ-

56. Evans and Novak, *Nixon in the White House*, 174; Osborne, *Third Year*, 11–14, 85–89, 95–98.

57. *National Review* 22 (22 September 1970): 1016, 986–88.

58. *Swann v. Charlotte-Mecklenburg*, 402 U.S. 1 (1971), 15, 26, 28.

il rights enforcement in the North as in the South, and in 1970 Mississippi's senator John Stennis demanded that HEW deal with northern schools that were racially imbalanced as a result of residential racial patterns, as well as southern schools that were racially imbalanced as a result of freedom of choice.[59]

Russell and Stennis were doubtless trying to ease integration pressures on the South, but some northerners conceded that the southern senators had a point. After admitting, "We're just as racist in the North as they are in the South," Senator Abraham Ribicoff of Connecticut scoffed at the usual distinction, saying, "*de facto, de jure,* I don't want to hide behind those two phrases." Minnesota's senator Walter Mondale also pushed for integration in the North, recommending the busing of students from suburbs to inner cities and extra spending for large "education parks" that would attract students from both areas. At the Supreme Court, Justice Lewis Powell said that racial imbalances throughout the nation were "largely unrelated to whether a particular State had or did not have segregative school laws." They were a result, rather, of the personal choices and the economic wherewithal of individual families.[60]

In 1973 the Supreme Court adjusted the legal rationale so that busing could be required outside the South, doing so in *Keyes v. School District No. 1,* a case that arose in Denver, Colorado. The schools in Denver had never been segregated on the basis of race, a practice that was explicitly prohibited by the constitution of Colorado. Nevertheless, Hispanic and African American students were disproportionately concentrated in downtown schools that served the areas where most Hispanics and African Americans lived. In 1969 attorneys for the NAACP went to court and argued that the racial imbalance that resulted from using neighborhood schools amounted to illegal segregation.[61]

59. *New York Times,* 23 February 1969, 1; 22 February 1970, E1.
60. Ibid.; *Wall Street Journal,* 28 June 1971, 1; 25 May 1972, 2; *Keyes v. School District No. 1,* 413 U.S. 189 (1973), 220, 223, 224. Some scholars have offered a different explanation of residential clustering. Instead of attributing the phenomenon to a combination of personal choices influenced by economic wherewithal, class consciousness, and racial identity, they emphasize that government policies are significantly responsible for the pattern of settlement. They note that municipal zoning laws made it difficult to build subsidized housing projects in many suburbs; that some government agencies built highways that facilitated the dispersion of people into separate areas; and other government agencies insured loans that made it easier for people to buy houses in racially imbalanced neighborhoods. Because government policies fostered a racially imbalanced pattern of settlement, they say, the public schools should now promote racial mixing by requiring students to attend racially balanced schools. For one of many statements of this rationale, see Lassiter, *Silent Majority.*
61. *Keyes v. School District No. 1,* 413 U.S. 189 (1973), 196.

After a lengthy lawsuit, the Supreme Court gave the NAACP a victory. A divided Court held that, despite appearances to the contrary, Denver had been practicing official segregation. The Court so held because the school board had opened a 450-student elementary school (the Barrett School) that was situated so as to serve a mostly black enclave. In his opinion for the Court's majority, Justice William Brennan developed what would be called the *"Keyes* presumption"—the presumption that if an attendance zone between two individual schools was gerrymandered to limit (or even to prevent maximization of) racial interaction, then the racial imbalance that prevailed elsewhere in a large metropolitan district was not adventitious. This problematical presumption paved the way for busing for racial balance in the North and West. It did so because civil rights lawyers could always find some instance of school location or attendance boundaries that contributed to racial imbalance. Once a school board was found to have committed such a "segregative act," *Keyes* authorized district judges to presume that racial imbalance elsewhere in the school district was the result of other segregative actions. Then, to correct such segregation, the judges were authorized to require affirmative policies such as busing for racial balance throughout the district.[62]

Thus busing came not only to Denver but to Boston and many other northern cities. As a dissenting Justice Powell had warned, however, many parents regarded such busing as an interference with "the concept of community" and with their "liberty to direct the upbringing and education of children under their control." The compulsory transportation of schoolchildren out of their neighborhoods to increase racial mixing touched off widespread, bitter resentment because busing affected the lives of average people significantly and directly. Busing gave rise to demonstrations, dissent, and middle-class flight. It became one of the most controversial social policies of the 1970s.[63]

The Supreme Court has said that the enforcement of constitutional principles cannot be compromised because of public opinion; but the justices were aware of the wide public opposition to busing and knew that in some ways the national mood in the 1970s was similar to that in the South in the late 1950s. In 1974 the House of Representatives voted, 293–117, to prohibit the use of federal funds to cover the cost of busing students past the nearest public school, and polls indicated that more than 80 percent of

62. Ibid., 201, 203–9.
63. There are many books on this subject. A good place to begin is a collection of essays edited by Nicolaus Mills, *The Great School Bus Controversy* (New York: Teachers College Press, 1973).

whites opposed busing for racial balance and less than half of the black population favored the policy.[64]

When the Supreme Court encountered opposition after the *Brown* decision of 1954, the justices allowed the nation time to adjust to new principles, saying that desegregation should be implemented "with all deliberate speed" and at "the earliest practicable date." When the busing cases of the early 1970s gave rise to complaints about judicial "usurpation" and "tyranny," the Court again drew back. It did so in *Milliken v. Bradley* (1974), a case that concerned busing for racial balance in the metropolitan region near Detroit.[65]

In Detroit the district judge, Stephen Roth, acknowledged that the city had never separated students on racial grounds and had made some efforts to promote integration. Nevertheless, the school board had built some schools in the center of racially concentrated areas, thereby minimizing integration and triggering the *Keyes* presumption. Yet since Detroit's overall enrollment had become 70 percent black by 1973, Judge Roth feared that affirmative assignments to achieve racial balance in each school would lead to massive white flight from the city to the suburbs. Thus a busing plan that was limited to the city of Detroit would probably lead to a resegregated school district that would be at least 90 percent black. Therefore, Judge Roth decided to look beyond Detroit. To get a 75 percent white majority in the schools, he ordered that black and white students should be dispersed through three counties and fifty-four school districts with a total enrollment of 780,000 students. Judge Roth said he would try to limit the students' busing time to eighty minutes a day but acknowledged that some youngsters would have to spend as much as three hours each day in transit to and from school.[66]

On appeal, a divided Sixth Circuit court voted 6–3 to affirm most of Judge Roth's order. The majority said that "any less comprehensive a solution than a metropolitan area plan would result in an all black school system immediately surrounded by practically all white suburban school systems."[67]

The Supreme Court then reversed and censured the lower courts for requiring a metropolitan plan simply because a plan that was limited to Detroit "would not produce a racial balance which they perceive as desir-

64. For a summary of the Gallup polls, see Ben J. Wattenberg, *The Real America* (Garden City: Doubleday, 1974), 252.

65. *Brown v. Board of Education*, 349 U.S. 294 (1955), 301, 300.

66. *Bradley v. Milliken*, 338 F.Supp. (1971), 587–92; *Bradley v. Milliken*, 345 F.Supp. 914 (1972); Graglia, *Disaster by Decree*, 207–15.

67. *Bradley v. Milliken*, 484 F.2d 215 (1973), 245.

able." Writing for the Court, Chief Justice Burger affirmed that racial balance was not required as such but only as a remedy for unconstitutional actions. Burger wrote that the logic of desegregation—the undoing of segregation—required that affirmative assignments to achieve integration must be limited to culpable school districts. Since the suburban districts near Detroit had never been found guilty of segregative actions, the Supreme Court insisted that they must be left out of any remedial plan. There was nothing in the Constitution, the Court held, that required that independent school districts must be consolidated to make all schools predominantly white. "The mere fact of different racial composition in contiguous districts does not itself imply or constitute a violation of the Equal Protection Clause."[68]

The Court's decision in the Detroit case hit integrationists like a slap in the face. The *Green* Court had sanctioned "whatever steps might be necessary" to achieve the "root and branch" eradication of dual school systems. The *Swann* Court told federal judges to "make every effort to achieve the greatest possible degree of actual desegregation." But those decisions were handed down in 1968 and 1971. In the Detroit case of 1974, the Court held that there was no warrant for an interdistrict plan to achieve integration unless there had been interdistrict actions to promote segregation. A dissenting Justice Thurgood Marshall complained that, because of *Milliken*, black and white children would grow up as strangers to one another, with most blacks attending schools in the central cities and most whites attending suburban schools. *Milliken* was a significant turning point. *Brown* had been the watershed of school desegregation. *Green, Swann,* and *Keyes* represented the high tide for integration. *Milliken* marked the water's edge.[69]

The Court's decision against metropolitan busing was by the narrowest of margins, 5–4, with all four of President Nixon's appointees voting with the majority. Chief Justice Warren Burger and Associate Justices Harry Blackmun, Lewis Powell, and William Rehnquist (as well as the veteran Justice Potter Stewart) essentially agreed with President Nixon's position on school desegregation: students should be assigned on a racially nondiscriminatory basis, but not by race to achieve proportional mixing. It was ironic that the Court's decision in *Milliken* was handed down on July 25, 1974, only two weeks before Nixon was forced out of

68. *Milliken v. Bradley,* 418 U.S. 717 (1974), 740, 744–47, 756 (concurring opinion of Justice Stewart).

69. *Green v. County School Board,* 391 U.S. 430 (1968), 438–38; *Swann v. Charlotte-Mecklenburg,* 402 U.S. 1 (1971), 26; *Milliken v. Bradley,* 418 U.S. 717 (1974), 808, 815.

office. *Milliken* was a signal victory for the soon-to-be-deposed president.

This made the decision all the more difficult for many people to accept. The battle over forced busing had been one of the major points at issue between liberals and conservatives during the early 1970s, and now, thanks to Nixon's justices, the Supreme Court had set up a roadblock that put most suburbs beyond the reach of liberal social engineering. Tom Wicker of the *New York Times* conceded that there was "no doubt whatever that public opinion has turned massively against the kind of cross-busing that would have been required to unify Detroit schools with 53 surrounding suburban school systems." But Wicker spoke for many integrationists when he also lamented that the Supreme Court had retreated from "a noble goal."[70]

The Supreme Court continued its retreat in 1977 in a case that involved the public schools of Dayton, Ohio. In Dayton, as in Detroit, there had been no formal segregation, but racial enrollments were not balanced because students were assigned to schools close to home and blacks were not evenly dispersed throughout the neighborhoods of the city. The district court also found that the school board had committed isolated acts (such as assigning 72 percent of the black teachers to schools in black neighborhoods) that contributed to the racial imbalance.

When the Dayton case finally got to the Supreme Court on appeal, the question concerned the nature of the remedy. Integrationists insisted that, in accordance with the *Keyes* presumption, district judges should require racial balance in each of Dayton's schools. In 1977, however, the Supreme Court ordered the district court to "tailor 'the scope of the remedy' to fit 'the nature and extent of the constitutional violation.'" Even if infractions were found, the Court said, judges should not impose a remedy that was out of proportion to the violation. They should require only the additional amount of mixing that would have occurred if there had been no infraction.[71]

"*Dayton* was a godsend to northern school districts," J. Harvie Wilkinson wrote. "It meant that school boards might indulge in . . . minor indiscretions without being subjected to city-wide busing as a result." Departing from the *Keyes* presumption, *Dayton* said federal judges should not use isolated infractions as justification for imposing citywide or district-wide

70. *New York Times*, 28 July 1974, IV, 7:1.

71. *Dayton v. Brinkman*, 433 U.S. 406 (1977), 412, 420, and passim; 443 U.S. 52 (1979), 525n11; *Brinkman v. Gilligan*, 503 F.2d 684 (1974); 518 F.2d 853 (1975); 539 F.2d 1084 (1976).

busing for racial balance. In the North and West, it seemed, busing would be limited. Thanks to *Milliken,* it would not extend into the suburbs. Thanks to *Dayton,* most cities in the region would be spared cross-town busing.[72]

In 1979, however, the Supreme Court adjusted its retreat. In considering a case from Columbus, Ohio, as well as additional litigation from Dayton, the high court allowed district judges to use the *Keyes* presumption, if they wished. Writing in dissent, Justice William Rehnquist noted that the Court had given lower courts such great latitude as to create the possibility that "very different remedies" would be "imposed on similar school systems because of the predilections of individual judges." Finding a metaphor in Roman literature, Rehnquist predicted that such latitude would lead to violations of Cicero's maxim against establishing "one rule in Athens and another in Rome." As it happened, district judges did just that. In the state of Georgia, Athens was required to have busing for racial balance, but Rome was not.[73]

At the end of the 1970s the Supreme Court had moved beyond *Brown.* In southern school districts racial balance was generally required, and busing could be used to achieve the necessary amount of mixing. Elsewhere, depending on the predilections of the judges, busing could be required either for racial balance (if the judge chose to exercise the *Keyes* presumption) or to eliminate the minor, incremental effect of isolated infractions (if the judge favored the Supreme Court's holding in *Dayton*). But the buses did not cross district lines—except in rare instances where outlying districts were guilty of segregation, or in cases where district judges were willing to engage in a sort of brinkmanship with the Supreme Court. After establishing this pattern, the high Court stepped back to see how things would work out. For more than a decade after 1979, the Supreme Court declined to hear cases that involved busing for racial balance.

Meanwhile, civil rights activists who had once demanded freedom had become so enamored of racial balance that they lost sight of *Brown*'s mandate for racial neutrality in student assignments. They demanded compulsory integration, assuming that black students would benefit and whites would not suffer. But was this true? This became a crucial question for a generation of educators, historians, and social scientists. The nation and the Supreme Court awaited the answer.

72. J. Harvie Wilkinson, *From Brown to Bakke* (New York: Oxford University Press, 1979), 246.
73. *Columbus Board of Education v. Penick,* 443 U.S. 449 (1979), 491, 525, 492; *Dayton v. Brinkman,* 443 U.S. 525 (1979).

6

Educational Reform in the 1960s

For many years black students had trailed whites in average academic achievement, a situation that most educators at the time of *Brown v. Board of Education* attributed to poor schools. Although an approximation of "separate but equal" had been achieved by then in some school districts, black children in other areas were still attending schools that were grossly inferior. With the equalization of facilities and with desegregation, many people thought that blacks would have better opportunities, would shed the feelings of inferiority that the Supreme Court had mentioned, and would do better in schoolwork.

James B. Conant and the Education of African Americans

These optimistic assumptions soon came into question. One of the first to express concern was the nation's most prominent educator, James B. Conant. As noted in Chapter 2, Conant's book of 1959, *The American High School Today,* had established his reputation as the nation's most influential school reformer. Conant had recommended that, in order to serve all the children of all the people, small high schools should be consolidated into comprehensive institutions that would have both ability grouping and democratic interaction. Yet Conant had considered the American public schools basically sound and not in need of changes other than consolidation and ability grouping.

Nevertheless, two years later, after taking a closer look at the education of African Americans, Conant reported that "social dynamite" was building up in the schools of the nation's inner cities. He called for decisive action "before it is too late"—a call that could not be ignored because, as the *New York Times* noted, it came from a man who, in his previous reports on the schools, had "earned a nation-wide reputation as a moderate and unemotional school reformer."[1]

In *Slums and Suburbs* (1961), Conant reported that public schools in the inner cities were doing quite well with young African American pupils. Before visiting elementary and middle schools in the nation's ten largest cities, Conant confessed that he had "expected to find blackboard jungles." Instead, he found schools "with high morale, tight discipline, imaginative principals and teachers." In fact, "the outward manifestations of discipline, order, and formal dress" were evident "to a greater degree in the well-run slum schools of a city than they are in the wealthier sections of the same city." The contrast was especially noticeable "between city slum schools and wealthy suburban schools, where informality in dress, deportment, and classroom procedure were the rule."[2]

Unfortunately, Conant reported, at about age twelve many black students lost interest in school. "At that time the 'street' takes over. In terms of schoolwork, progress ceases; indeed many pupils begin to go backward in their studies!" In accounting for the regression, Conant was told "privately even in the North . . . that a colored student on the average is inherently inferior to a white student." Conant nevertheless insisted that "no such generalization has been established, and in my view the difficulties in obtaining evidence that would validate or, for that matter, clearly negate such a position are virtually insurmountable." Rejecting the explanations of scientific racists, Conant approached the question of Negro education "with the background of a one hundred per cent New Englander" whose family tradition was "that of the strong abolitionists." He lamented that "for nearly a hundred years [white Americans] . . . accepted, almost without protest, the transformation of the status of the Negro from that of a slave into that of a member of a lower, quite separate caste." Conant thought the problems in inner-city schools were rooted in this history.[3]

As Conant saw it, one of the worst aspects of American race relations was job discrimination. Finding themselves excluded from many good jobs, a disproportionate number of black men turned to crime, and the situation with respect to the family was also bad. Because black men often earned less than black women, some men decided not to work at all.

1. James B. Conant, *Slums and Suburbs* (New York: McGraw-Hill, 1961), 2; *New York Times*, 17 October 1961, 38.
2. Conant, *Slums and Suburbs*, 23, 22.
3. Ibid., 21, 12, 8, 17–18.

"Racial discrimination on the part of employers and labor unions" had led to "many male Negro floaters." The streets were "full of unemployed men who hang around," and "the number of male *youth* in this category is increasing almost daily." Conant was especially concerned that the lack of good jobs was depressing the ambition of black teenagers. He reported that in "in some slum neighborhoods . . . over half of the boys between sixteen and twenty-one are out of school and out of work."[4]

Meanwhile, black women worked and earned "fairly good wages," but because they received little financial assistance from the fathers of their children, black mothers often moved "with their offspring from one rented room to another . . . and in so doing often go from one elementary school district to another." This made it difficult for many children to do well in school. Conant lamented that about a third of the African American pupils in the inner cities came "from family units (one hesitates to use the word 'home') which had no father, stepfather, or male guardian."[5]

From its first paragraph, *Slums and Suburbs* emphasized a main theme: that "the nature of the community largely determines what goes on in the school." Above all, Conant called for programs that would shore up beleaguered inner-city families. "Enforcement of anti-discrimination laws" was a good place to start, but hardly enough. Conant also recommended a massive public works program that would create 300,000 jobs in the nation's ten largest cities. This would be expensive, but Conant warned that the existing situation was "a menace to the social and political health of the large cities." To improve the quality of inner-city schools there had to be "an improvement in the lives of the families who inhabit the slums," and Conant insisted that little would be accomplished "without a drastic change in the employment prospects for urban Negro youth."[6]

Earlier in the twentieth century, immigrants from Europe had worked their way out of the slums without a public works program, but Conant said that, unlike the earlier era when "unskilled laborers were in demand, . . . today automation has affected the employment scene; there is much less demand for unskilled labor." The situation was especially difficult for African Americans because discrimination had left many with the conviction that it was not possible to work one's way out of poverty. In addition, the foreign immigrants of earlier generations usually came from a "stable society" with "pride of family and often strong church connections." Conant reported that in terms of social setting there was little

4. Ibid., 20, 2.
5. Ibid., 18, 19.
6. Ibid., 1, 20, 39, 2, 147.

resemblance "between the poor city districts of 1900 and those which are the sore spots of our modern cities." For Conant, there was no substitute for massive public works, however expensive such programs might be. These programs were the indispensable prerequisite for improving family life in the inner cities.[7]

In addition to a jobs program, Conant recommended policies that were designed to deal with special problems. "In the slum school," he wrote, "the development of reading skill is obviously of first importance." Conant did not endorse any particular method of teaching reading. He did not side with partisans of either "phonics" or "whole language." But he was "convinced that a common denominator among unsuccessful school children who later become dropouts and perhaps juvenile delinquents is the failure to develop reading skills." Part of the problem was that poor children rarely saw books in their homes, and they "never see anyone read anything—not even newspapers." Therefore, Conant proposed to hire social workers and visiting teachers "to do something with the mothers." This would not be easy, "for the almost illiterate parent may be frightened of anyone officially connected with education." But inducing a parent to take a positive attitude toward schooling would be a first step in the right direction.[8]

Conant also recommended that counseling be improved and vocational education upgraded in the inner cities. Because about half of teenage black boys did not graduate from high school, and only half of those who did graduate managed to find jobs, Conant called for "meaningful courses for pupils with less than average abilities," and especially for "the expansion of work-study programs for slow students." This would "cost money and . . . mean additional staff—at least a doubling of the guidance staff in most of the large cities." But Conant considered the expense necessary to establish "a much closer relationship than now exists among the schools, employers, and labor unions, as well as social agencies and employment offices." He wanted guidance officers and vocational teachers to take responsibility "for following the post–high school careers of youth from the time they leave school until they are twenty-one years of age."[9]

Conant also recommended higher salaries for the teachers and professional staff who worked in inner-city schools. He noted that teachers who had achieved some seniority often transferred "away from slum neighborhoods," leaving the inner-city schools staffed with either new teachers

7. Ibid., 37.
8. Ibid., 23, 56–57, 24, 25.
9. Ibid., 41. *New York Times*, 11 June 1961, E9; 17 October 1961, 35.

or substitute teachers. He recognized that unions generally favored a single pay scale for all teachers, but "the transfer requests speak for themselves." Teachers in the inner cities deserved extra pay because they had especially difficult jobs.[10]

Conant's emphasis was on money. He said "satisfactory education" could be provided, even in predominantly black schools, "through the expenditure of more money for needed staff and facilities." Because many children came to school ill-fed and poorly clothed, he wanted schools to provide meals and clothing. Because many youths had never been exposed to higher culture, he favored field trips to museums and concert halls. He also recommended tutoring and crash programs. And he thought the extra money could be found, if the nation's leaders recognized the gravity of the problem. After all, he said, some wealthy suburbs spent twice as much per student as some inner cities, even though "the pedagogic tasks which confront the teachers in the slum schools are far more difficult than those which their colleagues in the wealthy suburbs face."[11]

Conant's emphasis differed from that of many civil rights activists. Immediately upon publication of *Slums and Suburbs*, the Urban League of Greater New York noted that vocational education had sometimes been a "dumping ground" for Negro students, and also complained that Conant had not condemned *de facto* segregation. The American Jewish Congress emphasized the latter point, saying that Conant "failed to recognize an essential ingredient of the issue—the fact that racial segregation in public schools . . . has a damaging effect on the level of aspiration and educational attainment of minority children." New York's state commissioner of education, James E. Allen, said that schools were "racially imbalanced" if African Americans made up more than 50 percent of the student body, a statement that seemed to suggest that such schools were inferior, regardless of objective educational qualities. Conant later confessed, "the reaction of the outstanding leaders of Negro education disappointed me. They were highly critical. While acknowledging my service in awakening the public conscience, they found my point of view unacceptable. . . . [They] branded me as an advocate of the 'separate but equal' doctrine."[12]

Conant eventually came to think that it had been a mistake to express his belief that through the expenditure of more money a satisfactory edu-

10. Conant, *Slums and Suburbs*, 68.
11. Ibid., 29, 3.
12. *New York Times*, 22 October 1961, 53; 18 October 1961, 37; 23 June 1963, 151; Diane Ravitch, *The Great School Wars* (New York: Basic Books, 1974), 268; James B. Conant, *My Several Lives* (New York: Harper and Row, 1970), 623.

cation could be provided in a mostly or even all-Negro school. In 1961, however, Conant thought the racial imbalance theory had the potential to create a new form of educational racism, for it implied that a white majority was necessary for good schooling. He thought, in addition, that children from the inner cities had special handicaps that needed to be addressed before they could benefit from transfers to middle-class schools. Without remedial treatment, it seemed likely that many black children, if they were sent to schools in predominantly white suburbs, would wind up in segregated subsections of their new schools.

Conant thought it better to educate the children in their home communities, with special programs to compensate for shortcomings in the students' background and with teachers and counselors who were specially trained "to replace the lacking family influence in broken or inadequate homes." Conant condemned *de jure* segregation, which he considered "antithetical to our free society." But he thought it would be "far better for those who are agitating for the deliberate mixing of children to accept *de facto* segregated schools as a consequence of a present housing situation and to work for the improvement of slum schools whether Negro or white."[13]

Conant also mentioned the impracticality of racially balanced integration. Because of the distance between the predominantly black inner cities and the outlying white suburbs, Conant said the "transportation problem" was "quite insoluble." He was dismayed when he considered the amount of time that would be spent in transit in order "to move any appreciable number of white children by bus into what are now Negro schools or to move all the Negro children in a Negro neighborhood into what are now white schools." There was, in addition, the likelihood that many parents would resist any plan "for moving large groups of young children around a city for the sake of mixing." From the tone of his discussion, Conant conveyed the impression that he personally found it distasteful to "move children about as though they were pawns on a chessboard."[14]

In retrospect, many of Conant's comments seem prescient. At the time, however, *Slums and Suburbs* damaged Conant's reputation as an educational reformer. Because he questioned busing for racial balance and thought it possible to establish good schools in black communities, some reformers considered Conant little better than a sophisticated segregationist. "I had become *persona non grata*," Conant admitted.[15]

13. Ibid.; Conant, *Slums and Suburbs*, 29, 31; *New York Times*, 8 September 1963, E9.
14. Conant, *Slums and Suburbs*, 29, 31.
15. Conant, *My Several Lives*, 623.

Attitude Adjustments

Integrationists were not Conant's only critics. Others complained that *Slums and Suburbs* showed scant sympathy for inner-city children and their families. Conant seemed to evince attitudes that were patronizing if not contemptuous. He doubtless meant well. He had used the word *slum* because he wanted to convey the nature and gravity of educational problems in the inner city. For the same reason, he called attention to the problems of inner-city families—and he did so four years before the publication of Daniel Patrick Moynihan's controversial report, *The Negro Family*. Nevertheless, candor left Conant open to criticism from those who said that, "while there may be aspects of the [inner-city] culture . . . that would be better changed, it is necessary for the educator to work within the framework of the culture as it exists." To some observers it seemed that Conant lacked a sympathetic, noncondescending, understanding of the culture of the underprivileged.[16]

The Culturally Deprived Child (1962), by Frank Riessman, a psychologist at Bard College, was a widely read expression of this criticism. The very title of this book was itself insensitive—"very bad" and "entirely inappropriate," Riessman later conceded, especially for a book that blamed "priggish" teachers for failing to develop an "empathetic understanding" of the culture of lower-class black students. A revised version was eventually published under the title *The Inner-City Child*. There would be no progress, Riessman insisted, unless middle-class teachers developed "a different point of view." Inner-city youths knew they belonged to a despised group, and they quickly turned against teachers who manifested even a semblance of patronizing condescension. They refused to be "disrespected" ("dissed"). They would not cooperate with anyone who considered the style of the inner city deviant or inferior.[17]

Riessman conceded that few inner-city teachers were "white-color" racists. They wanted to help their students. But many were "white-collar" bigots. They stressed the liabilities of the underprivileged and believed that assimilating middle-class values was an essential prerequisite for upward mobility. In the process, middle-class teachers often alienated lower-class students. Riessman maintained that teachers could not teach effectively unless they established rapport with their sensitive pupils, and they could not do this without recognizing the strengths of inner-city culture.

16. Frank Riessman, *The Culturally Deprived Child* (New York: Harper and Row, 1962), 3, 2.

17. Ibid., 8, 16, xi, 24; Frank Riessman, *The Inner-City Child* (New York: Harper and Row, 1976), 1, x.

Black English admittedly differed from standard English, but it was also "vivid and expressive" and often superior to "the turgid prose of text-books." "The idealized construct of the independent, male-dominated nu-clear family" might be appropriate for middle- and upper-class neigh-borhoods, but teachers should understand that matriarchal, extended families were not necessarily dysfunctional in the inner city but rather were realistic adaptations to discrimination and poverty.[18]

Riessman thought urban teachers would also benefit from understand-ing the peculiarities of the inner-city style of learning. He counseled against "progressive approaches," saying that in the inner cities there was "practically no interest in knowledge for its own sake," and little concern for "self-expression, self-realization, growth, and the like." Underprivi-leged students were more oriented toward practical knowledge and vo-cational training. Riessman also recommended that inner-city teachers take account of the fact that their students were hyperkinetic ("much more physical or motoric"). Lessons should not require students to sit still and listen but should be designed to appeal to "the deprived child's love of action." Teachers should allow for "role playing" and other forms of in-teraction and movement. Such techniques were "uniquely appropriate for culturally deprived children and should be used as springboards for stim-ulating thinking."[19]

It was hard not to sympathize with Riessman's purpose. He said the ed-ucation of urban students could be improved if teachers recognized the cultural strengths that already existed in inner cities and if they used ap-propriate educational approaches. Riessman may have oversimplified the situation, and perhaps he had too much faith in what schools could ac-complish. But his work was well-intentioned and offered hope to those who were frustrated by the failure to do more for inner-city students.

Riessman's *Culturally Deprived Child* also shifted responsibility away from the attitudes that prevailed in the students' homes and neighbor-hoods and instead blamed the teachers for the low scores that inner-city students made on standard tests of reading and arithmetic. Kenneth B. Clark followed up in 1963, maintaining that the attitudes of teachers in-fluenced the self-image, academic aspirations, and achievements of black students. Then, in *Dark Ghetto,* a book of 1965, Clark criticized earlier writ-ers for incorrectly blaming inner-city children and their backgrounds for the widespread academic retardation in ghetto schools. Inner-city teach-ers and schools were responsible for the low achievement of their stu-

18. Riessman, *Culturally Deprived Child,* 20, xi; Riessman, *Inner-City Child,* 34.
19. Riessman, *Culturally Deprived Child,* 12–13, 32–33.

dents, Clark insisted. "[Black] children, by and large, do not learn because they are not being taught effectively and they are not being taught because those who are charged with the responsibility of teaching them do not believe that they can learn, do not expect that they can learn, and do not act toward them in ways which help them to learn." Teachers who focused on the deficiencies of the students' families and neighborhoods were offering an "alibi." They were "making the victims of poor education into its agents."[20]

A new conventional wisdom gradually emerged. Previously, it had been assumed that teachers assessed students on the basis of the students' work in school. But in the 1960s educational reformers increasingly said that the biases of middle-class teachers caused minority students to do poorly in school. The work of Harvard psychologist Robert Rosenthal and San Francisco school principal Lenore Jacobson was especially influential in establishing this view. "Kenneth Clark and others have been saying for a long time that some children are victims of educational self-fulfilling prophecies," Rosenthal told a reporter. "But they just haven't been able to come up with data to prove it. We think we have."[21]

Rosenthal and Jacobson's data came from a low-income school in San Francisco, where they told teachers that IQ tests had identified certain students as late bloomers who could be expected to experience an intellectual growth spurt. But the students thus identified had actually been selected at random, and the experiment had been designed to determine whether teachers expected more from students who had been identified as "potential academic spurters," whether such expectations would lead to differential treatment, and whether such treatment would cause students to do better in school. Rosenthal and Jacobson answered all three questions in the affirmative. "When teachers expected that certain children would show greater intellectual development, those children did show greater intellectual development."[22]

Rosenthal and Jacobson's study was remarkable. Without any enrichment programs or special tutoring, they reported, disadvantaged minority children made astonishing gains. The only variable was the teachers'

20. Kenneth B. Clark, "Educational Stimulation of Racially Disadvantaged Children," in A. Harry Passow, ed., *Education in Depressed Areas* (New York: Teachers College Press, 1963), 142–62; Kenneth B. Clark, *Dark Ghetto* (New York: Harper and Row, 1965), 131; Helen Gouldner, *Teachers' Pets, Troublemakers, and Nobodies: Black Children in Elementary School* (Westport, Conn.: Greenwood Press, 1978), 8.

21. *New York Times*, 8 August 1967, 1.

22. Robert Rosenthal and Lenore F. Jacobson, *Pygmalion in the Classroom: Teacher Expectation and Pupils' Intellectual Development* (New York: Holt, Rinehart and Winston, 1968), 82.

attitudes. Rosenthal and Jacobson entitled their book *Pygmalion in the Classroom*, because the situation reminded them of George Bernard Shaw's play, *Pygmalion*, in which a professor of linguistics and elocution succeeded in teaching a young woman from the slums to speak proper English—because the professor was convinced of his ability to do so, and because he conveyed that conviction to the woman.

Pygmalion in the Classroom came in for criticism in professional journals, and subsequent scholars have not been able to replicate the findings consistently. Nevertheless, the book received enormous publicity, perhaps because it offered assurance that the racial achievement gap could be closed if only teachers would change their expectations. "The power of stereotypes may explain the persistent gap between black and white kids," an article in *Newsweek* stated. A report in the *New York Times* cited the book as evidence "supporting the common thesis that many children, particularly minority-group children, turn out dull because their teachers expect them to be dull."[23]

A team of ethnographic researchers from Washington University also emphasized the importance of teachers' expectations. Financed by a grant from the U.S. Office of Education, these researchers spent about 500 hours observing the situation in kindergarten, first-grade, and second-grade classrooms in four St. Louis schools, and 270 hours visiting the homes of twenty-eight students. As reported by Helen Gouldner and Ray C. Rist, the observations led to an indictment of inner-city teachers. Most students failed to acquire "even the ordinary beginning skills" because the teachers "had decided quite openly . . . to teach only a very few of their pupils and not to teach the rest of them." The teachers then excused their neglect of the majority, saying "that poverty and disorganized homes are the source of educational failure" and that "there is really very little a teacher can do."[24]

A summary cannot convey the breadth of Gouldner and Rist's indictments. They reported that by the eighth day of school, kindergarten children had been divided into groups—not on the basis of objective tests of academic readiness but according to the teachers' perceptions of middle-class propriety. If the youngsters were dressed neatly and came from two-parent families, with at least one parent employed, the children would be

23. Samuel S. Wineburg, "The Self-Fulfillment of the Self-Fulfilling Prophecy," *Educational Researcher* 16 (December 1987): 28–37; Abigail Thernstrom and Stephan Thernstrom, *No Excuses: Closing the Racial Gap in Learning* (New York: Simon and Schuster, 2003), 195; *Newsweek*, 6 November 2000, 66; *New York Times*, 8 August 1967, 8.
24. Gouldner, *Teachers' Pets*, 17, 97, 137; Ray C. Rist, *The Urban School: A Factory for Failure* (Cambridge: Massachusetts Institute of Technology Press, 1973), 142–43.

placed in one group. If the youngsters came from female-headed welfare families, and especially if their clothing was disheveled or soiled, they would be placed in another group. The teachers would then devote far more time to teaching the first group, with the predictable result that by the end of kindergarten the "teachers' pets" were ahead of the others in readiness for reading. The separation was then extended when objective tests were administered at the end of the kindergarten year. The favoritism continued during the first and second grades and was rationalized with still more test scores.[25]

Disciplinary policies also differed. According to Gouldner and Rist, the teachers in the four St. Louis schools, all of whom were black, did not just devote more time to groups designated as "fast learners." They also adopted a repressive style of classroom management. Unlike many white teachers in upscale suburban schools, the inner-city teachers would not allow students to get out of their seats, wander around the room, and speak with other children. Sometimes suburban teachers embraced their students, and they often spoke sympathetically to a child. In the suburbs, teachers seemed "almost afraid of hurting a young child's feelings." By way of contrast, teachers in the inner city acted like "drill sergeant[s]." They insisted on "silence in the classrooms and halls and . . . tight control over the children." "There was no letup in the strict, punitive treatment of [inner-city] children."[26]

From the outset some black teachers were opposed to allowing the researchers in their classrooms. They recognized that systematic observations by outside witnesses might advance the careers of the visitors from Washington University, but they asked, "What are you going to do to really help these children and not just help yourself?" They also knew the researchers came from the world of educational sociology, a world that was not only predominantly white but also progressive in its child-rearing practices and left-of-center in political orientation. The black teachers therefore assumed that the researchers would be "soft on the children" and would not understand "why the [inner-city] teachers needed to be strict disciplinarians." They feared that the researchers would scorn the teachers as lower-middle class and *petit bourgeois*. They expected "another of 'those' books condemning ghetto schools."[27]

The fears and expectations were realized. Ray C. Rist's book *The Urban*

---

25. Gouldner, *Teachers' Pets*; Rist, *Urban School*; Ray C. Rist, "Student Social Class and Teacher Expectations: The Self-Fulfilling Prophecy in Ghetto Education," *Harvard Educational Review* 40 (August 1970): 411–51.

26. Gouldner, *Teachers' Pets*, 2, 25, 35, 37, 29.

27. Ibid., 22–23.

School: A Factory for Failure (1973) evinced not just a lack of sympathy but scorn for inner-city teachers. Their middle-class biases were responsible for the failure of lower-class black children. Although these black teachers thought they were trying to uplift their fellow African Americans, they were in fact traitors to their race. They were complicit "in the perpetuation of an unjust system." They were agents of the larger society, working "to ensure that proper 'social distance' was maintained between the various strata." The inner-city teachers were victims of false consciousness. They mistakenly subscribed to "the 'culture of poverty' notion, . . . that children fail because of the environmental obstacles they face in their homes and poverty-stricken communities." Because the inner-city teachers believed "the ghetto community inhibited the development of middle-class success models," they considered it their "duty to 'save' at least one group of children from the 'streets.'" Middle-class black children had to be segregated from the lower orders "to ensure that [they] would not be so influenced that they themselves become enticed with the 'streets' and lose their apparent opportunity for future middle-class status."[28]

Helen Gouldner was scarcely less critical. In her book *Teachers' Pets, Troublemakers, and Nobodies* (1978), she described inner-city teachers as "gatekeepers" who had to choose "between helping selected promising individuals and spreading scarce resources among the many." The teachers thought most urban families "provided such a bad environment for the children that it was hopeless for the school to counteract this." They therefore "felt they were justified in putting most of their time into teaching those children whose potential for learning seemed self-evident." To minimize the attraction of "the streets," middle-class teachers also encouraged children in the high groups to ridicule and belittle their fellow students, "to lord it over children in the low groups."[29]

The observations of the ethnographic researchers may have been distorted, but they reinforced belief in the Pygmalion effect. Although some researchers could not replicate the effect, educators increasingly came to attribute low student achievement to the expectations of teachers. According to Paul Vance, a superintendent of schools in Washington, D.C., "Research clearly reveals that students rise to the expectations that are set by their teachers and school." "Many black students miss the joy of learning because their teachers do not think them capable of it," journalist Sam Fullwood agreed. "Too many educators send signals—sometimes blatant

---

28. Rist, *Urban School*, 20, 7; Rist, "Student Social Class," 444, 446.
29. Gouldner, *Teachers' Pets*, 134, 12, 57.

and overt, but more often subtle and unconscious—to black students that they do not belong where learning is taking place." The Department of Education, which had funded the research of Gouldner and Rist, chimed in, saying that minority students often received "less encouragement [from] teachers who may harbor doubts about their abilities and thereby contribute to a self-fulfilling prophecy of underachievement."[30]

It was extraordinary for liberal white academics to have been so critical of black teachers who were working with minority students in the inner cities. But the ethnographic observations were interpreted to suit the zeitgeist of the late 1960s and 1970s. Against the background of the war in Vietnam and race riots in the cities, respect for established authorities declined and the schools came under attack. Dozens of writers were criticizing American teachers and schools—not just black teachers and schools—for being undemocratic, oppressive institutions. Marxist writers accused the schools of regimenting and sorting children to shore up an unjust social order. Neoprogressives found fault with the schools for being preoccupied with order and control, for being "grim joyless places" concerned above all with "docility and conformity." Other writers on the left said that, contrary to what many people believed, the schools did not foster social and economic mobility. They instead legitimized inequality—by appearing to offer the opportunity to succeed through education, and thus persuading students to blame themselves rather than the system if they failed to move ahead. The critics said the major function of the schools was to disguise "the 'oppressive' features of an undemocratic society." Teachers who "seemed to be helping the needy were only pacifying them and neutralizing their discontent."[31]

Community Control

While some white scholars emphasized class conflict, many blacks embraced a racialist perspective. This was especially apparent in Ocean Hill–Brownsville, the New York City district that became the most publicized example of the community control movement of the late 1960s and 1970s.

30. *Washington Post*, 6 December 2001, T3; Thernstrom and Thernstrom, *No Excuses*, 194; *Cleveland Plain Dealer*, 4 September 2000, 1B; National Center for Education Statistics, *Paving the Way to Postsecondary Education* (Washington: Department of Education, 2001), 9.

31. Diane Ravitch, *The Revisionists Revised: A Critique of the Radical Attack on the Schools* (New York: Basic Books, 1978), 3, 128, and passim; Ravitch, *The Troubled Crusade: American Education, 1945–1980* (New York: Basic Books, 1983), 246–47.

Here, as in many inner cities, the average achievement of African American and Puerto Rican children lagged behind that of white students. More than 70 percent of black students were below grade level in reading, and 85 percent in math. Yet, although nonwhites made up 95 percent of the population in Ocean Hill–Brownsville, most of the teachers were white. To complicate the situation, many of the white teachers in the district moved to mostly white schools as soon as they satisfied a union rule that allowed teachers to transfer after accumulating five years of service. "This stripped black-majority schools of teachers just as they were beginning to mature professionally."[32]

Although many of New York's black leaders initially had favored integrated education, after 1965 a preference for the community-centered approach was evident in many black neighborhoods. This preference coincided with the popularity of "black power" and its emphasis on building institutions in the black community. To the surprise of some, many business corporations also favored community control, believing that it offered social peace. The Ford Foundation threw its influence behind community control, and so did the *New York Times.* Community control also gained the support of the white New Left and was especially attractive to black intellectuals and activists. "By 1966 . . . a coalition of government, business, and media elites, white leftist intellectuals, radical teachers, and black activists and educators, had, for diverse reasons, formed around the idea of community control of education in black neighborhoods."[33]

Advocates of community control took exception to a merit system that had led, by the mid-1960s, to a situation where only 8 percent of the teachers, 2.5 percent of the supervisors, and 1 percent of the principals in New York City were black, although black youths by then constituted 30 percent of all students. Under a system that had been developed by the central school board and the mostly white teachers' union, the United Federation of Teachers (UFT), prospective teachers were required to graduate from college and pass a teachers' certification examination. To achieve tenure or to become a department head or school administrator, teachers had to take additional graduate courses and pass still more tests.[34]

The UFT conceded that individual tests could be improved but considered the test system basically fair. Supporters of community control, on the other hand, wanted to eliminate the examination requirements for hiring and promotion. It was all right, advocates of community control said,

32. Jerald E. Podair, *The Strike That Changed New York: Blacks, Whites, and the Ocean Hill–Brownsville Crisis* (New Haven: Yale University Press, 4, 16, 18, 19.

33. Podair, *Strike,* 5, 25, 32, 39–41, 42.

34. Ibid., 51, 92, 9, 87, 155.

to require that prospective teachers must be college graduates who had received a teaching certificate. But placements and promotions should depend on performance on the job and service to the community. Mindful of the students' low test scores, community controllers purportedly wanted "to rescue pupils from the stultifying grip of the white civil service bureaucracy." The UFT, however, said that community control would lead to teachers being "hired and fired not on the basis of educational competence, but on the basis of race, political conformity to parochial community prejudices, and favoritism."[35]

A brewing controversy came to a head in 1968, one year after the schools of Ocean Hill–Brownsville had become part of a Ford Foundation–funded experiment that created autonomous local boards of education in a few of the poorest school districts. The governing board in Ocean Hill–Brownsville then voted to end the employment of eighteen white teachers and supervisors (and one black who was mistakenly thought to be white). Later the local board also removed more than three hundred additional teachers who walked out in protest against what the board had done. The governing board also appointed several African Americans and one Puerto Rican as principals in Ocean Hill–Brownsville, even though their names were not on the list of those who had taken and passed the required examination. At the time, only four blacks were listed among the almost one thousand candidates on the elementary school principals' eligibility list.[36]

In its rush to provide more jobs for African Americans, the local board did not hold hearings, saying that the white teachers were simply being transferred or reassigned to other schools. Yet the UFT held that involuntary transfers were punitive and therefore required submission of charges and an impartial hearing. When evidence was belatedly presented to Judge Francis E. Rivers, who happened to be a black man, the judge ruled that the white teachers and supervisors were entitled to keep their jobs, finding that they had been singled out for retaliation, not because of incompetence but because they had criticized the idea of community control. Judge Rivers held that due process required that tenured teachers not be deprived of their jobs except for cause and with a hearing.[37]

When the local school board disregarded Judge Rivers' report as merely advisory, the UFT called a strike, and fifty-four thousand of New York's fifty-seven thousand public school teachers heeded the call. Eventually

35. Diane Ravitch, "Community Control Revisited," *Commentary* 53 (February 1972); 69; Podair, *Strike*, 93.

36. Podair, *Strike*, 1–2, 74–76, 231n33.

37. Ibid., 114–15; Ravitch, *Great School Wars*, 354–55, 358–59.

there were several strikes and complicated negotiations that have been described elsewhere.[38] Denying Mayor John Lindsay's charge that the strike was racially motivated, union president Albert Shanker insisted that it was about due process protections for teachers. If a white school board reassigned a black teacher arbitrarily, Shanker said, the union would support the teacher. "This is a strike to protect black teachers against white racists in white communities and white teachers against black racists in black communities."[39]

The strike was suspended when Mayor Lindsay offered assurance that the white teachers could return to their positions. Yet in Ocean Hill–Brownsville, the local board was adamant. "We do not want the teachers to return to this district," the board declared in one statement. When the returning teachers reported for work, they had to force their way through angry crowds. Once they entered their schools, they were told to attend orientation sessions, and as one group walked into the auditorium at Independent School 55, "approximately fifty community residents, most from the Brooklyn branch of CORE, surrounded them, brandishing sticks and bandoliers of bullets. While the men cursed the teachers, threw the bullets at them, and threatened to 'carry you out in pine boxes,' [the top local administrator] quietly observed the scene, offering no assistance to the frightened educators." After students attacked several white teachers at Junior High School 271, the school principal "herded them into a locked classroom for their safety. Police rescued them later in the afternoon."[40]

These scenes impressed some observers as a reversal of Little Rock, with black mobs now surrounding white teachers, but the union insisted it would not be intimidated by what UFT president Shanker called "a primitive type of tribalism." Because a disproportionately large number of the teachers were Jewish, as were the leaders of the UFT, the dispute also smacked of anti-Semitism. The local African-American Teachers Association (A-ATA) called for the separation of black and white teachers in cafeterias and lounges, and one leader of the group read aloud a student's poem dedicated to Shanker. The poem began, "Hey, Jew boy, with that yarmulke on your head / You pale faced Jew boy—I wish you were dead."[41]

The strike ended in November 1968, when the white teachers were re-

38. See especially Podair, *Strike*; Ravitch, *Great School Wars*; and Martin Mayer, *The Teachers Strike: New York, 1968* (New York: Harper and Row, 1969).

39. Podair, *Strike*, 115–16.

40. Ibid., 117.

41. Ibid., 44; Richard D. Kahlenberg, "Hire Education," *Washington Monthly*, January/February 2003, 56.

instated. At first it seemed as if the UFT had received most of what it wanted from the settlement. "The union won the right to return its members to the classrooms of Ocean Hill–Brownsville, as well as strong procedural protection for the future." But a form of decentralization persisted in New York, and eventually the community controllers also got much of what they had wanted. "The requirements for principal selection were revised to permit greater community involvement and the use of on-the-job performance tests," and "by the mid-1970s, 15 percent of the supervisors in the city's schools were members of minority groups, five times as many as had been in the system ten years earlier." In addition, by the 1990s, the public schools of New York had incorporated much of the multicultural curriculum and many noncompetitive hiring policies that community controllers had favored in 1968.[42]

The controversy in Ocean Hill–Brownsville would not have been so emotional at the time, or so significant in retrospect, if it had been merely a dispute over providing more jobs for blacks or protecting workers' rights. Its importance derives, at least in part, from the fact that the two sides had different opinions with regard to a basic question. Why did the academic achievement levels of blacks lag behind those of whites? Most teachers attributed the low test scores to disinterested students and parents, while most people in the community blamed disengaged teachers, especially white teachers. "Each side blamed the other for the poor performance of most black students. White teachers blamed black families and communities; black parents blamed the teachers and the schools."[43]

Many residents of Ocean Hill–Brownsville took exception to the teachers for allegedly "shift[ing] the blame for academic failure away from the school and teacher and toward the pupil's family and community." Thus Rhody McCoy, the top administrator in the district during the height of the controversy over community control, said that most white teachers, "for all their protests about supporting civil rights and admiring Martin Luther King, didn't believe in the ability of a black child to learn just as well as a white one." Elaine Rooke, the president of the Parent-Teacher Association at Junior High School 271, also accused the white teachers of having "bad attitudes." "They don't live in the neighborhood," Rooke complained, "and they rush out of the school and the neighborhood before three o'clock." Although Rooke conceded that white teachers rarely used overtly racist language, she said the teachers were "condescending

42. Ravitch, *Great School Wars*, 376–78; Podair, *Strike*, 151.
43. Podair, *Strike*, 19; Steve Golin, review of *The Strike That Changed New York*, *Journal of American History*, March 2004, 1539.

and patronizing toward black children." The teachers seemed to think that their middle- class way of life was superior to the customs that prevailed in Ocean Hill–Brownsville.[44]

In expressing these views, McCoy and Rooke were reiterating some of the points that psychologist Frank Riessman had discussed in *The Culturally Deprived Child*. They were emphasizing the importance of *respect*, saying that lower-class black children would do better in school if their middle-class teachers were more sympathetic and understanding. Residents of Ocean Hill–Brownsville said the teachers needed to change their ways, to become less "bourgeois," to transcend their "9 to 3 . . . then go home" culture. According to the African-American Teachers Association, the white teachers did not identify with the community in which they worked. They liked their jobs "because of the nice salaries, health plans, and medical coverage." Their "greatest joy" was "the security of the job." Residents of Ocean Hill–Brownsville thought black children were not learning because they were not being taught effectively; and they were not being taught effectively because teachers lacked sympathy for and confidence in their students and were not committed to inner-city communities.[45]

Although the UFT teachers were reinstated at the end of the 1968 strikes, over the next decades the local community gained more control over its schools. In time many white teachers moved to schools in more welcoming communities. More blacks and more residents of Ocean Hill–Brownsville were then hired as teachers, and newly hired white teachers adopted more positive attitudes. "If [students] think you like them, they respond a lot better," said one of the new teachers. Another attributed the success of his class to positive expectations, saying, "I decided mine was gong to be the brightest class and that's just what happened." In a newspaper advertisement, a group of new teachers declared: "We approach the children with an expectation of success which we communicate to them and to which they are responding." With community control, the schools also implemented many educational innovations: a new reading program that emphasized cooperative learning, Montessori-type kindergartens, Afro-American studies centers, and extensive employment of community residents as teachers' aides.[46]

For a while, the educational results seemed to be positive. After visiting Ocean Hill–Brownsville, the literary critic Alfred Kazin, who himself

44. Podair, *Strike*, 55, 4, 75, 76.
45. Ibid., 65, 171; Clark, *Dark Ghetto*, 129 ff.
46. Podair, *Strike*, 169; Ravitch, "Community Control Revisited," 69.

had attended school there when the district had been one of poor Jewish immigrants, assured readers of the *New York Times* that "the holy flame of learning" still "burns hotter than ever." Another visitor, the writer Dwight McDonald, returned from Ocean Hill impressed by "the friendly, serious, relaxed atmosphere" of the new teachers. Writing in the *Village Voice*, Nat Hentoff predicted a substantial rise in achievement. "I have no idea how many of [the new teachers] are fully licensed," Hentoff wrote, "and I don't think it matters in view of their attitude toward the children."[47]

Unfortunately, the overall quality of schoolwork, as measured by the performance of students on standard tests, did not improve. In 1971 historian Diane Ravitch reported that the average reading level had declined in all Ocean Hill–Brownsville schools during the four years since the experiment in community control had begun. By the early 1970s most measures of social and economic distress, including unemployment, crime, welfare assistance, and drug addiction, had also worsened. Dismayed by an academic failure that persisted for decades, in 1996 the state legislature put an end to community control and recentralized the public schools of New York City.[48]

Jerald E. Podair, the author of an able monograph, has perceptively explored the perceptual gulf that separated blacks and whites in Ocean Hill–Brownsville. Clearly, there were different explanations for the poor performance of most inner-city students, and many blacks and whites also differed in cultural values and styles. Yet an emphasis on differing "racial cultures" can obscure some key points even as it illuminates others. Clarence Taylor, the author of another able book, has concluded, "placing this confrontation into the context of a cultural war . . . is a misreading of history. African American and Puerto Rican parents were not fighting over culture; they were fighting to ensure their children a quality education."[49]

Demands for community control stemmed essentially from the public schools' failure to teach most black children to read and write, or to add and subtract, as competently as their white counterparts. This was the crucial factor that led many African Americans to believe that black teachers and principals should replace white ones. The fact that black students did not do any better in other cities with mostly or all-black staffs did not dis-

---

47. Ravitch, "Community Control Revisited," 69–70.
48. Ibid., 74; Podair, *Strike*, 152.
49. Ibid.; Clarence Taylor, review of *The Strike That Changed New York, Journal of African American History*, fall 1974, 376; Taylor, *Knocking at Our Own Door: Milton A. Galamison and the Struggle to Integrate New York City Schools* (New York: Columbia University Press, 1997).

suade community controllers, who suspected that there was a relationship between the dominance of middle-class white teachers and the relatively low academic achievement in Ocean Hill. Parents in the community were desperate. They wanted their children to have a good education, and they were willing to try almost anything to improve the public schools. If one "reform" did not work, they would try another. Thus the Reverend Milton Galamison, who previously had favored integration as the best method for improving the education of blacks, embraced community control in 1968 out of a sense that "something had to change, or an entire generation of black school children would be lost." And Rhody McCoy became the unit administrator in Ocean Hill–Brownsville because he thought that removing white teachers might be "a way to do something about the educational catastrophe he saw developing in the city's black community."[50]

Others supported community control for the jobs. Community control began during the era of President Lyndon B. Johnson's "war on poverty." Yet, as historian Gareth Davies has emphasized, the Johnson administration substituted a "service strategy" for the "public works" plan of President Franklin D. Roosevelt's New Deal. Instead of employing large numbers of unemployed men on government construction projects (as James B. Conant had recommended), the Johnson administration emphasized the importance of community services. It employed a legion of social workers to assist poor people. Some were teachers who worked with preschoolers in Head Start programs. Others were teachers' assistants who helped with reading and other school subjects. Still others were counselors in offices and centers that were established to compensate for family problems—alcoholism, drug addiction, spousal abuse, child neglect.[51]

Social workers also engaged in what was called "consciousness raising." A popular opinion at the time held that poor people suffered from defeatist attitudes—that they did not take jobs because they lacked confidence in their ability to control their futures, and thus saw no prospect of working their way out of poverty. To combat a sense of helplessness, and to instill a belief in poor people's ability to affect their future, social workers emphasized the importance of developing "assertiveness." They provided sports programs and cultural events and also organized rent strikes against slumlords and protests against police brutality. Getting rid

50. Ibid., 33, 4; Christopher Jencks, "Private Schools for Black Children," *New York Times*, 3 November 1968, 28ff.
51. Gareth Davies, *From Opportunity to Entitlement: The Transformation and Decline of Great Society Liberalism* (Lawrence: University Press of Kansas, 1996).

of the stigma of welfare also became a deliberate goal. Behind "community action" lurked two vague but inconsistent theories. For some officials in the Johnson administration, the goal was to alter deep-seated cultural patterns, to enable poor people to take advantage of opportunities by thinking and behaving like middle-class citizens. Many social workers, on the other hand, were contemptuous of middle-class values, celebrated what one black scholar called "the magnificent sexual vitality and sensualism of the underclass Negroes," and encouraged poor people to regard welfare as an entitlement.[52]

Civil rights leaders embraced many of these views. In 1966 George Wiley founded the National Welfare Rights Organization (NWRO), which lobbied for the expansion of welfare as a right. Insisting that income should be redistributed without any reciprocal obligation on the part of the recipients, the NWRO said a work requirement would be "an act of political repression . . . a flagrant example of institutional racism." Shirley Chisholm, the black congresswoman from Ocean Hill–Brownsville, similarly compared "compulsory work qualifications" with "involuntary servitude." Whitney Young of the National Urban League criticized proposals that distinguished between "the working [and] nonworking poor." And Martin Luther King asserted, "the solution to poverty is to abolish it directly by a now widely discussed measure: the guaranteed income." Under this proposal, the government would provide families with "a minimum—and *livable*—income," with no work required in return.[53]

Yet support for such ideas was limited. Civil rights activists embraced the concept, as did social workers, the intellectual class, and some members of the administrations of presidents Lyndon B. Johnson and Richard M. Nixon. But most Americans scoffed at the prospect of simply giving a living wage to able-bodied people. Political reality consequently militated against the guaranteed annual income. The most that could be obtained was a combination of welfare spending and the employment of thousands of people, not just social workers but also rank-and-file residents of many communities. One of the slogans of the "war on poverty" called for "maximum feasible participation" by poor people themselves.

52. Allison Davis, *Leadership, Love, and Aggression* (New York: Harcourt Brace Jovanovich, 1983), 115.

53. Steven F. Hayward, *The Age of Reagan* (New York: Prima Publishing, Forum, 2001), 239; Gareth Davis, *From Opportunity to Entitlement*, 211–33; Martin Luther King Jr., *Where Do We Go from Here: Chaos or Community?* (New York: Harper and Row, 1967), 162, 189.

Against this background, community control of the schools in Ocean Hill–Brownsville, and in many other places, became a *de facto* jobs program. Thousands of community residents were employed as teachers' aides, security guards, cafeteria staff, and maintenance workers. In addition, local contractors received favorable treatment when it came to providing the schools with supplies and needed repairs. Community control helped some people in the competition for jobs and contracts. This was yet another reason why disputes over community control became so heated.

Critics of local control later noted that spending per pupil in many inner cities was well above the statewide average, and sometimes as high as the amount spent in wealthy suburbs. In explaining the failure to improve student scores on standard tests, the critics then blamed local authorities for inefficiency—for hiring too many paraprofessionals and cafeteria staffers, and for not getting the most for the money spent for supplies and repairs. In some instances, the critics eventually abolished local control—by recentralizing the administration of schools, as in New York City, or by arranging for the state education department to take over inner-city schools, as happened in Newark, New Jersey.[54]

Community-controlled schools were not models of efficiency, but this critique seems wide of the mark. It might have been better if more people from the community had been employed as maintenance workers rather than as teachers' aides, and efficient workers are obviously better than those who are inefficient. Nevertheless, just as it is difficult not to sympathize with community residents who wanted to try a new educational experiment when old methods were not working well, so it is understandable that community schools would give local people as many jobs as possible—especially when so many local residents had difficulty providing food for their families.

Middle-class reformers had long lamented the inefficiency of using schools to provide jobs for needy workers. They had done so in the nineteenth century when public schools padded their payrolls to give jobs to immigrants from Europe. And they continued to do so in the civil rights era, when most of the African American and Hispanic workers were women who were hired as classroom aides or cafeteria helpers. The reformers complained about "patronage" and "meddling ward heelers" who decided "who gets to be a substitute teacher." But often these women were the only employees who actually lived near the school, and the only

54. *New York Times*, 23 July 1994, 1.

employees whose children attended schools in the community. One may wish that the private labor market had provided good paying jobs for these workers. Yet that was not the case, and school jobs came to play an important social role in minority communities.[55]

The Coleman Report, 1966

Section 402 of the 1964 Civil Rights Act provided one million dollars for a survey of educational inequalities, and Congress instructed the researchers to report on "the lack of availability of equal educational opportunities for individuals by reason of race [or] color." According to Alexander Mood, the director of the statistical center at the federal Office of Education, it was assumed "that schools in the cores of cities and in the rural South are inferior in terms of class size, teacher training, enrichment and remedial programs, and per pupil expenditures." Some people wondered if the researchers would not belabor the obvious, but Mood defended the project, saying that more needed to be known about "the relative importance of these things." "We're going to do some pretty sophisticated statistical analysis to identify them," he said. As it happened, the research was so comprehensive and of such high quality that it superseded all previous wok on school desegregation. Entitled *Equality of Educational Opportunity* and popularly known as "the Coleman report" for its principal author, James S. Coleman, then a professor of educational sociology at Johns Hopkins University, the study presented detailed information on 4,000 schools and test results from 570,000 students and 60,000 teachers. The report was of especially high quality because Coleman was the foremost mathematical sociologist of his age. His sophisticated statistical analysis of the quantitative information was evident on page after page.[56]

The Coleman report reinforced one aspect of conventional thinking. The evidence showed that the races were still educated apart from one another. Eighty percent of all white pupils in the first and twelfth grades attended schools that were from 90 to 100 percent white; while 65 percent of all African American first graders attended schools that were at least 90

55. Richard Rothstein, "The Other Role for the Schools," *New York Times*, 12 June 2002, B8.

56. Public Law 88–352 (1964); *New York Times*, 2 September 1965, 21; James S. Coleman et al., *Equality of Educational Opportunity* (Washington: Government Printing Office, 1966).

percent black, and 48 percent of black high school seniors attended schools that were at least half black.[57]

In another respect, however, the data contradicted the conventional wisdom. At the outset of the research, Coleman had predicted, "the study will show the difference in the quality of schools that the average Negro child and the average white child are exposed to." Speaking to a reporter, Coleman had said: "You know yourself that the difference is going to be striking. And even though everybody knows there is a lot of difference between suburban and inner city schools, once the statistics are there in black and white, they will have a lot more impact." Yet to Coleman's surprise, when the data were assembled they indicated that by 1966 there was substantial equality in facilities and other measurable resources at majority-black and majority-white schools. Although there were regional variations, with schools in the South less generously funded than schools in other sections, neither race suffered when it came to average expenditure per student, the size of the classes, the formal training of teachers, and many other factors. By 1966, the nation had come close to achieving the traditional notion of equality of educational opportunity.[58]

Equally surprising, the report also indicated that it would not have mattered very much if the resource distribution had been different. The average of academic scores varied from school to school, with students from middle- and upper-class families doing better than students from poor families. But after controlling for the students' socioeconomic background, there was no correlation between average achievement, as measured by scores on standard tests, and the facilities, amenities, or programs that schools provided or purchased.

Since most white students were from the middle class and most blacks were not, there were differences in the racial averages for student achievement. In fact, the differences were greater than most people had anticipated. On standard tests the average African American student consistently scored below 85 percent of the white students. At age six, the average black lagged behind the average white by one grade level, and by grade twelve, the gap separating the racial averages had increased to four

57. Frederick Mosteller and Daniel P. Moynihan, *On Equality of Educational Opportunity* (New York: Random House, 1972), 7.

58. Ibid., 8. More precisely, Coleman reported: "The facilities and resources of schools attended by black and white children in the same region and urban-rural setting differed very little. The principal differences in resources and facilities were between regions and between rural-urban settings, not among races within these settings. This did lead to inequalities of resources and facilities by race, but only through their different distributions across the country." James S. Coleman, "Sins of Sensitivity: A Quiet Threat to Academic Freedom," *National Review* 43 (18 March 1991): 28ff.

grade levels. Coleman understood that the report was "tread[ing] on sensitive ground." The differences could "lead to invidious comparisons between groups" and, even worse, might "lend [support] to racist arguments of genetic differences in intelligence." Nevertheless, Coleman decided that it would be a mistake not to mention the gap in academic achievement. "It is precisely the avoidance of such sensitive areas that can perpetuate the educational deficiencies."[59]

The achievement gap troubled Coleman. As a sociologist he was inclined to ascribe the difference in black and white test scores to the influence of the social environment, and he also knew that attributing even part of the difference to racial inheritance would place him outside the pale of his profession and render him ineligible for future grants. For Coleman and for many other educators and sociologists who studied his report, the key variables were family background and neighborhood. There was no correlation between test scores and per-pupil spending, age of textbooks, and a host of other measures. But there was a correlation with family background, the education and occupations of parents, and the number of books in the home. One prominent social scientist, Daniel Patrick Moynihan, noted that Coleman's report found that "per-pupil expenditure, books in the library, all that had but little impact. What mattered was family." At a reception at the Harvard Faculty Club, another eminent scholar, Seymour Martin Lipset, told a group of colleagues, "You know what Coleman is finding, don't you?" It was "all family." Writing in 2001, Richard D. Kahlenberg concluded: "Today, in public memory, Coleman's report has been largely reduced to [two] . . . proposition[s]: that 'family matters more than schooling' and that 'education spending is unrelated to achievement.'"[60]

For Coleman, these findings were unwelcome. Personally, he favored more spending for education. And Coleman's dismay was compounded by another correlation that emerged from the data. Both black and white children seemed to do better on tests if their teachers had done well on a standard test of vocabulary. This was especially problematical because black teachers were "on the whole less well prepared, less qualified, with lower verbal skills, than their white counterparts." This led to "the conjecture that [students] would do less well on average under black teachers than under white teachers." If so, "a major source of inequality of ed-

59. Mosteller and Moynihan, *On Equality of Educational Opportunity*, 23; James S. Coleman, *Equality and Achievement in Education* (Boulder, Colo.: Westview Press, 1990), 123.

60. *New York Times*, 31 December 1995, SM25; Richard D. Kahlenberg, "Learning from James Coleman," *Public Interest* 144 (summer 2001): 54–72.

ucational opportunity for black students was the fact that they were being taught by black teachers." Yet this possibility was so heterodox that
the Coleman report did not pursue the matter. In 1991 Coleman expressed
regret over the decision "not to ask the crucial question." "A dispassion-
ate researcher," he wrote, "would have gone on to ask the question we did
not ask."[61]

Instead, Coleman focused on another correlation, one that indicated
that black children who attended majority-white schools scored higher
than other blacks. To determine the effect of desegregation on student
achievement, the Coleman researchers compared the achievement levels
of African American students who attended schools that were mostly
white, half white, mostly black, and all black. They then reported that
African American students in mostly white schools generally had the
highest scores, although the difference was not great and the achievement
of African Americans did not rise in proportion to the presence of white
classmates. Black students in all-black schools actually scored as high as
or higher than those in schools that were half black or majority black. And
in the Middle West, African American students in all-black classes out-
performed blacks in majority-white classes.[62]

Yet the summary of the report did not stress the qualifications. It emphasized, rather, that black students learned more if they attended mostly white schools. To reinforce this point, Coleman gave interviews and
filed legal depositions in which he touted the benefits that black children
would receive if they were dispersed and educated in predominantly
white classrooms. This eventually became the most widely reported finding of the Coleman report. "One of the report's principal conclusions,"
the *New York Times* stated, "was that integration was by far the most important school-related factor in improving the achievement of poor children." When Coleman died in 1995, the *Times* recalled, "Dr. Coleman concluded that disadvantaged black children learned better in integrated
classes, and his findings became a manual for political and court actions
and were widely used to support busing to achieve racial balance in public schools."[63]

In making a case for racially balanced integration, Coleman emphasized the importance of social class. Although there was no correlation
between test scores and the measurable resources of the schools, the attitudes and values of fellow students seemed to make a difference. "The

61. Coleman, "Sins of Sensitivity," 28ff.
62. Kevin Brown, "Has the Surpreme Court Allowed the Cure for De Jure Segregation to Replicate the Disease?" *Cornell Law Review*, 78 (November 1992): 58–59.
63. *New York Times*, 21 March 1970, 15; 28 March 1995, B11.

educational resources provided by a child's fellow students are more important for his achievement than are the resources provided by the school board," Coleman wrote. "The social composition of the student body is more highly related to achievement, independent of the student's own social background, than is any school factor." "If [a] disadvantaged child went to school with children from better-educated backgrounds, he did somewhat better in school. It was the social class background of the schoolmates that seemed to make the difference." In thus emphasizing the influence of a student's peers, Coleman was returning to an old theme. In *The Adolescent Society* (1961), a book about white high school students of the 1950s, Coleman had also stressed the importance of peer pressure.[64]

Some civil rights leaders challenged Coleman's assertion that black and white schools had similar educational resources, and many school administrators criticized Coleman for saying that a student's peers mattered more than school programs. But Coleman was actually confirming what parents intuitively sensed. They knew that classmates influenced the aspirations of their fellow students. That was one reason why many parents, when they considered the things that were most important in selecting a good school for their children, often placed more emphasis on the quality of the student body than on the quality of the teachers or buildings.

As Coleman saw it, the characteristic that mattered least (school facilities) had been equalized for blacks and whites, but the factor that mattered most (the socioeconomic background of fellow students) was unequally distributed. From this Coleman concluded "that school integration across socioeconomic lines (and hence across racial lines) will increase Negro achievement." Although the report was written in a matter-of-fact style that befitted a scholarly work, Coleman himself spoke emphatically in support of integration. "School integration is vital," he said, "not merely for some vague, generalized social purposes, but because it is the most consistent mechanism for improving the quality of education of disadvantaged children." "Integration alone reduces the existing gap between black and white children by 30 per cent. All the other school factors together don't add up to nearly that much." Buoyed by such assurance, many people came to share the opinion of the editors of the *New York Times:* That "since home and environment do overshadow the impact of

64. Kahlenberg, "Learning from James Coleman," 54; *New York Times,* 24 August 1975, 191; James S. Coleman, *The Adolescent Society: The Social Life of the Teenager and Its Impact on Education* (New York: Free Press, 1961).

limited hours of schooling, it follows logically that, if disadvantaged children attend school in the company of their middle-class peers, then school and environment together will raise their achievement."[65]

The policy implication seemed obvious. Integrationist sociology assumed that the quality of a school depends largely on its youth culture, and that middle-class schools were better. Since "white" was presumed to be synonymous with "middle class" and "black" the same as "lower class," the purpose of integration was to create schools with enough middle-class white students to shape the prevailing attitudes and a substantial number of lower-class black children to benefit from being exposed to peers who recognized the importance of schoolwork. As explained by Coleman, "going to school with other children whose vocabulary is larger than one's own demands and creates a larger vocabulary. Sitting next to a child who is performing at a high level provides a challenge to better performance. The psychological environment may be less comfortable for a lower class child . . . , but he learns more."[66]

Because of Coleman's eminence as a sociologist and because he filed legal depositions in favor of integration, several federal judges cited his research and statements as justifications for deciding that court-ordered racial balance was required to give blacks an equal educational opportunity. In Washington, D.C., Judge J. Skelly Wright cited Coleman as support for his finding that "Negro students' educational achievement improves when they transfer into white or integrated educational institutions." In Charlotte, Judge James B. McMillan mentioned the "alarming contrast in performance" between black and white students, which, he said, "cannot be explained solely in terms of cultural, racial or family background" and could be reduced by "transferring underprivileged black children from black schools into schools with 70% or more white students." In Denver, Judge William E. Doyle said that racial imbalance was "a major factor producing inferior schools and unequal educational opportunity."[67]

According to Coleman, the best situation was one in which blacks made up between 20 and 30 percent of the total number of students in a school. In such a setting, blacks could escape the effects of being socialized in a lower-class culture that had little regard for education, without at the same time suffering from psychological isolation. The theory was that

65. *New York Times*, 9 March 1970, 1; 10 March 1970, 42.

66. *Brunson v. School Board No. 1, Clarendon County*, 429 F.2d 820 (1970), 824; James S. Coleman, "Toward Open Schools," *Public Interest* 9 (fall 1967): 23.

67. *Hobson v. Hansen*, 169 F.Supp. 401 (1967), 420; *Swann v. Charlotte-Mecklenburg*, 306 F.Supp. 1291 (1969), 1297; *Keyes v. School District No. 1*, 313 F.Supp. 61 (1970), 81.

"children who themselves may be undisciplined, coming into classrooms that are highly disciplined, would take on the characteristics of their classmates and be governed by the norms of the classrooms, so that middle-class values would come to govern the integrated classrooms. In that situation both white and black children would learn."[68]

Given the residential concentration of blacks in the inner cities and whites in outlying suburbs, such mixing could be achieved only through massive busing for racial balance. That policy became one of the hallmarks of liberal reform, and in 1975 the *National Observer* identified Coleman as "The Scholar Who Inspired Busing." When Coleman died in 1995, the obituary in the *New York Times* appeared under the headline, "Work Helped to Foster Busing."[69]

But with the passage of time, another aspect of the Coleman report seems even more significant. By the turn of the twenty-first century, busing for racial balance was no longer in fashion. Yet by then it was apparent that the Coleman report had caused a major shift in the way educators defined the concept of "equality of educational opportunity." Coleman himself regarded this shift as "the most important impact" of his study.[70]

In the past scholars had measured educational opportunity in terms of objective characteristics—the expenditure per pupil, the number of books in the library, the educational level of the teachers, and so on. The Coleman report assessed these matters and found less inequality than was commonly supposed. But its principal emphasis was not on the resources that went into education but on the students' achievement on standard tests. In the parlance of modern business, the Coleman report shifted the focus from "inputs" to "outputs."

Coleman also considered "equality" in the context of "effectiveness." For him, equality of educational opportunity implied not just equal schools but schools that were equally effective in preparing students to compete in the modern world. In the past, schools had supplemented the family in preparing a child for adult society, but Coleman envisioned a primary role for the school. In the past "the home itself and the cultural influences immediately surrounding the home" had been primary sources of education, but Coleman's goal was "to free achievement from the impact of the home."[71]

68. *National Observer*, 7 June 1975, 1.

69. Ibid.; *New York Times*, 28 March 1995, B11.

70. James S. Coleman, "The Evaluation of *Equality of Educational Opportunity*," in Mosteller and Moynihan, *On Equality of Educational Opportunity*, 150.

71. Ibid., 20; James S. Coleman, "Equality of Educational Opportunity, Reexamined," *Socio-Economic Planning Sciences* 2 (1969): 347–54.

This was a departure from the thinking of earlier civil rights leaders, such as W. E. B. Du Bois, who demanded that public schools "spend the same amount of money on the black child as on the white child for its education," but insisted that there should never be an opposition to racial congregation "unless that [congregation] does involve discrimination." "Never in the world should our fight be against association with ourselves because by that very token we give up the whole argument that we are worth associating with."[72]

Coleman, on the other hand, opposed congregation because he thought that predominantly black schools were inferior. Black students did not offer one another as much beneficial peer stimulation as was available in mostly white schools. In addition, Coleman thought that black teachers were problematical. Poring over the statistics, he noted that African American teachers, on average, had slightly more years of formal education that their white counterparts. But the black teachers lagged behind whites in vocabulary and reading comprehension. Although this finding was only mentioned and not stressed in the Coleman report, Coleman personally regarded it as another reason for integration. "To the extent that teacher verbal skills are important for student achievement, Negro students will be handicapped if they remain in schools whose faculties are . . . deficient."[73]

When Coleman said the schools were failing, he did not mean that students were stagnating. He recognized that students improved their academic performance each year, even in the inner cities. The average fourth-grade student was more advanced than the average third grader. Teenage students in the inner cities, as in the suburbs, knew some history, biology, and trigonometry. Coleman recognized that this would not have occurred without schools. He knew that children did not learn algebra by themselves.

Yet because the difference in racial averages remained great, Coleman disdained the educational progress that was being made. At the end of high school, as in first grade, 85 percent of African American students scored below the average for whites. In comparisons with white students, African American students did no worse at age eighteen than they had at age six. But they did not do any better, either. And for Coleman the important thing was not whether children improved when compared with themselves but whether they were prepared to compete when they left

72. *Crisis*, 41 (January 1934): 20.

73. Mosteller and Moynihan, *On Equality of Educational Opportunity*, 38–39; Coleman, *Equality and Achievement in Education*, 123, 124.

school. For Coleman, the schools had failed because they were unable to equalize achievement. As schools were then organized, they made no difference in the relative standing of the races. "Things end much as they begin." And, because schools did not overcome the differences in racial starting points, Coleman concluded that there was no equality of educational opportunity. The schools had failed because, despite desegregation, equalization of facilities, compensatory programs, community control, and other reforms, they had not closed the gap in racial averages on standard tests. Coleman embraced what could be called "statistical morality." He defined equality "in terms of outcomes, but not for individuals, rather for groups." For Coleman, "educational equality is reached only when the results of schooling (achievement and attitudes) are the same for racial and religious minorities as for the dominant group."[74]

Coleman's definition was at odds with the traditional American understanding of equality. Because the achievement differences among individual students in each school far exceeded the school-wide differences in average scores, many people assumed that learning—like skill in athletics or drama—depended on the aptitude and industry of individual students. They thought the school's job was to provide instruction and not worry much about those who lacked the talent or the interest needed to master the subject. This point of view was reinforced in the 1980s and 1990s, when many Asian immigrants did well in predominantly black, inner-city schools. Coleman, on the other hand, thought it was "the schools' responsibility to motivate the child to learn, to teach him reading and not merely to provide free facilities for learning to read." According to Coleman, "the responsibility to create achievement lies with the educational institution, not the child."[75]

Another traditional view, a view that many supporters of civil rights continued to embrace, and one that probably continued as the conventional wisdom of mainstream America, held that the status of African Americans could best be improved through nondiscrimination and equality of opportunity for individuals. But in the 1960s many civil rights activists shifted with Coleman and began think in terms of equality of results for groups. In fact, Coleman said, there was a "paradigm shift," and

74. Mosteller and Moynihan, *On Equality of Educational Opportunity,* 20, 21, 7; Coleman, *Equality and Achievement,* 25.

75. Coleman, *Equality and Achievement,* 65; James S. Coleman, "The Concept of Equality of Educational Opportunity," *Harvard Educational Review* 38 (winter 1968): 22; James S. Coleman, "The Concept of Equality of Educational Opportunity," in Harvard Eduicational Review, eds., *Equal Educational Opportunity* (Cambridge: Harvard University Press, 1969), 24.

this shift was especially apparent among intellectuals and policy makers in the universities, journalism, publishing, and the network of foundations and research centers. A similar shift occurred among civil service officers, especially those involved in the formation and shaping of public policy. A new "elite wisdom" became the prevailing opinion among the policy-making class. "The use of achievement outputs to measure . . . equality . . . bec[a]me conventional wisdom."[76]

Accounting for the popularity of the new thinking necessarily involves some speculation. One historian, Herman Belz, concluded that the meaning of equality was transformed because of the race riots of the 1960s. According to Belz, the leaders of the dominant institutions were truly frightened by the violence and devastation and came to regard the new way of thinking as "the price society had to pay to prevent further violence in the black community." "Considered in the abstract," Belz wrote in 1991, "few Americans then or now accept the notions of group rights and equality of results." But such notions were implemented because elite opinion after the 1960s considered this approach to be "a politically expedient response to the race riots." Two of Coleman's most influential disciples, Frederick Mosteller and Daniel Patrick Moynihan, expressed a similar view, writing that "racial peace" depended "on how well the American educational system succeeds in turning out students of approximately equal competence."[77]

Thanks to the Coleman report and the race riots, and thanks also to the Supreme Court's decisions in *Green v. New Kent County* (1968) and *Swann v. Charlotte-Mecklenburg* (1971), the stage was set for busing for racial balance. In the 1970s, social scientists and federal judges turned away from the color-blind ideal that had been the dominant goal of the civil rights movement for several decades. They rejected the argument that racial classifications were too arbitrary and irrational to pass muster under the Constitution. They turned the Civil Rights Act of 1964 on its head. Instead of demanding "the assignment of students . . . without regard to race . . . but . . . not . . . to overcome racial imbalance," they insisted that students should be assigned on the basis of race to achieve integrated education in schools that were predominantly middle class. Racial balance—rather

76. Coleman, "Concept of Equality of Educational Opportunity," 2; Charles Murray, *Losing Ground: American Social Policy, 1950–1980* (New York: Basic Books, 1984), 42; Coleman, *Equality and Achievement,* 3.

77. Herman Belz, *Equality Transformed* (New Brunswick: Transaction Publishers, 1991), 65; James S. Coleman, "Equal Schools or Equal Students?" *Public Interest* 4 (summer 1966): 75, 74; Mosteller and Moynihan, *On Equality of Educational Opportunity,* 45.

than racial neutrality—became the overriding concern. "Forced busing" became the nostrum of the 1970s.[78]

Coleman would not have enjoyed such influence had his research not been reinforced by other researchers who came to similar conclusions. Especially notable in this regard was *On Equality of Educational Opportunity* (1972), a reassessment of the Coleman report by several Harvard researchers; and *Racial Isolation in the Public Schools* (1967), a report by the U.S. Commission on Civil Rights. Using data from the Coleman report, the commission concluded that

> Negro children suffer serious harm when their education takes place in public schools which are racially segregated, whatever the source of such segregation may be. Negro children who attend predominantly Negro schools do not achieve as well as other children. . . . Their aspirations are more restricted. . . . When they become adults, they are less likely to participate in the mainstream of American society, and more likely to fear, dislike, and avoid white Americans. The conclusion drawn by the U.S. Supreme Court about the impact upon children of segregation compelled by law—that it "affects their hearts and minds in ways unlikely ever to be undone"—applies to segregation not compelled by law.[79]

Coleman and the report of the Civil Rights Commission did more than recommend racially balanced integration. They also challenged the other reform programs of the 1960s: the compensatory programs that James B. Conant had recommended, the attitude adjustments that Robert Rosenthal and others had touted, and the community control that activists in Ocean Hill–Brownsville had favored. Coleman understood that integration was not a panacea. By itself, it would not eliminate the racial achievement gap. But he thought integration made better sense than spending money on other programs. Integration was worth a try, Coleman insisted, and it received the trial during the generation after the Coleman report.

78. Public Law 88–352 (1964), 246.
79. Quoted in David J. Armor, "The Evidence on Busing," *Public Interest* 28 (summer 1972): 95.

7

The Travail of Integration

In making the case for integration, educational sociologists emphasized that the culture of the peer group influenced the attitudes of individual students. They said lower-class families and neighborhoods did not stress the importance of schoolwork, and that children from lower-class backgrounds would have a more positive attitude toward academic work if they were educated in classrooms where most children embraced the values of the middle class. Since blacks, on average, had less money and formal education than whites, it was assumed that most African Americans would benefit if they were dispersed and educated in predominantly white classrooms. Yet middle-class whites were assured that they would not suffer from integration. As long as middle-class students remained in the majority, middle-class values would continue to govern the integrated classrooms. "In that situation," James S. Coleman stated, "both white and black children would learn."[1]

Many federal judges embraced the premises of liberal sociology, citing the Coleman report as support for court orders that required busing to achieve racially balanced integration. The Supreme Court, however, never officially endorsed Coleman's rationale. The justices recognized that much had been written about whether black children learned more in predominantly white, middle-class schools. But the jurisprudence of the Supreme Court did not rest on this consideration.

In the landmark *Swann* opinion of 1971, Chief Justice Warren Burger stated that the high court "has not ruled, and does not rule that 'racial balance' is required." According to Burger, the Constitution required only

1. *National Observer*, 7 June 1975.

that students be assigned on "a non-racial basis." The Supreme Court officially held that there was no constitutional problem if racial imbalance
was the result of economic or geographic factors or of personal choices.
The justices said that court-ordered integration could be required only as
a *remedy* for official segregation. If government officials had done nothing
to keep the races apart, courts supposedly were not free to order integration simply for the sake of the educational benefits that might accrue from
the mixing. Court-ordered integration was sanctioned only as a remedy
for official segregation. Children were not to be assigned on the basis of
race simply to achieve more racial mixing than could be obtained by
racially neutral policies. This enabled the Court to maintain the advantage
of seeming to combat racism, as in *Brown v. Board of Education*. The
Supreme Court continued to insist that racial assignments were not allowed *for their own sake*.[2]

When it came to defining terms, however, the justices made words
mean what they wanted them to mean. Thus in a case from Denver, *segregation* turned out to mean "locating a school in the middle of a black
neighborhood when it would have been possible to achieve more racial
mixing by locating the school on the border of a white neighborhood."
And in litigation from Columbus and Dayton, *segregation* meant "assigning more than the district-wide proportion of black teachers to schools in
predominantly black neighborhoods." The Supreme Court then employed the *Keyes* presumption—the presumption that if "segregative
acts" could be identified in one school or in one part of a town, then the
racial imbalance that existed in schools throughout the region was a result of official segregation. In this way the Court arrived at what Justice
Lewis Powell called "the remarkable conclusion" that the absence of
racially balanced integration in Columbus, Dayton, and Denver was a result of government policies. Then, supposedly as a remedy for the governments' misdeeds, theoretically as a means of achieving the amount of
racial mixing that would have existed if there had been no official discrimination, the Supreme Court authorized racial balance in every grade
throughout entire school systems.[3]

Many Americans nevertheless recognized that official discrimination
was not the principal cause of racial imbalance. They knew that noninte-
gration resulted primarily from personal choices and socioeconomic factors—because some individuals preferred to live near others of their race;

2. *Swann v. Charlotte-Mecklenburg Board of Education*, 402 U.S. 1 (1971), 25n9, 26.
3. *Columbus v. Penick*, 443 U.S. 449 (1979), at 480, 481, or 482; *Dayton v. Brinkman*, 443
U.S. 525 (1979); *Keyes v. School District No. 1*, 413 U.S. 189 (1973).

because the races differed, on average, in financial means; because blue-collar industrial jobs were not evenly dispersed throughout metropolitan regions. Some observers therefore questioned the integrity of the justices. They said that when the justices imposed (or, in some cases, allowed other federal judges to impose) racial balance, the justices were requiring a degree of racial mingling "that no one honestly believed would have occurred in the absence of the alleged constitutional violations." They said that the effects of any official policies were slight indeed compared to the personal, social, and economic factors that were primarily responsible for racial imbalance. They accused judges of being "dishonest" when they said their goal was only to rectify the segregation that had been caused by state actions. In fact, liberal judges wanted to eliminate all racial clustering in schools, whether it resulted from individual actions of families or from state action. James S. Coleman said the justices had shifted the goal, without candidly admitting what they were doing, "from eliminating state-imposed segregation to instituting state-imposed integration."[4]

Some integrationists acknowledged that the remedy theory was a bad faith rationalization. Thus James S. Liebman of Columbia University advised judges and justices to proceed openly and to say candidly that racial justice required the United States to have integrated schools. Because students were young and impressionable, and because public education was a principal activity of local and state governments, Liebman thought schools were ideal places to inculcate a new standard of morality. Political scientist Jennifer Hochschild also considered racially balanced integration a moral imperative. She said the media elite and most members of the intelligentsia favored integration, and she quoted John Dewey: "What the best and wisest parent wants for his child, that must the community want for all its children." According to Hochschild, "democracy" should "give way to liberalism."[5]

The academic integrationists were in earnest. They did not equivocate. They openly expressed views that others were too circumspect to declare. But the Supreme Court never based its decisions for integration on either the argument from morality or the evidence from social science. The Bur-

---

4. Raymond Wolters, *The Burden of Brown* (Knoxville: University of Tennessee Press, 1984), 227, 289; Lino A. Graglia, "Race-Conscious Remedies," *Harvard Journal of Law and Public Policy* 9 (1986): 86; James S. Coleman, *Equality and Achievement in Education* (Boulder, Colo.: Westview Press, 1990), 211, 226.

5. James S. Liebman, "Desegregating Politics: 'All-Out' School Desegregation Explained," *Columbia Law Review* 90 (October 1990): 1496, 1595, 1597, 1617, and passim; Jennifer L. Hochschild, *The New American Dilemma: Liberal Democracy and School Desegregation* (New Haven: Yale University Press, 1984), 129, 124, 145, vii, 203.

ger Court of the 1970s continued to insist that integration could be required only as a *remedy* for official segregation. Eventually, after William
H. Rehnquist succeeded Warren Burger as Chief Justice, the Rehnquist
Court of the 1990s would use the remedy theory to undermine court-
ordered busing for racial balance. Yet the Rehnquist Court did not act in
a vacuum. By the time it turned the tide, the nation had extensive experience with racially balanced integration. This experience was exemplified
in several locales.

Racially Balanced Integration in Syracuse (New York)

In the 1970s and 1980s, Gerald Grant and his colleagues spent several
years observing the situation at Nottingham High School in Syracuse,
New York. Following the custom of ethnographic research, they changed
the name of the school to "Hamilton High," but that was one of very few
false notes in a book that presented an especially vivid description of
racially balanced, integrated education, *The World We Created at Hamilton
High* (1988).[6]

Nottingham High opened in 1953 in the hills of a newly developed
upper-middle-class area on the east side of Syracuse, a city of some
220,000 people. Most of Nottingham's 1,100 students came from up-
wardly mobile white Christian families, although there was a substantial minority of well-to-do Jews. Less than 15 percent of the students
came from working-class families. Some prosperous black families lived
in the Nottingham district, and in 1966 blacks made up about 8 percent
of the students.

During its first decade Nottingham was an elite public school. "The
competition for grades was keen." "Hallways glistened and lateness to
class was a rarity." "The students were neatly groomed and clean cut," including the black boys who, in yearbook pictures, "emulated Sidney Poi-
tier" and the black girls who "wore their hair like Jacqueline Kennedy."
Parents were pleased to know that the school supported middle-class
standards of courtesy and respect, provided good college prep courses,
and fielded winning teams. Teachers considered Nottingham an ideal
place to work—"orderly, with bright, willing students who showed deference and vied to serve, relieving the staff of many onerous policing
tasks." The teachers' style of dress "reflected social distance and respect

6. Gerald Grant, *The World We Created at Hamilton High* (Cambridge: Harvard University Press, 1988).

for authority," with "male teachers [wearing] jackets and ties, female teachers . . . skirts." There were some problems, of course, among them the excessive status that students bestowed on members of eight exclusive Greek-letter societies. Yet for most students, parents, and teachers, Nottingham High was just what they wanted. A statement in the 1954 school yearbook summed up a prevailing opinion: "We can hardly believe our good fortune."[7]

Civil rights activists nevertheless complained that the school was not fully integrated. In 1962 the Congress of Racial Equality (CORE) "began to press the issue of racial imbalance," noting that blacks made up 15 percent of all students in the city in 1960 (and 25 percent in 1970), but only 8 percent at Nottingham. The New York State Legislature then adopted a racial balance law that stated that the enrollment of minority students at individual schools should not depart by more than 15 percent from the minority's overall proportion in the local public school system. In response, authorities in Syracuse dispersed students more evenly by closing schools that were disproportionately black and busing the students to schools that were predominantly white. Black parents complained that only their children were bused, and white parents formed a Council for Better Education to preserve neighborhood schools. Yet the opposition to busing was thwarted by advocacy groups such as the Mayor's Commission on Human Rights and the Syracuse Committee for Integrated Education. The total number of students at Nottingham High continued at about 1,100, but the enrollment of African Americans increased from 90 in 1966 to 210 in 1970 and almost 500 by the mid-1970s.[8]

From the outset, integration was beset with problems, many of which concerned challenges to established standards of order and discipline. In the past the black students at Nottingham High had been "quiet, industrious, well-behaved, and eager to succeed." But the new black students were from a lower class with different customs. Teachers complained that the newcomers had "rough manners, were impudent, and were involved in frequent fights." The new black students were also described as hostile and exhibiting a "lack of respect for authority." One white teacher described a black pupil as "sullen," which she said was "very characteristic of these youngsters." Another white teacher said the new students came to school with chips on their shoulders. They wanted "to retaliate . . . to get even with teachers and students." Yet another teacher said, "I just

7. Ibid., 11, 7, 18, 13, 22; unsigned review of *The World We Created at Hamilton High, English Journal,* October 1989, 87–89.
8. Grant, *World We Created,* 25, 29.

don't know how to cope with it. It is difficult to discipline the Negro children. They are resentful and defiant of discipline."[9]

Racial tensions eventually boiled over. In October 1968 chairs were thrown and tables upended in the school cafeteria, and school principal William Massucco was clubbed over the head and sent to the hospital with a fractured skull. The following spring, after a memorial service for Martin Luther King, "black students rampaged through the school, breaking equipment in a physics laboratory and tearing into the library, where they overturned tables, swept books off the shelves, smashed windows, and tore up floor tiles." By then white students began to speak openly "of their fears of physical intimidation, of their resentment at lewd remarks in the hallways, and of a growing sense of territoriality in the school, with some bathrooms off limits for whites."[10]

As a result of the rioting, both whites and blacks were "radicalized." "Some liberal white students became racists." "Younger siblings of [white] students who [previously] had written editorials condemning racial segregation in the South now complained that black students were 'ruining our school.'" And "some middle-class blacks were torn apart by conflicting loyalties between the old world they knew and the demands of revolution." Previously the middle-class blacks had seemed to be assimilated at Nottingham, but after the school was massively integrated they were "ostracized as 'oreos' if they did not join the militants." According to one school administrator, "What often happened was that the black kid from the better background would pick up the speech pattern of the black kid from the poorer background and become one of the leaders . . . and in order to maintain that leadership would have to cut off his white friends, even to the point of attacking them physically, and that did happen."[11]

In an attempt to restore order, Principal Massucco limited the opportunities for informal contact between black and white students. All-school assemblies were cancelled for several years. There were no dances. And policemen were permanently stationed in the school to replace the student honor guides who had previously monitored the traffic during the few minutes when students passed one another in the halls. Yet these measures were not successful, and Massucco resigned after civil rights leaders pressured him to rescind his suspension of three black students (on the grounds that "the students had not been granted adequate due process

9. Ibid., 31, 26, 27.
10. Ibid., 34–35, 37.
11. Ibid., 44, 37, 35.

and should be presumed innocent until proven guilty"). Massucco went home and told his wife, "look, that's it. I can't deal with this anymore. I realized that whatever the problems were, they were bigger than me. . . . It was beyond my ability."[12]

Massucco's successor, Paul Cunneen, was "known for being a liberal" with a different approach. He began by banning social fraternities and sororities from using school facilities, and he proceeded to schedule communications meetings for white and black parents and biracial rap sessions for students. In addition, Cunneen made a point of hiring faculty who differed from many of the tenured teachers. Some of the new teachers were African Americans and others were whites who were "deeply sympathetic to the escalating protest movements." When compared with the older faculty, the new teachers had more generous grading policies and a greater tolerance for missed deadlines. "They were likely to be lenient with black students, out of what other faculty members felt was misguided and guilty liberalism."[13]

To promote integration, Nottingham also abolished ability grouping and established an elective system that increased the students' freedom to take whatever courses they wished. Surprisingly, the abolition of ability grouping did not lead to more racial mixing. "Instead, students now tracked themselves," with white students more inclined to choose academic subjects. After comparing the number of math, science, and foreign language courses taken by black and white students in 1967 and 1978, it turned out that "tracking actually increased slightly under the elective system." Whereas whites had taken an average of 3.75 years more of these subjects in 1967, a decade later the gap had increased to 3.96 years.[14]

Disorder persisted at Nottingham for several years. In the early 1970s, "'the school was in chaos . . . and riots in that time were a way of life unfortunately.' Instead of breaking up fights, whenever teachers heard a ruckus in the hall, they would automatically lock their door for fear the dispute would spill into their classroom. 'There was a true physical feeling of being afraid of black kids.' There were 'turf wars over control of the school not only between blacks and whites but also between blacks.' Weapons were brought into the school; knife and razor fights were not uncommon. . . . Student shakedowns of younger pupils, demanding money or a pen or a bicycle, were common. A few pimps were known to be operating in the school. When his life was threatened, [Principal] Cunneen

12. Ibid., 27, 8–29, 40.
13. Ibid., 40, 41, 49.
14. Ibid., 67.

had a bodyguard assigned to him. He had a heart seizure and fell unconscious after one particularly stressful period." In 1971 and 1972 the school
yearbooks "featured a grim portrayal of the violence in the school with
photographs of barred windows and barbed wire, with police in helmets
and riot gear lined up in front of the school."[15]

Eventually, a semblance of order returned. During the late 1970s and
1980s, there were fewer race riots in the nation and by then the black enrollment at Nottingham had increased to about 500—45 percent of the total enrollment. This may have led blacks to feel that they no longer had to
prove that they belonged at the school. In an ironic way, another aspect of
integration may also have contributed to the eventual return of order. As
part of the policy of maximizing diversity and integration, local authorities closed one of the vocational high schools and assigned sizable numbers of working-class white students to Nottingham. "Whereas middle-
class and upper-middle-class whites retreated from physical threats, these
ethnic whites were likely to respond and to initiate counterthreats. When
blacks at [Nottingham] planned to avenge their 'brothers' who had been
attacked by whites at another high school, the ethnic whites . . . got wind
of it. They knew the fight was planned for the cafeteria and about forty of
them took a stand. A leader of the white students had gone swinging into
the blacks with a chair leg.'" In language that suggested the racial tension
at the school, he told a researcher, "'By the time they got that thing stopped,
I think each of the white guys were on one knee. But we had fourteen or
fifteen of those coons spread out all over that floor. They were really out.'"[16]

> A sequel to this battle was planned for a few weeks later. About one hun-
> dred whites, armed with chains and tire irons, a few of them in hard
> hats, gathered behind the school at the prearranged time and place. An
> equal number of blacks came out from the gym. Threats were ex-
> changed, but no blows, before police broke it up. One of the hard-hat
> whites later claimed with pride that the blacks had "backed off" when
> the white ranks did not break. In reality, teachers felt both groups were
> relieved to have it called off. Although some tension remained in the
> school for years to come, this was the last large-scale confrontation.[17]

There were many explanations for the breakdown of order at Nottingham High. Some people probably regarded the situation as a vindication

15. Ibid., 41–42, 47.
16. Ibid., 43–44.
17. Ibid., 44.

of what the psychologist Henry E. Garrett had said in 1963. In his testimony in *Stell v. Savannah*, Garrett had predicted that with massive integration "neither group would be happy," since one group would be challenged above its ability level and the other group would not be challenged enough. As a result of "bringing the groups together . . . under classroom conditions," Garrett had said, many African American students would become frustrated, "and frustration leads to aggression and aggression leads to broken windows and muggings and crime."[18]

Garrett was a segregationist, but some liberals of the 1970s made similar points. One was Jerome Kagan, a professor of psychology at Harvard. Kagan noted that individuals of all races often ceased making an effort if they doubted their capacity for success in a particular endeavor. When it came to schoolwork, Kagan said, "the only way a child can tell if he is progressing adequately toward a goal is by checking to see how other children his age are doing." If the student was advancing at the same rate as his peers, "he feels confident and continues to work." But if the pupil perceived that he was far behind, "he is apt to conclude that he is incompetent and cease investing effort." Since the average black student lagged well behind his Caucasian age mate in academic achievement, the implication seemed obvious. Kagan thus turned the tables on James S. Coleman. Whereas Coleman had said that blacks students suffered if they were isolated from whites, Kagan said that blacks would suffer from congregation. One way or the other, African Americans would be disadvantaged.[19]

Few white teachers at Nottingham appear to have agreed with either Garrett or Kagan. If they did, they did not express such ideas openly. Among the old guard there was a tendency to blame the central school administration for not supporting teachers in disciplinary cases, for establishing cumbersome grievance procedures to deal with matters that previously had been left to the discretion of the teachers, and for generally telling teachers, "don't get too upset over this." Many teachers also took exception to parents who seemed not to care if their children misbehaved at school. When one teacher told a parent that a repeatedly tardy child should bring a note of explanation from her parent, the parent said no notes would be provided and advised the teacher to "stop worrying my child just because you have a middle-class hang-up about time." Other

18. Testimony of Henry E. Garrett, quoted in I. A. Newby, *Challenge to the Court: Social Scientists and the Defense of Segregation, 1954–1966* (Baton Rouge: Louisiana State University Press, 1967), 199.
19. Jerome Kagan, "The Poor Are Educable," *New York Times*, 16 January 1974, 57.

parents seemed not to care when informed that their children were sass-
ing teachers, and civil rights leaders complained when black students
were suspended for disruptive behavior.[20]

Black teachers, on the other hand, and some of the new white teachers
also, tended to make excuses for the students. One black chemistry
teacher attributed the bad behavior to "faculty racism," saying that black
students had been bused into "a foreign land" whose natives considered
the newcomers "unworthy." As this teacher saw it, the black students
knew of no other way to get the attention of the powers that ruled. This
teacher also commended the black students, saying that had it not been
for their disruptions, few blacks would have been hired as teachers or administrators.[21]

Whatever the correct explanation of the disorder, one thing was certain.
Massive integration was "a true social revolution" at Nottingham High.
"It resulted in the deconstruction of an old world. . . . By the fall of 1971
the former social and academic system of an elite public school was no
longer recognizable." "The old world had fallen apart." During the first
five years of integration, Nottingham "lost" 35 percent of its white students, and 72 percent of the teachers resigned, retired, or transferred to
other schools.[22]

The neighborhood around Nottingham High also changed as middle-
class whites moved out. Real estate prices declined by half, and blacks and
less affluent ethnic whites were able to purchase substantial homes at bar-
gain prices. Teachers said that much of the white exodus consisted of children from conservative families, with the remaining whites disproportionately drawn from a spectrum of groups. Some were from liberal families
associated with Syracuse University—some of whose children formed a
subgroup of strong students known as "The Achievers," while others took
frequent "reefer breaks" and gravitated toward the drug world. Other remaining whites were vocational students or the remnants of the social set
and athletes who had set the tone at Nottingham before integration. By the
1970s, among whites, there was no common ground at Nottingham High.[23]

The flight of conventional middle-class whites got to the point where,
in 1980, a new principal candidly stated, "I need [white] bodies." The central school administration then assigned a group of educable but mentally retarded white students to Nottingham. This might have happened

20. Grant, *World We Created*, 49, 50–51, 61, 54, 38–39.
21. Ibid., 29, 243–44.
22. Ibid., 45, 43, 46, 44.
23. Ibid., 62, 91, 89, 44.

even if there had been no desire to maintain a white majority at the school. A "mainstreaming" movement was evident throughout the country after 1980, and it aimed to place as many disabled students as possible in regular schools. Many teachers nevertheless thought that disabled students would be served better in special schools, and also feared that mainstreaming might lead to even more white flight. In any case, "mainstreaming" increased the diversity at Nottingham, as did the arrival of a sizable number of Asian students, who accounted for about 7 percent of the total enrollment in the 1980s.[24]

A certain stability eventually returned to Nottingham. Interracial hostilities declined as white enrollment held steady at slightly more than 50 percent, with blacks constituting about 40 percent of the students, and Asians making up most of the balance. In the 1970s the cafeteria had been "almost completely segregated," and "there was almost no informal interaction between blacks and whites." A decade later "the injunction against crossing racial boundaries was no longer in force." Some cafeteria tables were mixed, and interracial dating, while infrequent, was "not so rare as to draw special comment." "In the 1982 yearbook five interracial couples were selected to represent the most versatile, artistic, athletic, best-looking, and class couple categories."[25]

Some observers attributed the decline in interracial hostility to the fact that high school students of the 1980s were more likely than their counterparts of the 1960s and 1970s to have known classmates of another race since the earliest grades. Others praised the city of Syracuse for developing an all-choice school system that allowed parents and students to pick their school (within the bounds of racial quotas). About 37 percent then opted for schools outside their neighborhoods. The restoration of peace was also facilitated because, by the 1980s, there were so many diverse factions at Nottingham that no single group could impose its customs. There were no widely shared understandings. Each group did as it wished. Some students went to class; others did not. Some smoked dope; others did not. There was no common ethos, and no alternative to "live and let live."[26]

Although interracial relations at Nottingham were more amicable in the 1980s than in the 1970s, there was little progress in narrowing the racial gap in academic achievement. With whites from academic families forming a larger portion of the Caucasian cohort, and with Asians regarded as

24. Ibid., 46, 77–89.
25. Ibid., 46, 59, 95, 96.
26. Ibid., 46, 59, 95, 96, 97; Nicholas Lemann, review of *The World We Created at Hamilton High, Atlantic,* April 1988, 73–74.; Chester E. Finn Jr., review of *The World We Created at Hamilton High, Public Interest* 94 (winter 1989): 116.

"honorary Caucasians" for statistical purposes, the average score of whites on the Scholastic Aptitude Test (SAT) actually increased from 1,034 in 1967 to 1,061 in 1985. Meanwhile the average score of blacks declined, from 834 in 1967 (when most of the blacks students haled from the middle class) to 760 (after massive integration). By 1985, the difference in racial averages was 301 points, a margin that indicates that few black students scored higher than the lowest-scoring whites.[27]

The SAT results were especially disheartening because blacks were closing the gap in the average number of years of math and science that were successfully completed. When racially balanced integration began in the 1960s, whites, on average, took 2.35 more years of these subjects, and the difference increased to 2.55 years by 1978. In 1985, however, the gap in years of math and science had decreased to 1.78. In 1985 the average black student at Nottingham was taking more years of math and science than the average white student had taken in 1967. Some of the courses were watered down—as with "general science" or "basic algebra." Still, it was surprising to see that the difference in SAT scores remained so intractable.[28]

The accuracy of *The World We Created at Hamilton High* would have been questioned if the book had been written by a segregationist, or even by someone who favored mere desegregation rather than racially balanced integration. Yet, as Timothy Noah noted, the author of the book, Gerald Grant, "clearly believe[d] that, no matter how painful, integration was necessary and worthwhile." "[Grant] communicate[d] a true commitment . . . to the necessity of desegregation," wrote Nicholas Lemann, a writer who equated integration and desegregation. Critics of racial balance, on the other hand, may regard Professor Grant's point of view as an example of liberal dogma persisting despite the observed facts. For some observers, the history of Nottingham High was an example of reformers ruining a good school.[29]

New Castle County, Delaware

New Castle County, Delaware, provides another instructive example of racially balanced integration. After protracted litigation, a federal district

27. Grant, *World We Created*, 101.
28. Ibid., 100–105.
29. Timothy Noah, review of *The World We Created at Hamilton High*, *Washington Monthly*, June 1988, 57–58; Nicholas Lemann, review of *The World We Created at Hamilton High*, *Atlantic*, April 1988, 73.

court in 1975 dissolved eleven local school districts and established a single district that included more than 60 percent of all the public school students in the state of Delaware. Within this judicial district, students were assigned away from their local schools for several years. Students from Wilmington (90 percent black) were required to attend schools in the suburbs (90 percent white) for nine years, while students from the suburbs were to spend three years in Wilmington. The bus ride could amount to as much as two hours each day, but, as then Justice Rehnquist observed, "the plan [was] designed to accomplish a racial balance [of 80 percent white students and 20 percent black] in each and every school, in every grade, in all of the former eleven districts, mirroring the racial balance of the total area involved." Because the plan involved an entire metropolitan region, critics and proponents of racially balanced integration alike regarded New Castle County as a premiere case of court-ordered busing.[30]

Those familiar with *The Burden of Brown* (1984) will understand that this writer has previously questioned the rationale of the Delaware district court while also describing how racially balanced integration worked out in New Castle County. They will also understand that the point of view in *The Burden of Brown* differed from that of *The World We Created at Hamilton High*. Whereas Professor Grant considered balanced integration a moral necessity, I favored the position that Congress had established in the Civil Rights Act of 1964: "'Desegregation' means the assignment of students to public schools and within such schools without regard to their race . . . but 'desegregation' shall not mean the assignment of students to public schools in order to overcome racial imbalance."[31]

Despite the differences in the authors' points of view, *Hamilton* and *Burden* provided descriptions that were generally complementary. If anything, Professor Grant's account of what integration wrought at *Hamilton High* was even more alarming than my description of what transpired in New Castle County. There were no pitched battles in Delaware, and no principal was sent to the hospital with a fractured skull. Yet there were problems and a great deal of white flight.

The major problem in New Castle County did not revolve around interracial violence. There were some scuffles, of course, but nothing major. William Taylor, a committed integrationist, mentioned this when he cited the county as "one of the success stories of busing." The journalist Robert Hagar made the same point in one of his reports for NBC-TV. "[Integration] went smoothly," Hagar said. "For 21 years Wilmington's white sub-

30. *Delaware State Board of Education v. Evans*, 446 U.S. 923 (1980), 923.
31. Public Law 88-352 (1964), 246.

urbanites had fought against busing in the Court, but now it was a reality and all was going well." Delaware senator Joseph R. Biden, on the other hand, questioned this. "It is true that there has been no violence," Biden said. "[But] this doesn't mean there haven't been other serious negative impacts on the community. Anyone who talks with parents, teachers, and students, both black and white . . . will agree."[32]

Among the problems were petty theft, vandalism, and defiance. During the first year of busing, the number of criminal complaints in what had been the suburban Newark School District increased from about 10 to 165, while throughout the county there was a fourfold increase in the number of thefts reported at the schools. Nothing like this had happened before, and it was widely assumed that black students were responsible. "We'd arrest guys for stealing twenty jackets at a time," police major John Lingo recalled. "Twenty lockers would be cleaned out, and girlfriends would conceal the stolen goods when they boarded the buses back to Wilmington. Some youths were coming to school primarily to steal merchandise that could be sold in the city." Laboratory equipment also was pilfered, a form of theft that was difficult to measure because suburban schools had not previously kept a careful inventory of their supplies. At one suburban high school even the brass plates behind the door knobs were stolen and fenced.[33]

Thefts declined in frequency as students and teachers learned to leave their valuables at home or to keep them securely locked. Nevertheless, vandalism and disorder persisted. At Newark High School stalls in the lavatories were ripped from the walls and auditorium seats were kicked to pieces. False fire alarms were common, and during class time many black students roamed the halls. "From the appearance of things in the hallways, you'd think our school had become all black," teacher Dorothy Munroe said. Between classes and during lunch periods, the students from Wilmington congregated in separate groups, often to gamble, and the noise level was "simply deafening."[34]

Teachers were especially troubled by the pettiness of much of the misbehavior. Dan Defoe quit teaching after being sassed by students who refused to clear the halls and go to their classes. And Gladys Sharnoff encountered defiance when she came upon students who had stolen balloons and aluminum foil needed for a physics experiment. "Their attitude was, 'If you didn't lock it up in your desk, it's your fault. And if you

---

32. Wolters, *Burden of Brown*, 250, 230. This book mentions various theories that have been adduced to explain the relative infrequency of violence in New Castle County.
   33. Ibid., 242.
   34. Ibid.

didn't see us take it, you should shut up because you've got no proof.'"
In some schools teachers could not walk the halls without being called
names.[35]

Some teachers were simply incredulous when school administrators offered soothing assurance that court-ordered busing was going well. Anna
Hayes Owens, a veteran of seventeen years in the classroom, said that
such statements reminded her of "a general behind the lines who doesn't
really know what is happening to the soldiers on the front line." She offered the following description of conditions at her suburban school:

> The problems involving discipline are so acute in many classes that the
> teacher's role is changing to that of a policeman but with none of the
> safeguards. The problems of vandalism, violence, drug abuse and thiev-
> ery seem to get worse each year. Cheating and copying have become en-
> demic diseases. Graffiti appear on the walls, desks, and books. Litter
> piles up—a daily burden for overworked janitors. Too many students
> are absent or late for class. Noise in many classrooms has to be experi-
> enced to be believed. There is constant gossiping, bickering, intermin-
> gled with threats and obscenities.[36]

Court-ordered integration brought about a clash of cultures, and on occasion black students took exception to improper white behavior. Most
black students frowned on hugging and kissing in public, and sometimes
they complained when whites did so. When blacks took exception, however, they touched a raw nerve among whites who felt that blacks had intimidated school authorities and were having almost everything their
way. In November 1979, suburban Christiana High School was closed for
a week to allow for an easing of tensions that erupted after black girls as-
saulted a white girl who told them to mind their own business when they
complained about her kissing her boyfriend in a hallway. Whites then organized a protest with impromptu signs. "Why can't people who are repeatedly causing trouble be expelled?" they asked. "They are infringing
on the rights of others who want to learn." The school administration was
accused of covering up problems and taking too much from repeat offenders. Similar protests later occurred at other schools.[37]

Despite the administrators' reluctance to punish transgressions, black
students in the racially balanced New Castle County school district were

35. Ibid., 242–43.
36. Ibid., 243.
37. Ibid., 243–44.

suspended twice as often as whites, a ratio that was about the same as the national average. But the overall proportion of students suspended in New Castle County (8.7 percent) was double the national average (4.2 percent). Whereas 6 percent of the nation's black students and 3 percent of the whites were suspended from school at least once each year, in New Castle County (after counting repeat offenders) the figures were 14 percent and 7 percent respectively. In 1975–1976, before busing began, 1,637 black students and 4,555 whites had been suspended, a total of 6,292 of the 79,039 students then enrolled in the district. In 1978–1979, the first year of court-ordered busing, the number of students had declined to 63,558, but the number of suspensions had increased to 10,906 (5,442 whites, 5,291 blacks, 162 Hispanics, and 9 Asians). Before busing for racial balance, about 25 percent of the suspensions were given to black students; afterwards, blacks received 50 percent of the suspensions.[38]

Black students said they were being treated unfairly, and a federal district judge ordered school authorities to commission an independent study of possible discrimination. Yet the ensuing study by Charles M. Achilles and a biracial team of educational researchers from the University of Tennessee found no evidence of racial bias. White students were disciplined as frequently as blacks for truancy, cutting classes, and using drugs, but the overall black suspension rate was greater because blacks were disproportionately punished for theft, fighting, and defiance. "Defiance" was not precisely defined but often involved the use of vulgar language when a student was told to stop talking, leave the halls, or go to class. Many teachers considered profanity "as offensive . . . as some epithets are to Blacks," the researchers reported. However middle class the teachers might have been, the researchers thought "very, very few" were racially prejudiced. They also noted that blacks made up 56 percent of those found guilty of fighting and assault and that during the second and third years of court-ordered busing blacks made up 75 percent of those who were expelled after hearings that left "little room for error or bias."[39]

There were various explanations for the disproportionate incidence of misbehavior among black students. Some people said the misbehavior was a consequence of poverty and other social disparities. Civil rights activists, on the other hand, tended to attribute the disproportionate disciplining of black students to narrow-minded, middle-class white teachers who did not understand the cultural style of youngsters from the inner cities. According to Derrick Bell, at one time a lawyer for the NAACP, "the high levels of

38. Ibid., 244.
39. Ibid., 244–45.

disciplinary action against black children" were evidence that "racism" was prevalent at predominantly white schools. The Children's Defense Fund also attributed disciplinary problems to "racial discrimination, insensitivity, and ignorance as well as to 'a pervasive intolerance by school officials for all students who are *different* in a number of ways.'"[40]

In stressing these points, Bell and the Children's Defense Fund were not breaking new ground. In 1935 the venerable W. E. B. Du Bois had warned that there was "no magic . . . in mixed schools," especially if the white teachers felt little empathy for black students. Martin Luther King also had reservations about predominantly white schools, although King generally remained steadfast in his support for integration. On one occasion King told two members of his congregation:

> I favor integration on buses and in all areas of public accommodations and travel. I am for equality. However, I think integration in our public schools is different. In that setting, you are dealing with one of the most important assets of an individual—the mind. White people view black people as inferior. A large percentage of them have a very low opinion of our race. People with such a low view of the black race cannot be put in charge of the intellectual care and development of our boys and girls.[41]

40. Derrick Bell to *Yale Law Journal* 86 (December 1976): 383; Bell, "Serving Two Masters: Integration Ideals and Client Interests in School Desegregation Litigation," *Yale Law Journal* 85 (March 1976): 488n52. Based on research conducted by the Office of Civil Rights (in the U.S. Department of Education), Abigail Thernstrom and Stephan Thernstrom concluded, "African Americans are two-and-a-half times as likely to be disciplined as whites and five times as likely as Asians." *No Excuses: Closing the Racial Gap in Learning* (New York: Simon and Schuster, 2003), 137–42.

41. W. E. B. Du Bois, "Does the Negro Need Separate Schools?" *Journal of Negro Education* 4 (July 1935): 328, 335; Bell, "Serving Two Masters," 515; Martin Luther King, as quoted by John Feagin Sr., in Wally G. Vaughn, ed., *Reflections on Our Pastor* (Dover, Mass.: Majority Press, 1999), 129. Feagin quoted King as continuing to say, in 1959: "I don't see school integration successfully happening right now and being beneficial. I think the school system will have a problem. It will be disastrous. Training will be necessary. White educators especially will need training in how to deal with Black children. They will have to come to grips with their prejudices. Without such training I don't think it will work" (129–30). In his speech at the 1963 March on Washington, King spoke about his "dream that one day . . . little black boys and black girls will be able to join hands with little white boys and white girls as sisters and brothers." And in one of his books he wrote in favor of "educational parks which bring together in one place all the students of a large area." Even while endorsing integrated education, however, King also stressed the need to improve the quality of education in predominantly black schools. See James M. Washington, ed., *I Have a Dream: Writings and Speeches That Changed the World* (New York: Harper Collins, 1992), 105; and Martin Luther King Jr., *Where Do We Go from Here: Chaos or Community?* (New York: Harper and Row, 1967), 193–96.

Like Bell, Du Bois, and King, the (mostly white) administrators who were implementing racial balance in Delaware tended to blame middle-class white teachers for the problems that accompanied integration. When court-ordered busing began, they hired ninety-eight full-time human relations specialists and established workshops and seminars to discourage disciplinary policies that affected minority students disproportionately. Many black students would feel uncomfortable after being assigned to schools in suburban neighborhoods, the teachers were told, and numerous workshops were held to encourage the teachers to develop better "consultation skills" and "multicultural sensitivity."[42]

Gloria Grantham, a black educational psychologist who worked for the integrated school system in New Castle County, explained the rationale for the sensitivity training. If blacks were punished more frequently than other students, she said, it was because many white teachers were narrow-minded and did not understand the distinctive cultural style of African Americans. Therefore, in addition to encouraging teachers to become more "sensitive," Grantham's office required teachers to prepare written accounts and to list witnesses to student misbehavior. Her assistant explained that they were "piling on the paperwork to discourage teachers from suspending unruly children."[43]

Proponents of racially balanced integration also pushed for a legally binding consent order that would have stigmatized the police. The proposed order would have prohibited police forces from responding to crimes committed at the public schools—because the police supposedly were prejudiced against blacks. The consent order also called for the expenditure of about two million dollars for "intervention specialists," whose job was to come to the defense of minority youths who had a problem with teachers or principals.

Many Delawareans nevertheless questioned the prevalence of "insensitivity" and blamed integrationists for undermining order and disci-

42. Wolters, *Burden of Brown*, 229–230.

43. *Wilmington News Journal*, 30 December 1994; *Wilmington Morning News*, 9 August 1979; Wolters, *Burden of Brown*, 245–46; Raymond Wolters, *Right Turn: William Bradford Reynolds, the Reagan Administration, and Black Civil Rights* (New Brunswick: Transaction Publishers, 1996), 462–63; Gloria Grantham and Lisa Bullock, interview with the author, 5 March 1982. Grantham's comments prompted one committed integrationist, journalist Ralph Moyed, to confess that he was "utterly baffled." Moyed recalled, "in the '30s and '40s, long before I learned to deal with my temper, I'd slug someone at the drop of an insult," as he continued to do until he learned that he might be hit back or otherwise punished. It never occurred to Moyed that he might have been "a victim of cultural bias against violence in schools." *Wilmington Sunday News Journal*, 15 January 1995.

pline. They said that well-behaved students were being compelled to sacrifice part of their education so that disruptive students could stay in school. They said that because misguided officials would not crack down on classroom disrupters, a handful of hoodlums had been allowed to destroy the other children's education. John C. Still, a state legislator and former teacher, characterized the integrationists' approach as an absurd combination of providing "'advocates' for students who cause trouble" while sending teachers away for "cultural sensitivity training." Although the integrationists' disciplinary policy was strongly supported by a popular governor, Tom Carper, and by Delaware's most influential newspaper, the state legislature killed the proposed consent order.[44]

While integrationists and state legislators debated, many middle-class parents removed their children from the public schools. Rather than cope with cultural conflict and a breakdown of order, they sent their children to private schools or moved to more distant, predominantly white regions in nearby states. During the decade after the beginning of litigation that sought court-ordered integration, white enrollment in the public schools of New Castle County declined from 70,173 to 35,764, while enrollment in private schools increased from 17,235 to 21,598. Some of the reduction was due to a decline in the white birth rate, but the 50 percent decline in the white public school enrollment (along with an increase in private enrollments) was also evidence that resourceful parents could evade the best-laid plans of sociological jurisprudence.[45]

The extent of the middle-class flight surprised many integrationists. They had made New Castle County a *cause célèbre* because conditions there seemed to offer the prospect for achieving stability as well as racially balanced integration throughout a metropolitan region. In *Milliken v. Bradley* (1974), a narrowly divided Supreme Court had ruled against metropolitan busing in Detroit. But to obtain a 75 percent white majority in Detroit, blacks would have had to be dispersed through three counties and fifty-four school districts with a total enrollment of 780,000 students. By contrast, integrationists noted that an 80 percent white majority could be achieved in metropolitan Wilmington by busing only the 80,000 students who lived in that portion of New Castle County that lay to the north of the Chesapeake and Delaware Canal. The prospect for achieving a stable racial balance was further enhanced because geographic and demo-

44. Raymond Wolters, "The Consent Order as a Sweetheart Deal," *Temple Political and Civil Rights Law Review,* 4 (spring 1995): 271–99; Thomas Sowell, "Judicial Havoc," 6 July 2005, Sowell Archive, Townhall.com; Charles Murray, *Losing Ground: American Social Policy, 1951–1980* (New York: Basic Books, 1984), 199–201.
45. Murray, *Losing Ground,* 246–47.

graphic considerations made it difficult for families to flee. South of the canal the public schools already enrolled a larger proportion of blacks than the newly created New Castle County School District. To the north, east, and west lay rural regions of Pennsylvania, New Jersey, and Maryland, where there were not enough schools to enroll large numbers of people fleeing from Delaware. Given the manageable size of the busing area, the preponderance of whites, and the shortage of other predominantly white public schools nearby, New Castle County seemed to be the sort of area the U.S. Civil Rights Commission had in mind when it said that metropolitan integration would be "quite stable . . . because there is simply 'no place to flee.'"[46]

The reasons for the flight were as diverse as the individual families. "You can say I'm chicken and that I'm running away, but I don't want to get involved in the whole thing," said a textile research specialist at Du Pont. A white teacher who had worked in inner-city schools was convinced that her children's education would suffer under busing. A Chinese American father was upset when his son described the disruptive behavior and disrespectful attitudes of some of his classmates. A Railway Express worker complained that the federal court had misinterpreted the Constitution. A black father wrote, "Assignment of students on the basis of the color of their skin is an American and South African indignity to which no children should be subjected."[47]

Many middle-class parents had purchased homes in the suburbs because they feared the pull of downward mobility. They thought bad attitudes and low achievement were endemic in the black areas of Wilmington, and they were adamantly opposed to having their children associate with lower-class pupils. A university professor said that under busing his daughter "would have a 30 to 45 minute drive into a neighborhood where I wouldn't want to spend the day." A suburban mother recalled that "once the school nurse telephoned and said my daughter was sick and I was afraid to go down to Wilmington and pick her up. I had to call my husband and have him leave the office and get her from school. I was that afraid." Another mother, a native Delawarean whose son had been enrolled in the same elementary school she had once attended, said she "love[d] this little state, but I'll be darned if I'll stay around to pay for the busing. I won't fight. I'll just move out." Many suburbanites felt cheated of something they had worked hard to obtain. "Oh, believe me, there is

46. *Milliken v. Bradley*, 418 U.S. 717 (1974); Wolters, *Burden of Brown*, 228, 247–48; *With All Deliberate Speed* (Washington, D.C.: Clearinghouse Publication 69, 1981), 34.
47. Wolters, *Burden of Brown*, 247–48.

resentment here," one of them declared. The flight from the public schools was testimony to that.[48]

When it came to academic achievement, for a while it seemed that students were doing better. But that apparently was a result of teaching to the test. During the first few years of court-ordered integration, the school district administered a California Achievement Test. That test, however, was discarded when it became known that high school students took exactly the same test each year. Elementary students took a different examination as they progressed through their grades, but the same test was given at each grade level every year. Fourth-grade students took a different test than they had taken the year before, but the fourth-grade teacher administered exactly the same examination that she had given the previous year.[49]

When different tests were administered, the overall average hovered around the national mean, but the customary gap in black-white test scores was also evident. This was especially disappointing because, as sociologist David Armor observed, "if any school system should have been able to show improved black achievement," it would have been New Castle County, where "black students spent 9 out of 12 years in (mostly) middle class suburban schools, and there were sufficient whites so that, despite white flight, nearly all schools remained majority white and highly balanced." Yet, despite these conditions, "achievement trends and the achievement gap remained constant after desegregation." In 1994 and 1995, pro-busing plaintiffs returned to court and complained that the court-supervised school district had done little to reduce the gap between the average scores of black and white students on academic achievement tests. In 2004, Leland B. Ware, a University of Delaware professor who had previously been an attorney for the NAACP, reported that the "educational disparities persist[ed]." "The empirical evidence indicates that educational equity has not been achieved in Delaware's public schools. Today, educational attainment averages for African Americans in Delaware still lag far behind white averages."[50]

48. Ibid. 248.

49. *Wilmington Sunday News Journal*, 12 August 1979, 17 August 1979, 30 August 1981; *Wilmington Morning News*, 2 August 1979; Robert L. Green, "Metropolitan School Desegregation in New Castle County" (paper presented at Rockefeller Foundation Conference, October 1981); *Wilmington News Journal*, 10 October 1981.

50. David J. Armor, "Reflections of an Expert Witness," in Stephen J. Caldas and Carl L. Bankston III, *The End of Desegregation?* (New York: Nova Science Publishers, 2003), 17; Armor, "Desegregation and Academic Achievement," in Christine H. Rossell, David J. Armor, and Herbert Walberg, *School Desegregation in the 21st Century* (Westport, Conn.: Praeger, 2002), 147–87; Leland B. Ware, "Educational Equity and *Brown*

Nevertheless, racially balanced integration was not a complete failure in New Castle County. Black and white students were attending school together, and demographic stability was eventually achieved, with the enrollment of black students leveling off at about 40 percent—twice the proportion that had existed when the federal court first ordered busing for racial balance. Most residents of the county were opposed to busing for racial balance, but by the year 2000, the people who felt deeply about this had either transferred to private schools or moved to other states. Among those who remained with the public schools, the prevailing mood was a combination of acceptance, acquiescence, and apathy.

Dallas, Texas

In *Disruptive School Behavior* (1988), Judith Lynne Hanna provided another account of racially balanced integration, one that is especially valuable because, unlike authors whose descriptions of integrated education dealt primarily with high schools, Hanna focused on an elementary school in Dallas, Texas. Hanna's account was of special interest because of the author's background and the distinguishing characteristics of the school.[51]

The Hamilton Park Elementary School appeared to be an almost ideal setting for successful integration. It was located in a lower-middle-class black area of Dallas and was integrated as a magnet school under a court order of 1975. Instead of forcing students to attend a school outside their neighborhood, magnet schools were structured to attract students by offering special features. Blacks who lived in the vicinity of Hamilton Park were assigned to the school; but to achieve a student body that was 50 percent white, a federal district judge ordered that the facilities at Hamilton Park should be "clearly superior," with "a spacious gym . . . art barn, large lunchroom-cafeteria, [and] media center." By order of the court, special teachers were also available in art, physical education, music, and Spanish. Another feature, to attract white volunteers, was an extended day program, which offered activities and child care from 7:00 a.m. to 6:00 p.m. "Between 3:30 and 5 p.m., there were classes in astronomy at the planetarium, gymnastics, private piano, class piano, chess, computer work-

---

v. Board of Education: Fifty Years of School Desegregation in Delaware," *Howard Law Journal* 47 (winter 2004): 319; *Wilmington News Journal,* 18 December 1994, 13; 20 December 1994, 1; 22 January 1995, 1.

51. Judith Lynne Hanna, *Disruptive School Behavior: Class, Race, and Culture* (New York: Holmes and Meier, 1988).

shops, arts and crafts, drama, intramural athletics, bowling, and dancing." Twenty of the twenty-four teachers were white, and another twenty adults, including some regular teachers, were on the extended day
staff.[52]

Thanks to the incentives, Hamilton Park opened in 1975 with a biracial
student body that was 50 percent white and 50 percent black. "Some
black community residents felt their school was being invaded," but liberal whites appreciated the special benefits and welcomed the "opportunity for children to learn to get along with different groups of people."
Judith Lynne Hanna and her husband were a white couple who had only
recently moved to Texas, having previously lived in New York City.
When they lived in New York, their two sons "frequently played with
black houseguests" and attended a school that was "mixed, with Afro-
Americans, Filipinos, Chinese, Koreans, Greeks, French, Germans, and
Italians of varied educational background." Hanna herself was a cultural anthropologist and the author of several books on nonverbal communication, especially dancing, in Nigeria and other countries.[53]

Hanna was taken by surprise when her two sons, after attending
Hamilton Park for only a short time, "began speaking negatively about
black children . . . [s]uch statements as—'They get me in trouble,' 'They're
dumb,' 'They're mean,' 'I don't like HP,' 'I'm sick. I can't go to school,' 'It
was so noisy in class I got a headache.'" At first Hanna disregarded the
comments, knowing that "children often fluctuate in their attitudes toward peers." She also feared that she might be accused of prejudice, since
it was "conventional wisdom that children commonly reflect their parents' values." But Hanna's children were not reflecting the attitudes of
their parents. Nor were they continuing with the patterns of speech and
behavior they had established at their former school in New York.[54]

Hanna's curiosity and training as a cultural anthropologist led her to
look closely into what was happening. With the approval of school authorities, in 1977–1978 she observed patterns of behavior at Hamilton
Park and interviewed students and teachers. Employing what she called
"the standard ethnographic research methods common in traditional
fieldwork settings," Hanna went to school every day and took notes on
what she observed at Hamilton Park. Initially, she assumed that the black
and white students had "different communication styles (especially nonverbal ones)." Eventually, she concluded that the behavior she observed

52. Ibid., xiii, 41.
53. Ibid., 43, 42, 7.
54. Ibid. 8.

was "part of a wider problem facing not only [Hamilton Park] but the U.S. educational system as a whole."[55]

Many observers considered the Hamilton Park program an example of successful integration, and *Newsweek, Time,* and the *Christian Science Monitor* all published favorable reports about the school. Yet from Hanna's observations as well as her sons' experiences, Hanna determined that there were problems behind the orderly facade, the most serious of which the students called "meddlin'." As Hanna saw it, many black boys had adopted a style that combined fighting and verbal intimidation. Unlike the white pupils, who came from families that "usually emphasize[d] verbal negotiation and academic prowess over physical 'street' prowess," the black students at Hamilton Park were "socialized to more aggression." They would be swiftly slapped if they misbehaved at home, and they seemed to be primed to resort to fighting when at school. In addition, with the average black student at Hamilton Park lagging well behind his white age mates, there was a tendency for blacks to devalue academic achievement. Fellow students often chided blacks who did well in school, saying that "intellectual achievement" amounted to removing oneself "from the black brotherhood."[56]

Much of Hanna's book was devoted to examples of black children's disruptive behavior, and most of the incidents were minor infractions such as children wandering around the classroom when they were supposed to be seated, speaking to other students, and copying others' work when they were supposed to do their own. The children sometimes "chucked" books across the room and blew pins through straws at one another. "Tripping children going about their business" was another pastime, and there was a good deal of pushing and shoving. According to Hanna, "black boys were demonstrably more [aggressive] than white boys."[57]

In accounting for the aggression, Hanna emphasized the importance of "cross-cultural misunderstandings." Of course Hanna was not the first observer to discuss a clash of cultures. As noted, some authorities on education had been blaming teachers, especially insensitive middle-class white

55. Ibid., 17, 9, 8.

56. Ibid., 42, 53, 73, 115, 59.

57. Ibid., 63, 90. Hanna was a white observer, but black teachers were even more likely than whites to report that black students were more disruptive than others. That, at least, was the conclusion that George Farkas came to after surveying seventh- and eighth-grade students in the Dallas Public Schools and after asking teachers to indicate which of their students were disruptive. Some black teachers, however, blamed white teachers for "not know[ing] how to discipline black students. They let them walk all over them." See Farkas, *Human Capital or Cultural Capital: Ethnicity and Poverty Groups in an Urban School District* (New York: Aldine de Gruyter, 1996), 102–4, 100.

teachers, for the problems associated with integrated education. Hanna, however, did not attribute "meddlin'" to the insensitivity of middle-class teachers. As she saw it, black students did not feel out of place at Hamilton Park. The school, after all, was located in their neighborhood. In this instance the white students were the interlopers, and the blacks were striving to maintain the ascendancy of their values and style. One black girl expressed a prevailing view when she told a white newcomer, "you gonna sing this way, you in soul country now."[58]

Hanna provided an elaborate and creative analysis of the origins and significance of "meddlin'." Some of her explanations were dubious, but she wrote candidly about aspects of integration that many others considered taboo. Hanna's purpose was to make integration succeed, which she thought could be accomplished if blacks and whites had a better understanding of each other's customs. Her descriptions, however, were such that one reviewer feared that the book would "reinforce racial stereotypes."[59]

There were enough white liberals to allow for stable integration at the Hamilton Park school. Yet, rather than deal with the problems that accompanied racially balanced integration, many parents elsewhere in Dallas either moved away from the city or sent their children to private schools. Between 1971 and 1985, the white enrollment in the Dallas Independent School District declined from 54 percent of all students to 22 percent. In 2003, whites were only 6.7 percent of the more than 161,000 students enrolled in the public schools of the district. There has been much discussion of whether the departing parents and children were motivated by racial bigotry, were concerned about disruptive school behavior, or were repelled by some of the educational "reforms" that were introduced to "make integration work." Whatever the mixture of motives, racially balanced integration set the stage for massive white flight.[60]

Portland, Oregon

The Brush Elementary School in Portland, Oregon, was the site of yet another early experience with integrated education. In some ways what transpired at Brush School resembled the situation at the Highland Park

58. Hanna, *Disruptive School Behavior*, 44.

59. Ibid., 55, xii, 44; Judith Raferty, review of *Disruptive School Behavior, Journal of American History* 76 (December 1989): 996.

60. Joyce E. Williams and Lisa Garza, "A Case Study in Change and Conflict: The Dallas Independent School District," *Urban Education* 41 (2006): 459–81.

School in Dallas, and in other respects the situation was quite different. Integration at Brush was on a small scale, with thirty black volunteers bused daily to a previously all-white, upper-middle-class school of about five hundred students. All the teachers at Brush were white, and the ethnographic observer was Ray C. Rist. Rist was the sociologist who (as noted in Chapter 6) observed and severely criticized the black teachers who were working at predominantly black elementary schools in St. Louis. When it came to criticizing teachers, it turned out that Rist was color-blind.

Even before the first transfer students arrived at Brush School in September 1973, the principal confessed that he had one worry. "I hope they can make it academically," the principal said. "You know, the students at this school are really good. I would guess that a third of them have IQs above 130. There may be only twenty or twenty-five children in the whole school with an IQ below 85. And these kids really get pushed, not only by the teachers, but by their parents. Everyone expects these students to be achievers. What worries me is that I have looked at the records on the new transfer students and of the whole group, and it looks on paper like only three or four are going to be able to keep up. What I mean is that they are the only ones with an IQ above 110, and I figure you need at least that to make it here."[61]

Perhaps because segregationists had stressed the importance of intelligence tests, liberal social scientists generally avoided any discussion of IQ. Ray Rist was far from alone in implying that IQ did not matter. Nevertheless, judging from what transpired during the school year, the concern of the Brush principal was well-founded.

Thus one black girl with a high IQ, Gloria, did well throughout the school year and received high marks from her teachers. But most of the transfer students had problems. They were generally assigned to the lowest reading group in their classes, and even then they had trouble keeping up. A second-grade student named Jeff fell so far behind his low-level group that by February he was no longer trying. When the teacher called out "Blue Group," he "moved not a muscle." Although it was Jeff's group, Rist observed, "he stays [lying] on the floor. . . . The group no longer had significance for him, and he no longer considered himself a member. He belonged nowhere."[62]

Jeff became more energetic during recess. One mother called the school

61. Ray C. Rist, *The Invisible Children: School Integration in American Society* (Cambridge: Harvard University Press, 1978), 69.
62. Ibid., 139–41, 195–96.

to complain that Jeff was intimidating her son in the bathroom and beating him on the playground. Believing that Jeff probably was guilty, school authorities thereafter kept a close watch over Jeff. But Jeff was far from the only problematic transfer student. Donald was "always talking and 'pestering' the other children"—pulling their hair and stealing crayons and pencils. On the fourth day of school he was "pushing other children at the water fountain," even though "he didn't want to drink himself, but just to cause trouble by breaking into line." Two months later Donald "graduated" to stealing from the milk fund in the teacher's desk. "When he sees something he wants, he just takes it," the teacher said. "But no more. Now things get locked up."[63]

Other transfer students in Portland also repeated a pattern that Judith Hanna had observed in Dallas. One child was "in an almost constant state of motion, . . . moving through the room from one student's desk to another, to the teacher's desk, and on to another." Another pupil wandered about his classroom "creat[ing] disturbances," and yet another, according to his teacher, was "totally uncontrollable," "just wild." "There were days when we did not get a thing done because I had to constantly deal with his disruptions."[64]

According to the principal of the school, the problems were the result of "putting low achieving black students in rooms with high achieving white students. So many of the black students had such low ability that they just couldn't keep up. Then they started to cause problems because they were frustrated and discouraged." Many of the teachers concurred, although one was perplexed by a transfer student who had the ability to keep up with the class but nevertheless would not stay in his seat. The teacher said she "could understand if he was constantly moving because he couldn't do the work, but . . . he won't concentrate when he has the ability to do the class assignments." The teacher was further bewildered when she found the youngster "using a sharp piece of metal to gouge out a piece of wood from his desk top" and making "two deep scratches in one of his books." "I can't understand what makes a child do that," the teacher said. "He's too young to be angry at the world."[65]

Despite the problems, most teachers at Brush School thought that, on the whole, the transfer program was a success. They believed the black students at Brush had "somewhat assimilated the dominant values . . . — speaking more clearly, starting to be proud of one's work, and trying to

63. Ibid., 92, 120, 135, 142.
64. Ibid., 96, 145, 146, 124.
65. Ibid., 235, 206.

do one's work well." They thought that black students were more likely to succeed in the United States if they broke away from the culture of the ghetto and assimilated conventional values. The assumption was paternalistic. In the opinion of Ray Rist, and of many other New Left scholars of the 1960s and 1970s, it reeked of cultural imperialism. Yet the teachers' goals were egalitarian. They were trying to prepare students for life outside the slums, in the mainstream of American life.[66]

At the same time, some teachers also expressed reservations. At the beginning of the school year, one teacher had said, "I don't think with this small number of [transfer] students that there should be any problems. Now if there were seventy-five or a hundred, it would be different. But I don't think twenty-eight will make any difference at all." At the end of the year, another teacher was less sanguine: "I can't see what good integration does. . . . What will the white children think when the blacks they see are so academically poor? And what about the black child's self-image? What is he going to think about himself when he compares his work with the work of the white students around him, and finds out he is at the bottom of his class?"[67]

As Rist saw it, opinions such as these poisoned the experiment with integration at Brush School. One reviewer noted that Rist also regarded "the assimilation model employed in Portland as a grand failure, since it seeks to deny the cultural distinctiveness of children." Instead of recognizing and affirming the valuable diversity of cultural life in America, the curriculum and activities at the school gave scant attention to the history and cultural contributions of African Americans. Nor did the teachers recognize and try to eliminate their own cultural biases and racial insensitivity. In addition, Rist thought the teachers were far too bourgeois. In many respects they resembled the black teachers he had observed in St. Louis and had criticized for attending church regularly and for living in spacious homes in comfortable middle-class sections of the city. Whether the teachers were black, as in St. Louis, or white, as in Portland, Rist thought that they were not prepared to deal with impoverished black students from the inner cities.[68]

Rist also found fault with the curriculum at Brush School. The teachers there organized their classes with different groupings for students who

66. Ibid., 239.
67. Ibid., 83, 143.
68. Meyer Weinberg, review of *The Invisible Children, Change,* May 1978, 49; Ray C. Rist, "Student Social Class and Teacher Expectations: The Self-Fulfilling Prophecy in Ghetto Education," *Harvard Educational Review* 40 (August 1970): 411–51; Rist, *Invisible Children,* 252.

were reading at different levels, and so also with arithmetic. But Rist considered this a form of institutional racism, since it led to a situation where black students were assigned disproportionately to the slower groups. It amounted to "segregation by performance level." For integration to succeed, Rist wrote, teaching should be "individualized," less emphasis should be placed on academic subjects, and more attention should be given to "the socialization component"—to teaching children how to "live with others." Rist criticized the Brush teachers for stressing "academic material above all else," and for expecting "punctuality, neatness, and deference to be displayed by the students as a matter of course." This approach might work with middle-class students, but it was not appropriate for students from the ghetto.[69]

Most parents disagreed. They liked Brush School as it was. They did not want to compromise on the basics of academic education, and they were skeptical about "individualization." They understood that individualized instruction was an ideal, but they nevertheless sensed that most children learned more when students were taught as a group. Admittedly, this was a paradox, but many parents intuited that it was not possible to provide effective one-on-one instruction to an entire class of about twenty-five students. While one student was being coached individually, the others would be left to work alone—or, more likely, not to work at all but to fritter away the time. On the other hand, when the entire class was taught effectively, more students would be learning. Yet Rist believed that good students "would succeed regardless of what the school did." His concern was with uplifting weak students and protecting their self-esteem.[70]

White parents were not alone in supporting the traditional emphases and methods of instruction. Toward the end of the school year, when Rist asked parents for their views on the programs at Brush School, he discovered that the black parents were "uniformly positive." Without exception, they said they "would send their children back, and they all said they would do it again if they had to begin anew."[71]

Rist could hardly believe what he heard from the black parents. "It could be argued," Rist wrote, "that the parents were not 'really aware' of what was happening to their children at Brush. If they were, they would not have responded as they did." "Or, perhaps, the black parents who sent their children to Brush School, much like parents everywhere, hardly paused to consider what happened to them when they got there. The par-

69. Rist, *Invisible Children*, 250, 267, 247.
70. Ibid., 247.
71. Ibid., 242–43.

ents' expectations may have been rather basic: so long as the teachers tried to teach and the children could stay out of trouble . . . the school was doing a good job."[72]

As Rist saw it, the neglect of black studies in the curriculum, the emphasis on academic subjects, the system of grouping students by ability, and the insistence on middle-class manners and customs had a devastating effect on Brush's young black transfer students. Brush School exemplified how not to treat black children in mainly white schools.[73]

Success Stories?

Despite the problems in Syracuse, New Castle County, Dallas, and Portland, there were instances where integration fared better. Janet Ward Schofield, a professor of social psychology, has described one such case. Alan Peshkin, an education professor, described another. In each instance, they assigned pseudonyms to their schools and locales. Schofield spent several months observing classes at "Wexler Middle School," which was located in a large, northeastern city that she called "Waterford." Peshkin spent a year at "Riverview High School" in a smaller California city, "Riverview."

When Wexler Middle School opened in 1975, the student body was "almost exactly 50 percent white and 50 percent black," and a number of factors contributed to minimizing white flight. One was a "lavish" physical plant that included a "swimming pool and tennis courts . . . comparable to or better than those at most high schools in the city." Wexler also contained a media center that was "the envy of some commercial TV studios." The school board and the principal were "almost emotional" in expressing support for integration, the academic programs were of high quality, and teachers (three-fourths of whom were white) were carefully chosen "on the basis of judgments about their ability to work effectively in a desegregated setting." On standardized tests, Wexler was "the only one of Waterford's middle schools in which average scores . . . were essentially equal to or above the national norms."[74]

72. Ibid., 243.
73. According to Derrick Bell, "what Rist observed . . . has been replicated in many school integration efforts across the country." *Silent Covenants: Brown v. Board of Education and the Unfulfilled Hopes for Racial Reform* (New York: Oxford University Press, 2004), 123.
74. Janet Ward Schofield, *Black and White in School* (Westport, Conn.: Praeger, 1982), 6–7, 40, 210.

Nevertheless, there were problems. If teachers followed the traditional practice of presenting information, asking questions, and grading tests, the academic differences between black and white students became apparent to the entire class. On one "fairly typical math test," for example, almost 50 percent of the white students received A's, compared with about 7 percent of the black students. "It is just so obvious that the whites are smarter than blacks," one white student said, adding that her mother had assured her that this was due to "socioeconomic background," not race. If students were asked to do group projects, the disparity was still evident to the smaller number of students in the group. To counter negative impressions, the principal urged teachers to "individualize" instruction; but many teachers refused to do so because they believed that individualization caused academic progress to be "sacrificed to promote . . . social goals." Instead of "structur[ing] their classes in a way specifically designed to promote positive relations," most of the teachers at Wexler did "all they [could] to promote the students' academic achievement."[75]

As Schofield reported with dismay, parents, "especially white parents," generally supported this academic emphasis. Some complained when they learned of practices that were intended to foster good race relations rather than promote "their children's immediate academic achievement." What did "learning stations" have to do with math? one parent asked. Stellar students, too, were quick to react if they believed their academic progress was being "sacrificed to promote others' achievements or more general social goals." According to Schofield, this emphasis on academics was partly responsible for an increasing difference in the achievement of black and white students.[76]

As a result of the widening gap in the quality of schoolwork, many white students concluded that members of their race were generally brighter than blacks, and also more interested in learning. Speaking to this point, one white girl said, "[integration] changed [me]. It made me prejudiced really." A white boy similarly told his father, "Dad, I know you won't like this but I think I'm becoming a racist." When the father inquired further, it turned out that the boy believed that "the black kids . . . were neither academically talented nor motivated." At the same time, Schofield reported, many black students also came to think that whites were brighter, more hard-working, or both. Some African American students even regarded academic effort and achievement as "characteristi-

75. Ibid., 78, 43, 76; Janet Ward Schofield and H. Andrew Sagar, "The Social Context of Learning in an Interracial School," in Ray C. Rist, ed., *Desegregated Schools: Appraisals of an American Experiment* (New York: Academic Press, 1979), 164.
76. Schofield and Sagar, "Social Context," 162, 163.

cally white," and others believed that white children worked for good grades "in order to look better than [blacks]."[77]

According to Schofield, the black students' concern about being disrespected led many of them, girls as well as boys, to develop a tough, intimidating style. Like Judith Lynne Hanna in Dallas, Janet Ward Schofield observed a great deal of physical intimidation. "There is no doubt," Schofield wrote, "that both black and white students at Wexler saw blacks as physically tougher than whites and as inclined to use this toughness to . . . dominate others." However, the misbehavior of the older middle school students went beyond the activities that Hanna had seen at her elementary school. By middle school, the problem students had "graduated" from throwing books and tripping one another; they had moved on to fighting and the extortion of food and money. Yet Schofield maintained that whites were partially responsible for their victimization. With a glance or a facial expression, whites sometimes conveyed the impression that they considered blacks mentally slow. And the whites' participation in class discussions impressed some blacks "as an arrogant display, a deliberate flaunting of knowledge that downgrades other class members." When one black girl was asked why she had frightened a smaller white girl in the bathroom, the black girl explained that she had been annoyed by the white's "attitude in class. She knows all the answers. She gets them right all the time."[78]

Since the racial gap in academic achievement increased as students proceeded through school, and some racial tensions were exacerbated, many observers would have considered the experience at Wexler Middle School another example of integration gone awry. Schofield, however, pointed to "a definite, but relatively modest, improvement in relations between black and white students." Over the course of six years, she reported, white students became more likely to see blacks as individuals. They came to recognize that not all African Americans were mentally slow and physically intimidating. There was a "diminution of whites' fears of blacks."[79]

Thus, Schofield concluded, integration was not a failure at Wexler. Things could have been worse. The whites' assessment "of what blacks were like showed little if any positive change and in some cases became quite negative." Yet although "white ideas about what blacks were like changed little, if at all, for the better," more white students were "willing

77. Schofield, *Black and White in School*, 93, 94; Schofield and Sagar, "Social Context," 197.
78. Schofield, *Black and White in School*, 222–23, 108; Schofield and Sagar, "Social Context," 194, 171–72, 177.
79. Schofield, *Black and White in School*, 156, 161.

to interact with blacks as they progressed through Wexler." "Although the school . . . did not completely fulfill the extremely optimistic prediction of its strongest proponents, neither did it fail miserably, as others thought it would." This was faint praise, of course, as Schofield acknowledged: "The extent to which [integration at Wexler] is judged a success or failure clearly depends on one's expectations and point of view."[80]

For Schofield, the experience at Wexler pointed to the need for more careful planning to make integration work. She emphasized the importance of "social learning"—that is, learning how to get along with others. She urged schools to turn away from "a narrow concentration on the academic outcomes of schooling" and to focus "on other nonacademic outcomes such as intergroup relations." To this end, Schofield offered several suggestions: students should not be allowed to choose their own seats (since they usually chose to be near others of their race), they should be seated at tables rather than at individual chairs with arms, and teachers should move away from group instruction and toward "individualization." Honor rolls should be abolished. Everything possible should be done to foster equal status for all students, regardless of their academic achievement. Otherwise, integrated education would lead to "increased intergroup hostility." "Unless interracial schools are carefully planned," Schofield wrote, "they can exacerbate the very social tensions and hostilities that they initially hoped to diminish."[81]

Alan Peshkin was more enthusiastic in assessing integrated education. In the preface to his book *The Color of Strangers, the Color of Friends* (1991), Peshkin boldly asserted that what transpired at California's Riverview High School (RHS) amounted to "an American success story." It was a peculiar sort of "success," however.[82]

RHS had been desegregated for decades, with a mix of Caucasian, Hispanic, African American, and Asian students. Over the years there had been a decline in the number of white students, as wealthier families moved to suburbs outside Riverview. As this occurred, the enrollment at RHS increasingly became a mix of working-class youths from diverse ethnic groups. Indeed, many families settled in Riverview because housing prices were lower there than elsewhere in the region. When RHS teams played away games, they sometimes heard shouts, "Go back to Riverview where you belong." But conditions in the school did not change

80. Ibid., 162, 231.
81. Schofield and Sagar, "Social Context," 155, 156.
82. Alan Peshkin, *The Color of Strangers, the Color of Friends* (Chicago: University of Chicago Press, 1991), ix.

markedly until the civil rights movement crested in the 1960s and 1970s. Before then, one former student recalled, "everybody got along fine . . . as far as friendship in classrooms, lunchrooms, and dances," but "as for dating, everybody stayed in their own group—the color barrier."[83]

In April 1968, after the assassination of Martin Luther King, there was a race riot at RHS. About two hundred black students stormed the lunchroom, where they broke chairs and windows, fought with nonblack students, and shoved and jostled teachers. Repairs cost $4,600, and sixteen black students were expelled for their behavior.[84]

By comparison with uprisings that occurred elsewhere, the riot at RHS was a small, short-lived affair that did little damage. But it loomed large in the consciousness of the school and the community. Within a few months, both the high school principal, who had been at RHS for sixteen years, and the school district superintendent, who had twenty-two years of local experience, resigned their positions. The school then hired four minority assistant principals, implemented an affirmative action hiring policy, and added courses in ethnic studies. At the same time, RHS abolished its policy of grouping students according to academic achievement. To improve human relations, the school also set up encounter groups and sensitivity training programs. There, Peshkin noted, teachers were taught how to respond to provocations such as students who told teachers to "Take your fucking white hands off me." During the 1970s several white students were "jumped" while walking in the corridors, and the local newspapers described conditions in the school as "violent."[85]

Against this background, the school became less Caucasian, with the white percentage of the student body declining from 48 percent in 1971 to 31 percent in 1987. Meanwhile, the Asian (mostly Filipino) percentage increased from 1 to 17, and the black and Hispanic portions remained constant (with blacks declining from 30 percent to 29, while Hispanics increased from 21 to 22). Despite the increase in Asian students, in 1980 the test scores at RHS were the lowest in the county and at the 5th percentile for the state of California.[86]

Given all this, one might wonder why Peshkin considered RHS "an American success story." Again, as with the situation at the Wexler Middle School, part of the answer is that ethnic tensions subsided with the passage of time. "Had I been present in Riverview during the 1975–1976 school year rather than the 1985–1986 school year," Peshkin wrote, "I

83. Ibid., 21, 77.
84. Ibid., 78–79.
85. Ibid., 79–87, 104.
86. Ibid., 101, 99.

would have had to write about outrage, violence, and disorder, perhaps the greatest share of it ethnicity-based. Ten years later, the *Sturm und Drang* had dissipated, replaced by a much less newsworthy, and much more appreciated, ethnic peace."[87]

But for Peshkin, there was something more important than a decline in racial tensions. For Peshkin, integration was a success at RHS because it also included "mingling." And "mingling," he explained, was the gerund that people at RHS used to characterize "the close contact among students from different ethnic groups." As Peshkin viewed the scene, he observed a sort of mixing that was conspicuously absent at many other schools: interracial groups were eating at the same tables in the cafeteria, playing on the athletic teams, and participating in social clubs. Most significantly for Peshkin, the mixing extended to interracial romances. He was pleased to report that when he observed a group of students sitting in the bleachers at a Friday night basketball game, with the girls seated in front of their dates, "a white girl [was] leaning back against the legs of her Filipino boyfriend" while a "Filipino girl lean[ed] against the legs of her black boyfriend." According to another white girl, whom Peshkin quoted with approval, "Everybody just seems to socialize. . . . Everybody mingles. Nobody goes by race."[88]

Peshkin readily conceded that many of the predominantly working-class parents were opposed to "intimate black-nonblack relationship[s]." If the parents could have done so, they would have drawn a line "between friendship and intimacy." After all, it was affordable housing, not the prospect of racial mixing, that had led most parents to settle in Riverview. Many of the teenage students recognized this and therefore made a point of hiding interracial romances from their parents. Yet, to Peshkin's evident satisfaction, the students continued with relationships that they knew their parents disapproved. At Riverview High School, there was "not a mere absence of [ethnic and racial] conflict . . . but interethnic mingling, an infinitely more positive state of affairs."[89]

Peshkin recognized that "the foundation for mingling at RHS [was] the students' compulsory presence in public schools." Because students were required to attend school, and because parents did not control RHS, students there were being prepared "for a world of friends their parents never bargained for." For Peshkin, this trumped all else. Peshkin acknowledged the usual "statistics of failure"—the tallies that showed "black and

87. Ibid., ix.
88. Ibid., 217, 218.
89. Ibid., 227, 243.

Mexican students . . . disproportionately high in the ranks of dropouts, suspensions, expulsions and assignment to special programs, and disproportionately low in test scores, eligibility for college-prep classes, and college attendance." Nevertheless, Peshkin considered integration a success at RHS because students there formed the sort of interracial relationships that their parents would not countenance. Students at RHS had been "liberated" from their parents' sense of exclusiveness as to those outside the family's social circle.[90]

Unlike the working-class whites of Riverview, most middle-class whites had the financial wherewithal to thwart the designs of integrationist social engineers. H. G. Bissinger recorded a notable example of this at Proviso West High School in the western suburbs of Chicago. Unlike Schofield and Peshkin, Bissinger was neither a university professor nor a social scientist. He was, rather, a writer whose best-selling book on high school football in Texas, *Friday Night Lights,* was later made into both a motion picture and a TV series.

When it opened in 1958, Proviso West appeared to be a place where $6.75 million in taxpayers' money had been well spent. With more than half a million square feet, the school was "a kind of mini-Pentagon." The indoor pool was "sparkling," the tiled outdoor mall could be used for student dances, and there was an impressive atrium "with floor-to-ceiling glass and sweeping curves and airy space." Viewing the school thirty-six years later, Bissinger observed that the physical plant was still in good shape, with "well-kept wooden benches, an outdoor stage, [and] the Senior Circle courtyard . . . filled with the chirping of birds."[91]

Yet over time, and especially after 1980, Proviso West experienced an enormous amount of demographic and socioeconomic change. In 1973–1974, 98 percent of the 4,500 students had been white, and less than 1 percent black. Twenty years later, only 2,300 students remained at the school, of whom 56 percent were black, 22 percent Latino, 18 percent white, and 4 percent Asian. In terms of home ownership and residence in the township, whites remained the predominant racial group. But Bissinger observed "a kind of negative synergy . . . at work." When sizeable numbers of blacks enrolled at Proviso West, whites responded by sending their children elsewhere.[92]

90. Ibid., 266, 268.
91. H. G. Bissinger, "We're All Racist Now," *New York Times Magazine,* 29 May 1994, SM26.
92. Ibid.

In explaining their decisions, many whites alluded to the bad behavior and low academic standards of the African American students. Yet most of the incoming black youths were themselves from middle-class families that were "seeking suburban refuge from the crime and chaos of the city [Chicago] just as whites did twenty years earlier." When black youths enrolled at Proviso West, however, they soon found themselves almost as racially concentrated as they had been in Chicago. One exasperated integrationist, Gary Orfield of Harvard, urged blacks to continue to chase after whites, predicting, "The places [whites] are moving to will go through the same process in 10 to 15 years."[93]

Bissinger provided a balanced account of integration at Proviso West. He acknowledged that the school had a reputation for violence and turmoil, but from what he observed personally the school was "orderly and quiet." Test scores were admittedly lower than those in most other suburbs, but this was hardly surprising since so many of Proviso's students had come only recently "from the difficult streets of Chicago." Proviso West also offered an expansive curriculum, with demanding honors courses for those interested in and capable of achieving academic excellence. In the honors courses, the racial enrollments were "almost the opposite of the makeup of the school." At a time when whites and Asians accounted for 22 percent of the total enrollment, they constituted about 80 percent of the students in honors classes.[94]

Yet Bissinger did not disregard white complaints about the bad behavior of black students. To convey the flavor of white attitudes, he mentioned a boy who said that attending Proviso West was "like going to hell . . . I get pushed, and because I'm white I can't say anything because there's too many of 'em. I'll get my butt kicked." Bissinger also quoted a white girl: "[Blacks] think they can touch you, they think they can do anything to you. I cannot stand the race. I'll never date anyone who isn't white." When asked to describe a typical black student, one white student responded: "Ignorant, rude, loud." "Ignorant and scum," said another. A third brought up a scene from the movie *2001: A Space Odyssey* when a group of apes went out of control: "In a typical day in the hallways, that's what it looks like here." When other white students heard this comment, they laughed and nodded their heads approvingly. At least one white teacher agreed. Bill Paterson, a veteran of twenty-three years at Proviso West, acknowledged that when it came to behavior in the hallways, "The

93. Ibid.
94. Ibid.

conduct of some of these black males is incredibly immature—the yelling, the screaming, the way they hit girls."[95]

Bissinger also recorded the depth of the whites' concern about academic standards. He quoted one white student as saying, "You know, I'm sitting in an English IV Academic class, and I'm sitting here with these black kids who can't even write a complete sentence." Bissinger even provided examples from student essays: "The pepel from wen Martin Luther King Jr. Lived did not wrly get along"; "If a person do a job, be the best they can be, so I am." Similarly, in a class in American history, one black boy identified Herbert Hoover as "the vacuum guy," and a girl yawned as a teacher tried to spark a discussion about the millions of soldiers who were killed in World War I. Many black students were "actively resisting learning," said Dennis Bobbe, who had taught social studies at Proviso West for twenty-eight years. "They just don't want to learn." The black students who enrolled in the honors classes also talked about the way other black students treated them—about how they were accused of being "nerds" and "sellouts" because they took honors classes. "We're not accepted by the white people because they think we're not smart enough," said one of the black honors students, Loura Banks. "We're not accepted by black people because they think we're too smart."[96]

As Bissinger saw it, the facilities at Proviso West were well-maintained, most students usually behaved in an orderly fashion, and the academic classes (at least in the honors track) were of good quality. Nevertheless, Bissinger understood that many whites who had attended the school in the 1970s "would never, ever send their children there." To illustrate this point, he cited the case of Al and Becky Lasky, a liberal white couple who had insisted that their two daughters continue at Proviso West until graduation, because "we wanted our kids to be in . . . a multicultural environment." Looking back, Al Lasky said, "We fought the war and we lost. That's how I feel. If we had [another chance] to do it differently, I think we would." Lasky said the problems at Proviso West stemmed from socioeconomic considerations, not race. But his wife, Kim, disagreed. In a conversation with Bissinger, she insisted, "It's all about race. . . . You don't start out as racist, [but] we're all racist now."[97]

Racism may not be quite the right word, since it implies the existence of both bigotry and a conscious set of beliefs. *Ethnocentrism* may be a better

95. Ibid.
96. Ibid.
97. Ibid.

term, since it conveys a set of implicit attitudes and behaviors that make for racial identity and loyalty. In the modern United States, African Americans and Hispanics have celebrated their sense of racial identity and pride, as is reflected in popular slogans like "black is beautiful" and in the very name of one influential Mexican American organization, La Raza. Since about the time of World War II, however, elite opinion has insisted that, at least for whites, neither race nor ethnicity is a legitimate consideration.

In his book *White Guilt* (2006), the black writer Shelby Steele has emphasized this point: "[B]eyond an identity that apologizes for white supremacy, absolutely no white identity is permissible. In fact, if there is a white racial identity today it would have to be white guilt—a shared, even unifying, lack of racial and moral authority." By way of explanation, Steele called attention to "the extraordinary human evil" that whites have exhibited at one time or another. Steele made light of instances of slavery, conquest, genocide, and repression by nonwhites—instances that persist to this day in parts of Africa and Asia. Instead, he declared, "no group in recent history has more aggressively seized power in the name of its racial superiority than Western whites. This race illustrated for all time—through colonialism, slavery, white racism, Nazism—the extraordinary human evil that follows when great power is joined to an atavistic sense of superiority and destiny. That is why today's whites, the world over, cannot openly have a racial identity."[98]

Some white writers have agreed. James Traub, a liberal writer, has asserted that accepting "collective [white] responsibility—guilt"—is an essential "precondition" for whites who wish to enter "the contemporary discussion [about race]." Joe Klein, another liberal writer, has insisted that whites must begin a discussion of race with a confession: "It's our fault; we're racists." Writing from a different perspective, Jared Taylor has lamented, "Every other race is thought to have good reason to speak of collective achievement, to have collective interests, and to have collective goals as a group. For whites all of this is washed away in an ocean of collective guilt for having oppressed non-whites. This . . . is the only way in which whites are allowed . . . to have a group consciousness. The meaning of whiteness . . . consists of affirming collective guilt. . . . For almost all whites . . . the only occasion in which they speak as *whites* is to apologize."[99]

98. Shelby Steele, *White Guilt* (New York: Harper Collins, 2006), 107–8; Steele, quoted by Samuel Francis, ed., *Race and the American Prospect* (Mount Airy, Md.: Occidental Press, 2006), 5, 3.

99. James Traub, "Never Angry, Often Disappointed," *New York Times Book Review,* 7 September 1997, 14; Joe Klein, "Deadly Metaphors," *New York Magazine,* 9 Septem-

In modern America (and in Europe as well), white leaders are no longer celebrated for defending the interests of people of European descent. Of course it was not always thus. The historical record contains many examples of white leaders who were considered heroes because of their racial or ethnic loyalties. One thinks of King Leonidas and the Spartans, who stood at Thermopylae to defend Greece against an invasion from Persia; of Charles Martel and Jan Sobeiski, who defended Europe against the Muslims; of William Wallace and Robert Bruce, who battled for the Scots against the English. For thousands of years, ethnic groups have honored leaders who defended the interests of their people.

Although tendencies toward white ethnocentrism have been "delegitimized" in the modern West, vestigial remnants persist and continue to influence the behavior of people. The power of ancient attitudes has been suppressed by the cultural programming of the modern elite, but evolution may have equipped groups with unconscious dispositions to combat the displacement of their own people. That, at least, is the opinion of some psychologists. Kevin MacDonald, for example, has noted that many rank-and-file whites have rejected the exhortations of their elite and are "gradually coalescing into . . . communities that reflect their ethnocentrism." When it comes to choosing friends, neighborhoods, and schools, "there is a profound gap between the implicit attitudes and . . . behavior [of whites] (which show ingroup racial preference) . . . and the explicit attitudes (which express the official racial ideology of egalitarianism)."[100]

For MacDonald, white identity and separatism are the deeply ingrained results of a long evolutionary process. Perhaps. Whatever the reason for white flight, it does seem that, with some exceptions, whites who could afford to do so generally found ways to evade the plans of liberal educational sociology.

---

ber 1991, 28; Jared Taylor, "The Racial Revolution: Race and Racial Consciousness in American History," in Francis, *Race and the American Prospect*, 143–44.

100. Kevin MacDonald, "Psychology and White Ethnocentrism," *Occidental Quarterly* 6 (winter 2006–2007): 7–8, 18.

8

Controversy over White Flight and the Effects of Racially Balanced Integration

The evidence of white flight had been accumulating for some time. As early as 1958 the psychologist Bruno Bettelheim noted an irony. While "the liberal North [was] excitedly telling the South what ought to be done," many northern parents were ensuring that their children did not attend school with lower-class black students. Either by patronizing private schools or by moving to predominantly white suburbs, these parents were making sure that their children did not have to go to school "with children from 'undesirable' homes." Sometimes the parents defended the moves by saying their children would enjoy better cultural opportunities in the suburbs, although historically cultural advances had been associated with urban and not rural life. But the real motive became apparent when many parents moved back to the city, once the children were no longer of school age, "precisely because commuting is a bother and the cultural advantages of the city are more available." In 1967 the journalist Joseph Alsop also noted that whites in the District of Columbia had only one-fifth as many children as blacks. Most whites in the District were older people who had already reared their children or childless younger couples. To Alsop, the statistics indicated "that just about every white couple . . . has moved to the suburbs, at least as soon as it came time to send the children to school."[1]

---

1. Bruno Bettelheim, "Sputnik and Segregation," *Commentary* 26 (October 1958): 332–33; Joseph Alsop, "No More Nonsense about Ghetto Education!" *New Republic* 157 (22 July 1967): 19.

Another Coleman Report

The impressions of Bettelheim and Alsop were confirmed in 1975 when James S. Coleman released a second report. After analyzing data from twenty large school districts, Coleman concluded that court-ordered busing fostered "resegregation" by increasing the incidence of white flight. Coleman reported, in essence, that the more blacks enrolled in a school system, the more whites left. Specifically, he found than an increase of 5 percent in the average white child's black classmates would cause an additional 10 percent of white families to leave. Thus the nation faced "an insoluble dilemma." There would be no racially balanced integration without court-ordered busing, but such busing had the overall effect of defeating integration. The official push for school integration was offset by the actions of white families who moved from areas where there was a large enrollment of black students to areas in where there was less racial mixing.[2]

Civil rights leaders were shocked. In his report of 1966 and in several legal depositions, Coleman had supplied a scholarly rationale for busing for racial balance. Now, it seemed, he had switched sides and joined with whites who opposed integration. Kenneth Clark charged that Coleman's new report was "part of an extremely sophisticated attempt on the part of Northern urban communities to do successfully what Southern communities could not do, namely to evade the effect of the 1954 *Brown* desegregation decision." Clark was so disgusted with Coleman that he warned of the danger of "over-relying" on "inconclusive" and "flawed" social science research. Clark, the designer of the doll studies that the Supreme Court had cited in *Brown*, now said that "courts and political bodies . . . should decide questions of school spending and integration, not on the basis of uncertain research findings, but on the basis of the constitutional and 'equity rights of human beings.'"[3]

Coleman insisted that he still favored integration. But Coleman was concerned because, despite good intentions, court-ordered busing for racial balance achieved an effect that was not intended. "We need an approach that is more stable," Coleman said, "because if integration is going to come to exist in this country, we have to devise ways where after two or three years of integration we won't end up with resegregation." "If we abandon integration," Coleman said, "we strongly risk creating all

2. Coleman's new report was entitled, "Recent Trends in School Integration" and was delivered to the American Educational Research Association on April 2, 1975.
3. *New York Times*, 28 June 1975, 49; 11 June 1972, 37; Biloine Whiting Young and Grace Billings Bress, "A New Educational Decision," *Phi Delta Kappan*, April 1975, 517.

over the country [a] kind of apartheid." Coleman favored racial mingling "for general social purposes." "If we go the anti-integration way," he said, "we risk the most serious widening of the racial and territorial isolation that is already evident."[4]

As an alternative to court-ordered racial balance, Coleman favored an open enrollment plan that would allow inner-city students to transfer to suburban schools, with the provision that the suburban schools would have to accept outsiders up to 20 percent of their total enrollment. Coleman also noted that some schools had "made themselves more attractive and [were] holding white populations" by staying "open from the time parents went to work until they got back." To allow for this and other attractive features, Coleman proposed that integrated schools be given budgets that would be 50 percent larger than the expenditure per pupil in nonintegrated schools.[5]

Coleman wanted to make integration work, and in the 1970s he added to his earlier argument that racial integration would improve the education of black students. He said, in addition, that school integration should be structured to work against racial separation and polarization. He could not foresee "any but the most sullen and corrosive scenarios of the future if the multi-colored and multicultured children of this . . . nation are not permitted to get to know one another as individuals." Coleman also found some grounds for optimism, especially in statistics that pointed toward an increase in interracial dating and marriage. Coleman described this trend as "very encouraging"—saying, "no society is going to be completely integrated until there is widespread interracial marriage."[6]

In contrasting the flight from court-ordered busing with the increase in interracial marriage, Coleman harkened back to the "contact theory" that Harvard psychologist Gordon W. Allport had popularized in the 1950s. This theory held that if different groups of people were brought together in "equal status" contact they would like and respect each other more than before contact. To achieve better relations, however, the contact had to involve groups of equal status. As Coleman saw it, court-ordered busing for racial balance was problematical because it mixed lower-class blacks with

4. *New York Times*, 7 June 1978, 25; James S. Coleman, "Toward Open Schools," *Public Interest* 9 (fall 1967): 23; *New York Times*, 9 March 1970, 1; Walter Goodman, "Integration? Yes. Busing? No: An Interview with James S. Coleman," *New York Times*, 24 August 1975, sec. 6, p. 10.

5. *New York Times*, 28 October 1975, 16; 24 August 1975, 191.

6. James S. Coleman to Editor, *Public Interest* 28 (summer 1971): 128, quoting a statement of the New York Board of Regents; *New York Times*, 7 June 1975, 25; 24 August 1975, 191.

middle-class whites at a time when there was a substantial difference in the customs and in the average academic achievement of the two groups. In attempting "class integration as opposed to racial integration," Coleman said, the courts were trying something new. In the past "ethnic integration came as people moved from lower class to middle class." "There has never been a case of lower-class ethnic integration in the schools."[7]

In the 1960s, Coleman himself had recommended class integration. His theory had been that lower-class black children would benefit if they attended school with more academically oriented middle-class white students. He said it was "very much a function of the proportion of lower-class pupils in a school," and he assumed that if middle-class students remained in the majority they would continue to set the tone for the school. "In that situation, both white and black children would learn." As it happened, however, sometimes "the characteristics of the lower-class black classroom" took over and constituted the values in the integrated school, even if middle-class students remained in the majority. Middle-class parents then transferred their children to private schools or moved to predominantly white suburbs. The problem, Coleman said, was "the degree of disorder and the degree to which schools . . . have failed to control lower-class black children." It was "quite understandable," he said, for middle-class families "not to want to send their children to schools where 90 percent of the time is spent not on instruction but on discipline."[8]

For years integrationists had cited Coleman as support for their contention that blacks would learn more in integrated schools. Drawing on the first Coleman report, integrationists also insisted that white students would not suffer from integration. *Newsweek* expressed this view when it reported, "educationally, integration has been shown to be at worst harmless and often beneficial. Repeated studies have nearly always reached the same conclusion: black children profit from integration efforts, while white children do not suffer." The *New Republic* told its readers, "Research overwhelmingly indicates that blacks in a desegregated environment learn more than their segregated peers, and that white students do not suffer at all."[9]

In 1978, however, Coleman said that the most that could be said for large-scale integration was that academic scores usually did not decline. The worst, and a result that Coleman acknowledged after reading some careful studies of court-ordered integration, was that sometimes the aca-

7. *New York Times*, 7 June 1975, 25.
8. *National Observer*, 7 June 1975, 1.
9. *Newsweek* 96 (15 September 1980): 101–10; *New Republic* 186 (24 February 1982): 5–7.

demic scores of whites declined after integration. What once appeared to be fact—that integration would improve the achievement of lower-class black children without damaging middle-class whites—turned out to be fiction.[10]

This point remained controversial, although it received support from studies of integrated schools in California and Louisiana. Coleman had initially hypothesized that lower-class black students would benefit from greater exposure to middle-class norms. But if lower-class students gained from a redistribution of what is sometimes called "social capital," middle-class students might suffer from exposure to a peer group that did not value academic achievement highly or perhaps did not value it at all. To test that possibility, three Louisiana professors distributed a questionnaire to 172 teachers at schools in Lafayette, a city that had been integrated by court order. According to a majority of the teachers, "the white children . . . did not benefit by the influx of bused students, and . . . a major reason for this could be tied to increased discipline problems." The teachers emphasized two points: the "bad influence" of black students on whites; and the lowering of academic standards to accommodate weaker students.

- "I find that many of our [white] students, perhaps those who were on the 'edge,' are emulating the behavior and disrespectfulness that many of the [black] students brought with them."

- "Our [white] students were exposed to a lot of [negative] things they were never exposed to before. Some of them acted out because of it."

- "The [black] students I taught were very, very disruptive and took away the learning for other students."

- "Instead of bringing [black students] up and making them better students by modeling, [white] students are acting like [blacks]."

- "There has been an explosion of profanity / vulgarity, and disrespect . . . the students who care and do have respect are exposed to these outbursts."

10. James S. Coleman, "School Desegregation and City-Suburban Relations," 1978 paper reprinted in "Court-Ordered Busing," *Hearings before the Subcommittee on Separation of Powers*, Senate Judiciary Committee, 97th Congress, 1st Session (1981), 454–59.

● "Academically the teachers are having to move at a slower pace. They are having to water down the curriculum causing our brighter children to be held back."

● "Students that can accelerate do not due to constant review for weaker students."[11]

More Evidence on Busing

Integrationists received another setback in 1972 when David J. Armor published an influential article, "The Evidence on Busing." Like Coleman, Armor was a liberal integrationist. In the late 1950s and early 1960s he had been a leader of SLATE, a radical student party at the University of California, Berkeley. Later in the 1960s he was a member of the team of researchers who produced the first Coleman report. And in a book published in 2003, Armor would call for extraordinary measures to close the gap between the academic achievement of blacks and whites. Yet Armor turned against court-ordered busing for racial balance, which he considered counterproductive—not only because it stimulated middle-class flight but also because it seemed to aggravate race relations while damaging the confidence of African American students and doing nothing to improve their academic achievement.[12]

In the 1972 article Armor summarized research that had been done on integration in six northern cities, focusing especially on METCO, a voluntary program that he had helped to design and that bused approximately fifteen hundred black students from Boston to its suburbs. In terms of academic achievement, Armor reported, "None of the studies were able to demonstrate conclusively that integration has had an effect . . . as measured by standardized tests." "The bused students did not gain significantly more than the black control group, nor did their gains diminish the black/white gap in the integrated schools."[13]

The results with respect to self-confidence were also discouraging.

---

11. Stephen J. Caldas, Carl L. Bankston III, and Judith S. Cain, "Social Capital, Academic Capital, and the 'Harm and Benefit' Thesis," in Stephen J. Caldas and Carl L. Bankston, *The End of Desegregation?* (New York: Nova Science Publishers, 2003), 135–37.

12. David J. Armor, "The Evidence on Busing," *Public Interest* 28 (summer 1972): 90–126; Armor, *Maximizing Intelligence* (New Brunswick: Transaction Publishers, 2003).

13. Armor, "Evidence on Busing," 99. The other reports dealt with integration in White Plains, New York; Ann Arbor, Michigan; Riverside, California; and two Connecticut cities, Hartford and New Haven.

When questions were posed about the students' occupational aspirations and when the students were asked to rate "how bright they were in comparison to their classmates," the bused blacks were less positive than the control students who remained in inner-city schools. This may have been because the average control student was able to maintain a B average in the central city, while the average for bused students was just above C level. This was hardly a surprise. "Since black students are behind white students [on standard achievement tests]," Armor explained, "we should expect their grades to fall when they are taken from the competition in an all-black school to the competition in a predominantly white school."[14]

Armor also reported that experience with integration heightened the racial consciousness of blacks and led whites to become more negative in their attitudes toward blacks. This finding was especially surprising, Armor wrote, for "the idea that familiarity lessens contempt has been a major feature of liberal thought." Yet it turned out that "contact under the wrong conditions" reinforced negative impressions. For black students, "initial stereotypes about white students as snobbish, intellectual, and 'straight'" were confirmed by actual experience, while the same seemed to be true for white stereotypes of black students as "non-intellectual, hostile, and having different values."[15]

Armor's article was a blow to the pro-busing movement. Joseph Alsop publicized the article in one of his op-ed essays in the *Washington Post*, and Lawrence Feinberg, an education reporter for the *Post*, discussed Armor's work in two widely read news stories. As a result, Armor later recalled, "my telephone rang constantly for the next several weeks, and I believe I heard from virtually every school system in the nation that was involved in school desegregation litigation."[16]

Armor had reported on the situation in only six cities, but his conclusions were reinforced in 1975 when Nancy St. John, another committed integrationist, reviewed 120 studies of the relation of school racial composition and the achievement, attitudes, and behavior of students. St. John also found that integrated education did not boost the academic performance of black children and had negative effects on their self-esteem and vocational aspirations.[17]

14. Ibid., 102, 100; Lawrence Feinberg, "Study Casts Doubt on Busing," *Washington Post*, 21 May 1971, A1.

15. Armor, "Evidence on Busing," 110–11.

16. David J. Armor, "Reflections of an Expert Witness," in Caldas and Bankston, *End of Desegregation?* 4–5.

17. Nancy St. John, *School Desegregation: Outcomes for Children* (New York: John Wiley and Sons, 1975).

In addition to reporting on racial averages, St. John noted that integration had disparate effects on different black students. Strong black students sometimes benefited from the experience, while weaker students became more dispirited. In social life, black boys seemed to fare better than black girls, perhaps because the athletic prowess of many black boys gave them a certain prestige, while black girls sometimes suffered because feminine beauty was judged by the standards of white society. Although the amount of interracial dating was small, enough white girls and black boys crossed the color line to leave "some black girls with resentful feelings over white girls 'stealing their men.'" According to St. John, "Among blacks the social threat of desegregation is almost universally reported to be greater for girls than boys." Considering everything, St. John concluded, "During the past twenty years considerable racial mixing has taken place in schools, but research has produced little evidence of dramatic gains for children and some evidence of genuine stress for them."[18]

The evidence on busing thus seemed to contradict the prediction of the first Coleman report. Coleman had reported that black children who attended integrated schools scored higher on achievement tests than similar children who were educated in predominantly black schools. When Coleman had collected that data in 1965, however, nearly all the black children attending integrated schools in the South were volunteers who had enrolled under freedom-of-choice plans, while almost all integration in the North had occurred in neighborhood schools where blacks and whites lived in the same vicinity. Moreover, the first Coleman report was based on data collected at one time, with inferences drawn by comparing students in schools with different proportions of black and white pupils. It was not a "longitudinal" study that followed carefully controlled groups of children for several years after they did or did not attend integrated schools.[19]

Coleman recognized that integration had turned out to be "much more complicated than any of us ever realized." The desegregated black students of 1965 were unusual in that they had come disproportionately from middle-class families that considered education important. They had either volunteered to attend mostly white schools or had lived in mostly white neighborhoods. It had been "wishful thinking," Coleman admitted, to believe that other black students would make similar gains if they were integrated under mandatory court orders. Yet Coleman did not have that

18. Ibid., 119, 110, 136; Armor, "Evidence on Busing," 108.
19. Lawrence Feinberg, "Coleman Now Discounts Advantage of School Desegregation," *Washington Post*, 18 September 1978, A1.

much to recant, for the improvement that the first report had noted among desegregated black students had been quite small.[20]

Coleman's turnabout naturally displeased integrationists. "In 1966, we cited you as proof that [integration] worked," NAACP attorney Charles Morgan told Coleman. "We don't cite you as proof any more."[21]

After Coleman's second report, the evidence against court-ordered integration continued to mount. In 1978 Walter Stephan of New Mexico State University published an evaluation of predictions implicit in *Brown* and concluded that, while integration "sometimes" led to increased black academic achievement, it did not improve the self-esteem of blacks, did not reduce white prejudice toward blacks, and as often as not increased black prejudice toward whites. Then, in 1984, the National Institute of Education convened a panel of seven social scientists to review the research on how integration affected academic achievement and race relations. The panel included two scholars whose own previous research had indicated that integration had positive effects on black achievement; two who had found negative effects; two who had discovered no significant effects; and a seventh member who served as a moderator. After reviewing 157 separate studies and focusing on 19 studies that were deemed especially "rigorous" and "scientific," only one member of the panel (Robert L. Crain) concluded that blacks benefited substantially from integration.[22]

Still later, in a 1995 review of the evidence from hundreds of studies, David Armor reported that during the 1970s and 1980s there had been a narrowing of the racial gap in academic achievement, as measured by the standard tests of the National Assessment of Educational Progress (NAEP). For thirteen-year-old students, the gap in reading and math scores was reduced by about 60 percent. Integrationists emphasized that the 1970s and 1980s were decades when court-ordered integration was in fashion, but Armor stressed that the trend in academic achievement was similar for all black students, regardless of whether they were attending schools that were mostly white or almost entirely black. Since the test scores of black students in racially concentrated inner-city schools improved as much as those of blacks who were attending integrated schools, Armor concluded, "school desegregation is unlikely to have contributed significantly to na-

20. Ibid.; *National Observer*, 7 June 1975, 1.
21. *New York Times*, 12 December 1975, 31.
22. Walter G. Stephan, "School Desegregation: An Evaluation of Predictions Made in *Brown v. Board of Education*," *Psychological Bulletin* 85 (1978): 217–38; National Institute of Education, *School Desegregation and Black Achievement* (Washington: Government Printing Office, 1984). In addition to Crain, the panelists were David Armor, Thomas Cook (the "referee"), Norman Miller, Walter Stephan, Herbert Walberg, and Paul Wortman.

tional black achievement gains." In the 1990s, moreover, the racial gap widened again, erasing about half of the progress that had been achieved in the 1970s and 1980s. As had been the case with the achievement gains, the retrogression occurred among both integrated and concentrated black students.[23]

If integration did not account for the gains (or declines) in black achievement, what did? Armor noted that by the 1970s black parents, on average, had more years of schooling, and he speculated that this might have led them to instill in their children a greater regard for the importance of schoolwork. He also opined that "improvement in black family socio-economic status" was a key variable, although that seemed questionable in light of the persistence of poverty and an increase in the number of female-headed single-parent families. Another possibility, Armor suggested, was that compensatory educational programs finally began to show a lasting effect. Officials of the federal government were especially attracted to this possibility, since it provided a justification for billions of dollars that Congress had spent on programs that were intended to reduce the black-white achievement gap. There was some research, however, that reported that compensatory programs produced only a short-term "spike" in test scores, but that after a few years the children who were exposed to Head Start and other compensatory programs lost much of the benefit that they had enjoyed for a while. The decline in test scores of the 1990s may have been related to this pattern.[24]

Controversy would continue over the actual effects of integrated education. By the 1990s, however, the major premises of integrationist sociology were widely disputed. Integrationists had predicted that academic achievement would improve as black students moved to integrated schools, but, after controlling for differences in family background and socioeconomic standing, many social scientists reported that there were no significant differences between integrated black students and those who attended racially concentrated schools in the inner cities. Integrationists also predicted that busing would enhance interracial harmony, but instead of reducing racial hostility, the mixing of groups with different mores and levels of achievement often aggravated negative feelings. Integrationists had predicted that busing would bolster the confidence and

23. David J. Armor, *Forced Justice: School Segregation and the Law* (New York: Oxford University Press, 1995), 96.

24. "A study by the Congressional Budget Office estimated that federal Chapter 1 programs had reduced the black-white achievement gap by about 10 percent." Armor, *Forced Justice*, 98; Daniel Koretz, *Educational Achievement: Explanations and Implications of Recent Trends* (Washington: Congressional Budget Office, 1987).

aspirations of black youngsters, but the competition and higher academic standards in predominantly white schools seemed to have the opposite effect. One positive finding that emerged from the research was that black students who attended predominantly white schools were more likely to attend college and to enroll in what were generally considered higher-quality institutions. This could be interpreted as evidence that integrated education made black youths more at ease among whites and more confident of their ability to succeed in the white world. But even this was a mixed blessing, because so many blacks dropped out of predominantly white colleges that they graduated at a lower rate than blacks who attended predominantly black schools.

Breaking Ranks

Already reeling from the defection of James S. Coleman, Nancy St. John, and David J. Armor, integrationists received yet another setback when many blacks questioned the policy of seeking court orders to require racial balance in the schools. One Gallup poll reported that by 1981 half the black population in the United States believed that busing to achieve school integration "caused more difficulties than it is worth." In another poll, 75 percent of African Americans agreed with the assertion that "the schools work so hard to achieve integration that they end up neglecting their most important goal—teaching kids."[25]

There were many reasons for an increase in black criticism of, or disillusionment with, integration. Some African Americans pointed to a problem created by demography, saying that it was impossible to achieve balanced integration when black youngsters made up the great majority of students in many large urban school districts. Benjamin E. Mays, a former president of Morehouse College, mentioned this in 1974 when he explained his support for an "Atlanta Compromise," in which local civil rights groups gave up their demands for city-suburban busing in return for assurances that more blacks would be hired as teachers and administrators in Atlanta. "It is the most viable plan for Atlanta—a city school system that is 82 percent Black and 18 percent white and is continuing to lose whites each year to five counties that are more than 90 percent

25. *New York Times*, 2 March 1981, B4; Greg Winter, "Long after *Brown*, Sides Switch," *New York Times*, 16 May 2004, summarizing the results of a poll by Public Agenda, a nonpartisan research group. Pollster Samuel Lubell reported that about 50 percent of African Americans were opposed to busing for racial balance. See Ben J. Wattenberg, *The Real America* (Garden City: Doubleday, 1974), 252.

white." In addition, Mays insisted, "Black people must not resign themselves to the pessimistic view that a non-integrated school cannot provide
Black children with an excellent educational setting. Instead, Black people . . . should recognize that integration alone does not provide a quality education, and that much of the substance of quality education can be
provided to Black children in [predominantly black schools]."[26]

The black economist Thomas Sowell endorsed Mays's point in an article that celebrated the excellence of Dunbar High School, a segregated
school in Washington, D.C. Over a span of eighty-five years, most of Dunbar's graduates went on to college and, although financial limitations required most to attend low-cost colleges nearby, an impressive minority
achieved academic honors at prestigious schools like Harvard, Amherst,
and Oberlin. According to Sowell, the graduates of Dunbar excelled "in
their careers, as in their academic work." "The first black general (Benjamin O. Davis), the first black federal judge (William H. Hastie), the first
black Cabinet member (Robert C. Weaver), the discoverer of blood plas-
ma (Charles Drew), and the first black Senator since Reconstruction (Edward W. Brooke) were all Dunbar graduates. During World War II, Dunbar graduates in the Army included . . . a substantial percentage of the
total number of high-ranking black officers at that time."[27]

Of course Dunbar was only one school. But in 1976, Ron Edmonds, an
influential black educator and school administrator in New York, identified several other successful black schools. In a letter that was placed on
file with the *Yale Law Journal*, Edmonds listed seventy-one public schools
in the Northeast that he said were effective in teaching basic skills to poor
children. Thirty-four of these schools had student bodies that were 50 percent or more black, and blacks made up more than 75 percent of the students in sixteen of the schools. Rather than continue to emphasize the
need for racially balanced integration, Edmonds recommended that emphasis be shifted to educating black children where they were, in the inner cities.[28]

Edmonds insisted that it was a mistake to think that poor black children
could not be educated effectively unless they were integrated with children from "better" family backgrounds. After studying the test scores of
disadvantaged black students who had attended schools with different

26. Benjamin E. Mays, "Comment: Atlanta—Living with *Brown* Twenty Years Later," *Black Law Journal* 3 (1974): 184, 190–92.
27. Thomas Sowell, "Black Excellence—The Case of Dunbar High School," *Public Interest* 35 (spring 1974): 13, 2–4, 5–6.
28. Derrick Bell, "Serving Two Masters: Integration Ideals and Client Interests in School Desegregation Litigation," *Yale Law Journal* 85 (March 1976): 479.

proportions of white or middle-class students, Edmonds reached two conclusions: that "desegregation alone has little effect on pupil performance"; and that schools could succeed, even if all the students were poor and black, if the teachers had positive attitudes, maintained order, focused on basic skills, and monitored their pupils' progress with periodic testing.[29]

This message resonated in many black communities where older blacks often had fond memories of their segregated schools. "The teachers we had in those days, they knew you personally," recalled an African American from Florida. "It was like having your dad at school all day." During the era of segregation black teachers were "important people" who actually "liv[ed] in your community," added a black Texan. "We didn't have the same resources that the white students had," one North Carolinian recalled. "But we had teachers who made sure you did the very best you could with what you had." A black woman who had attended segregated schools in Missouri during the 1940s, and whose daughter attended an integrated school in the 1960s, summed it up this way: "We had teachers who were interested in us getting the best and doing our best . . . I would not trade my education that I received . . . for the education kids are receiving today."[30]

It is hard to know how many black people felt this way. Nevertheless, several scholars have used these and similar statements to challenge the idea that desegregated or integrated schools were better than the segregated schools of yesteryear. With integration, these scholars have noted, many black neighborhoods suffered a loss of community as black students were dispersed to provide "a better racial mix" at predominantly white schools. When one of the many schools named for Booker T. Washington was integrated, a former student said, "We lost the name of the school, the name of the newspaper, . . . the name of the football team, we lost school colors, we lost everything that was associated with Black History. Everything was lost because of integration." "It was not simply the end of an era," one researcher wrote of the closing of a black high school in Nashville. "It was the loss of tradition, ownership, and the collapse of a school community." "We were segregated," said a black

29. Ronald R. Edmonds, "Effective Education for Minority Pupils," in Derrick Bell, ed., *Shades of Brown* (New York: Teachers College, 1980), 110, 121.

30. *Florida Times Union,* 26 July 2001, M1; Peggy B. Gill, "Community, Commitment, and African American Education: The Jackson School of Smith County, Texas, 1925–1954," *Journal of African American History* 87 (2002): 261–62; "Teachers Weigh the Impact of *Brown* Decision," *All Things Considered* (National Public Radio, 13 December 2003); Tracey Berry, "Inherently Unequal," *Missouri Resources* (winter, 2000–2001).

graduate of Lincoln High School in Tallahassee, "but we were a good school."[31]

Some skeptics have dismissed such recollections as "a trek down nostalgia lane." Nevertheless, despite the problems that accompanied segregation, many African American communities had created good schools. "In spite of . . . inequities," Emile V. Siddle Walker has written, "the principal, parents, and teachers forged a system of education that has been documented to have been highly valued by those who were participants." "Institutional caring" was the foundation for this success. "Before school desegregation," Patricia Walker has written, black teachers were actively engaged with many activities and groups in the community—with adult organizations as well as with youth clubs. As a result, African American parents "felt comfortable coming and going in the school," and there was much "collaboration" and many "co-generative discussions with teachers." Afterwards, black students often were bused away from their neighborhoods, "disproportionately track[ed] into lower academic tracks . . . [and] disproportionately [subjected to] disciplinary actions." According to Mwalimu J. Shujaa, "the result of school desegregation . . . was a cruel irony. The cost of being integrated in schools was the disintegration of community. The children were separated from their culture."[32]

Wilmington, Delaware, provided an example. Before integration, the racially imbalanced, mostly black schools had served as centers for social activities in black neighborhoods. One community activist, Jea P. Street, recalled that when he had attended the predominantly black Wilmington High School in the 1960s, "I didn't have any talent for basketball, but I

31. Stuart Buck, "Acting White" (unpublished manuscript), chap. 5, p. 41. I am indebted to Buck's work for pointing me to many sources. He, in turn, expressed special indebtedness to the work of Vanessa Siddle Walker, *Their Highest Potential: An African American School Community in the Segregated South* (Chapel Hill: University of North Carolina Press, 1996); Vivian Gunn Morris and David L. Morris, *Creating Caring and Nurturing Educational Environments for African-American Children* (Westport, Conn.: Bergin and Garvey, 2000); David S. Cecelski, *Along Freedom Road: Hyde County, North Carolina, and the Fate of Black Schools in the South* (Chapel Hill: University of North Carolina Press, 1994); and Barbara Shircliffe, *The Best of That World: Historically Black High Schools and the Crisis of Desegregation in a Southern Metropolis* (Cresskill, N.J.: Hampton Press, 2006). See also *Charlotte Observer*, 2 April 1995; and Carter Julius Savage, "Cultural Capital and African American Agenda: The Economic Struggle for Effective Education for African Americans in Franklin, Tennessee, 1890–1967," *Journal of African American History* 87 (2002): 229.

32. Emile V. Siddle Walker, "Can Institutions Care?" in Mwalimu J. Shujaa, *Beyond Desegregation: The Politics of Quality in African American Schooling* (Thousand Oaks, Calif.: Corwin Press, 1996), 210, 215; Patricia A. Edwards, "Before and After School Desegregation," in ibid., 147; Christine J. Faltz and Donald O. Leake, "The All-Black School," in ibid., 231; Van Dempsey and George Noblit, "Cultural Ignorance," in ibid., 136.

went to all the games because the social life was the best I've known." After Wilmington's black students were dispersed in the suburbs, there was less participation in school activities, and Street maintained that the youngsters had been "systematically deprived of fun." Street's friend, Theo Gregory, a councilman in Wilmington, also noted the disadvantages of what he called "forced integration." While conceding that some black students did well in "diverse schools," Gregory said that others thrived "in an environment free of racial conflict, surrounded by those of similar background." "Some children need an incubator," Gregory said. "You go to school to learn, not to be exposed to all of society's ills." Some people said that racially concentrated schools did not prepare students "for what they're going to encounter in the real world," but Gregory feared that with fewer social activities and less sympathetic teachers many black students "might not even get out of the ninth grade." After 1978, Wilmington's public school students attended high school in the suburbs. But half of these students dropped out of school before graduating.[33]

With desegregation and integration, most black students were no longer taught by black adults who served as role models of academic success. Instead, black students were assigned to white instructors who allegedly "did not relate to the black children" and did not provide "the same nurturing of the children that the older children got from their teachers in the black schools." One black student expressed this point of view when he remarked, after transferring from an all-black school to one that was desegregated, "Today's schools don't provide black children with the support that existed during segregation, when black teachers were part of the community and kept in contact with parents. Today, black students often do not relate to white teachers."[34]

The best research indicates that, after controlling for the relevant variables, blacks who attended desegregated or integrated schools did just as well on standard tests as blacks who remained in predominantly black institutions. Nevertheless, many African Americans believed that white teachers did not push black children to succeed academically. "Whether this was because of outright racism, lower expectations, disillusionment, liberal paternalism, or whatever other cause you can imagine, the result was the same: teachers that often didn't inspire the best performance out of their students."[35]

33. Jea P. Street, interview with the author, 7 March 1982; *Wilmington News Journal*, 28 October 2005, A2.

34. Beth Roy, *Bitters in the Honey* (Fayette: University of Arkansas Press, 1999), 347; *Virginia Pilot*, 18 April 2004; *Orlando Sentinel*, 16 May 2004.

35. Buck, "Acting White," chap. 6, p. 23. For impressive research on this point, see James S. Coleman et al., *Equality of Educational Opportunity* (Washington: Government

Before the 1950s, grouping students by ability was rare in segregated black schools. But this changed after *Brown*. With blacks trailing whites in average achievement and with *Sputnik* spurring the United States to challenge the brightest students, the use of "tracking" exploded. As noted in Chapter 2, ability grouping had been a controversial subject in the early 1950s, but by the mid-1960s the controversy had subsided and "96.5 per cent of the principals responded affirmatively" when asked, "Do you group students by ability in one or more academic subjects?"[36]

Given the range of academic aptitude and achievement, it is hard to see how high schools could have done otherwise. But "tracking" had a disparate racial impact. When high schools grouped students by levels in reading and math, the highest group usually was disproportionately white and the lowest disproportionately black. One study that looked at nationally representative data reported that 15 percent of black students were in high-level English classes, compared to 32 percent of whites. Another study found that "Asians have over an 80 percent chance of being in college prep math, whites have a 43 percent chance of taking college prep math, and blacks and Latinos have less than a 15 percent chance of taking college prep math."[37]

The statistics with respect to discipline were also skewed, with black students in desegregated or integrated schools about twice as likely as whites to be punished for infractions. Researchers have investigated this matter with an eye to possible racial discrimination but have reported that the disparity occurred because black students committed more offenses than whites.[38]

Many black students and parents nevertheless believed that African Americans were being disciplined unfairly in desegregated and integrated schools. As Stuart Buck has written, "Even if discrimination were completely absent in each and every case of school discipline . . . , black parents and children might very naturally *suspect* that discrimination had played a role. If you're a black parent, and you hear from a black principal that a black teacher has had problems with your son talking back, you

Printing Office, 1966); David J. Armor, *Forced Justice: School Segregation and the Law* (New York: Oxford University Press, 1995); and Abigail Thernstrom and Stephan Thernstrom, *No Excuses: Closing the Racial Gap in Learning* (New York: Simon and Schuster, 2003).

36. James B. Conant, *The American High School Today* (New York: McGraw-Hill, 1959), ix–x; Conant, *The Comprehensive High School* (New York: McGraw-Hill, 1967), 30.

37. Buck, "Acting White," chap. 7, pp. 7–8.

38. Charles M. Achilles et al., "A Study of Issues Related to Discipline, Grouping and Tracking, and Special Education" (1982 report in files of New Castle County, Delaware, public schools); Thernstrom and Thernstrom, *No Excuses*, 55–57, 137–42.

have no reason to think that racism is involved. But if you hear from a white principal that a white teacher saw your son get in a fight, you may have more trouble trusting that the principal and teacher are being totally fair."[39]

Many African Americans also took exception to what they considered the condescending and misleading implications of seeking racially balanced integration. To assume that African Americans could not learn unless white students were present in the classroom seemed to suggest that there was something wrong with blacks. According to Malcolm X, "what the integrationists . . . are saying, when they say that blacks and whites must go to school together, is that the whites are so much superior that just their presence in the black classroom balances it out. I can't go along with that."[40]

Malcolm was a black separatist, but when it came to the need for racial balance in the schools, many more moderate blacks agreed him. The mainstream black journalist William Raspberry said it was "damaging" to tell black children "that what is wrong with their predominantly black school is that it has too many kids who look like them." According to Raspberry, this was almost as damaging as it had been in the days before *Brown,* when black children were told they could "not attend certain schools (or must attend certain other schools) because they are black." Raspberry also criticized black leaders for giving the false impression that learning was "a passive enterprise . . . something that happens to children." He said civil rights leaders were using racial imbalance as an excuse, when they should have stressed that black youths could learn, even in mostly black schools, if they had good teachers and worked conscientiously.[41]

Supreme Court Justice Clarence Thomas expressed similar views in one of his concurring opinions. "It never ceases to amaze me that the courts are so willing to assume that anything that is predominantly black must be inferior," Thomas wrote. Some integrationists assumed "that blacks cannot succeed without the benefit of the company of whites"; that "blacks, when left on their own, cannot achieve." The black economist Glenn Loury made the same point in pithy language: "We need better schools, not racial condescension."[42]

39. Buck, "Acting White," chap. 6, p. 42.

40. George Breitman, ed., *Malcolm X: By Any Means Necessary* (New York: Pathfinder Press, 1970), 17.

41. *Washington Post,* 19 December 1987, A25; 16 September 1985, A17b.

42. *Missouri v. Jenkins,* 63 USLW 4486 (1995), 4498–4500; Glenn C. Loury, "Integration Has Had Its Day," *New York Times,* 23 April 1996, A23.

In addition, many African American parents were practical people who thought it made more sense to devote scarce resources to addressing their children's educational needs directly. Instead of stressing the long-term benefits that might accrue from gaining greater familiarity with the ways of the white world, they stressed the importance of improving their neighborhood schools. They also recognized that there was an important difference between schools that were black because the neighborhood was black and the dual school systems that had existed in many states before *Brown.* Biloine Whiting Young and Grace Billings Bress, two black teachers who wrote about education, insisted that it was inappropriate to extend the word *segregation* "beyond the specific Southern *de jure* meaning to include this Northern *de facto* imbalance." They said the semantic conflation was misleading, because it "conveyed the assumption that the problem in the North was identical to the Southern situation." This was "dangerously simplistic," because it suggested "that if the correct racial mix can be provided in a classroom, problems of low achievement and racial tensions will disappear."[43]

The growing defection of former supporters alarmed traditional integrationists, who were especially startled when Ruby Martin joined "the opposition." Martin had headed the Office of Civil Rights in 1965–1966, when the administration of President Lyndon B. Johnson rejected freedom-of-choice plans and demanded racially balanced integration as proof that schools were truly desegregated. In 1975, however, Martin told old friends in the civil rights movement that she "no longer consider[ed] integration a high priority." She said she preferred to concentrate her efforts "on black children where they are, in the slums."[44]

Derrick Bell experienced a similar change of mind. At one time Bell had supervised three hundred school desegregation and integration lawsuits for the NAACP. He spent so much time in Mississippi during the early 1960s that he paid income taxes there, "based on the percentage of my income earned while in the state." Bell also possessed a combative temperament. He delighted in challenging the white power structure. His goal was "organized resistance to racial subjugation."[45]

Nevertheless, Bell eventually concluded that he had been "more committed than wise." "The belief that I was doing the Lord's work did not relieve me of the obligation to consider . . . what I was doing." "Why was

43. Young and Bress, "New Educational Decision," 516, 519.
44. Robert Reinhold, "Busing: Integrationists Now Have Their Doubts," *New York Times,* 22 June 1975, 194.
45. Derrick Bell, *Silent Covenants: Brown v. Board of Education and the Unfulfilled Hopes for Racial Reform* (New York: Oxford University Press, 2004), 98, 103.

I trying to get [black] children admitted to schools where they were not wanted?" Why push for admission of blacks to schools where, "unless they were exceptional, they would fare poorly, perhaps responding to their hostile treatment and getting into difficulties that would result in their expulsion?" Bell suspected that he had been "blinded" by his "zealous faith in integration." In the 1970s he came to the conclusion that "a singular focus on racial balance" was actually counterproductive, because it distracted attention away from efforts to improve education "and led us to pursue integration without regard to, and often despite, its ultimate impact on the well-being of students."[46]

In explaining his turnabout, Bell reiterated some of the explanations that others had offered. He noted that the rationale for racial balance perpetuated "the demeaning and unproven assumption that blacks must have a majority-white presence in order either to teach or to learn effectively." He recognized that "few ... desegregated districts show black scholastic achievement scores equal to those of whites," a result that he considered "the most distressing aspect of school desegregation." He said that integrated black students usually did "not receive ... the spiritual uplift and self-assurance that come from being a part of an institution where persons like themselves are in charge, and where the rank and file of students and teachers share their interests, view, and expreiences."[47]

Bell, however, emphasized *legal* points, as befitted an attorney who, after leaving the NAACP, became a law professor at Oregon, Stanford, Harvard, and NYU. In an article entitled "Serving Two Masters," Bell challenged the propriety of using class action lawsuits to obtain court-ordered, racially balanced school integration. When civil rights lawyers petitioned courts for such orders, they claimed to be acting on behalf of the entire class of African Americans. In point of fact, Bell wrote, these lawyers answered only to the people who financed the NAACP—"middle class blacks and whites who believe fervently in integration."[48]

According to Bell, the civil rights lawyers ignored the fact that substantial numbers of African Americans did not favor the racial balance that was being sought in their behalf. In the case of school-integration law-

46. Bell, *Silent Covenants*, 106, 113.
47. Derrick Bell, "A Reassessment of Racial Balance Remedies," *Phi Delta Kappan*, November 1980, 177; Bell, "Learning from Our Losses," *Phi Delta Kappan*, April 1983, 575; Bell, "A Model Alternative Desegregation Plan," in Bell, *Shades of Brown*, 138.
48. Bell, "Serving Two Masters," 489. In making this argument, Bell was developing and quoting from an article of Ron Edmonds, "Advocating Inequity: A Critique of the Civil Rights Attorney in Class Action Desegregation Suits, *Black Law Journal* 3 (1974).

suits, the fee-paying minority was "impos[ing] its will on the majority of the class on whose behalf [the] suit [was] presumably brought." As Bell saw it, the civil rights lawyers failed to reflect the significant changes that had occurred in black thinking. In the 1950s and early 1960s, "virtually all blacks" had assumed "that integration was the best means of achieving a quality education for black children." Yet the NAACP continued to seek the same remedy decades later, "when many black parents are disenchanted with the educational results of integration." Bell urged the courts to "develop greater sensitivity to the growing disagreement in black communities over the nature of school relief."[49]

Civil rights lawyers predictably rejected Bell's argument. Nathaniel R. Jones of the NAACP insisted that "the overwhelming number of blacks" continued to support the policy of his organization. He rejected "Professor Bell's allegation that civil rights lawyers do not ethically represent the interests of the black community." In response, Bell reiterated that "a substantial percentage of black parents have become disenchanted with the results of relief based on racial balance and busing, and thus politics and professional ethics dictate reassessment of that policy." "Most black and white parents are more concerned with the quality of their children's education than with either integration or separation."[50]

While some black educators and lawyers were expressing these reservations, two black anthropologists sparked another controversy that eventually led to additional questions about the value of integration. Writing in the *Urban Review* in 1986, John Ogbu (an African immigrant) and Signithia Fordham (an African American) focused on what they called "the burden of 'acting white.'" Because of the past history of racial discrimination in employment, Ogbu and Fordham maintained, black students did not expect to benefit from doing well in school. As a result, African American youths had developed a peer-group culture that discouraged academic effort as "acting white." According to Ogbu and Fordham, black teenagers went beyond the teasing and nerd bashing that is common in most high schools. They regarded outstanding black students as racial turncoats of a sort. By doing well in school—by reading books, getting good grades, and speaking standard English—stellar black students were

49. Bell, "Serving Two Masters," 491, 492.
50. Nathaniel R. Jones to *Yale Law Journal* 86 (December 1976): 380, 381; Derrick A. Bell to *Yale Law Journal* 86 (December 1976): 384. Drew S. Days is another former NAACP litigator who has expressed doubts about his work for racially balanced integration. See Days, "In Search of Educational E/Quality," *Southern Methodist University Law Review* 54 (fall 2001): 2089–99.

said to evince a desire to separate themselves from their racial brother-hood.[51]

At first "acting white" was a phrase used mostly by scholars writing in academic journals. During the 1990s, however, the term came into common parlance as a way of describing high-achieving but allegedly snobbish black students who were shunned by their peers. By the end of the decade, negative peer pressure had emerged as a common explanation for the failure of blacks to do better on standard achievement tests. In order to avoid the social sanctions of their peers, many able African American students were said to have deliberately decided not to do their best in school.

Eventually "acting white" became the subject of a contentious academic dispute.[52] More immediately, it influenced the intra-black debate on desegregation and integration. Ogbu and Fordham's initial research had focused on inner-city schools that were almost all black, and some observers attributed the culture of antiachievement to the fact that, with desegregation, many academically oriented middle-class black professional people had fled to the suburbs. "That left fewer role models whose success reinforced the importance of education and more children from families who found little grounds for hope in schools." Thus the dispersion of middle-class blacks arguably aggravated conditions in the inner cities—a result that some observers considered an unintended happenstance but one that W. E. B. Du Bois had predicted. In the 1980s and 1990s, the Harvard sociologist William Julius Wilson documented the emergence of delinquent subcultures in black neighborhoods that were bereft of middle-class role models. University of Pennsylvania sociologists Douglas Massey and Nancy Denton also noted that "an alternative status system has evolved within America's ghettos that is defined *in opposition to* the basic ideals and values of American society."[53]

With the passage of time, it became apparent that "acting white" was not limited to the predominantly black, inner-city schools that the black

51. John U. Ogbu and Sinithia Fordham, "Black Students' School Success: Coping with the Burden of 'Acting White,'" *Urban Review* 18 (1986): 176–206.
52. Stuart Buck's forthcoming book ("Acting White") provides an excellent discussion of the scholarly studies on this subject. See also Erin McNamara Horvat and Carla O'Connor, eds., *Beyond Acting White: Reframing the Debate on Black Student Achievement* (Lanham, Md.: Rowan and Littlefield, 2006).
53. *Time*, 16 March 1992, 45; William Julius Wilson, *The Truly Disadvantaged* (Chicago: University of Chicago Press, 1987); Wilson, *When Work Disappears: The World of the New Urban Poor* (New York: Alfred A. Knopf, 1996); Douglas S. Massey and Nancy A. Denton, *American Apartheid: Segregation and the Making of the Underclass* (Cambridge: Harvard University Press, 1993).

middle class had abandoned. In one suburb after another, the children of successful African American professional people also lagged far behind their white classmates on almost every measure of academic success. In fact, in many middle- and upper-class schools, the children of black professionals trailed their white classmates by greater margins than those that separated inner-city and rural black students from their white classmates. This became a matter of grave concern to the black doctors, lawyers, judges, and other professional people who had moved to upscale suburbs specifically because of their supposedly outstanding school systems.[54]

Some observers wondered if integration was not responsible for some of the problems of black students. In most high schools, students attended classes with peers who were at similar levels of academic achievement. But this grouping had a disparate racial effect—with relatively few black students enrolled in higher-level courses but instead disproportionately concentrated in lower-level ones. Consequently, one researcher in North Carolina noted, "low achievers develop[ed] strategies to help them maintain positive perceptions of themselves (including pretending they do not care about achievement or rewards)." Beverly Daniel Tatum, the president of Spelman College, pointed out that "An oppositional identity that disdains academic achievement has not always been a characteristic of Black adolescent peer groups. It seems to be a post-desegregation phenomenon."[55]

Many African Americans were ambivalent about the "acting white" theory. It shifted blame for the racial achievement gap away from white racism and discrimination and instead attributed the gap, at least in part, to the attitudes of blacks themselves. Some people also attributed the phenomenon not to desegregation but to the practice of grouping students by ability—a practice they considered nefarious. Others qualified the theory. After interviewing about 140 integrated black students in Charlotte, North Carolina, sociologists Roslyn Arlin Mickelson and Anne E. Velasco reached a measured conclusion: "while some students may avoid academic achievement and difficult classes due to the fear of being labeled [mentally slow], others find the cultural stereotypes of Blacks as less intelligent and the acting-white epithet motivating. They interpret

54. For extended discussion of this point, see John U. Ogbu, *Black Americans in an Affluent Suburb: A Study of Academic Disengagement* (Mahwah, N.J.: L. Erlbaum Associates, 2003).

55. Karolyn Tyson, "The Making of a 'Burden,'" in Horvat and O'Connor, *Beyond Acting White*, 71; Beverly Daniel Tatum, *Why Are All the Black Kids Sitting Together in the Cafeteria?* (New York: Basic Books, 1997), 64–65.

these aspersions as a personal challenge, goading them to excel in school and to embrace academic success as a way of 'acting black.'"[56]

Despite the qualifications, many blacks embraced the "acting white" theory. One young black scholar, John McWhorter of Berkeley, wrote at length about "self-sabotage in black America." Henry Louis Gates of Harvard said that fear of "acting white" was one of the ways blacks themselves had "'reforged the manacles' of the slave era." Hugh Price, the president of the National Urban League, urged black youths to put "a stop to the anti-achievement peer culture in our own community." In syndicated opinion columns, William Raspberry and Thomas Sowell referred to "acting white" while urging fellow blacks to take personal responsibility and stop assuming the role of victims.[57]

Roland Fryer of Harvard provided some of the most persuasive support for the "acting white" theory. Unlike ethnographers and journalists who based their conclusions on personal observations and interviews, Fryer presented empirical evidence to demonstrate that "acting white" was real. To measure the phenomenon, he developed "an index of social popularity" and asked 90,000 students at 175 schools to list their closest male and female friends, up to five of each sex. Students who were listed as a friend by many peers were then regarded as the social elite, while those who were listed by only a few peers stood out as marginal members of the community. Fryer then tabulated whether high-achieving African American students were less popular than lower-achieving black students. And he compared this result with the result for white students.[58]

Fryer's data indicated, first, that "acting white" was real. Among students with low grades, there was little difference among ethnic groups, with blacks and whites enjoying about the same degree of popularity. Middling students of both races also turned out to be more popular than those with lower grades. But Fryer reported that the experience of black and white students diverged as their grade averages climbed above B+.

56. Roslyn Arlin Mickelson and Anne E. Velasco, "Diverse Responses to 'Acting White,'" in Horvat and O'Connor, Beyond Acting White, 30.

57. John McWhorter, Losing the Race: Self-Sabotage in Black America (New York: Free Press, 2000); McWhorter, Authentically Black (New York: Gotham Books, 2003); Henry Louis Gates, quoted by M. Jogger, Guardian, 6 July 2002, 20; Hugh Price, quoted by Brian Mooar, Washington Post, 4 August 1997, A12; William Raspberry, column in Washington Post, 23 December 1989, A19, and 9 December 2002, A23; Thomas Sowell, columns in Columbus Dispatch, 25 May 1997, G3, and Chicago Sun-Times, 30 September 1997, 25.

58. Esquire, December 2005, 218, 229; Roland G. Fryer, "'Acting White,'" Education Next 6 (winter 2006): 53–59; Roland G. Fryer and Paul Torelli, "An Empirical Analysis of 'Acting White,'" NBER Working Paper W11334, 2005.

"As the GPAs of black students increase beyond this level, they tend to have fewer and fewer friends." "Social penalties [were] imposed for acting white." Fryer further reported that "acting white" was "unique to those schools where black students comprise[d] less than 80 percent of the population." In schools that were almost all black, he found "no evidence at all that getting good grades adversely affects students' popularity."[59]

It was controversial for Fryer to validate the existence of "acting white"—since the corroboration emphasized problems created by the attitudes of blacks themselves rather than difficulties that might be ascribed to white people or to other social barriers. Some saw in Fryer (and Ogbu, too) another instance of "blaming the victim." And Fryer's second conclusion—that opposition to "acting white" was more prevalent when schools were integrated—was especially contentious. It was also at odds with the reports of Ogbu and other ethnographers who had lived among black students and personally observed the interactions at schools that were almost all-black. Fryer nevertheless insisted, "the evidence indicates that the social disease [criticism of peers who were successful at school work] . . . is most prevalent in racially integrated public schools. It's less of a problem in the private sector and in predominantly black public schools."[60]

Fryer understood that his data raised troubling questions. "That acting white is more prevalent in schools with more interethnic contact hardly passes the test of political correctness," he conceded. Nevertheless, it seemed that avoiding intellectual engagement and disparaging academic work was a defense mechanism for black students who had been forced to compete with better-prepared whites and Asians. One black teacher recalled that when she graduated from a segregated high school in Virginia, she "could see these kids walking up there with these four-year scholarships to places like Fisk and Howard or A&T or wherever." After desegregation and integration, however, "the only kids I see getting the scholarships are white kids."[61]

Fryer emphasized yet another point. Whenever a cohesive group faced the danger of losing its most successful members to outsiders, he said, "then the group will seek to prevent the outflow." The Amish, for example, were known "for limiting their children's education for fear that too much contact with the outside world risks the community's survival." Similarly, Fryer speculated, many African Americans feared that their

59. Fryer, "'Acting White,'" 56, 57.
60. Ibid., 54.
61. Ibid., 58; Michele Foster, *Black Teachers on Teaching* (New York: New Press, 1997), 60.

most successful students would no longer identify with their race. They feared that, rather than provide leadership for the black masses, the educated elite would scatter and attempt to escape from their race. They regarded residence in a mostly white neighborhood or attendance at an integrated school as a first step in this direction. "To forestall such erosion [of racial or group identification]," Fryer reasoned, "groups may try to reinforce their identity by penalizing members for differentiating themselves from the group." Thus the social sanctions for acting white were especially severe in integrated schools.[62]

There was yet another consideration that contributed to black opposition to integration. In 1966 James S. Coleman had reported that predominantly black schools were funded at about the same level as other schools in their region, and with time the funding for inner-city schools became still more generous. President Lyndon B. Johnson's Elementary and Secondary Education Act of 1965 provided billions of dollars for what were called "Title I programs"—programs that provided breakfasts and lunches for poor students and paid for teachers' assistants and cultural enrichment at schools with sizeable enrollments of students from families with low incomes. The Supreme Court of Chief Justice Warren E. Burger then gave added impetus to this approach. After ruling against interdistrict busing between Detroit and its suburbs, the Court ordered the state of Michigan (and later, other states) to appropriate more money for remedial education in schools that were "racially isolated." President Richard M. Nixon also endorsed this policy. Even as he criticized busing for racial balance, Nixon directed an additional two billion dollars of federal aid to poor and inner-city schools. In a nationally televised address, Nixon declared: "It is time for us to make a national commitment to see that the schools in the central cities are upgraded so that the children who go there will have just as good a chance to get quality education as do the children who go to school in the suburbs."[63]

In the 1980s and 1990s, the funding for inner-city schools was increased again—as a result of lawsuits in which civil rights lawyers demanded that states make good on the equal protection provisions that most state constitutions contained. In response, several state supreme courts required that districts throughout the state should spend approximately the same amount per student or required, as in New Jersey, that the expenditure

62. Fryer, "'Acting White,'" 58–59.
63. Elementary and Secondary Education Act, Public Law 89–10 (1965); *Milliken v. Bradley*, 418 U.S. 717 (1977); Milliken II; "Transcript of President Nixon's Statement on School Busing," *New York Times*, 17 March 1972, 22.

per pupil in poor districts should exceed statewide averages and match the amount spent in the wealthiest suburbs.[64]

After achieving the equalization of school funding, and emboldened especially by their victory in New Jersey, civil rights lawyers proceeded with demands for extra funding. In addition to equal protection clauses, many state constitutions also contained provisions that required the state to provide an "adequate public education," a "thorough and efficient system of free schools," or "an educational program of high quality." Such statements had previously been considered vague generalizations, but in the 1980s and 1990s, litigators persuaded several courts to interpret this language to mean that states must move beyond equalization and provide the extra funds that were required to make public education "adequate" or "sufficient" for students who had suffered the disadvantages associated with living in poverty.[65]

One wonders how long the populace will support allocating resources disproportionately to urban schools. Nevertheless, the successes of "equity" and "adequacy" litigators had the short-term side effect of undermining black support for integration. As the legal scholar Robert A. Garda has explained, "With the hope that all schools will be sufficiently funded to yield adequate educational outcomes, parents have little reason to demand integration." In 1994, a Gallup poll reported that 64 percent of African Americans chose "increased funding" as the best way to help minorities, while only 25 percent favored "integration." Sixty-four percent also said they would choose local schools over integrated schools outside of their community.[66]

The Case for Integration

The proponents of racially balanced integration did not suffer in silence. They responded to every point, and then some. Perhaps because

64. James E. Ryan and Michael Heise, "The Political Economy of School Choice," *Yale Law Journal* 111 (2002): 2059.

65. There is a large and growing literature on this subject. See Peter Schrag, *Final Test* (New York: New Press, 2003); and James S. Liebman and Charles F. Sabel, "A Public Laboratory Dewey Barely Imagined," *New York University Review of Law and Social Change* 28 (2003): 183–304. The quotations are from the constitutions of Georgia, New Jersey, and Virginia.

66. Robert A. Garda Jr., "Coming Full Circle: The Journey from Separate but Equal to Separate and Unequal Schools," *Duke Journal of Constitutional Law and Public Policy* 2 (2007): 54.

James S. Coleman had formerly been their ally, perhaps because Coleman had spoken candidly about the misbehavior of black students, and perhaps because they feared that Coleman's turnabout would serve as a precursor for additional criticism of racially balanced integration, the civil rights establishment not only challenged Coleman's research on white flight but also cast aspersions on his character.

Civil rights activists began by disregarding Coleman's insistence that he was still an integrationist—that he was simply trying to identify policies that would work as distinguished from policies that were counterproductive. NAACP executive Roy Wilkins denounced Coleman's traitorous "defection," and the Brookings Institution, the Notre Dame Center for Civil Rights, and the Catholic University Center for National Policy Review organized symposia to refute Coleman's findings on white flight. The *Harvard Educational Review* also featured an article that criticized Coleman's research on white flight.[67]

The civil rights establishment also went to work on the media. Over the course of several decades, the establishment had cultivated connections and had used its influence to shape the public perception of the social science research on integrated education. Thus, as historian Diane Ravitch has noted, in 1966 journalists lauded Coleman's first report as "firm evidence" for busing and generally treated Coleman himself "as a giant in his field, a social scientist with a progressive agenda." After the second Coleman report of 1975, however, the liberal media "turned hostile," "questioned [Coleman's] findings," and "frequently quoted critics."[68]

Most of the criticism focused on the statistics pertaining to white flight. Critics said that Coleman did not look at enough cities and that he confused a long-term trend toward moving to the suburbs with a flight from court-ordered racial balance. The most highly regarded of these critiques was by Christine H. Rossell, then an assistant professor of political science at Boston University. Gary Orfield, the editor of a volume of anti-Coleman papers, called Rossell's study "particularly impressive," and Robert L. Green, a social scientist who himself had denounced Coleman's claim that court-ordered busing led to white flight, described Rossell's work as "the most serious challenge to the Coleman position." According to Rossell, "School desegregation cause[d] little or no significant white flight, even

67. Thomas F. Pettigrew and Robert L. Green, "School Desegregation in Large Cities: A Critique of the Coleman 'White Flight' Thesis," *Harvard Educational Review* 46 (February 1976): 1–53.

68. Diane Ravitch, "The Coleman Reports and American Education," in B. Sorenson Aage and Seymour Spilerman, eds., *Social Theory and Social Policy: Essays in Honor of James S. Coleman* (Westport, Conn.: Praeger, 1993), 129–41.

when it is court ordered and implemented in large cities." She said her data "contradict almost every claim Coleman has made regarding school desegregation and white flight."[69]

It turned out, however, that the statistics in Coleman's second report were sound. Eventually most experts—regardless of their policy preferences—acknowledged the problem of middle-class flight. By 1980, most of the nation's large cities had lost more than 40 percent of their white students. Eventually even Professor Rossell conceded that Coleman had been right.[70]

It is rare for a scholar's major critic to concede that she had been mistaken, but Professor Rossell's concession did not rehabilitate Coleman—at least not in some quarters. One persistent critic was Alfred McClung Lee, a sociologist who had worked with Kenneth Clark in the 1950s on the social science statement that the NAACP had submitted in the *Brown* litigation. In 1976 Lee became the president of the American Sociological Association, and he used his new position to denounce Coleman at a press conference and then to ask the Ethics Committee of the association to censure Coleman. Still later, Lee asked the general membership of the organization to condemn Coleman. Cooler heads ultimately prevailed, and Coleman eventually confronted his critics at a plenary session of the association. The walls at that session were plastered with posters bearing Coleman's name, Nazi swastikas, and various epithets. For some time thereafter, Coleman suffered through "a tortured period of intellectual isolation." "We should not forget," Coleman later wrote, "how strong the consensus was at that time among social scientists that bussing was an unalloyed benefit, and a policy not to be questioned."[71]

Coleman survived the censure. His standing as a sociologist remained high, and he himself later became the president of the American Sociological Association. Accepting an award in 1988, Coleman acknowledged that "recognition by one's fellow researchers is one of the highest honors

69. Diane Ravitch, "The 'White Flight' Controversy," *Public Interest* 51 (spring 1978): 136–37; Christine H. Rossell, "School Desegregation and White Flight," *Political Science Quarterly* 90 (winter 1975): 688; Diane Ravitch, "Reply to Rossell," *Public Interest* 53 (fall 1978): 111–13.

70. Christine H. Rossell, *The Carrot or the Stick* (Philadelphia: Temple University Press, 1990), xii, xiv; *New York Times*, 26 November 1978, E7. In unpublished papers and in a 1978 letter to *Public Interest* 53 (fall 1978, 109–11), Professor Rossell admitted that Coleman's second report was essentially correct. For a more recent, well-informed assessment of the "white flight" controversy, see Charles T. Clotfelter, *After Brown: The Rise and Retreat of School Desegregation* (Princeton: Princeton University Press, 2004), chapter 2.

71. James S. Coleman, letters to the American Sociological Association, published in *ASA Footnotes*, November 1976, 4; January 1989, 4–5.

that can be bestowed." Yet he also recalled that it had been difficult to withstand the criticism of peers, and he lamented that others, including "some of the most original and brilliant sociologists," had been "driven to the periphery or to adjacent disciplines because the implication of their work runs counter to the current intellectual fashion." In the academic world, Coleman noted, "the threat posed by fellow faculty members is probably greater than that posed by the usual villains." In sociology, academic freedom had been constricted, not by external pressures from either the right or the left, but by fellow scholars who were predisposed against research that challenged the conventional wisdom of the liberal mainstream.[72]

When Coleman spoke of sociologists who were driven from academe, he might have had in mind the case of David Armor, the author of "The Evidence on Busing." That article had enjoyed tremendous influence because, as noted by Oscar Cohen of the Anti-Defamation League, "it's been seized on by the opponents of busing and desegregation all over the country to further their cause." Like Coleman, Armor said he was simply an honest scholar who was trying to determine what really worked. "I have to believe that knowledge in the long run can't hurt," Armor said. "I support voluntary busing programs, but we have to know the facts to make intelligent decisions. . . . If you don't know what's true, you stand the danger of doing harm despite the best intentions."[73]

Proponents of racially balanced integration had no choice but to answer Armor's influential article. One of the first responses came in the winter of 1973 when Thomas F. Pettigrew and three other professors at Harvard published a critique that called attention to what they called "extremely serious methodological problems" and further complained that Armor had presented "selected findings from selected studies." They said that integration could not be expected to work unless there was "*classroom—* not just school—desegregation," and unless there was "avoidance of strict ability grouping" in the integrated classrooms. They noted, in addition, that the ambitions of bused black students remained high, and argued that the slight decline in this respect "should be considered a positive, not a negative effect," in that it indicated that bused black students were becoming more realistic about their prospects in the wider world. Pettigrew and his coauthors also stressed a point that would receive greater emphasis with the passage of time: that "the most significant ef-

72. *ASA Footnotes*, January 1989, 4–5; James S. Coleman, "Sins of Sensitivity: A Quiet Threat to Academic Freedom," *National Review* 43 (18 March 1991): 28–32.
73. *Washington Post*, 11 June 1972, A1.

fect of integrated schools is probably not 'educational.'" It was "that Negroes who attend integrated schools will have more contact with whites" and therefore would be more comfortable in the white world when they were adults.[74]

Pettigrew and his coauthors did not present evidence to show that integrated education had enhanced the academic achievement of black students. They had, instead, picked at methodological flaws to show that the absence of benefits had not been proven. To this they added that the whole question of mandatory busing was really a constitutional issue, to be decided by the judiciary's interpretation of the Fourteenth Amendment. The civil rights establishment had initially used social science to promote desegregation or integration, as with Kenneth Clark's doll studies in *Brown* and James S. Coleman's pro-busing testimony in later cases, but now Pettigrew and his coauthors maintained that the burden of social science proof should fall on those who opposed busing for racial balance; and that the whole matter was really a constitutional issue that should be determined on a strictly legal basis. In reply, Armor said that Pettigrew was applying a "double double standard."[75]

There was more. When he published "The Evidence on Busing" in 1972, Armor was a junior professor at Harvard, with an office two doors away from Pettigrew, who had been one of Armor's professors when Armor was a graduate student. On more than one occasion in the past, Pettigrew had recommended Armor for research positions, but now the senior professor said that going through Armor's work was "like cleaning out the Augean stable, an incredible job. We keep shoveling away and there just turns out to be more of it yet." Some Harvard professors, including Daniel Bell and Christopher Jencks, defended Armor's integrity and competence, but others, while praising Armor's work privately, refused to be quoted by name. "Only a damn fool would talk," one said. "I don't want to pay the price."[76]

After leaving Harvard in 1972 to take a teaching position at UCLA, some of Armor's colleagues in California boycotted and demonstrated against Armor's course on race relations. In the meantime, Armor received a job offer from the Rand Corporation, and because of the contro-

74. Thomas F. Pettigrew, Elizabeth L. Useem, Clarence Normand, and Marshall S. Smith, "Busing: A Review of 'The Evidence,'" *Public Interest* 30 (winter 1973): 89, 107, 108, 111.

75. David J. Armor, "The Double Double Standard," *Public Interest* 30 (winter 1973): 119–31.

76. Lawrence W. Feinberg, "Busing Study Stirs Anger," *Washington Post*, 11 June 1972, A1; Armor, "Reflections," 5.

versy his research had caused at both Harvard and UCLA, he decided that a research institute might be a better place to do his work. He did not return to an academic position until 1989, when he accepted a visiting professorship at Rutgers University. In 1992 Armor became a regular member of the faculty at George Mason University.

Because the civil rights lobby was adept at intimidation and at ad hominem criticism, there is a temptation to disregard the substance of their statements. In the case of court-ordered integration, however, this would be a mistake, for the lobby also mounted a scholarly defense of the policy. One pithy expression of this was a "Social Science Statement" that was signed by fifty-two scholars in 1991 and submitted as an appendix to the brief of the NAACP in a school-integration case, *Freeman v. Pitts.*[77]

Drawing on the research of several pro-integration stalwarts, the NAACP's new social science statement reiterated a point that integrationists had been disseminating for years: that there was "wide agreement on the basic conclusion: 'Desegregation is generally associated with moderate gains in the achievement of black students and the achievement of white students is typically unaffected.'" Nevertheless, the district judge in *Freeman v. Pitts* recognized that many scholars would not accept this as a fair summary of the relevant research. After listening to the testimony of opposing experts, Judge William C. O'Kelley sided with those who disputed the alleged benefits of balanced racial mixing, finding "the evidence presented by the defendants' experts to be more reliable on this issue."[78]

A careful reading of the NAACP's social science statement suggests that the fifty-two social scientists tried to reconcile their policy preference with the evidence by redefining the meaning of *desegregation*. They began by equating *desegregation* and *integration*. Then, while saying that *desegregation* was generally associated with moderate gains for black students and no losses for whites, the NAACP's social scientists also said that a school was not truly *desegregated* unless the school had abolished ability grouping, scrapped the traditional lecture method in favor of "innovative teaching techniques such as cooperative learning groups," adopted "multi-ethnic texts," implemented new grading policies, established "empathetic human relations programs for teachers," and changed the

77. "School Desegregation: A Social Science Statement," in brief of the NAACP as amicus curiae in support of respondents, *Freeman v. Pitts*, 503 U.S. 467 (1992). This statement drew especially on research by Robert Crain, James McPartland, Gary Orfield, Karl Taeuber, and Meyer Weinberg.

78. Ibid., 7a; Armor, "Reflections," 16 (quoting *Pitts v. Freeman*, Civil Action 11946, Northern District of Georgia, Atlanta Division [1988], 23).

school's mascots and symbols "to create an inclusive community and minimize racial and social tensions." Only after implementing these and other policies, the statement implied, would it be possible to determine how *desegregation* affected academic achievement. Since no schools had implemented all the conditions that the signatories considered essential for *desegregation,* the statement essentially sidestepped the evidence that busing for racial balance had not boosted the academic achievement of black students.[79]

By the 1990s, the social science evidence was mixed. Much of it either cast doubt on the value of racially balanced integration or was inconclusive (if one believed that integration had yet to be implemented). Proponents of busing for racial balance then shifted to another argument, a celebration of "diversity." This point of view had been percolating for years and came into vogue in the 1990s. The NAACP's social science statement of 1991 emphasized that truly integrated education would "motivate minority students, giving them hope that they will have an opportunity as adults to escape segregated job markets." The statement asserted, in addition, that white students would "benefit from learning to function in a racially diverse setting that can prepare them for the workforce of the future." According to the statement, "Whites who know how to function effectively in a multiracial setting will have substantial advantages in the job settings of the future," and integrated blacks were more likely to acquire the social skills needed for easy interaction with whites.[80]

The NAACP's social science statement emphasized that students of both races suffered from isolation. Whites lacked familiarity with the racial and ethnic minorities that were becoming a larger proportion of the American population, and impoverished minorities were immersed in a dead-end world. In important respects, the statement harkened back to the Coleman report of 1966. It said that values and culture influenced academic achievement, and the best strategy for improving the schoolwork of minority students was to expose them to the ways of the mainstream, white world. With reciprocal exposure, each group would benefit from becoming more familiar with the ways of the other. Without such exposure the nation would remain, in the words of the Johnson-era Kerner commission, "two nations, separate and unequal."[81]

The argument for "diversity" had been building for years. In imple-

79. "School Desegregation: A Social Science Statement," 14a–21a.

80. Ibid., 8a, 11a.

81. For additional statements of this view, see James Traub, "Can Separate Be Equal?" *Harper's Magazine,* June 1994, 36–47; and Jonathan Kozol, *The Shame of the Nation* (New York: Crown Publishers, 2005).

menting the orders that the Supreme Court handed down in *Green v. New Kent County* (1968) and *Swann v. Charlotte Mecklenburg* (1971)—the orders that called for the maximum feasible amount of racial interaction—several federal judges stressed the need to prepare students for democratic interaction in a multiethnic society. Thus Judge Luther Bohanan, when ordering busing for racial balance in Oklahoma City in 1970, emphasized the importance of giving students "the experience of functioning in a multiethnic situation similar to that of the larger society." According to Judge Bohanan, "extensive contact with other children at an early stage" was "indispensable" if youngsters were "to become inculcated with a meaningful understanding of the essentials of our democratic way of life."[82]

The celebration of "diversity" would receive special emphasis in *The Shame of the Nation,* a book that the best-selling author Jonathan Kozol published in 2005. According to Kozol, all children suffered from racial insularity. But African American children suffered especially, because their isolation in predominantly black schools left them with "little knowledge of the ordinary reference points" that one had to be familiar with in order to succeed in the American mainstream. To illustrate his point Kozol mentioned the case of Roger Wilkins, a black lawyer who became an assistant attorney general in the administration of President Lyndon B. Johnson. Wilkins had spent his early school years in segregated Missouri and racially concentrated Harlem. In high school, however, his family moved to Grand Rapids, Michigan, where Wilkins attended "an almost totally white high school." At first Wilkins felt isolated socially, but then he started making friends and learned how to function in the white world. "If I had not had that kind of education," Wilkins said, he would have been less "at ease among white people" and less likely to succeed in his career.[83]

Kozol and other integration enthusiasts shifted the grounds when they stressed "diversity" as a rationale for balanced mixing. Although this justification had been mentioned for years, before the 1990s it had been a subordinate consideration. The justices of the Supreme Court had regarded integration as remedial—restoring a notional status quo—while most civil rights activists had believed that balanced mixing enhanced the academic achievement of minority students. When the evidence of educational improvement turned out to be thin or nonexistent, however, diversity for its own sake became a spearhead argument. As will be noted in Chapter 9 and especially in Chapter 10, the standard argument for racial-

82. *Dowell v. Oklahoma City,* 219 F.Supp. 427 (1970), 599; Raymond Wolters, *Right Turn: William Bradford Reynolds, the Reagan Administration, and Black Civil Rights* (New Brunswick: Transaction Publishers, 1996), 447, 449.

83. Kozol, *Shame of the Nation,* 17, 238–39, and passim.

ly balanced integration shifted from "it will lift the academic achievement of black students" to the contention that balanced mingling would better equip all students to make their ways in a multiracial world. The new rationale, unlike the "enhanced performance" argument, had the advantage of being hard to disprove. The predictions of improved academic performance, after all, were testable. They could be verified or disproved. The diversity argument, on the other hand, was almost impossible to establish or to discredit. When the argument for improving the academic education of minority children washed out, integration enthusiasts celebrated diversity as a policy for cultivating social skills. Beginning in the 1990s, they increasingly insisted that their policy would enable students to get along better in a multicultural globalized world. The "Roger Wilkins story" became a familiar refrain. It was against this background that the Supreme Court of the 1990s returned to the question of busing for racial balance, a subject that the Court had not addressed since 1979.

9

From *Brown* to *Green* and Back

It was inevitable that local people eventually would ask to be released from busing decrees. For a generation, the Supreme Court had emphasized that the courts' jurisdiction over "desegregating" districts should be only temporary. *Brown* had said the district courts should "retain jurisdiction" during the "period of transition" between segregation and desegregation. *Swann* had said, "[A]t some point, these school authorities and others like them should have achieved full compliance with this Court's decisions," at which point "further intervention by a district court should not be necessary." In 1985 former solicitor general Rex E. Lee identified the termination of court orders as "the most important unresolved issue in the school desegregation area." The key questions were, "When, and on what showing, should the governance of school systems be restored to elected officials?" "Under what conditions, if any, should court-ordered busing yield to local preferences for neighborhood schools?" The Supreme Court answered these questions in three important cases of the 1990s, *Oklahoma City v. Dowell* (1991), *Freeman v. Pitts* (1992), and *Missouri v. Jenkins* (1995).[1]

The public schools of Oklahoma City had been desegregated in 1955 and integrated via court-ordered busing in 1972. Then in 1977 the local district court terminated the case after holding that the city had established a "unitary system." At one time this term was used to describe school districts that operated only one set of schools (unlike "dual" sys-

---

1. *Brown v. Board of Education,* 349 U.S. 294 (1955), 301; *Swann v. Charlotte-Mecklenburg,* 402 U.S. 1 (1972), 31–32; *New York Times,* 4 November 1985, 1; *Oklahoma City v. Dowell,* 111 S. Ct. 630 (1991); *Freeman v. Pitts,* 60USLW (1992) 4186; and *Missouri v. Jenkins,* 63 USLW 4486 (1995).

tems that had separate schools for blacks and whites); but by the 1970s *unitary* was a legal term to describe formerly dual systems that had taken whatever steps the courts had required to create "a unitary system in which racial discrimination would be eliminated root and branch." Courts awarded unitary status to school districts that had satisfied six criteria the Supreme Court had mentioned in *Green v. New Kent County* (1968). In addition to achieving racially balanced student enrollments, the districts had to eradicate the vestiges of past segregation with respect to "faculty, staff, transportation, extracurricular activities and facilities."[2]

In holding that the schools of Oklahoma City had become unitary, the district court was saying that the school board had satisfied the six indicia of *Green.* The NAACP then appealed, maintaining that a broader definition of *unitary* was needed—one that would require the maintenance as well as the establishment of racially balanced schools. Civil rights activists said there were "'surface' vestiges [of segregation] that are amenable to relatively swift remedial action." These were the *Green* factors. In addition, the activists maintained, there were "'underlying' vestiges" that would take generations to correct. These included racial clustering in different neighborhoods and the performance of black students on standardized tests. Until racial disparities in these areas were eliminated, the underlying vestiges of past discrimination would not have been eradicated. The stalwarts said that even if black youngsters attended racially balanced schools, their academic performance would still suffer from the lingering influence of parents, grandparents, and more distant ancestors whose education had suffered because they had not attended integrated schools. NAACP lawyers insisted that court-ordered racial balance should continue until *all* the effects of past segregation had been eliminated— that is, until blacks and whites lived together in proportionally balanced neighborhoods and until their average scores on standard tests were similar.[3]

The NAACP and its supporters said "resegregation" would ensue if federal courts did not require the maintenance of racially balanced integration. If local districts were released from court orders after only a few years of racial balance, "the promise of *Brown*" would be "thwarted in the final hour." If school districts no longer had to comply with court orders for racial mixing, most students would once again be assigned to school on the basis of nonracial considerations such as choice or residence in a particular neighborhood. And that would lead to "resegregation" because

2. *Green v. New Kent County,* 391 U.S. 430 (1968), 435, 439, 442.
3. *Columbia Law Review,* 87 (1987): 799; *George Washington Law Review* 58 (1990): 1142.

most neighborhoods were racially imbalanced and few students would choose to attend a school where their race was in the minority. More legalistically, the NAACP's lawyers said that requests for unitary status were unconstitutional because they were animated by a discriminatory intent that could be inferred from the racial imbalance that would ensue after a finding of "unitariness."[4]

Most local communities, on the other hand, said they were entitled to return to local control. They recalled that the Supreme Court, in the landmark busing case, *Swann v. Charlotte-Mecklenburg* (1971), had said that after school districts had complied with court orders their systems would be "unitary" and it would not be necessary "to make year-by-year adjustments of the racial composition of student bodies once the affirmative duty to desegregate has been accomplished." They recalled that the *Swann* Court said it had "not ruled, and does not rule that 'racial balance' is required under the Constitution." The Court had ruled only that local districts must remove the effects of official segregation, and local communities said that racially imbalanced neighborhoods and disparities in test scores were too attenuated to be considered vestiges of state-imposed segregation. In legal language, *attenuated* meant that a vestige was too remote or weak to warrant legal action.[5]

As has been noted, the Supreme Court's opinion in *Swann* was a negotiated document. At the time (1971) Chief Justice Warren Burger had wanted to rule against busing for racial balance, but he discovered that he and Justice Hugo Black were the only members of the Court who were satisfied with racially neutral policies (like assigning children to schools in their neighborhoods) that did not lead to substantially proportional racial mixing. Burger therefore voted with the pro-busing majority so that he could assign himself the job of writing the Court's opinion. He hoped to limit the damage. The Court's majority made Burger say that local authorities must make "every effort to achieve the greatest possible degree of actual desegregation." They made him approve busing as one way to do this. Burger nevertheless was able to put some restrictions in the opinion, and the Rehnquist Court later made much of these points. The three cases that brought an end to court-ordered busing for racial balance can be seen as "Burger's revenge."[6]

4. *Oklahoma Law Review* 40 (1987): 587. For similar views, see *Case Western Reserve Law Review* 37 (1986): 57, 70; and *North Carolina Law Review* 65 (1987): 643–44; and 70 (1992): 615.

5. *Swann v. Charlotte-Mecklenburg*, 402 U.S. 1 (1971), 23–24, 5–6, 31–32.

6. Ibid., 26, 27. For more on this, see Bernard Schwartz, *Swann's Way* (New York: Oxford University Press, 1986).

In *Oklahoma City v. Dowell* (1991), the Supreme Court held that school systems that once practiced racial discrimination should be released from court-ordered busing if they had complied with court orders and had taken all "practicable" steps to eliminate the vestiges of their former discrimination. Writing for the Court's majority, Chief Justice William H. Rehnquist said federal court supervision of local school systems had always been "intended as a temporary measure to remedy past discrimination" and was not meant "to operate in perpetuity." The Court also rejected the NAACP's argument that the vestiges of discrimination would not be removed as long as the pattern of residential settlement was racially imbalanced, saying that it was impermissibly "Draconian" for lower courts to consign school districts "to judicial tutelage for the indefinite future." The Court reiterated the importance of eliminating the vestiges of segregation "as far as practicable," but it indicated that the pattern of residential concentration "was the result of private decisionmaking and economics, and that it was too attenuated to be a vestige of former school segregation." Writing in dissent, Justice Thurgood Marshall complained that the *Dowell* Court had backed away from "lasting integration" and no longer insisted on "preserving an integrated school system."[7]

One year later, in *Freeman v. Pitts* (1992), a case that pertained to DeKalb County, Georgia, the Supreme Court again emphasized that judicial supervision of public education should be temporary and should last only until local authorities had eliminated the effects of discrimination to the extent practicable. Writing for the Court, Justice Anthony M. Kennedy emphasized that "federal judicial supervision of local school systems was intended as a 'temporary measure,'" that "local autonomy of school districts is a vital national tradition," and that "the ultimate objective" was "to return school districts to the control of local authorities." Kennedy further disavowed the argument that school districts must continue with af-

7. *Oklahoma City v. Dowell*, 111 S.Ct. 630 (1991), 636–43. Some proponents of racially balanced integration say that government agencies are responsible for the pattern of racial clustering in different residential neighborhoods. They say that such clustering would be more difficult if government agencies had not facilitated the clustering by building roads, underwriting loans, concentrating public housing in certain areas, and assigning students to the nearest public schools. Therefore, they say, if the government assigns students by race to increase racial mingling, the government is not practicing racial discrimination but is simply remedying the effects of its own prior discrimination. Others, however, emphasize that personal choice and economic wherewithal are of crucial importance in choosing a neighborhood. They note, moreover, that social scientists have not been able to determine the precise extent of the government's responsibility for the pattern of settlement. Whatever the extent of the government's responsibility, the Supreme Court, in *Dowell* (and later in *Freeman v. Pitts*), held that the effects of government policies were too "attenuated" to be decisive.

firmative policies until residential integration had been achieved. Instead, he said judges would exceed proper limits if they went beyond remedying discrimination in the schools and tried to shape general social conditions. If the judiciary tried to counteract demographic shifts, Justice Kennedy explained, local school districts would be subjected to "ongoing and never-ending supervision by the courts."[8]

Then, in *Missouri v. Jenkins* (1995), a case that pertained to integration in Kansas City, Missouri, the Supreme Court rejected the argument that federal courts should enforce racially balanced integration until black and white students made similar average scores on standard tests. In this case the district judge had identified the low average scores of black students as a continuing vestige of past segregation, and he proposed to continue the court's supervision until the local schools had attained "educational achievement results more in keeping with the national norms." The Supreme Court then overruled the district judge, saying that federal courts should not use racial scores on examinations to determine whether a school system had achieved unitary status. In his opinion for the Court's majority, Chief Justice Rehnquist said that test scores were "simply too far removed" to be considered a vestige of discrimination. They were "clearly . . . not the appropriate test to be applied in determining whether a previously segregated district" had desegregated its schools.[9]

The Kansas City case was one of the Supreme Court's most important decisions on school desegregation. In its first decision that dealt explicitly with the racial gap in academic achievement, the Court absolved the schools. Instead of holding the schools responsible for eliminating the gap, the Court held that the lingering influence of segregation was "attenuated" and implied that the gap resulted from things schools could not control—things such as child-rearing practices, family relationships, and cultural values. "This is the first Supreme Court decision to consider explicitly that educational deficiencies are due to a lot more than segregation," one observer noted. The Court deliberately chose not to saddle school districts with the "incredible burden" of achieving "equality of test results."[10]

Thus the jurisprudence of the Supreme Court shifted decisively in the

8. *Freeman v. Pitts*, 60 USLW 4286 (1992), 4292, 4294.

9. *Jenkins v. Missouri*, 639 F.Supp. 19 (1985), 24; *Missouri v. Jenkins*, 63 USLW 4486 (1995), 4491, 4494; Raymond Wolters, *Right Turn: William Bradford Reynolds, the Reagan Administration, and Black Civil Rights* (New Brunswick: Transaction Publishers, 1996), 428n43.

10. David Armor, quoted in *USA Today*, 13 June 1995, 5A; *Toronto Globe and Mail*, 5 July 1995.

1990s. In the late 1960s and early 1970s, the Court had authorized busing for racial balance as a way to eradicate the last vestiges of segregation. But in the 1990s the Court settled for correcting the remnants of segregation "to the extent practicable." The Court still required desegregation, but it rejected a rationale that would have required the maintenance of racially balanced integration. To balance the conflicting requirements of desegregation and local control over education, the Court held that local districts that had complied with a court-ordered desegregation plan should be declared "unitary" and should be released from judicial supervision even if a return to neighborhood schools would lead to a retrogression from the racial balance that a formerly segregated district had to attain to qualify for unitary status.

The new trend was evident in Charlotte-Mecklenburg, the county-wide North Carolina school district where the Supreme Court had first authorized busing for racial balance in 1971. Charlotte-Mecklenburg had desegregated its schools in the 1960s when all students, irrespective of race, were assigned to neighborhood schools. Yet because of racially concentrated residential patterns, in 1968 only 28 percent of the city's black students attended a majority-white school. This was more racial mixing than occurred in most large cities, but it was not enough to satisfy people who equated desegregation with racially balanced integration.[11]

After *Green v. New Kent County* (1968), advocates of balanced integration challenged the Charlotte system. They said it was one thing to require, as *Brown* had, that children must be assigned to public schools on a nondiscriminatory basis; it was something else to require, as *Green* had, that school boards must take affirmative steps to achieve substantial integration. Agreeing with this argument, District Judge James B. McMillan held that "the rules of the game have changed, and the methods and philosophies which in good faith the Board [of Education] has followed are no longer adequate to complete the job which the courts now say must be done."[12]

Judge McMillan then imposed a busing program, the goal of which was to achieve an even dispersion of blacks and whites throughout an area that ranged over 550 square miles and enrolled 84,000 students in its public schools. Judge McMillan started with the thought that the racial balance in each school should mirror the county-wide racial ratio, 71 percent white and 29 percent black. He recognized that natural and man-made ob-

11. Davison M. Douglas, *Reading, Writing, and Race: The Desegregation of the Charlotte Schools* (Chapel Hill: University of North Carolina Press, 1995), 123–24.
12. *Swann v. Charlotte-Mecklenburg*, 300 F.Supp. 1358 (1969), 1372.

structions—ravines, bridges, interstate highways—made some "variations from [the] norm . . . unavoidable." But he ordered that "pupils of all
grades [must] be assigned in such a way that as nearly as practicable the
various schools at various grade levels have about the same proportion of
black and white students."[13]

On appeal, the Supreme Court affirmed Judge McMillan's orders—although with the aforementioned qualifications. Once Charlotte-Mecklenburg had complied with the orders of the district court, Chief Justice Burger wrote, it would become a unitary system and would not have to make
yearly adjustments of the schools' racial composition. In theory, the purpose of busing was to *remedy* the official discrimination of the past, not to
achieve racial balance.[14]

Initially, there was much grumbling in Charlotte-Mecklenburg, and
several rallies were held in opposition to court-ordered busing. Judge
McMillan was hanged in effigy, the law office of pro-busing attorney
Julius Chambers was set on fire, and there was some interracial fighting
at the newly integrated schools. White parents in the suburbs also established an anti-busing organization called the Concerned Parents Association (CPA). The CPA insisted that there was a difference between *desegregation,* assigning children to school in a racially nondiscriminatory
manner, which it accepted, and assignment on the basis of race to achieve
balanced *integration,* which it opposed.[15]

President Richard M. Nixon endorsed the position of the CPA in a policy statement of 1970, and the Supreme Court seemed to agree in its 1974
Milliken decision—which essentially held that racial imbalances in the
suburbs and inner cities resulted from personal choice and economic
wherewithal, not from state action. Then, after 1990, the Supreme Court
more explicitly held that federal courts had no authority to require liberal social experimentation to counteract residential clustering.[16]

Although the arguments of the CPA eventually prevailed, in the short
term the organization failed to prevent comprehensive integration in
Charlotte-Mecklenburg. In 1969 and 1970, community leaders understood the temper of their times. They sensed that defiant opposition to integration would stifle economic growth. They knew that Little Rock,

13. *Swann v. Charlotte-Mecklenburg,* 306 F.Supp. (1969), 1312, 1313–14.
14. *Swann v. Charlotte-Mecklenburg,* 402 U.S. 1 (1971).
15. Stephen Samuel Smith, *Boom for Whom? Education, Desegregation, and Development in Charlotte* (Albany: State University of New York Press, 2004), 61; Matthew D.
Lassiter, *The Silent Majority: Suburban Politics in the Sunbelt South* (Princeton: Princeton
University Press, 2006).
16. Matthew D. Lassiter, "The Suburban Origins of 'Color-Blind' Conservatism,"
Journal of Urban History 30 (May 2004): 549–82.

Arkansas, had experienced a severe decline in new business after its well-publicized resistance to school desegregation in the 1950s, and Virginia also had economic problems after it flirted with interposition and massive resistance. Leaders in Charlotte-Mecklenburg therefore were concerned about the reputation of their community. Some even calculated that busing would turn out to be a blessing in disguise. They predicted that the city and county would enjoy an economic boom if it became known not only for its mild climate, low taxes, and low cost of living, but also (and perhaps most importantly) for progressive racial policies.

Most whites would have preferred neighborhood schools and only grudgingly decided that it was futile to defy the federal courts. But many of Charlotte's leaders and a sizeable minority of white liberals went beyond acquiescence and tried to make the best of the situation. They would do more than obey the court orders; they would make integration work. They would show that racially balanced integrated schools could provide high quality education.[17]

For liberal Charlotteans, integration became a source of civic pride. A large sign at the headquarters of the Charlotte-Mecklenburg School District announced the goal of becoming "the premier, integrated urban district in the country." When protests against busing erupted in Boston, Charlotte dispatched a group of students to help the New England city through its crisis. When President Ronald Reagan criticized judges for taking "innocent children out of the neighborhood school and mak[ing] them pawns in a social experiment that nobody wants," the *Charlotte Observer* published an indignant editorial under the headline, "You Were Wrong, Mr. President." According to the *Observer*, "Charlotte-Mecklenburg's proudest achievement of the past 20 years is not the city's impressive new skyline or its strong, growing economy. Its proudest achievement is its fully integrated school system." Thanks to "courageous elected officials, creative school administrators and dedicated teachers and parents," the public schools of Charlotte-Mecklenburg were "recognized through the United States for quality, innovation and, most of all, for overcoming the most difficult challenge American public education has ever faced."[18]

Although the rhetoric smacked of politics and public relations, there was substance behind the claims. The population of Charlotte increased from 354,656 in 1970 to 613,310 in 1997—the second greatest rate of

17. Lassiter, *Silent Majority*, 169.

18. *Houston Chronicle*, 16 April 2002, A5; *Newhouse News Service*, 29 June 2005; Frye Gaillard, *The Dream Long Deferred* (Columbia: University of South Carolina Press, 2006), xi.

growth among all American cities with more than 500,000 people. Charlotte boomed especially as a center for banking, and in 2000 the chief executive officer of the Bank of America, Hugh L. McColl, credited school integration with igniting the economy "like a wildfire in the wind."[19]

Such praise was not limited to members of the local Chamber of Commerce. One sober scholar, Stephen Samuel Smith, expressed the same opinion in academic prose: "the busing plan fueled Charlotte's reputation as a city characterized by racial harmony and progressive race relations. In the intense competition for mobile capital, Charlotte benefited greatly from its image as 'The City That Made It Work.'"[20]

The mainstream media tended to agree. Writing in the *New York Times* in 1992, journalist Peter Applebome lauded the quality of the public schools in Charlotte-Mecklenburg. "If integrated education has been a priority anywhere in America, it has been in this shiny new banking center in western North Carolina, where busing . . . became a source of civic pride at the same time it was met with fierce opposition around the nation." Articles in the *Charlotte Observer* described the nature of the success. To begin, the *Observer* said there was a minimum of white flight because Charlotte's busing plan was county-wide and there were no independent suburbs to escape to. In addition, according to reporter Frye Gaillard, "test scores were good and generally getting better, and nobody doubted the intangible advances—those changes in mood and climate that . . . 'made Charlotte-Mecklenburg synonymous with trying to do what's right.'" Charlotte-Mecklenburg was a place where, thanks to busing, whites had learned "that they could live peacefully in the presence of blacks," a place that "had finally come to terms with the old problems of race." Throughout the nation, Charlotte-Mecklenburg was widely regarded as the example par excellence of the success of court-ordered busing.[21]

Nevertheless, most residents of Charlotte-Mecklenburg, like most Americans elsewhere, chose to live in racially concentrated communities. Whites increasingly congregated in the far southeastern and northern parts of the county, in distant areas where livestock had recently grazed. This left blacks disproportionately concentrated in the city of Charlotte. Many affluent African Americans moved into what had been white suburbs, but many of these areas eventually became predominantly black.[22]

19. *Capacchione v. Charlotte-Mecklenburg*, 57 F.Supp. 228 (1999), at LexisNexis 8 of 55; *Newshouse News Service*, 29 June 2005.

20. Smith, *Boom for Whom?*, 4.

21. *New York Times*, 15 April 1992, B11; Frye Gaillard, *The Dream Long Deferred* (Chapel Hill: University of North Carolina Press, 1988), 156, 158, 172–73.

22. Gaillard, *Dream Long Deferred* (2006), 150.

Until 1992 school authorities managed to achieve racial balance (plus or minus 15 percent) in the great majority of schools. Because of the pattern of settlement, however, the time in transit became longer. When busing began, the commutes rarely exceeded thirty minutes, but by the 1990s some students were spending two hours a day on a bus. At first school authorities refused to build new schools in predominantly white areas, but that led many whites to enroll in new private schools, more than thirty of which were established after 1970. After busing began, the number of white students in the public schools decreased by more than 15,000, while the number of whites attending private schools increased from 2,150 to 15,835. By 1997, about 25 percent of the white students in Charlotte-Mecklenburg were enrolled in private schools—more than double the national average for private school enrollment and ten times what the rate had been in Charlotte-Mecklenburg in 1970. A new sort of racial imbalance had emerged in Charlotte-Mecklenburg, one that resulted not from the segregation of yesteryear but from choice, demographic shifts, and population growth after 1970.[23]

There were other circumstances that also contributed to the shift. Some whites said the public schools were falling short in basic education, even as they succeeded in attaining racially balanced integration. "We may be number one in integration," one candidate for the school board declared, "but we have low teacher morale . . . and students aren't performing." Some parents said that "forced busing" did more than inconvenience children with long-distance transportation. It also "damaged educational quality by mixing students of vastly different academic abilities." "Because ability levels pretty much go down black-white lines," one mother explained, "This is a quality-of-education issue."[24]

Other white parents complained about the number of crimes in Charlotte, where, according to an article in *Newsweek*, the homicide rate was nearly twice the average for large urban areas nationwide, and where crime among black youths increased to the point where, according to *Newsweek*, Charlotte was on the verge of becoming a "fortress city." Within the schools, blacks were disciplined at a rate disproportionate to their presence in the schools. Of the 13,205 students who were disciplined between 1995 and 1998, for example, black students received 66 percent of the penalties although at the time they made up only 40 percent of the students. Some people said the disproportionate discipline resulted from dis-

23. Ibid.; *Capacchione v. Charlotte-Mecklenburg*, 57 F.Supp. 228 (1999), at LexisNexis 9 of 55, 17 of 55, and passim; *Belk v. Charlotte-Mecklenburg*, 269 F.3d 305 (2001), at Lexis-Nexis 19 of 78; *Wall Street Journal*, 21 January 1985, 22.

24. *New York Times*, 15 April 1992, B11; Lassiter, *Silent Majority*, 218.

crimination against blacks, but after considering the evidence a local district judge held that the disparity was "probably due to a disproportionate incidence of infractions committed by black students."[25]

Some observers also pointed to an irony. Charlotte-Mecklenburg's progressive reputation had helped the county lure many new businesses. Nevertheless, after the newcomers settled in the area, many of them criticized busing for racial balance. More than a century after the end of the Civil War, a new invasion of Yankees seemed to be undermining school integration. When they had lived in the North, most of the affluent newcomers had sent their children to predominantly white suburban public schools, and when they moved to North Carolina they demanded schools like those they had left behind. "When people move, they are looking to go from like to like," said one school board member, referring not just to the situation in Charlotte-Mecklenburg but to a similar pattern in the suburbs of Nashville and Atlanta. According to journalist Jonathan Tilove, the recently arrived Yankees saw "only their obligation as parents to secure the best possible education for their children." Roslyn Arlin Mickelson, a professor at the Charlotte campus of the University of North Carolina, similarly noted that newcomers "familiar with their former homogeneously white, middle-class high quality school systems . . . were dissatisfied with the . . . less rigorous southern education they found in . . . schools desegregated by race and social class." One mother expressed the sentiment of many parents when she told Professor Mickelson, "If I wanted my children to attend school with students who live in trailer parks or [public housing] projects, I'd have moved next to one."[26]

Executives of the Royal Insurance Company—which moved its headquarters from New York to Charlotte-Mecklenburg in 1985 and 1986— were especially vocal in complaining that "the quality of education for college-bound students" was being sacrificed "for integration goals." In addition, the insurance executives said, the schools were "not adequately preparing non–college bound students for the job market." School board member Susan Burgess noted that most of the people who worked for Royal had previously "had their children in public schools in suburban systems [which were] for the most part self-contained, high-budget,

25. *Charlotte Observer*, 31 December 2006; *Newsweek*, 10 June 1991, 17; *Capacchione v. Charlotte-Mecklenburg*, 57 F.Supp. 2d 228 (1999), at LexisNexis 43 of 55.

26. *Newhouse News Service*, 29 June 2005; Roslyn Arlin Mickelson, "White Privilege in a Desegregating School System," in Stephen J. Caldas and Carl L. Bankston III, eds., *The End of Desegregation?* (New York: Nova Science Publishers, 2003), 100; Mickelson, "Do Southern Schools Face Rapid Resegregation?" *North Carolina Law Review* 81 (May 2003): 1520n35; Smith, *Boom for Whom?* 92.

all-white systems and then they came here, and many of them bought [houses in an outlying suburb] not realizing that they were in a paired situation with [a school located in mostly black areas in the city]." When they discovered what was in store for their children, they said, "your schools are bad. And we really don't give a flip about your desegregation, we're not busing our kids down to the ghetto." One newcomer lamented, "When we moved down here from Albany [New York], we bought a house [in a mostly white suburb] so we could get our kids out of inner-city schools. But dammit, you got us anyway."[27]

Despite the mounting complaints, the school board continued to work for integration. After 1980 almost all the new public schools were built in predominantly white areas but, at a time when almost half of the of census tracts in Mecklenburg County were less than 10 percent black, the board voluntarily resolved to build schools only in areas where blacks constituted at least 10 percent of the population. In addition, the school board adjusted attendance boundaries and paired schools that were in neighborhoods that were mostly black or mostly white. It reassigned teachers to achieve racial balance (plus or minus 15 percent).[28]

Yet with many whites transferring to private schools, and others complaining about the length of commutes and the quality of the education, leaders in the community believed that the time had arrived to try new approaches. As Professor Smith has noted, in the early 1970s Charlotte's business elite had "milk[ed] the city's reputation for progressive race relations for all it was worth." By 1990, when they feared that compulsory integration was making it more difficult to attract new businesses, "the established business elite threw its support behind dismantling the busing plan." All along, the business elite's support for racially balanced integration had been "largely ancillary to its pursuit of development."[29]

In 1992 the school board heeded the new demands of business leaders. To placate the suburbs and maintain support for the public schools, several new policies were implemented. The board sharply reduced the amount of forced busing and instead fostered integration by establishing racially balanced "magnet" programs at about one-half of the district's schools. At the same time, the board also adjusted the curriculum in all schools to correspond with standard exams that would be given regularly. It established a system of financial bonuses for schools, teachers, and

27. Smith, *Boom for Whom?* 102, 92.
28. *Capacchione v. Charlotte-Mecklenburg*, 57 F.Supp. 228 (1999) at LexisNexis 20 of 55 and 27 of 55; Amicus Brief of Julius Chambers et al., *Parents Involved v. Seattle School District* (U.S. Supreme Court, 2006), 16.
29. Smith, *Boom for Whom?* 66, 222–23.

principals whose students showed progress on the exams. And it provided extra funds for nonmagnet schools.[30]

Magnet schools had been around for years, although before they were used to promote integration they were usually called "specialty schools." Two famous examples were the Boston Latin School and the Bronx School of Science. Charlotte's magnet schools became so popular with suburban whites that waiting lists grew longer every year. There were problems nonetheless. Because many magnets were situated in black neighborhoods, African American children often were displaced and had to be bused elsewhere to make space for whites. And to maintain integration, the school board established a quota system for the magnet schools: 60 percent white, 40 percent black. It turned out, though, that comparatively few blacks wished to attend magnet schools. Consequently some of the spaces that had been reserved for black students went unfilled while hundreds of whites were placed on waiting lists.[31]

Magnet schools were also established in many other cities, with the general purpose of appealing to white families who otherwise would not send their children to schools in black neighborhoods. Rather than depart for private schools, it was thought, white families would patronize integrated schools if they knew that there would be special academic programs, that the black enrollment would be limited to pupils who were interested in such programs, and that white students would make up a substantial proportion of the student body. One white proponent of magnet schools candidly explained, "the idea was to create a program where schools were so special that white parents who would otherwise flee the system to avoid mandatory busing would voluntarily put their kids in these schools, even if it meant sending them half way across town." A black member of the NAACP in Charlotte concurred, saying the "plan was to try to make black communities palatable to white children."[32]

Magnet programs generally managed to maintain racial balance, at least in some schools, if the black proportion of the student enrollment did not become too large. One close student of the magnets, Christine Rossell of Boston University, said her research indicted that only 18 percent of white parents would send their children to magnet schools if the enrollment was evenly divided between blacks and whites; and if the black enrollment exceeded 50 percent, even fewer whites would do so. In affluent

30. Ibid., chapter 5.
31. Gaillard, *Dream Long Deferred* (2006), 153–55; *Atlanta Journal and Constitution*, 24 August 1999, 3A.
32. Christine Rossell, quoted in *Washington Post*, 25 January 1990, D1; Sylvester Vaughns, quoted in *Washington Post*, 24 June 1996, BO1.

but predominantly black Prince George's County, Maryland, for example, school administrators found themselves unable to fill 500 openings for white students at a time when 4,100 black students had been placed on waiting lists.[33]

In predominantly white areas like Charlotte-Mecklenburg, however, the magnet program succeeded in placating whites who were concerned about the quality of education in regular, racially balanced schools. Indeed, the magnets were so popular in Charlotte-Mecklenburg that the number of white applicants exceeded the slots that had been set aside for white students. Eventually this "success" led to a lawsuit by white parents whose children had been passed over. The lead white plaintiff, William Capacchione, filed a complaint in 1997, protesting that his daughter had been denied admission to a magnet school because of the racial enrollment quota. According to Capacchione, the equal protection clause of the Fourteenth Amendment prohibited racial quotas, unless the quotas were tailored to remedy the effects of racial discrimination. But Charlotte-Mecklenburg had long since corrected its transgressions and was widely recognized as one of the nation's most thoroughly integrated school systems. Therefore, Capacchione said, the school system should be declared unitary and, as a unitary system, should be prohibited from discriminating on the basis of race.[34]

Yet the school board was dominated by integrationists who would not seek a declaration of unitary status. They recognized that once such status was awarded, a slide toward racial imbalance probably would ensue. This had already happened in many once-integrated metropolitan regions, and a study by the *Charlotte Observer* predicted that, if racial assignments and quotas ended in Charlotte-Mecklenburg, more than half of the public school students would attend schools with little racial diversity.[35]

Therefore, in April 1998 the school board declared that it had not yet desegregated its schools—and therefore was not eligible for unitary status. Despite thirty years of trying, the board said, it had failed to eradicate numerous aspects of segregation. To support this claim, the board presented data that touched on academic achievement, teacher training, school construction, and school discipline. If true integration would erase the racial gap in academic achievement, as the school board maintained it would, then Charlotte-Mecklenburg had not achieved real integration. In

33. *Washington Post*, 25 January 1990, D1.

34. *Capacchione v. Charlotte-Mecklenburg*, 57 F.Supp. 228 (1999), at LexisNexis 10 of 55 and passim.

35. Gaillard, *Dream Long Deferred* (2006), 162ff; *New York Times*, 11 September 1999, A1.

1978, after eight years of busing, 80 percent of the school district's black high school juniors, twice the number of whites, failed the minimum competency examinations that were required for high school graduation, and in almost every category the gap between the average score of blacks and whites was greater than it had been before busing. Academic scores improved after that, with blacks in Charlotte-Mecklenburg outperforming the statewide and nationwide averages for African American students. The school board nevertheless castigated itself for not eliminating the black-white achievement gap, saying that its system of ability grouping perpetuated the racial gap in academic achievement. In courtroom testimony an associate superintendent also implied that middle-class white teachers did not know how to teach black students. Some teachers took exception to this testimony, with one saying that the associate superintendent "should get out of her office in the Education Center and come see where the real work takes place and where the total child is being taught by excellent teachers who don't look at the color of a child's face."[36]

The school board had additional complaints about its own policies. It berated itself for allowing a situation to develop where teachers in the mostly white suburbs had an average of about twelve years of experience while teachers in the city of Charlotte had only ten. It found fault with itself for building new schools in the newly settled, mostly white suburbs, while the existing school buildings in Charlotte were merely renovated. The board said it was guilty of racial discrimination because it allowed schoolteachers and principals to discipline a disproportionately large number of black students. In making this last point, the board endorsed the position of black activists who appeared at disciplinary hearings on behalf of black children whom they said had been punished unfairly by "white teachers who were inadequately prepared for dealing with multiracial educational settings."[37]

In arguing that even Charlotte-Mecklenburg had failed to desegregate

36. Gaillard, *Dream Long Deferred* (2006), 165; *Capacchione v. Charlotte-Mecklenburg*, 57 F.Supp. 2d (228) at LexisNexis 37 of 55. According to the district court, "the black-white achievement gap has remained relatively constant . . . because white students have made progress as well." Smith, *Boom for Whom?* 170–71. For more on the test scores and academic programs, see Smith, *Boom for Whom?* Stephen Samuel Smith and Roslyn Arlin Mickelson, "All that Glitters Is Not Gold: School Reform in Charlotte-Mecklenburg," *Educational Evaluation and Policy Analysis* 22 (summer 2000): 101–27; and Amicus Brief of Julius Chambers et al., n. 9. Despite the academic gains, some observers condemned grouping and tracking as sophisticated forms of segregation. See Roslyn Arlin Mickelson, "Do Southern Schools Face Rapid Resegregation?" *North Carolina Law Review* 81 (May 2003): 1513.

37. Smith, *Boom for Whom?* 214.

its schools, and in accusing itself of racial insensitivity and bias, the school board left itself open to criticism that bordered on contemptuous ridicule. "All over Charlotte," Frye Gaillard observed, "there was jeering and dismay at a system that declared that it couldn't get it right." By exaggerating its failures, the board created a public relations disaster. One commentator characterized the board's contentions as "The We-Stink Defense." Another noted that "critics called the school system's emphasis on its own failures a 'doofus defense,' a term that quickly caught on in the court of public opinion."[38]

The argument did not impress Judge Robert D. Potter, the senior judge of the federal district court in Charlotte. In 1999, after listening to hours of testimony and sifting through documents that ran to thousands of pages, Potter characterized the school board's arguments as "bizarre" and a "pretext" for continuing "race-conscious, diversity-enhancing policies in perpetuity." Potter concluded that the Charlotte-Mecklenburg schools were unitary and probably had been so for years. He found that Charlotte-Mecklenburg had "eliminated . . . the vestiges of past discrimination." It had "complied in good faith with the desegregation orders [of the federal courts]." It had "achieved unitary status in all respects." Therefore, Potter enjoined the school system from continuing to assign children to schools or to allocate educational opportunities and benefits "through race-based lotteries, preferences, set-asides, or other means that deny students an equal footing based on race."[39]

On appeal, the judges of the Fourth Circuit Court of Appeals eventually affirmed Judge Potter's decision by a vote of 7 to 4. In 2002 the Supreme Court let the decision stand in an opinion that was just one line long. Although the Supreme Court's decision was devoid of explanation, it was consistent with other cases that the Court had decided since the *Dowell* case of 1991. Nevertheless, even though the Charlotte case broke no new legal ground, the denouement of busing for racial balance in that city was especially significant. The school system that pioneered busing for integration in the 1970s had been ordered to halt its affirmative admissions policies. The courts' decisions marked the end of an era in American social policy. After once signaling the start of a national era in school integration, Charlotte-Mecklenburg helped mark its end.[40]

As had been predicted, the return to nonracial assignments led to an in-

38. Gaillard, *Dream Long Deferred* (2006), 174; Smith, *Boom for Whom?* 170–71.
39. *Capacchione v. Charlotte-Mecklenburg*, 57 F.Supp. 228 (1999), at LexisNexis 4 of 55 and 54 of 55; Gaillard, *Dream Long Deferred* (2006), 178.
40. *Belk v. Charlotte-Mecklenburg*, 269 F.3d 305 (2001); *Cappachione v. Charlotte-Mecklenburg*, 535 U.S. 986 (2002); *New York Times*, 11 September 1999, A1.

crease in racially imbalanced enrollments. Within a few years the proportion of black children who were attending schools that were at least 80 percent black increased from 3 percent to 15 percent. The average black student went from attending a school that was 52 percent white to one that was 35 percent white. By 2004 only one-third of the district's 148 schools had racially balanced enrollments (plus or minus 15 percent). The situation at the Marie G. Davis Middle School was extreme but symptomatic. In 2002, 44 percent of the students at this magnet school had been white, even though the school was located near public housing projects. Two years later, after the courts had ruled against the school district's affirmative racial policies, whites made up only 1 percent of the students at the school. Meanwhile, white enrollment in the suburbs soared, with one elementary school that had been built for eight hundred students having to use thirty-four trailers to accommodate an additional eight hundred students.[41]

At Harvard University, the Civil Rights Project documented the trend. In 2007 one of its reports stated that more than half the public elementary schools in Charlotte-Mecklenburg were either more than 90 percent black or 90 percent white. "What is going on is a stunning historical reversal," lamented Gary Orfield, the project's most prominent scholar. "Some of the desegregated parts of the South, especially metro areas that were fully desegregated," were developing "resegregated schools."[42]

Others had a different point of view. Observing the situation with a combination of realism and optimism, the black economist Glenn Loury said that in mostly black cities it "made more sense to address . . . students' educational needs directly, rather than to spend scarce resources trying to get white families to send their children to the same schools as minorities." According to Loury, most African American parents were "more concerned about the quality of their children's schools than about racial balance for its own sake." Whether or not one approved of the trend toward racial imbalance, the experiment with racially balanced integration was coming to an end, and "the weight that was borne by school desegregation as the vehicle for trying to equalize opportunity will now have to be borne elsewhere."[43]

Recognizing this, some school officials insisted that all was not lost.

41. *Newhouse News Service*, 29 June 2005; *New York Times*, 18 January 2004, A4; *Cleveland Plain Dealer*, 17 May 2004, A1.

42. *Newhouse News Service*, 29 June 2005; *St. Petersburg Times*, 29 September 2002, 1D; *Christian Science Monitor*, 28 January 2008. Not everyone agreed with Professor Orfield. Attorney Roger Clegg questioned some of the research and also noted that in many areas the percentage of white students declined because whites had become a smaller part of the population.

43. *New York Times*, 23 April 1997, A23; 11 September 1999, A1.

Some even said that education would improve, once schools no longer had to proceed with one eye trained on court orders. After they were liberated from a preoccupation with achieving racial balance, they said, schools could focus more attention on the educational needs of low-performing students. Although it is too soon to know for certain, this may have happened in Charlotte-Mecklenburg. In 2005, when school administrators were no longer engrossed with planning bus routes and keeping racial records, they developed an incentive plan that provided a $750 bonus for teachers whose students showed improvement on standard tests. The following year the number of African American students who were reading at grade level increased to an all-time high in Charlotte. And in 2006, Charlotte-Mecklenburg generally beat North Carolina's average on standard tests that were given to fourth- and eighth-grade students. When Charlotte-Mecklenburg's black and Latino students were compared with students from ten other big-city districts, the students from Charlotte compiled the highest average scores.[44]

Integrationists nevertheless remained despondent. "I've always said that test scores were the least interesting story," said Robert L. Crain of Columbia Teachers College. As Crain saw it, other matters were more important—especially the cultivation of interracial friendships. A white parent in Charlotte also made this point when she implored the school board to maintain racial "diversity." Speaking in a trembling voice, Jane Henderson declared, "I'm so grateful that I was able to go to school with people who were not from my exact background, and I've wanted that for my children."[45]

44. *PR Newswire US*, 12 June 2007; *Charlotte Observer*, 23 September 2005, A1. For a different assessment of test scores, see Amicus Brief of Julius Chambers et al., 24, 27.
45. *St. Petersburg Times*, 17 November 1996, 1D; *Newhouse News Service*, 29 June 2005.

10

The Diversity Rationale

In the Charlotte-Mecklenburg case, District Judge Robert D. Potter concluded that the public schools were thoroughly desegregated. Therefore, Judge Potter reasoned, the school district should be granted unitary status and should also be prohibited from continuing to consider race when assigning students to schools. The decisions seemed logical. In *Brown* the Supreme Court had ordered schools to admit students "on a racially nondiscriminatory basis." The Court's decisions in *Green* and *Swann* had required policies that pointed toward a different policy—assigning students by race to achieve proportional mixing. But that was what the Court required, not what it said. Even in *Green* the Court professed that the purpose of desegregation was to eliminate all the vestiges of prior discrimination. And in *Swann,* the Court ostensibly maintained that the goal of desegregation was not to achieve racial balance but to remedy the segregation of the past. If that was so, and if the schools of Charlotte-Mecklenburg were fully desegregated, then the time had come to assign students on a racially nondiscriminatory basis.[1]

In ruling as he did, Judge Potter also made much of two opinions that the Supreme Court had handed down in cases that involved affirmative action for minority contractors. In *Richmond v. Croson* (1989), the Court had said that racial classifications must pass the test of "strict scrutiny" and should be "reserved for remedial settings." Writing for six members

---

1. *Brown v. Board of Education,* 349 U.S. 294 (1955), 301. For an impassioned critique of Judge Potter's ruling opinion, and of the similar decisions by two panels of judges of the Fourth Circuit Court of Apeals, see John Charles Boger, "Willful Colorblindness: The New Racial Piety and the Resegregation of Public Schools," *North Carolina Law Review* 78 (2000): 1719–96.

of the Court, Justice Sandra Day O'Connor said it was a serious matter for the government to classify citizens racially; that the Constitution did not permit such classification as part of an effort to redress general societal discrimination; that racial classifications had to be tailored to correct instances of proven, identified discrimination. Then, in *Adarand v. Pena* (1995), the Court reiterated that "all racial classifications . . . must be analyzed by a reviewing court under strict scrutiny" and that "any preference based on racial or ethnic criteria must necessarily receive a most searching examination."[2]

Judge Potter was not alone in holding that *Croson* and *Adarand* pointed to the conclusion that public schools could not classify students by race except as part of an effort to remedy previous discrimination. In well-publicized cases involving the Boston Latin School and the University of Texas Law School, and in several less publicized cases as well, other federal judges also ruled against race-conscious policies that were designed to achieve racial balance rather than to correct previous discrimination. As a result, after the mid-1990s many local authorities shied away from officially taking account of race. For fear of lawsuits, they discontinued practices such as establishing racial guidelines for enrollments and holding separate lotteries for popular magnet programs, with members of one race assigned to waiting lists while places were held open for members of another race. In the past, federal courts had sanctioned such policies as creative strategies for dealing with racial imbalance. But after *Croson* and *Adarand*, there was a fear that such policies would make school districts legally vulnerable. According to NAACP attorney Dennis Parker, "What you have are school boards that are so afraid of being sued that they are running away from [such policies]."[3]

Nevertheless, some judges were loath to change course until they received explicit instructions as to whether the Supreme Court's holdings in *Croson* and *Adarand* applied to public schools. After all, for years the Supreme Court had allowed school districts to take race into account in order to promote racial mingling—even if the districts had never been found guilty of segregation or, if they had been judged guilty, had remedied the situation and had been awarded unitary status. To achieve more mixing than could be obtained by racially neutral policies, the court had allowed policies that permitted students to transfer from schools in which their race was a majority to schools where their race was a minority; it had

---

2. *Richmond v. Croson,* 488 U.S 469 (1989); *Adarand v. Pena,* 515 U.S.200 (1995).
3. *Wessman v. Gittens,* 160 F.3d 790 (1998); *Hopwood v. Texas,* 78 F.3d 932 (1996); *St. Petersburg Times,* 29 September 2002, 1D.

approved when school boards deliberately chose to build new schools at locations that were likely to maximize racial mixing; it had permitted local authorities to gerrymander attendance areas to promote mixing. In addition, as five former secretaries of education noted in 2006, for forty years agencies of the federal government had "interpreted . . . the Civil Rights Act of 1964 not to prohibit consideration of race," as the act had specified, but to reduce "racial isolation regardless of whether the racial isolation was the result of proven discrimination."[4]

After the Supreme Court's decisions of the 1990s, the federal judiciary removed itself from the business of judicially enforced racial integration. The high court made it clear that court-ordered mixing was not required except as a remedy for past discrimination. And even remedial orders were to be temporary, lasting only until school districts had corrected the effects of their own prior discrimination "to the extent practicable." In the great majority of cases, the "reformed" districts then assigned students in a racially nondiscriminatory manner—usually to the nearest neighborhood schools. In some instances, however, local communities voluntarily continued with race-conscious plans to promote mixing, even after courts no longer required them to do so. One administrator in Louisville, Kentucky, explained that his school board chose to keep its schools racially balanced, even after the system had been declared unitary, "because we believe it is the best way to educate all our children academically and the best way to prepare them to be citizens and employees in our community." Increasingly, the districts that persisted with racial assignments cited "diversity" as the justification for their policy.[5]

Previously, the Supreme Court had held that the Constitution generally prohibited the government from classifying citizens racially, but the Court had allowed exceptions in two circumstances. Government agencies that had engaged in racial discrimination could be required to consider race in order to remedy their prior practice. And in cases that concerned the internment of Japanese Americans during World War II, the Supreme Court had allowed for racial considerations that were deemed essential to protect national security. In the Japanese internment cases, the Court said that "pressing public necessity may sometimes justify the existence of [racial discrimination]," and in later cases "pressing public necessity" morphed into the doctrine that "racial and ethnic distinctions of any sort are inherently suspect and . . . call for the most exacting judicial

4. Amicus Brief of David Mathews et al., *Parents Involved v. Seattle School District*, U.S. Supreme Court, 2006.
5. Pat Todd, quoted in *Richmond Times Dispatch*, 3 December 2006, A4.

examination." In its *Adarand* decision of 1995, the court held that "more than good motives should be required when the government seeks to allocate its resources by way of an explicit racial classification system," "government may treat people differently because of their race only for the most compelling reasons," and "all racial classifications by government" should be "analyzed by a reviewing court under strict scrutiny"— which meant that such classifications were constitutional only if "searching judicial inquiry" established that the classifications had been tailored to further a compelling interest.[6]

In the 1990s, proponents of racially balanced integration advanced "diversity" as a third compelling justification for racial classifications. Some scholars had reported that children who attended racially balanced schools were more comfortable around people of other races and, after they became adults, more likely to live and work in integrated settings. Therefore, one lawyer maintained, "racial classifications are justified by the school board's compelling interest in preparing its students for life in a multicultural world." "We are trying to prepare students to live in diverse communities," another lawyer said.[7]

"Diversity" eventually became a popular refrain. Many proponents of integration insisted that society had greater objectives to achieve than ensuring that public school students were treated in a racially nondiscriminatory manner. According to an editorial in *USA Today*, the nation had "a compelling interest in . . . turning out graduates who are comfortable with diversity." Predicting that "fully one-third of those entering the work force" would soon be minorities, an editorial in the *New York Times* said that racially balanced integrated education was vital to the health of the American economy. "It is easier for a diverse group of employees to work together if they share common educational experiences," the *Times* maintained.[8]

The diversity rationale owed much to the work of Professor Robert L.

---

6. *Korematsu v. United States*, 323 US 214 (1944), 216; *Miller v. Johnson*, 515 U.S. (1995), 904; *Adarand v. Pena*, 515 U.S. (1995), 226–27. As noted in Chapter 1, during the *Brown* litigation Thurgood Marshall had urged the Supreme Court to prohibit state-sanctioned racial classifications. The Court decided *Brown* on other grounds but, in the companion *Bolling* case, held that racial classifications must satisfy strict scrutiny. In the 1960s, when the high court ruled against miscegenation laws, the justices again applied the strict scrutiny test to invalidate racial classifications. See Reva B. Siegel, "*Brown* at Fifty: Equality Talk: Antisubordination and Anticlasification Values in Constitutional Struggles over *Brown*," *Harvard Law Review* 117 (March 2004): 1470–547.

7. Francis J. Mellen and Michael Madden, as paraphrased and quoted in *Chicago Daily Law Bulletin*, 4 December 2006.

8. *USA Today*, 19 June 2006, 10A; *New York Times*, 19 December 1993, E12.

Crain. Crain achieved wide recognition in 1978 with research that purported to show that the academic achievement of black students improved if they attended integrated schools. Yet the evidence was far from conclusive. In 1982, when the National Institute of Education convened a panel of seven social scientists to review 157 studies of the matter, only Crain concluded that integration boosted the achievement of black students substantially. In its final report the panel concluded, "on average, desegregation did not cause an increase in achievement in mathematics" but did give a small boost ("estimated to be between two to six weeks [of a school year]") to reading levels. Eleven years later, after reviewing another 250 studies, Janet Ward Schofield echoed this conclusion: "research suggests that desegregation has had some positive impact on the reading skills of African American youngsters. The effect is not large. . . . Such is not the case with mathematics skills, which seem generally unaffected by desegregation." In 2003, after the relation between racial mix and educational achievement had been studied by an army of social scientists, Abigail Thernstrom and Stephen Thernstrom reported that there still was "no scholarly consensus that a school's racial mix has a clear effect on how much children learn." If one controlled for relevant variables, the Thernstroms said, there was no evidence of a clear and consistent relationship between the racial mix of students and their academic achievement.[9]

Yet Professor Crain was not dissuaded. On the basis of additional studies, he maintained that the long-term benefits of attending racially balanced schools were greater than any effect on test scores. He reported that black students who attended racially balanced high schools were more likely to prefer predominantly white colleges and to choose integrated settings later in life. In addition, both black and white students who attended racially balanced schools had to interact with people from different racial groups and therefore were better prepared to function effectively in a multicultural world.[10]

9. Robert L. Crain and Rita E. Mahard, "Desegregation and Black Achievement," *Law and Contemporary Problems* 42 (1978): 17–56; National Institute of Education, *School Desegregation and Black Achievement* (Washington: Government Printing Office, 1984); Janet Ward Schofield, "Review of Research on School Desegregation's Impact," in J. A. Banks and C. A. McGee Banks, eds., *Handbook of Research on Multicultural Education* (New York: McMillan, 1995), 597, 610; Abigail Thernstrom and Stephan Thernstrom, *No Excuses: Closing the Racial Gap in Learning* (New York: Simon and Schuster, 2003), 179–80.

10. Robert L. Crain and Rita Mahard, "School Racial Compositions and Black College Attendance and Achievement Test Performance," *Sociology of Education* 51 (1978): 81–101; Amy Stuart Wells and Robert L. Crain, "Perpetuation Theory and the Long-Term Effects of School Desegregation," *Review of Educational Research* 64 (1994): 531–56.

Once again, critics challenged Professor Crain's conclusions. They admitted that there was a "significant relationship between black students attending a desegregated high school and attending a predominantly white college, and a somewhat weaker relationship with working in predominantly white employment settings." But the critics attributed this to "self-selection." They said that black youths who attended mostly white high schools were more likely to be from families who preferred such schools, and thus the children also tended to prefer predominantly white settings when they became adults. Critics also said that interracial contact was likely to reduce prejudice only when the contact involved people who had similar values and interests—which often was not the case when students were assigned by race to achieve a proportional mix.[11]

Professor Crain's critics may have had the better of the scholarly dispute. Nevertheless, Crain's contention soon became popular not only with liberals but also with many people who had no ideological axes to grind. In part this was because Crain's thesis was intuitively appealing. To many observers, it seemed commonsensical that schools that contained substantial percentages of students from different groups would do a better job of reducing prejudice and promoting interracial understanding. This impression was reinforced when one of Crain's coauthors, Amy Stuart Wells, interviewed students who had graduated from racially balanced schools. Wells, who had previously worked as a reporter for the *New York Times*, understood the importance of public relations. Her interviews were a triumph in this respect. Unlike the students who attended the integrated schools in many of the communities discussed in previous chapters of this book, Wells's graduates recalled only occasional racial tensions and emphasized that "cross-racial friendships were not uncommon and that diverse cliques formed on a regular basis." Students who had attended racially balanced schools said they were "more open-minded and less fearful of other races than peers who went to segregated schools." They said they were "far more accepting of and comfortable with people of other racial background than those who lack an integrated K–12 experience." "I think I'm a stronger person for having dealt with such a diverse background and having friends of all different backgrounds," one grad-

---

11. Amicus Brief of David Armor, Abigail Thernstrom, and Stephan Thernstrom, *Parents Involved v. Seattle School District* (U.S. Supreme Court, 2006); Nancy St. John, *School Desegregation: Outcomes for Children* (New York: John Wiley and Sons, 1975), 72; Walter G. Stephan, "The Effects of School Desegregation: An Evaluation 30 Years after *Brown*," in M. Saks, ed., *Advances in Applied Social Psychology* (Hillsdale, N.J.: Erlbaum Associates, 1986), 181.

uate said. "I feel definitely more confident every day that I walk around in any kind of area."[12]

Sociologist Gary Orfield, the head of the Civil Rights Project at Harvard, concurred. "You should listen to the young people," Orfield said. "We are actually surveying young people in schools, high schools around the country, and in colleges, and those who've been in interracial backgrounds deeply appreciate it. They believe that they're better able to understand each other. They believe that they've learned about each other's culture. They're comfortable working together; they look forward to living in the society that we're going to have, which is going to be half nonwhite in the middle of [the twenty-first] century."[13]

Orfield also weighed in with additional research. Shortly after the Supreme Court's decision in *Dowell v. Oklahoma City* (1991), Orfield complained that the phenomenon of "resegregation" was not being discussed widely. He was determined that this would no longer be the case. Over the next decade Orfield and his colleagues at Harvard's Civil Rights Project published several studies with a common theme: as federal courts bestowed unitary status, the number of schools with racially balanced enrollments declined. *Dowell* "authorized a return to neighborhood schools," Orfield wrote, and resegregation ensued. The percentage of black students who attended majority white schools in the South declined from 43 percent in 1986 to 30 percent in 2001, and for the United States as a whole the percentage of black students attending schools where most students were nonwhite increased from 66 percent in 1991 to 73 percent in 2003.[14]

As Orfield saw it, the Supreme Court of Chief Justice William H. Rehn-

12. Amicus Brief of Amy Stuart Wells et al., *Parents Involved v. Seattle School District*; Associated Press State and Local Wire, 5:41 p.m., 2 December 2006.

13. *CNN Sunday Morning*, 19 January 2003 (transcript 011903CN.V46).

14. *New York Times*, 19 January 1992, E5; Gary Orfield and Chungmei Lee, *Brown at 50* (Cambridge: Harvard Civil Rights Project, 2004), 19, 3, and passim; *London Guardian*, 17 January 2006, 16. Although blacks were having less contact with whites, it was also true, as *National Review Online* noted on April 27, 2007, that "today white students are more likely to go to school with non-white students than at any other time in American history." Immigration was the reason for the apparent paradox. Because of an influx of nonwhites (and also, differentials in birth rates) the proportion of nonwhite students increased markedly after 1990. The Civil Rights Project at Harvard has published many additional studies that call attention to "resegregation"; see Gary Orfield, *Schools More Separate: Consequences of a Decade of Resegregation* (2001); Erica Frankenberg, Chungmei Lee, and Gary Orfield, *A Multiracial Society with Segregated Schools* (2003); Gary Orfield and Chungmei Lee, *New Faces, Old Patterns? Segregation in the Multiracial South* (2005); and Gary Orfield and Chungmei Lee, *Racial Transformation and the Changing Nature of Segregation* (2006). See also Gary Orfield and Susan E. Eaton, *Dismantling Desegregation: The Quiet Reversal of Brown v. Board of Education* (New York: New Press, 1996).

quist was largely to blame. "I don't think the nation has given up on [racially balanced integration]," Orfield said, citing polls that reported that most white people favored "diversity" and "integrated education." He brushed over the fact that the same polls also indicated that most people preferred programs that tried to improve the quality of education in neighborhood schools rather than programs that bused children away for racial balance. For Orfield the problem was that the nation was "being pushed into segregation by the [Rehnquist] Court. There are five members of that court that really don't see any racial problems in this country except discrimination against whites. They really don't see desegregation as a long-term goal." The Rehnquist Court viewed racial integration "as a merely temporary punishment for historic violations, an imposition to be lifted after a few years." Going beyond the preceding Supreme Court of Chief Justice Warren E. Burger, which had limited the reach of racially balanced integration by prohibiting busing across school district lines in metropolitan areas, the Rehnquist Court refused to persist with racially balanced integration in areas where balanced mixing had been required by court orders. In doing so, Orfield said, the Rehnquist Court placed its seal of approval on educational "apartheid."[15]

To reverse the trend toward racially imbalanced neighborhood schools, Crain, Wells, Orfield, and other proponents of integration resurrected the argument that James S. Coleman had developed in the 1960s (but had retracted in the 1970s). They said black youngsters learned more, and whites did not suffer, when students were required to attend racially balanced, predominantly white schools. Like the early Coleman, they emphasized that students learned from one another and that a child's peer group was of key importance in influencing attitudes toward academic achievement. According to Orfield, "all of the research, starting with the Coleman Report of the late 1960s, shows that low socioeconomic students get some measurable benefit from being in schools that are predominantly middle class, and race is an additional factor." "From an educational standpoint," black youngsters did better when they attended "schools that have middle-class norms and middle-class expectations."[16]

15. In 1999 a CNN/USA Today/Gallup Poll reported that 59 percent of Americans believed that more, not less, should be done to integrate the nation's schools. Nevertheless, when given the choice of "stepping up efforts to integrate white students with minority students" or increasing "funding and other resources for minority schools," 60 percent of those polled—with blacks and whites splitting evenly—favored increasing the funding for minority schools. *USA Today*, 22 July 1999, 1A; *New York Times*, 26 September 1995, 1A; Orfield and Eaton, *Dismantling Desegregation*, passim; Nat Henthoff, "Back to Separate and Unequal," *Village Voice*, 31 May 1994, 22.

16. *Boston Globe*, 26 December 1991, 1.

Nevertheless, in many places demography precluded the sort of integration that Orfield envisioned. In most big cities, there were not enough middle-class white students. By the mid-1990s, Harvard's Civil Rights Project reported, whites made up an average of only 15 percent of the public school students in the nation's ten largest cities, with the proportion ranging from a high of 31 percent in San Diego to a low of 6 percent in Detroit. Orlando Patterson, an African American scholar at Harvard, acknowledged that court-ordered integration was being abandoned in Boston and other large cities "because there is nothing for busing to do, there being hardly any white students left in the system for minorities to integrate with."[17]

Beyond this, many black people questioned integration, with one 1998 poll indicating that only 51 percent of African Americans favored the policy. As has been noted, the opposition was especially prevalent among older people who had grown up with segregated schools. Some contrasted the quality of the education they had received at all-black schools with the experience their children had with white teachers who allegedly did not have high expectations or did not care about black students. Others said that predominantly black schools did a better job of teaching African Americans to appreciate their own history and culture. Some complained that their children had to make "a car ride an hour across town to a high-achieving school with white kids," only to end up grouped with other black students in less-demanding sections of many courses. One black student returned to her neighborhood school saying, "People just go where they're comfortable." Another declared, "I appreciate being around all types of people . . . but . . . there are times when I just want to be around people that are like me."[18]

Most of all, many black people rejected the assumption that the quality of education depended on the number of white students in a classroom. They considered it insulting to suggest that black children needed to have white role models sit near them. They said the notion that blacks had to have the civilizing influence of middle-class whites was paternalistic, if not racist, and a vestige of bygone times. Barbara Sizemore, the former superintendent of schools in Washington, D.C., expressed this sentiment in blunt language when she said that integration "promote[d]

17. For discussion of these statistics, see *Newsweek*, 29 September 1997, 52. Orlando Patterson, "What to Do When Busing Becomes Irrelevant," *New York Times*, 18 July 1999, WK17.

18. *Cleveland Plain Dealer*, 28 February 1994, 5A; John A. Powell, quoted in *Atlanta Journal Constitution*, 22 June 2003, 1F; Ashley Parkins, *Boston Globe*, 16 May 2004, CW1; Fatima McKindra, quoted in *Newsweek*, 29 September 1997, 52.

the society's value of white superiority and confirm[ed] its value of black inferiority."[19]

There were so many questions about busing for racial integration that sometimes it seemed that the only people who continued to support the policy were liberal professors and lawyers who worked for civil rights groups. And even some of them had second thoughts. At the NAACP, attorney Dennis Parker acknowledged that many black parents (as well as black mayors in several cities) had asked that busing for racial balance be ended. "There is a lot of frustration with the way desegregation worked out," Parker said. "There is frustration and justified offense taken at the idea that you find yourself . . . chasing white students, as . . . white students flee the system." Another NAACP officer, education director Beverly Cole, noted that the NAACP "still support[ed]" what she called "desegregation efforts," but then she added, "at the present time we are more concerned with the quality of education, and this has to take precedence over whether schools are integrated."[20]

Integrationists therefore adjusted their arguments. One tactic was to emphasize the importance of socioeconomic class. "What I say to black parents," Gary Orfield explained, "is that it's not magic to sit next to a white kid. But to be in a middle-class school rather than a poverty school makes a huge difference." "The basic damage inflicted by segregated education comes not from racial concentration but from the concentration of children from poor families."[21]

Like James S. Coleman, Orfield believed that schoolwork was affected by the socioeconomic status of a student's classmates—"that who you go to school with matters." It was a disadvantage if bright students had classmates who misbehaved or were mentally slow. It was a handicap if most of one's fellow students came from families that did not stress the importance of going to college. Unlike Coleman, however, Orfield said little about the problematical behavior and the antiacademic attitudes of many students. Recognizing the sensitivities of minority communities, Orfield pointed instead to other problems. Occasionally he mentioned instances where inner-city schools were inadequately funded—although this argument failed to impress critics who noted that in most cases the expenditure per student in the inner cities exceeded the statewide average for expenditure per student. More frequently, Orfield emphasized that even if high-poverty schools spent more per

19. *Pittsburgh Post-Gazette*, 16 May 2004, A1.
20. *Houston Chronicle*, 2 June 2002, A1; *New York Times*, 14 December 1993, A1.
21. *Atlanta Journal-Constitution*, 22 June 2003, 1E; Richard D. Kahlenberg, "Stay Classy," *New Republic*, 18 December 2006, 14.

pupil, these schools were beset with a welter of problems that stemmed from poverty.[22]

Eventually this became a theme in the arguments for integration. Predominantly black schools were unsatisfactory because so many of the students came from families that had to grapple with problems that stemmed from poverty—poor nutrition, lack of health care, housing evictions, job losses, and problems with alcohol and drugs. Yet, for fear of frightening middle-class parents or antagonizing minority groups, most integrationists did not belabor these points. Instead, they emphasized that black and Latino students in the inner cities were "getting worse teachers because they're getting the rookie teachers." Because union rules allowed teachers to transfer to different schools after acquiring a few years of seniority, Orfield noted, inner-city schools had disproportionately large numbers of "less-experienced teachers" with "less adequate college preparation." Children in mostly black schools experienced "conditions of concentrated disadvantage, including . . . unqualified teachers, fewer demanding pre-collegiate courses and more remedial courses." They were not doing well in school because their teachers, on average, were not as good as the teachers in the suburbs. Drawing on Orfield's research, columnist Karin Chenoweth made the same point in the *Washington Post*: the "least experienced, least knowledgeable teachers" were "systematically assigned" to teach "African American, Latino and poor children."[23]

Orfield also insisted that the nation's shifting demographics made integration a matter of national importance. At the time of *Brown*, about 10 percent of America's public school students were nonwhite. But in the future an increasing proportion of the nation's workers were going to be black and brown. In these circumstances, the nation's schools should do more than teach the basics of academic education. "Our schools need to prepare our children for life in a multicultural world," Orfield said. He insisted that racially balanced integration would help children learn about one another and empathize with members of other races. "If you go to an integrated school," Orfield said, "you're much more confident in integrated settings later in life."[24]

22. *Atlanta Journal-Constitution*, 22 June 2003, 1E; *St. Petersburg Times*, 29 September 2002, 1D; *Boston Herald*, 16 May 2004, 27; Jonathan Kozol, *Savage Inequalities* (New York: Crown Publishers, 1991); Kozol, *The Shame of the Nation* (New York: Crown Publishers, 2005).

23. Ben Scafidi, quoted in *Atlanta Journal Constitution*, 22 June 2003, 1E; ibid., 18 January 2004, 9A; *Washington Post*, 24 April 2003, T12; *Boston Herald*, 27 March 2005, O21.

24. *Boston Globe*, 12 November 2006, D1; *Atlanta Journal-Constitution*, 18 January 2004, 9A.

While Orfield generally stressed the benefits of mixing, he also mentioned another side of the story—the problems that allegedly resulted from "racial isolation." "You can't learn to live in an interracial society growing up in segregated neighborhoods and going to segregated schools," he said. Other civil rights activists agreed. Education writer Jonathan Kozol emphasized that black children from the inner cities suffered from a separation that "divorced them from the mainstream of American society." And civil rights lawyer John Boger said that "white people who grow up in racially isolated schools, however excellent, are increasingly going to be out of step in the world in which they are going to live."[25]

Integrationists made these arguments with an eye on the Supreme Court. Orfield's great desire was to persuade the high court to reverse its ruling in *Milliken v. Bradley,* the 1974 decision that placed legal barriers in the way of busing students to and from inner cities and distant suburban school districts. In the long run, such a reversal was a prerequisite for achieving substantial integration. Orfield recognized, however, that the majority of the Court had turned away from judicially enforced integration. Therefore, as a short-term goal, Orfield and other integrationists hoped to persuade the justices simply to allow "diversity" as a rationale that would permit schools to use race to promote racial mixing, if the schools chose to do so voluntarily.

One case that eventually presented this issue involved the University of Michigan, where authorities had developed a system of racial double standards and bonus points to foster what they considered a good racial mix. The details of the system were complex, but the issues were clear. Did the Constitution's equal protection clause allow an agency of the state to consider race and ethnicity when admitting students? If so, how far could a university go in trying to promote diversity? In 2002, the Supreme Court granted *certiorari* to consider the case.

Initially, the Michigan case did not look good for integrationists. The Supreme Court had previously held that there was "no way to determine what 'classifications are "benign" or "remedial" and what classifications are in fact motivated by illegitimate notions of racial inferiority or simple racial politics.'" The Court had said that "all racial classifications imposed by government 'must be analyzed by a reviewing court under strict scrutiny.'" It had said that "government may treat people differently because of their race only for the most compelling reasons."[26]

25. *Boston Globe,* 18 January 2004, B7; Kozol, *Shame of the Nation,* 5, 6; *Atlanta Journal-Constitution,* 22 June 2003, 1E.

26. *Adarand v. Pena,* 515 U.S. 200 (1995), 227; *Richmond v. Croson,* 488 U.S. 469 (1989), 493.

Thus the question before the Court was whether the case for affirmative racial policies at Michigan was compelling. The answer seemed to be "no." "Strict scrutiny" and "proof of a compelling interest" supposedly required state universities to present consistent, unequivocal evidence to show that race-conscious policies actually led to enhanced academic achievement or better race relations. And this was far from the case.

The social science arguments for integration were plausible, but as has been noted, the evidence with respect to academic achievement had given rise to a complex debate among scholars. The best study of the subject, David Armor's book *Forced Justice* (1995), had concluded that there were no gains that resulted simply from racial diversity. "Certainly there's no evidence that [balanced integration] has anything more than a trivial effect," said Christine Rossell, a Boston University scholar who had studied the matter for three decades.[27]

The evidence with respect to race relations was also disputed. As noted in Chapter 8, even committed integrationists had come to question the relation of school racial composition and the attitudes of students. Thus, after reviewing 120 studies, Nancy St. John had reported that the evidence did not show that racial mixing led to better race relations. Another scholar, Walter G. Stephan, reported that integration led black students to have slightly more favorable attitudes toward whites, but the reverse was true for whites. Many other scholars concluded that the evidence on this topic was far from conclusive, among them David Armor, Christine Rossell, Abigail Thernstrom, Stephen Thernstrom, and Herbert Walberg.[28]

In a sober, legal analysis of the arguments for integration, University of Virginia law professor James E. Ryan noted that courts were "awash in social science evidence." Hundreds of scholars had tried to measure the connection between racially balanced integration and academic achievement and race relations. But for all the effort, there was no consensus. "More often than not" the evidence was "conflicting or inconclusive." Those who favored mere desegregation presented the courts with expert witnesses who said the social and academic gains from integration are limited at best. Those who favored integration then called on experts who painted a more favorable picture. Given the inconclusive nature of the evidence, the case for integration did not seem likely to withstand strict scrutiny. Indeed, Ryan wrote, "the evidence regarding the benefits of school desegregation is not sufficiently clear to dislodge any but the most weakly held

27. *St. Petersburg Times,* 17 November 1996, 1D.
28. St. John, *School Desegregation;* Stephan, "Effects of School Desegregation"; amici briefs of David J. Armor, John Murphy, Christine Rossell, Abigail and Stephan Thernstrom, and Herbert Walberg, *Parents Involved v. Seattle,* U.S. Supreme Court, 2006.

beliefs about the propriety of using race as a criterion in education pro-grams."[29]

Many observers were therefore surprised when the Supreme Court, by a vote of 5 to 4, paid scant attention to the research of scholars who had questioned the purported benefits of integrated education. In *Grutter v. Bollinger* (2003), a case that dealt with admission policies at the Universi-ty of Michigan Law School, the court endorsed the arguments for inte-gration while ignoring the fact that these contentions were the subject of a spirited scholarly disagreement. The court did so, it seems, because lead-ers of several major corporations and of the U.S. armed forces filed briefs in support of Michigan's racial policies. The benefits of balanced integra-tion were "not theoretical but real," Justice O'Connor wrote in her opin-ion for the Court. American businesses had made it clear "that the skills needed in today's increasingly global marketplace can only be developed through exposure to widely diverse people, cultures, ideas and view-points. What is more, high-ranking retired officers and civilian leaders of the United States military assert that, 'based on [their] decades of experi-ence a highly qualified, racially diverse officer corps . . . is essential to the military's ability to fulfill its principal mission to provide national securi-ty.'" Therefore, O'Connor concluded, the law school had a "compelling interest in securing the educational benefits of a diverse student body."[30]

Grutter marked a departure from the sort of "strict scrutiny" that, at least since the *Croson* case of 1989, the Supreme Court had accorded in oth-er cases involving consideration of race. To be sure, *Grutter* purported to subject Michigan's policy to exacting judicial review, but as Chief Justice Rehnquist noted, the court actually accorded the law school "an un-precedented display of deference." Justice Clarence Thomas similarly chided the court's majority for allowing a degree of deference that was "antithetical to strict scrutiny." In a sharply worded dissent, Justice An-thony M. Kennedy said the court had "abandoned or manipulated" strict scrutiny "to distort its real and accepted meaning." A cynic might say this was nothing new. The combination of "compelling interest" and "strict scrutiny" was a reformulation of the "pressing public necessity" that an earlier Supreme Court had mentioned when it approved another of the government's race-based policies—the internment of Japanese Ameri-cans during World War II.[31]

There were some qualifications in the opinion that Justice O'Connor

29. James E. Ryan, "The Limited Influence of Social Science Evidence in Modern De-segregation Cases," *North Carolina Law Review* 81 (2003): 1660, 1664, 1689–91.
30. *Grutter v. Bollinger*, 539 U.S. 306 (2003), 330–31.
31. Ibid., 378–87, 349–78, 387–95.

crafted for *Grutter*. She said the court was deferring to the law school because the school's admissions committee purported to consider students
individually, with race being only one of several matters than were taken
into account. To accentuate the importance of this point, the Court (in a
companion case decided on the same day) ruled against the practice at
Michigan's college of arts and science, which gave "bonus points" automatically to all applicants from certain racial or ethnic minority groups.
O'Connor also emphasized that *Grutter* dealt with "higher education,"
where it was important "to select those students who will contribute the
most to the 'robust exchange of ideas.'" [32]

Integrationists, however, largely disregarded the limitations that Justice O'Connor included in *Grutter*. Instead, they stressed that the Supreme Court had held that diversity was a compelling justification for
race-conscious policies, and they insisted that the rationale also applied
to public elementary schools and high schools. Indeed, they said, these
schools had "an even greater interest in maintaining racial diversity than
do colleges," since the K–12 years were the "critical formative period in
the development of young minds and future citizens." "If diversity in
higher education has value," they said, "then these concerns operate
even more strongly in the context of K–12 integration." [33]

Even before the Supreme Court handed down its opinion in *Grutter*,
some federal courts had cited diversity as a justification for policies that
used race to promote racial mixing in elementary schools and high
schools. Thus a district judge in Massachusetts had allowed the public
schools in Lynn to take account of race when considering student requests
to transfer to schools outside their neighborhood. With references to the
research and testimony of Professor Orfield, the judge held that there was
compelling evidence "that side-by-side learning with students of other
races confers substantial citizenship benefits on all students." [34]

After *Grutter* additional federal courts approved still more plans to promote mixing. Thus the Ninth and Sixth Circuit Courts of Appeal, in cases

32. Ibid.; *Gratz v. Bollinger*, 539 U.S. 244 (2003).
33. Brief of Julius L. Chambers et al., *Parents Involved v. Seattle*; Brief of Amy Stuart
Wells et al., ibid.; Lia B. Epperson, "True Integration: Advancing *Brown*'s Goal of Educational Equity in the wake of *Grutter*," *University of Pittsburgh Law Review* 67 (2005):
175–224.
34. *Comfort v. Neumyer*, 263 F.Supp. 2d (2003), 209nn50–51. On the other hand, Pacific Legal Foundation attorney Paul Beard distinguished *Grutter*, where the Supreme
Court accepted diversity in the context of promoting robust debate in institutions of
higher learning, from regular public schools, saying, "In the second grade, you're
learning the multiplication tables, not discussing the effects of slavery in the 20th century." *San Francisco Chronicle*, 3 December 2006, A1.

that involved Seattle, Washington, and Louisville, Kentucky, allowed local school districts to rely on race to determine which public schools certain children could attend. In Seattle some schools were more popular
than others, and the goal was to keep oversubscribed schools within ten
percentage points of the district's overall white/nonwhite racial balance.
In Louisville and its surrounding Jefferson County, 34 percent of the students were black, and students were assigned to ensure that the proportion of black students at each school was not less than 15 percent or more
than 50 percent.

Critics took exception to these race-conscious policies, sometimes in
scathing terms. The black economist and public intellectual Thomas Sowell mocked judges who were "pondering whether there is a 'compelling'
government interest in creating the educational benefits of racial 'diversity.'" "What are those 'compelling' benefits?" Sowell asked. After considering the relevant social science research, Sowell bluntly declared: "there
is no evidence that mixing and matching black and white kids in school
produces either educational or social benefits." The alleged benefits were
an artifact of disingenuous research. To anyone who did not share a bias
in favor of the policy, the benefits were "as invisible as the proverbial emperor's new clothes. Yet everyone has to pretend to believe in those benefits, as they pretended to admire the naked emperor's wardrobe."[35]

Other critics said it was morally wrong for the government to engage
in any sort of racial discrimination. One lawyer for the Pacific Legal Foundation asked, "If we don't want our children to judge people based on
the color of their skin, why are educators doing just that?" A reporter for
the online magazine *Slate* noted that critics were "essentially saying . . .
that . . . race is race, and you can't use it—not for good reasons, not for
bad reasons, particularly when it's not clear . . . that it even worked."[36]

Critics of race-conscious policies often quoted statements of Supreme
Court justices and civil rights leaders. They recalled that Justice O'Connor had once warned that race-based policies divided the nation "into
racial blocs, thus contributing to an escalation of racial hostility and conflict." They remembered that Justice Antonin Scalia had said that such
policies "reinforce the belief, held by too many for too much of our history, that individuals should be judged by the color of their skin." Critics
also recalled that in his oral argument for the NAACP in *Brown v. Board of
Education*, attorney Robert L. Carter had insisted: "We have one funda-

35. Thomas Sowell, "Supreme Farce," Townhall.com, 12 December 2006.
36. Sharon L. Brown, quoted in *Augusta Chronicle*, 4 December 2006, AO5; Dahlie
Lithwick, statement on NPR Broadcast, 4 December 2006.

mental contention . . . that no State has any authority under the equal-protection clause . . . to use race as a factor in affording educational opportunities among citizens." Critics especially liked to quote from the legal brief that Thurgood Marshall wrote for *Brown*: "Distinctions by race are so evil, so arbitrary and invidious that a state bound to defend the equal protection of the laws must not invoke them in any public sphere."[37]

In 2006 the Supreme Court agreed to consider an appeal from disgruntled parents in Seattle and Louisville. The legal points at issue were straightforward. Could a public school system that had not operated segregated schools in the past, or a formerly segregated system that had since been found to be unitary, classify students by race and then rely upon the classifications in making school assignments?

Integrationists sensed trouble ahead. In 2005, when Sandra Day O'Connor was still a member of the Court, the justices had refused to consider a similar appeal from parents in Massachusetts. But after Samuel A. Alito Jr. replaced O'Connor, the justices agreed to consider the question. Civil rights stalwarts understandably feared that Justice Alito would tip the balance of the Court. They recalled that O'Connor had supplied the crucial fifth vote for diversity in *Grutter*. And Alito, in his younger days as an attorney for the Reagan administration, had written that he was particularly proud of his efforts opposing "racial and ethnic quotas."[38]

The integrationists' fears turned out to be well-founded. In 2007, by another vote of 5 to 4, the Supreme Court ruled against the race-conscious programs that Seattle and Louisville had developed. In explaining themselves, the justices published a judgment, a plurality opinion, two concurrences, and two dissents. One key point touched on the social science evidence for integration. Did it amount to a "compelling" rationale for racial discrimination?

The principal dissent, by Justice Stephen Breyer, acknowledged that careful scholars had reached different conclusions about the way balanced mixing affected academic achievement and interracial attitudes. Nevertheless, Breyer considered the evidence for integrated education "strong enough to permit a democratically elected school board reasonably to determine that this interest is a compelling one."[39]

---

37. *Metro Broadcasting v. Federal Communications Commission,* 497 U.S. 547 (1990), 603; *Shaw v. Reno,* 509 U.S. 630 (1993), 657; Transcript of Oral Argument in *Brown v. Board of Education,* 9 December 1952, 7; George F. Will, "The Court Returns to *Brown,*" *Washington Post,* 5 July 2007, A17.

38. *American Bar Association Journal* 92 (December 2006): 16; *San Francisco Chronicle,* 3 December 2006, A1.

39. *Parents Involved v. Seattle,* 127 S.Ct. 2738 (2007), 2821.

In his plurality opinion for the court, Chief Justice John G. Roberts also acknowledged that there was much disagreement over "whether racial diversity in schools in fact has a marked impact on test scores . . . or achieves intangible socialization benefits." Roberts, however, concluded that the debate was "not one we need to resolve." The court need not do so because neither Seattle nor Louisville had shown that its preferred level of diversity was related to the alleged educational benefits. In Seattle the benefits of racial diversity required an enrollment of between 30 and 50 percent white students, while in Louisville the benefits supposedly would accrue only in schools where white students made up between 50 and 85 percent of the enrollment. Instead of tailoring their programs to achieve the level of racial diversity needed to obtain the asserted educational benefits, the plans were designed to achieve "a level of diversity within the schools that approximates the district's overall demographics." [40]

Roberts called this the "fatal flaw" in the districts' plans, for the Supreme Court had "many times over reaffirmed that 'racial balance is not to be achieved for its own sake.'" In addition, Roberts wrote, if the court accepted racial balancing as a compelling state interest, it would provide a justification for imposing "racial proportionality throughout American society." And this would be contrary to the court's repeated recognition that "at the heart of the Constitution's guarantee of equal protection lies the simple command that the Government must treat citizens as individuals, not as simply components of a racial, religious, sexual or national class." [41]

In concurring comments, Justice Kennedy also stressed that government agencies must treat citizens individually. Kennedy would have allowed the government some leeway in taking race into account. He said the Constitution allowed racial policies to promote mixing, if the policies pertained to impersonal matters such as where to build a new school or where to offer certain academic programs. He said schools could even consider race as one of many factors that were taken into account when assigning individual students. But if the court approved Seattle and Louisville's programs for racial balancing, it would allow government agencies to use race, not to remedy discrimination, but to allocate "benefits and burdens." It would allow school authorities to tell students that they were "defined by race." Like Chief Justice Roberts, Justice Kennedy also feared that approval of the Seattle and Louisville plans would propel

40. Ibid., 2755–56.
41. Ibid., 2757.

the nation toward accepting racial classifications "in areas far afield from schooling."[42]

In another concurring opinion, Justice Thomas insisted that the evidence from social science was too inconclusive to satisfy the judicial standard of strict scrutiny. Personally, Thomas was skeptical of social science theories. He knew that scientific racism had been in vogue through much of the nineteenth and twentieth centuries, and he did not wish to place the Court's equal protection jurisprudence "at the mercy of . . . the evanescent views of a handful of social scientists." Even if the evidence for racially balanced integration had been stronger, Thomas said he would not "constitutionalize today's faddish social theories." "If our history has taught us anything, it has taught us to beware of elites bearing racial theories." Thomas insisted that "the Constitution enshrines principles independent of social theories."[43]

The immediate reaction to the court's decision was predictable. Critics of racially balanced integration were pleased, and proponents were dismayed. Some critics wished that the Supreme Court of 2007 had gone even further and completely disavowed the diversity argument that the court had endorsed four years earlier in *Grutter*. Most, however, were pleased to know that the Roberts Court had affirmed strict scrutiny and had placed some guardrails around diversity. Syndicated columnist George F. Will praised the court for recognizing a point that some earlier Supreme Court opinions had ignored: "that race must not be a source of government-conferred advantage or disadvantage." Ward Connerly, a prominent African American critic of double standards, agreed: "We're clearly moving in the direction of a color-blind government," Connerly said. "The court is finally starting to catch up with what the American people have known for years: Race has no place in American life."[44]

Advocates of balanced mixing naturally disagreed. After listening to the oral argument, when several justices gave indications of how they would later decide, Harvard professor and civil rights attorney Charles Ogletree confessed, "this was the most depressing moment that I have had as a lawyer." When the court's decision was announced, Gary Orfield was disconsolate. He thought Louisville "should have been given a pat on the back rather than being punished." Schools were "the only integrated things in a lot of our inner cities," Orfield noted, and a policy that guaranteed that whites would make up a sizeable portion of the total

42. Ibid., 2792, 2793, 2797.
43. Ibid., 2778, 2787.
44. Will, "Court Returns to *Brown*," A01.

enrollment in at least some schools was "one of the only ways to keep middle-class kids involved in big-city school systems."[45]

Some observers discounted the importance of the litigation. Robert Lowe, an expert on race and education policy at Marquette University, considered the court's decision "a step backward from [the] expansive notion that public schools are here to educate all together." Nevertheless, the points at issue in *Seattle* and *Louisville* were of concern only to the relatively small number of school districts that wished to implement racial balance policies of their own free will. Therefore, Lowe said, "I honestly don't think these cases make an enormous amount of difference. For a long time courts have been releasing schools from [racial balance] orders. What's left are voluntary programs that don't include very many students overall."[46]

Yet the symbolic significance was considerable. David G. Savage, an astute legal affairs reporter for the *Los Angeles Times,* thought the decision might "herald a new era." With Justice Alito as the newest member of the Supreme Court, conservatives were shaping the jurisprudence on racial matters—much to the dismay of the Court's four liberal justices, one of whom lamented, "it is not often in law that so few have quickly changed so much." Ronald Walters, the director of the University of Maryland's African American Leadership Institute, thought the decisions in *Seattle* and *Louisville* marked "the end of the *Brown* era assumption that . . . dispersion of African-American kids . . . could be a mechanism for them to achieve academic excellence and advancement."[47]

Technically, the debate in *Seattle* and *Louisville* had concerned the sort of evidence that was necessary to justify policies that were intended to promote balanced racial mixing. In his dissent, Justice John Paul Stevens noted that the court had not been unanimous in its previous rulings that racial classifications should be analyzed under strict scrutiny, and Stevens repeated that he personally believed that policies that were intended to promote mixing need not satisfy such an exacting standard. In another dissent, Justice Breyer acknowledged that he also thought the policies in Seattle and Louisville should be considered under "a standard of review that is not 'strict' in the traditional sense." In his argument before the court, on the other hand, Solicitor General Paul Clement said "the lesson of history . . . is that racial classifications are not ones where . . . we

45. National Public Radio, 5 December 2006; Associated Press State and Local Wire, 29 June 2007.

46. *U.S. News and World Report,* 28 June 2007, 2 October 2006.

47. *Los Angeles Times,* 29 June 2007, 1; Stephen G. Breyer, quoted by Jeffrey Toobin, *The Nine* (New York: Doubleday, 2007), 336; *Newhouse News Service,* 26 June 2007, n.p.

should just let school board officials do what they think is right. . . . The Constitution puts a particular premium on avoiding racial classifications."[48]

The debate touched on more than the choice of the correct legal standard for judicial review. At a deeper level, *Seattle* and *Louisville* raised questions about the purpose of public education. The Seattle School Board insisted that "the function of modern public schools extends beyond basic education." In its legal brief, the board mentioned the desirability of increasing its students' learning and achievement, but it emphasized the importance of "preparing students for work and citizenship in our multiracial and multicultural democracy." Some observers, however, noted that as often as not racial mixing led to increased racial tension and hostility. After reviewing the data from 120 studies, Nancy St. John concluded, "for either race positive findings are less common than negative findings." Other observers predicted that schools that were organized to promote multicultural sensitivity would fail to achieve the main purpose to education—teaching basic academic subjects. This was hardly a new idea. In 1935, W. E. B. Du Bois had told the National Education Association, "the school has but one way to cure the ills of society and that is by making men intelligent. To make men intelligent, the school has again but one way, and that is, first and last, to teach them to read, write and count. And if the school fails to do that, and tries beyond that to do something for which a school is not adapted, it not ony fails in its own function, but it fails in all other attempted functions. Because no school as such can organize industry or settle the matter of wage and income, can found homes or furnish parents, can establish justice or make a civilized world."[49]

The Seattle and Louisville cases also concerned the meaning of *Brown v. Board of Education*. The dissenting justices disregarded the specific language of *Brown* and focused instead on what they called the "moral vision" of the Fourteenth Amendment and "the hope and promise of *Brown*." In their view, *Brown* did not stand for the principle that the government should not discriminate among citizens on the basis of race. It stood for the combating of racial separation and clustering by achieving racially balanced enrollments.[50]

48. *Parents Involved v. Seattle*, 127 S.Ct. 2738 (2007), 2798–99, 2819; *New York Times*, 5 December 2006, 1A.

49. Brief of Seattle School Board, quoted in *St. Petersburg Times*, 3 December 2006, 5a; St. John, *School Desegregation*, 67–68; W. E. B. Du Bois, quoted by Diane Ravitch, "A Bifurcated Vision of Urban Education," in Jane Newitt, ed., *Future Trends in Educational Policy* (Lexington, Mass.: Lexington Books, 1979), 80.

50. *Parents Involved v. Seattle*, 127 S.Ct. 2738 (2007), 2836.

For the Court's majority, on the othe rhand, *Brown* meant what it said. The Constitution required public schools to assign pupils on "a racially nondiscriminatory basis." "History will be heard," Chief Justice Roberts wrote. "The way to stop discrimination on the basis of race is to stop discriminating on the basis of race."[51]

51. Ibid., 2767, 2768.

Conclusion

When considering the course of the law on race and education, it is well to recall an often-quoted statement of Charles Evans Hughes, a former chief justice of the Supreme Court: "We are under a Constitution, but the Constitution is what the judges say it is." Until the middle twentieth century, the Supreme Court interpreted the equal protection clause to allow public schools to practice racial discrimination to separate the races, as long as the separate facilities were (theoretically) equal. The *Brown* opinion of 1954, however, was originally understood to prohibit racial discrimination in assigning children to public schools. This understanding was then inverted with the *Green, Swann,* and *Keyes* opinions of 1968, 1971, and 1973, which required school districts to take race into account in order to increase racial mixing. Then, in the *Dowell, Jenkins,* and *Freeman* cases of the 1990s, and in the *Seattle* and *Louisville* cases of 2007, the Supreme Court moved back toward the original understanding of *Brown*.[1]

To understand the trends, it is well to recognize that social science theories, whether they are right or wrong, are more influential than is commonly acknowledged. The law on race and the schools is based on the U.S. Constitution, but individual judges have interpreted the Constitution in light of their understanding of social science. Sometimes, it seems, they were influenced by little else.[2]

Thus in 1969, when busing for racial balance began in Charlotte-

1. Speech, May 3, 1907, quoted in William Lockhart, Yale Kamisar, and Jesse Choper, *Constitutional Law,* 3d ed. (St. Paul: West Publishing, 1970), 7.
2. "Sometimes" is not "always," and there are instances when courts have determined that the accepted legal standards do not leave much room for social science. There are other instances when judges appear to be manipulating social science evidence to bolster conclusions that are based primarily on moral or philosophical

Mecklenburg, the first Coleman report was in vogue. At that time, according to Judge James B. McMillan, "the experts all agree[d] . . . that a racial mix in which black students heavily predominate tends to retard the progress of the whole group, whereas if students are mingled with a clear white majority, such as a 70/30 ratio . . . the better students can hold their pace, with substantial improvement for the poorer students."[3]

In 1975 Professor Coleman backed away from this contention, and by the 1990s the best social science evidence indicated that, after controlling for relevant variables, there was no correlation between the performance of black students and the racial balance of schools. Integrationists still believed that African Americans fared badly in what they called "racially isolated" schools. But the test scores were such that even supporters of racially balanced integration shifted their emphasis and instead identified more general changes in attitude, ambition, and race relations as the chief benefits of integration. Even there, however, the evidence was mixed. In this new social science context, the Supreme Court adjusted the constitutional requirements once more.

One could say that the course of the law on school desegregation has proceeded from *Brown* to *Green* and back to *Brown* again. The road was windy and bumpy, but a majority of the justices of the Supreme Court eventually decided that prudent social policy and a proper interpretation of the Constitution required the *sub silentio* repudiation of *Green v. New Kent County,* the tacit rejection of integrationist social science, and a return to what most people thought *Brown v. Board of Education* meant in 1954 and what Congress certainly intended when it enacted the Civil Rights Act of 1964: the prohibition of official racial discrimination but not the prohibition of racially neutral policies that do not lead to a substantial amount of racial mixing.[4]

Integrationists have condemned the Supreme Courts of William H.

---

grounds. See James E. Ryan, "What Role Should Courts Play in Influencing Educational Policy? The Limited Influence of Social Science Evidence in Modern Desegregation Cases," *University of North Carolina Law Review* 81 (May 2003): 1659–702.

3. *Swann v. Charlotte-Mecklenburg,* 300 F.Supp. 1358 (1969), at 1371, 1373.

4. For more on this point, see Raymond Wolters, "From *Brown* to *Green* and Back: The Changing Meaning of Desegregation," *Journal of Southern History* 70 (May 2004): 317–26. In private correspondence, one of my friends, an eminent authority on constitutional law, has suggested that the Court's recent rulings against racial discrimination were accidental—a result of "the fortuitous replacement of [Justice] O'Connor." Perhaps I am too optimistic. The appointment of different justices could lead the Supreme Court to change its jurisprudence once again. If the Court returns to social engineering for integration, however, it will ignite another wave of political protest. In California, Washington, and Michigan, voters have already amended the state constitutions to prohibit government officials from discriminating on the basis of race or ethnicity, and other states are poised to do likewise.

Rehnquist and John G. Roberts for "dismantling desegregation." Other observers are more upbeat. This writer believes the *Brown* Court deserves praise for putting the nation on the road toward removing racial barriers and dismantling a system of mandatory segregation laws. But the *Green, Swann,* and *Keyes* opinions involved a different principle. *Brown* required that segregated school systems be disestablished, in the sense that the assignment of children to particular schools should not depend on race. But *Green, Swann,* and *Keyes* required school officials to consider race and to strive for racially balanced enrollments.

Outside the South most Americans quickly accepted *Brown,* and even in Dixie the great majority eventually came around. Desegregation was necessary in light of emerging moral values, and most Americans went beyond grudging acceptance of the nondiscrimination principle. They favored the idea that the government should not treat citizens on the basis of race. Desegregation was in tune with the larger trends of the time. Scientific racism had been called into question by recent scholarship and discredited by the excesses of Adolf Hitler. The Great Migration of blacks out of the rural South had led to black voting in urban areas and black control of the balance of political power in some cities. The Cold War had brought about competition for influence in the Third World. And African Americans had mobilized their own resources—their churches, colleges, and racial-betterment organizations—to establish the foundation for a powerful civil rights movement. Had these other factors not existed, the *Brown* Court would not have prevailed against segregation.

But most Americans never accepted *Green* and its progeny. *Green* was at odds with larger trends. It could not be reconciled with pluralism and freedom of association. Racial identity persisted, despite the pleas of integrationists and court orders that required racially balanced enrollments. Most adults chose to live in neighborhoods that were populated by people of their own race and class, and they wanted their children to have similar associates. Racially balanced schools also contravened the expectation that schools should provide order and safety as well as a good basic education. In theory, integration required only that schoolchildren be exposed to an approximately proportional number of children from other races and classes. In fact, integrated education often exposed children to influences that many parents considered anathema—racial snobbery and condescension as well as disorder and disdain for academic achievement and middle-class values.

For one reason or another, most Americans never embraced the principle of *Green v. New Kent County.* Court-ordered integration gave rise to flight, initially among whites and eventually among middle-class blacks as well. During the years after court-ordered busing plans were implemented, middle-class enrollments declined precipitously. "School integration is just not stable where the proportion of blacks in the district is very large," James S. Coleman noted. Whites were voting "with their feet," political scientist Christine H. Rossell observed, and there was little that courts could do about it. To maintain balanced integration, judges would have had to "go into private schools and put a noose around white kids' necks and pull them back into public schools."[5]

This writer believes the Rehnquist and Roberts courts should be commended for recognizing that there are limits to what courts can accomplish and for returning to the principle of nondiscrimination. The Rehnquist and Roberts courts have also propelled the nation toward experimenting with what may turn out to be more effective methods of improving America's schools. Because of the Rehnquist and Roberts courts, educators can no longer regard getting the "right" racial mix as the key to better education. They have to experiment with other approaches. At the turn of the twenty-first century, the stage is set for a new era in the history of American education, an age of school reform—which I plan to discuss in another book.

5. *National Observer*, 7 June 1975, 1; *St. Petersburg Times*, 17 November 1996, 1D; *Cleveland Plain Dealer*, 7 November 1997, 2B.

Index